LEGACY

CHARLES FOX
&
SARAH ELEANOR

PARHAM

AND THE RACIAL ROOTS OF THE
PENTECOSTAL MOVEMENT IN THE
UNITED STATES

BISHOP BERNIE L. WADE, PHD

Legacy
Charles Fox & Sarah Eleanor Parham
And the racial roots of the pentecostal movement in the United States
Copyright © 2022 Bishop Bernie Wade

All rights reserved. No part of this publication may be reproduced, distributed or transmitted in any form or by any means, without prior written permission.

Published by
Dreamer Reign Media, LLC
P.O. Box 291354
Port Orange, FL 32129

www.dreamerreign.com

For Worldwide Distribution
Printed in the U.S.A.

ISBN: 9781952253256
Library of Congress Control Number: 2023900837

Cover Design: C Marcel Wiggins

TABLE OF CONTENTS

Special Thanks 4

Preface: A LETTER TO BISHOP WADE 5

Foreword 6

Introduction 8

Chapter One: APOSTOLIC FAITH 17

Chapter Two: WILLIAM JOSEPH SEYMOUR 25

Chapter Three: INFLUENCER 47

Chapter Four: THISTLETHWAITE SISTERS 69

Chapter Five: SLAVERY 89

Chapter Six: RACIAL SEGREGATION – THE NEW SLAVERY 97

Chapter Seven: RELIGIOUS EXCUSES FOR WHITE SUPREMACY ... 105

Chapter Eight: BETHEL 119

Chapter Nine: TOPEKA OUTPOURING 133

Chapter Ten: EVIDENCE OF SPIRIT BAPTISM GOES GLOBAL 144

Chapter Eleven: LOS ANGELES OUTPOURING 151

Chapter Twelve: ZION CITY 167

Chapter Thirteen: WHITES ONLY 191

Chapter Fourteen: TEXAS SYNDICATE 207

Chapter Fifteen: APOSTOLIC FAITH COGIC SCHEME 221

Chapter Sixteen: THE RULE IN TEXAS 239

Chapter Seventeen: THE SYSTEM 263

Chapter Eighteen: HOLY ROLLERS 275

Chapter Nineteen: ALL-WHITE KANGAROO COURT 287

Chapter Twenty: NEW PENTECOSTALS AND THE KKK 311

Chapter Twenty-One: THE BIG LIE 331

Chapter Twenty-Two: BAPTIZED IN JESUS' NAME 353

Chapter Twenty-Three: LYNCH MOB JUSTICE 369

Chapter Twenty-Four: DETRACTORS 387

Endontes 407

SPECIAL THANKS

Special thanks to those who helped me with this project. My father, Bishop Sanford L. Wade, my wife, Daisy R. Wade, PhD, my good friends, Drs. Gary and Deborah Garrett of Apostolic Archives.[1] Students of Apostolic Faith or Pentecostal history will enjoy the work that the Garrett's are doing through Apostolic Archives, the Heritage Museum and more. Thanks to John Collins of the William Branham Historical Research[2] and others. Till we all get to Heaven!

PREFACE
(A letter to Bishop Wade)

Dear Dr. Wade (Bro. Bernie)

"I'm 238 pages into your book, and all I keep saying is 'WOW' as history falls into place and Holy Spirit is teaching me not only what I need to know, but also providing me confirmation as to 'what's wrong with America?'" Shortly after the George Floyd killing, I cried out, "Lord, what's wrong with America?"...Two days later Holy Ghost dropped this answer into my spirit - 'White Christianity'...Not 'Jesus Christianity,' but a twisted 'another Gospel, doctrines of demons, Christianity,' promulgated by the likes of such treacherous men as Warren Carothers...Your book rolls away the stones from such whited sepulchers, and rips off the lids of such dens of vipers...It has also educated me about Charles F. Parham whom I'd read/heard some racist things about, but really knew very little of him. About ten years ago, Holy Spirit had me discover two audio books (1) - W.E.B. Dubois "Souls of Black Folk" and (2) - Booker T. Washington's "The Negro Problem," both of which circa 1903 had both men pleading with their White Christian siblings to en'masse help the stranded Negro people so as not to have so many of 'the wretched' we have today...I'd been thinking ever since about the blatant inactions of American White Christianity, then and now, toward Blacks in general, but even more specifically about their apathy concerning "the least of these" their Black siblings in Christ...Now Holy Ghost, via this book through you, has made everything crystal clear to me!

-Prophet Rahman Reuben

FOREWORD

I once remember hearing that truth stands on its own and will bear witness in time. I must say that Bishop Wade has brought forth a new perspective of truth by shining the light upon a deep darkness that has clouded the legacy of Charles and Sarah Parham and their role in one of the greatest moves of God in the 20th century. For those who have a heart for truth and history, you will find this book will be a great resource documenting some of the findings associated with what we come to know as Azusa Street Revival.

I must say, as someone who did not have roots in neither Pentecostal nor Apostolic foundations, this read was very enlightening. Bishop revealed matters lying dormant for many years that include historical events of great church movements and birthing. Indeed, some material will be very disturbing, and seem offensive and harsh, but it spoke into areas that has plagued our nation for centuries, and in the Church today as well.

Just like the prophet Habakkuk, who bore a burden, Bishop Wade himself bore a burden framing for the truth surrounding the life and legacy of Charles and Sarah Parham. He established a great axiom—that if you ever want to know the intent and purpose of a thing involving visionaries such as Charles and Sarah, then you must not start in the middle, nor at the end, but go back to the very beginning. The beginning of their ministry reveals the intent of their heart of having a multicultural outpour on the move of God that rooted itself in having White people, Black people, Mexicans, men and women all working together in ministry, during one of the most segregated times in American history.

This book is necessary for all believers, especially those whose foundation is in a Apostolic and Pentecostal denomination.

—Apostle Deddrick Perry
Glory International Harvest Church, Joliet, Illinois

INTRODUCTION

Two men sat with their hats in their hands in the office of a prominent Pentecostal pastor in Michigan. They explained that they had been unhappy with a spiritual brother. As a result, they formulated and spread lies about him. Among the lies they told, "he had been unfaithful to his wife." Now, the man was dead from suicide; the aftermath of the lies they had forged about him.

"How can we fix this?" They asked their pastor. In response, the pastor walked to a closet and pulled out a feather pillow. He handed the pillow to one of the men. Then he gave the pair this instruction: "Drive to Chicago. Go to the Chicago tower.[3] Go up to the top floor and pour all the feathers in this pillow out the window. Then, go down to the ground and retrieve all the feathers."

"Pastor!" one of the men exclaimed, "We would never be able to retrieve all the feathers!"

"Yes," the pastor acknowledged. "You will also never fix all the mess you have created through your lies and deceit."

This is the task with which we find ourselves confronting. Many people have spread falsehood about Charles and Sarah Parham and their family. We will only be able to retrieve some of the 'feathers,' but we will pick up the ones that we are able. For more than one hundred years, those who have been interested in the Apostolic Faith or Pentecostal Movement have been subjected to storylines about Charles Parham that are fundamentally unethical. No man or woman should be held hostage by unproven claims, predisposed to support a denominational agenda. Volumes have been written about Charles Parham. Nearly all of them are filled with spurious claims about his personal life. We are not proposing that anyone is above scrutiny. What we are saying is, no one should be ill-famed based on undocumented or unprovable allegations. Further, any claim against a person that derives from their sworn enemies (especially political or religious foes) should be regarded with great suspicion and presented as such. For example: When visiting websites and the subject is Charles Parham, you get a disclaimer ostensibly accusing the Parhams of being racists.[4] Strangely, there is no such disclaimer for William Branham who was part of the Ku Klux Klan (KKK).[5] None of the Assemblies of God's racist hall of shame who hold the same ideology as the KKK are gaslighted in that same manner.[6] No disclaimers for them. The point is the disclaimers are a part of continued diatribe of innuendo started by the all-white Texas Syndicate and propagated by religious hate groups like the Assemblies of God (A.G.)[7], the United Pentecostal Church (U.P.C.I.)[8], and many others. Christian magazines like Charisma routinely print articles allowing Charles Parham to be labeled as "infamous" while they routinely promote others with sordid pasts.[9]

Scripture supports the idea of innocent until proven guilty. While legitimate legal processes declared the Parhams innocent, religious bigots, and xenophobes have conducted a campaign to smear, libel, and slander the Parhams in the fugazi *Court of Public Opinion*. Charles and Sarah Parham have been denied a fair defense of unfounded charges against their family, persons, lives, and character. This author has no legal education, but regards it reasonable to give the Parhams an opportunity for a fair-minded and impartial defense as protected in the Bill of Rights.[10] Further, where appropriate give the benefit of the doubt, show mercy, and expect that those who are genuinely filled with the Holy Ghost are imperfect but forgiven.[11] As Citizens of Heaven, we are cleansed by the blood of Jesus Christ.[12] Citizens of the United States of America hold to a cardinal principle of justice; every person accused of a crime is presumed to be innocent unless—and until his or her guilt is established beyond a reasonable doubt.[13] The presumption is not a mere formality. It is a matter of the most important substance. *"Although the United States Constitution recognized a right to a jury trial in criminal cases, the states demanded a constitutional amendment to guarantee a jury trial in civil cases as well, leading to the creation of the Seventh Amendment."*[14] Thankfully, these are fundamental rights afforded all Citizens.[15] *Trial via media circus* is purely evil. those who employ such methods should by right be treated in a manner equal to those who use mob justice and lynching.[16]

When Job's life was in turmoil, his friends assumed he had done wrong and was being divinely punished. Many allegations were made against his character, though each was incorrect. The book ends with God chastising Job's friends for their rush to judgment. Even as wild allegations were made against Jesus, the legal expert Nicodemus spoke: "Does our law condemn anyone without first hearing him to find out what he is doing (John 7:51)?"[17]
"If anyone says, 'I love God,' and hates his brother, he is a liar; for he who does not love his brother whom he has seen cannot love God whom he has not seen."[18]

Innocent If Not Proven Guilty

A man, or woman is presumed innocent if not proven guilty by a legitimate court of their peers.[19] The opportunity for them to legally defend themselves is paramount.[20] The presumption of innocence alone may be sufficient to raise a reasonable doubt, and to require the acquittal of a defendant. In a trial of any kind, it should be expected that the defendant has the benefit of that presumption of innocence. You are not to convict of a particular charge unless you are persuaded of guilt of that charge beyond a reasonable doubt.[21] History is full of false witnesses, liars, and perjurers.[22]

"From Cain to Potiphar's Wife to the pig and chicken laws of the Lex Salica of Clovis I."[23] "Bearing false witness is mentioned many times in the Bible, exclusively as something terrible. "You shall not bear false witness against your neighbor" is the ninth of the Ten Commandments that Moses brought back with him from his encounter with God on Mount Sinai (Exodus 20:16). False witness, or spreading a false report, is associated with being allied with the wicked (Exodus 23:1), willing to do violence to others (Psalm 27:12), and sowing discord among brothers (Proverbs 6:19). The Bible calls bearing false witness lying (Proverbs 14:5) and compares a man who bears false witness against his neighbor to a violent weapon (Proverbs 25:18). Lies harm people.[24]

    A false witness is one who stands up and swears before others that something untrue is true, especially with the intention of hurting someone else or ruining his reputation.[25] This is a crime called Perjury. "Whoever (1) having taken an oath before a competent tribunal, officer, or person, in any case in which a law of the United States authorizes an oath to be administered, that he will testify, declare, depose, or certify truly, or that any written testimony, declaration, deposition, or certificate by him subscribed, is true, willfully and contrary to such oath states or subscribes any material matter which he does not believe to be true; or (2) in any declaration, certificate, verification, or statement under penalty of perjury as permitted under section 1746 of title 28, United States Code, willfully subscribes as true any material matter which he does not believe to be true; is guilty of perjury and shall, except as otherwise expressly provided by law, be fined under this title or imprisoned not more than five years, or both. This section is applicable whether the statement or subscription is made within or without the United States."[26]

    This type of crime happened to David (Psalm 27:12), Jesus (Matthew

26:60; Mark 14:56), and Stephen (Acts 6:13). When the wicked Queen Jezebel wished to procure a vineyard for her sulking husband, King Ahab, she employed two false witnesses. Naboth, the rightful owner of the vineyard, was seated in an honorable place on a day of fasting, but "then two scoundrels came and sat opposite him and brought charges against Naboth before the people, saying, 'Naboth has cursed both God and the king.' So, they took him outside the city and stoned him to death" (1 Kings 21:13). What the "scoundrels" said against Naboth was absolutely untrue; they were bearing false witness with impunity and with the queen's blessing. As a result, an innocent man was killed. When a person is righteous and his enemies can find nothing with which to blame him, bearing false witness is a common weapon.

> The lies told by a false witness come from the sinful human heart—along with murder, adultery, sexual immorality, theft, slander, and evil thoughts (Matthew 15:19). Jesus said that man is defiled by these evil things that come from the heart."[27]

The presumption of innocence until proven guilty, means that the burden of proof is always on those bringing the charge to satisfy that the defendant is guilty of the crime with which he or she is charged beyond a reasonable doubt. This burden never shifts to the defendant. It is always the government's burden to prove each of the elements of the crime charged beyond a reasonable doubt by the evidence. The defendant has the right to rely upon the failure or inability of the government to establish beyond a reasonable doubt, any essential element of a crime charged against them.[28] No one shall be subjected to arbitrary interference with his privacy, family, home or correspondence, nor to attacks upon his honor and reputation.[29]

Since the false arrest of Parham was in Texas, we investigated that legal action. Unfortunately, the State of Texas has made the spotlight for leading the way with a glut of wrongful convictions, executions and mishandling of cases.[30] The problem in Texas has been prevalent for more than one hundred years.[31] Texans are historically all too tolerant of the innocent being exploited. There are too many cases of innocent people being accused of crimes that they did not commit.[32] To be an accomplice, accessory, or aide and abet the persecution of someone not convicted of a crime as in the case of Charles Parham is corrupt.[33] Those who conspired against the Parham family in a secret cabal perpetrated by those we have dubbed The Texas Syndicate acted in a manner that is unconscionable.[34] This organization did what was all too common in Texas history; they attempted to lynch an innocent man.[35]

Real witnesses have a responsibility to first hear all evidence and then give fair and impartial consideration.[36] If you have a reasonable doubt as to a defendant's guilt of a particular crime, it is your duty to acquit him or her of that crime.[37] Once acquitted, the matter is over.[38] This is a civility we must afford all mankind. As followers of Jesus Christ, we are commanded to conduct our lives in such a manner that we are not judgmental.[39] Charles and Sarah Parham have been denied this civility.[40] The outrageous accusations against them, based on the word of their political enemies in collusion with unknown contrived witnesses, met only the lowest standards.[41]

This treatise will attempt to begin to set the record straight. There is no effort to hide any truth, but there is a deliberate endeavor to lay to rest lies, innuendo, libel, slander, backbiting and all other works of the flesh.[42] Included in the works of the flesh are hatred, contentions, jealousy, outburst of wrath, selfish ambitions, dissentions, heresies, envy, murderers,

revelries, etc. Apostle Paul warned that those who practice such things will not inherit the Kingdom of God![43]

There are fundamental questions raised about the activity and character of the Parhams' detractors and accusers. We are not here to judge them, but we will not shy away from an honest assessment of their actions. Aiding and abetting against an innocent person was and remains criminal activity.

"Under the Texas penal code, if you help another person commit a crime or knew about it, you may wind up in jail. Examples: You purposely helped facilitate a crime by assisting, encouraging, directing or hiding the truth. You solicit someone else to engage in a crime on your behalf. The law does not care that you did not directly participate in a crime."[44]

Our response is not meant in the same manner as the unfounded allegations of the Parhams' enemies. Rather, this written account is presented as the rightful defense everyone should be granted. These historical facts and information are not intended as indictments. Yet, they may present that way in areas where the historical record implicates the character and/or motive of those who have borne false witness.[45] For our part, we have given the historical record. We cannot answer for the actions of others. We can, and will continue to assert, that we are not those people. It is fair, and honorable that we should be purveyors of truth. We are not of those who would purposely bring hostility to any group, race or gender. We are for all women, called of God, to walk in their calling.

To the horrible abuse by those claiming Christ, even further presenting to have been born of the water and Spirit, we offer no excuses. The actions of such are indefensible. We offer only sorrow at their reprehensible actions, that officials and leaders of religious organizations, denominations, their proxies, and surrogates would do these things *in the name of God* are embarrassing blemishes to the Body of Christ.[46] We join in solidarity with all minorities (including women, African-Americans, Japanese, Native-Americans, Mexicans, Chinese, all people of Africa and others) especially those who have been maligned by these religious groups. We are not willing that anyone should use falsehood to torment anyone as these have done and apparently still practice in too many cases. Further, we will not be those who make excuses for those who have committed criminal and civil offenses based on the color of one's skin, race, or one's gender.

In this treatise, we take a stand for those who have been slandered, libeled, defamed in any manner. We continue to take such a stand in their defense. To God be the Glory!

CHAPTER ONE

APOSTOLIC FAITH
"There are no small parts, only small actors."[47]

Charles Fox and Sarah Eleanor Parham waltzed onto the pages of history because of the Topeka Outpouring.[48] "The Parhams' importance to the Apostolic Faith and Pentecostal movement is clearly recognized, particularly their central role in establishing the doctrine of tongues as the initial evidence of Spirit baptism. What detractors fail to recognize, is that the Pentecostal movement for the volatile first-generation period, and indeed throughout much of its subsequent history, has been freewheeling; indeed, much of its dynamic growth can be attributed to this interpretive freedom. What mattered was the crux of the Pentecostal message – the baptism of the Holy Ghost. Spirit baptism was understood by ALL in the Apostolic Faith Movement [A.F.M.] and Pentecostals adopted this as their identifying badge, and the consensus formed quickly, that this experience came to a believer with the accompanying biblical sign of speaking in tongues.[49]

As a result, Parham's position as the initial Pentecostal theologian, and the most prominent spokesman of the pioneering generation, cannot be obscured."[50]

Charles Fox and Sarah Eleanor Parham, like their fellow Methodists were, "as John Wesley (taught) downright Bible-Christians; taking the Bible, as interpreted by the primitive church [early church fathers] ... for their whole and sole rule."[51] Likewise, Martin Luther called it "Sola Scriptura."[52] One of the Parhams' early converts, Howard Goss, confirmed Charles Fox Parham as "personable, gifted, accomplished, original, and forceful thinker with a vivid magnetic personality, and superb, versatile platform ability."[53] Parham was humble, meek, and consecrated in a way that was favorable; he became "father to us all."[54] Sarah Parham echo's these sentiments writing, "...his spiritual children everywhere, who looked to him for spiritual food affectionately called him 'Daddy Parham.'"[55]

Like John Wesley, Charles and Sarah Parham, First, rejected the Reformers "notions of election, predestination, irresistible grace and the like as matters of opinion. He believed that these ideas did not reflect the teaching of the Bible and the early Church. Also, they did not portray accurately the character or work of a loving God. Instead, following Apostle Paul's discussions of law and gospel, sin and justification in Galatians and Romans, Wesley insisted that the grace of God is freely available to all who would *hear the gospel, repent, and believe*; grace precedes faith so that the choice to believe is uncoerced and free. The doctrine of prevenient grace (grace that goes before), which Wesley gleaned from the church fathers, points to a God who saves the lost without transgressing their moral freedom to choose. Such grace enables the individual to repent of their sins and to believe in Jesus Christ."[56] "Second, Wesley taught that salvation, or justification as it is termed, comes by faith alone."[57] "Third, Wesley taught that genuine faith produces inward and outward holiness. The regenerative process inwardly cannot help but find expression in an improved moral character outwardly. The doctrine of holiness is grounded in the command to be holy as God is holy (Lev. 19:2). Therefore, whenever Wesley discussed holiness, sanctification or perfection (all theologically synonymous), he preferred the expression "Christian Perfection." The Parhams' found Christian Perfection through the indwelling of the Holy Ghost.

Charles and Sarah Parham, like pious Christ followers of their day, wanted to better understand how someone could know for certain that they had been filled with the Holy Ghost. They challenged their students, at their Bethel Bible College (later Apostolic Faith Bible College[58]) to study and determine *what is the evidence of the Holy Spirit?* These students began to fast and pray to that end. Rather, simply trusting by faith that the Holy Spirit had come, they sought some type of evidence that would leave no doubt. It is unlikely they had any sense of the impact their efforts would create. Spirit baptism was destined to become the crown jewel of the Apostolic Faith Movement and all those who sought a Pentecostal experience.[59] The result was the students received what Methodists like Henry Clay Morrison and others called their **Pentecost**.[60]

Dwight Moody preaching- Internet Archive- from A Full History of the Wonderful Career of Moody and Sankey by E. J. Goodspeed

Pentecost referenced the outpouring of the Holy Spirit on the Day of Pentecost in the New Testament Book of the Acts of the Apostles. It is unclear who coined the concept of "seeking a personal Pentecost" but John

Wesley spoke of the Holy Ghost in such terms.[61] Adam Clarke, Francis Asbury, William Arthur, Charles Finney, Charles Spurgeon, Dwight Moody, and a long list of others expected that the Holy Spirit comes by faith and all expected to receive the Holy Spirit in great measure.[62] "Wesleyans are Holy Spirit people. From its inception, the Methodist Revival was a Spirit-born resurgence of scriptural Christianity."[63]

Henry Clay Morrison makes the case for a personal Pentecost in his book, **Baptism with the Holy Ghost (1900)**.[64] This and other writings were catalysts that caused the Parhams' students (many with Methodist background) to seek their own Pentecost. Henry Clay Morrison, the most published Methodist of his day, taught that the Baptism of the Holy Spirit is necessary for every believer. Among those whom he cites as having received their own Pentecost is Methodist minister William Arthur, a Presbyterian minister friend, the Evangelist Dwight L. Moody and himself. Morrison expected, Christians should seek a post conversion religious experience called baptism with the Holy Ghost. Recalling the Holy Spirit's descent upon the first Christians in Jerusalem on the day of Pentecost, or Shabuoth (Acts of the Apostles 2-4), this experience appears to have been common in the Christian movement during its first generations.[65]

Morrison unalterably taught that what the Apostles experienced was still in force for believers. Morrison was so impassioned about the necessity of Pentecost that he changed the name of his publication from *The Old Methodist* to *The Pentecostal Herald*.[66] Morrison's writings positioned him like John the Baptist to be the forerunner of a global outpouring where millions would receive their Pentecost. Morrison expected a personal Pentecostal experience was the destination of every believer. He quoted from the book **Tongue of Fire**[67] by fellow Methodist William Arthur. Arthur wrote, "Eyesight is the necessary basis of what is called a painter's or a poet's eye, the sense of hearing, the necessary basis of what is called a musical ear; yet eyesight may exist where there is no poet's or painter's eye, and hearing where there is no musical ear. So, may the human soul be *filled with the Holy Ghost*, having every faculty illuminated, and every affection purified, without any miraculous gift. On the other hand, the miraculous power does not necessarily imply the spiritual fullness; Paul puts the supposition of **speaking with tongues,** prophesying, removing mountains, and yet lacking charity, that love which must be shed abroad in every heart that is full of the Holy Ghost." "Filled with the Holy Ghost!" Thrice blessed word! Thanks be to God that ever the tongues of men were taught it! It declares not only that the Lord has returned to His temple in the human soul, but that He has filled the house with His glory; He has pervaded every chamber, every court, by His manifested presence."[68]

William Arthur

Consider the conversion of a man who became a powerful missionary to India, E. Stanley Jones. "Jones met Henry Clay Morrison (1857-1942)—soon to be president of Asbury College in Wilmore, Kentucky—while Morrison was holding meetings in a Methodist church in Baltimore. Jones was impressed. If he could learn to preach like that at Asbury, then to Asbury he would go. Probably in 1903, but perhaps as late as 1905, the first Asbury Revival struck the campus and then the entire town of Wilmore. There Jones recorded that he experienced the filling of the Holy Spirit." He and four or five of his classmates were praying in one of their rooms when something happened, without provocation, that would change his life. As they prayed, he felt the Holy Spirit sweep them off their feet and fill them all. It seemed to him a new Pentecost and would become one of the most sacred and formative moments in his life.[69]

Writers like Arthur and Morrison helped to create an expectation for another global outpouring of the Holy Spirit just like the Apostles and others experienced in the New Testament Church.[70] In their preaching for one to surrender to the Holy Ghost they did not give proper consideration that would include the tongue. Morrison and others were on the cutting edge of Christian leaders who expected that there was more to the Second **Distinct Work of Grace**.[71] Morrison's fellow Methodists, Charles and Sarah Parham, queried others for the evidence that one had received the Holy Ghost. The collective answer was that they had received the Holy Ghost in faith. For the Parhams, that was simply not thorough enough. They sought demonstrative evidence. Thus, they encouraged their students at Bethel Bible College to determine the Biblical evidence of the Holy Ghost. The unanimous answer from the student's study, was the Holy Ghost was evidenced by *speaking in other tongues*[72] as the Spirit gives utterance, just like the Apostles and others on the Day of Pentecost.[73] Most of the theologians and religious leaders of their day did not believe tongues were available to the believer. These expected tongues had ended in the Apostolic Age—traditionally, the years following Jesus until the death of the last of the Twelve Apostles.[74]

"There has never been a time in history when the gifts of the Holy Spirit completely ceased to function in the Church of Jesus Christ. History undeniably refutes the claims of cessation.[75] At no time has God ceased to give good gifts to His people. God will have His witness."[76]

The contribution of **Charles and Sarah Parham** in recognizing that the Biblical expectation of speaking in other tongues for the recipient of the Holy Ghost was and remains epic! Charles Fox Parham is rightfully recognized as being the first in the modern era to develop the Apostolic Faith Movement's doctrine of speaking in tongues.[77]

The Parhams are equally given due credit as well as laboring to lend this understanding to expand the emerging Pentecostal Movement.[78] William Joseph Seymour wrote of Charles Parham, "He was surely raised up of God to be an Apostle of this doctrine of Pentecost."[79] Pentecostal Historian, Walter J. Hollenweger said, "Pentecost is that event which broke down the walls of the nations, colour, language, sex and social class."

Charles Parham blossomed in his own right because of his willingness to teach that the Holy Spirit is still available to the Believer in Jesus Christ, just as it was in the days of the Apostles, evidenced by speaking in other tongues.[80]

Charles Fox Parham

Charles and Sarah Parham dared to hope that their efforts would usher in a new wave of the Holy Spirit.[81] They held a vision of restoration expecting that what had been lost or explained away was being restored.[82] They envisioned that there would be a new outpouring of the Apostle's doctrine. To that end, Charles and Sarah Parham named their movement, Apostolic Faith. The Parhams began printing a magazine in 1897.[83] Its purpose was to declare the faith of the Apostles: the tenets and doctrines they preached and experienced. Those doctrines included divine healing, justification, entire sanctification, and the baptism of the Holy Ghost as received on the day of Pentecost and recorded in Acts 2, accompanied by the initial witness of speaking in tongues. Parham called his magazine *"The Apostolic Faith,"* and used a portion of Jude 3 as a motto: "Earnestly contend for the faith which was once delivered unto the saints."[84] In the tradition of John Wesley, the Apostolic Faith was organized in Bands.[85] From these Apostolic Faith Bands would come a plethora of outpourings, Revivals, Encampments, Camp meeting, and other gatherings. These events produced a generation of people who, just like John Wesley, Henry Clay Morrison, and others imagined, would seek their own personal Pentecost that even great men of God like Charles Spurgeon had preached.[86]

This vision of a Personal Pentecost became the life's work of Charles and Sarah Parham. The manifestations at The Topeka Outpouring prompted people to refer to the experience of the Apostolic Faith Movement as *Pentecostal*.[87] There had been other groups called Pentecostal but after the events of the Topeka Outpouring the word had new (or restored) meaning. For his global contribution to the Kingdom of Jesus Christ, Charles Parham would be remembered as the Father of the Modern Pentecostal Movement.[88] He is not such because of personal elevation or expectation. In fact, he would likely chide his posterity for referring to him in this manner.[89] Yet, no one is more deserving.

Render therefore to all their dues: tribute to whom tribute is due, custom to whom custom, fear to whom fear, honor to whom honor (Romans 13:7)

CHAPTER TWO

APOSTOLIC FAITH

"If you don't know where you are going then any road will get you there."

-Bishop Bernie L. Wade

The most renowned of the disciples of Charles and Sarah Parham is William Joseph Seymour. Yet, it must be noted that he was far from the first minority that was ministered to by the Parhams. The Parhams ministered to minorities in Topeka and many other areas. The campaigns in Texas were different because there were larger populations of minorities hungry for the baptism of the Holy Ghost. Blacks (African-Americans and Hispanics were very responsive to Charles Parham's ministry.[90] While Seymour did not invest years at the Parhams' sides, he certainly made the most of his time he had with them. Blessed with an eidetic memory, he so dedicated himself to his studies, as to be able to recite verbatim what Charles Parham taught in the Houston Bible College. Time and chance brought them together to fulfill the work of the Lord.[91]

"In 1903, W. E. B. Du Bois prophetically stated: "The problem of the twentieth century is the problem of the color line."[92] Thankfully, someone was working on the problem. Charles and Sarah Parham were already focused on a Christocentric Gospel that dispelled the long-held traditions of men and devils that helped to keep non-whites "in their place." Charles and Sarah Parham had long ago celebrated their Homegoing. Nevertheless, there remains no shortage of performers who are eager to cast lots for a piece of one of their garments.[93] While they lived it was much the same. They wholly dedicated their lives for the cause of the gospel of Jesus Christ. Terms that the Parhams used or were attributed to their movement like Apostolic, Apostolic Faith, Pentecostal have been pirated but their Apostolic Faith Movement (A.F.M.) is the originator. Some sought to remove deserved

> "Parham did not seek recognition; he left no trail of being self-serving."

honor from Charles Parham and place it on one of his representatives, disciples, followers, or even his enemies. Parham did not seek recognition; he left no trail of being self-serving. In fact, even those who opposed him and chose to become his enemies referred to him as humble.[94] The idea of dishonoring his legacy is born from a plethora of un-scriptural agendas, attention seeking, greed, racism, hatred, and historical ignorance. [95]

It has been offered that his student, William Joseph Seymour, fathered the Pentecostal movement.[96] No offence to Bishop William Joseph Seymour, but he came at least ten years too late to be the father of the Pentecostal movement. Seymour was under no illusion that he birthed the Apostolic Faith Movement (A.F.M.). He acquiesced to Parham in person as well as in writing. He proclaimed Parham as his spiritual father.[97] Most who offer these theories pretend that Seymour has been deferred from the honor because of racial discrimination. Sadly, this is very prejudicial to Bishop Seymour. This reduces Brother Seymour as unable to stand with his equals in a place he earned. These attempts of history revision are the societal and racial bias that Charles and Sarah Parham battled to expel through the A.F.M. These theories have been perpetuated by those with various agendas. Opponents of righteousness revel in such conflict-ridden diminishment.[98]

These impressions are extremely disrespectful to Brother Seymour's considerable contribution to the **Apostolic Faith Movement** and subsequent Pentecostal Movement. Such a position lends critics the opportunity to discount Seymour's significance. His church, Apostolic Faith Gospel Mission, began as a mission work of Charles and Sarah Parham's A.F.M. This came at Seymour's own request to Charles Parham. The work that became the mission began a year before Seymour arrived in Los Angeles. In January 1905, William F. Manley of the A.F.M. began tent meetings in the area known as Little Tokyo in Los Angeles. From these tent meetings a prayer meeting started in the home of Richard Asberry[99] at 214 Bonnie Brae Street.[100] The seed for the A.F.M. outpouring in Los Angeles was planted.[101] In 1906 Lucy Farrow, William Seymour (and others) joined these nascent prayer meetings and the Holy Ghost began to fall![102]

William Seymour

The decision by the Apostolic Faith Gospel Mission in Los Angeles to become independent and separate from the international body did not change their church's genesis, name, mission, or doctrine. Seymour did not call the events at his church, The Azusa Street Revival. It was decades before that title was applied by denominations seeking to take credit for the work of the A.F.M.[103] Azusa was a street. The revival was at the church led by Bishop Seymour, **Apostolic Faith Gospel Mission.** Historian, Frank Bartleman understood the big picture and properly titled his book, *How*

Pentecost came to Los Angeles.[104] These meetings were generally referred to as the **Los Angeles Pentecostal outpouring.** The Azusa Street Revival moniker was later created to take credit from the A.F.M. and Seymour. The goal was transferring the credit and the emphasis to the new Pentecostals. Most of the new Pentecostals were not directly involved with The Apostolic Faith Gospel Mission in Los Angeles, but have often taken credit for the same.

William Joseph Seymour joined the Apostolic Faith Movement In 1905, as William F. Manley was holding tent meetings in Los Angeles, down in Houston, Texas **William J. Seymour** became a student and a disciple of the **Apostolic Faith Movement.** This was primarily because of his connection to **Pastor Lucy Farrow,** an adopted member of the Parham family.[105] This connection would change Seymour's life and destiny. Seymour was considered an equal by the Parhams. This was the culture of the Parhams' A.F.M. to expect that God was not a respecter of persons, especially regarding race or gender.[106] Seymour deemed Charles Parham his spiritual father.[107] Parham was known to many as a spiritual father. Howard A. Goss said that Parham became "father to them all."[108] Yet, Goss and many of his friends, were not pleased when the Parhams brought people of color into the A.F.M. as contemporaries. Goss never saw non-whites as his equals and soon joined a faction to oppose the same. Seymour's multicultural impact would likely had been non-existent without his time with Charles Parham. Yet, they complimented each other. Seymour gave Parham more credibility with the black community in the Houston, Texas area and Parham gave Seymour credibility as a minister in the A.F.M. Seymour needed direction for his life and through Parham he became connected to his destiny. The A.F.M.'s influence among black communities saw exponential growth starting in 1905.[109]

At age 36, Seymour, having lived two-thirds of his life, had only recently come to Christ.¹¹⁰ Seymour was still searching for direction when through the influence of the beloved Pastor, Lucy Farrow he met Charles Parham.¹¹¹ Charles Parham was not a Texan. The Parhams were from Kansas. When and where possible, they disregarded the Jim Crow restrictions. A restriction was ignored when they permitted Seymour to enroll and participate in their Bible College just like any other student. Both Charles and Sarah were struck with the man's humility, hunger, and willingness to learn. It is self-evident Seymour applied the lessons he learned in Charles and Sarah Parham's Bible College.¹¹² Seymour was more than a student to Charles Parham. He was treated like family.¹¹³ In spite of the fact that it was a violation of Jim Crow laws for a black man to eat at the same table with white people, Seymour was a daily guest to the Parhams' breakfast table before school at the Houston Bible College.¹¹⁴

Pauline Parham, later mentioned in a lecture, "William Seymour humbly asked Bro. Parham if he could sit outside and take in the lessons, but Bro. Parham gave him a place in the classroom with the other students to learn the truths about the Pentecostal message."¹¹⁵ Like so many parts of Charles and Sarah Parham's history, this part has often been distorted. To this point, Dr. Gary W. Garrett wrote, "Probably the most recognized individual to attend the Parhams' Bible Training School in Houston was **William J. Seymour.**" Sarah Parham recalled the events. *"One colored man, William J. Seymour, became a regular attendant each day for the Bible lessons. In Texas, you know, the colored people are not allowed to mix with the white people as they do in some of the other states; but he was so humble and so deeply interested in the study of the word that Brother Parham could not refuse him. So, he was given a place in the class and eagerly drank in the truths which were so new to him and found for his hungry soul."*¹¹⁶ Sarah also wrote affectionately, *"W. J. Seymour, the colored man who had attended the school (AFM in Houston) so faithfully, had received all the truths and teachings that we* *had held from the beginning."*[117]

"Some historians are writing a different story concerning Seymour being constrained to the hallway and not allowed to enter into the class with the other students."[118] "This story has never before been written about with such clarity concerning the facts from those who were present. A third confirmation of this story comes from the late Howard Goss. *"A negro Baptist preacher from Houston was selected - a Brother Seymour, who had often attended the morning session of the school..."* [119] Notice Goss wrote, "selected." While most had just joined the A.F.M., like Joseph from Scripture, Parham selected this spiritual son, William Joseph Seymore. Even more confirmation from, **The Apostolic Faith Report,**[120] *"For the benefit of many who have been misled, we'll right here drop a word that our readers may fully understand the matter thoroughly. In this training school in the city of Houston, Texas, one negro man by the name of Seymour, became a regular attendant, taking his seat in the classes: and it was here that he gained the full knowledge of the Full Gospel message."*[121]

The reader should wonder, Who was spreading the misinformation and why? Charles W. Shumway was the original source of all the falsehood on this topic. In 1914, Shumway led the way as the first of many proxies that did the dirty work for the white supremacists that had taken the preeminence that same year. He assumed that Seymour was allowed to attend Parham's meetings but was relegated to a separate section. This was based on Shumway's knowledge of Jim Crow laws in Texas. He wrote this with no evidence and no collaboration. This assumption by Shumway was repeated by subsequent historians and is the origin of the story that Seymour had to sit outside the classroom at Parham's Bible School.[122] This single accusation is the cornerstone of an overabundance of false assumptions and the further denigration of Charles and Sarah Parham's character. This is a blatant example of the misinformation that has been propagated against the Parham family. Based on the whole of Mr. Shumway's work, it would seem it is simply character assassination; it is like a drive by shooting.[123] Shumway fancied himself a critic. He was definitely critical. This is the kind of horrible assumption that causes unspeakable hardship and anguish. It is too easy to disparage a man's character. *A froward man soweth strife: and a whisperer separateth chief friends.*[124]

The Parhams did not believe in the *separate but equal Jesus*. Historians busy themselves looking for proverbial needles in haystacks[125] seeking, in like manner as they did Jesus, to bring accusation to some word or statement from the Parhams.[126] The Parhams said probably millions of words and what the proxies offer in criticism is infinitesimal in comparison.[127] I challenge all to look at what the Parhams accomplished! In contrast to Mr. Shumway's raging assumptions about the Parhams, we have truth.[128]

"It was Parham who first reached across racial lines to both African-Americans and Mexican-Americans and included them in the fledgling Pentecostal movement. It was Parham, a native of Kansas, who offended southern whites by preaching in black churches and allowing a black pastor to enroll in his Bible school in segregated Houston, TX. It was Parham who did the "unheard of" and invited a black woman, Rev. Lucy Farrow, to preach in his Apostolic Faith Camp Meeting in south Texas in 1906. And it was Parham who, until his death in 1929, maintained cordial relations with the black community in his hometown of Baxter Springs, KS, often preaching in the local black Pentecostal church."[129] Charles Parham "emerges as an individual who, at critical times, was willing to break with cultural mores and reach across racial lines when it was not the popular thing to do. It is for this reason that Charles Parham deserves credit for setting the tone for the inter-racial openness and

harmony that prevailed for a time in early Pentecostalism."[130] **If anyone thinks he is religious and does not bridle his tongue but deceives his heart, this person's religion is worthless.**[131]

In Texas, Seymour and Parham often preached meetings to black congregations in the Houston area ministering side by side.[132] When the opportunity presented, through one of Parham's followers, Julia W. Hutchins,[133] for Seymour to go to Los Angeles to potentially pastor her church Warren Faye Carothers[134] was not in favor of sending him as representing the A.F.M.[135] Seymour was dispatched to Los Angeles as a representative of the Apostolic Faith Movement.[136] When Seymour needed funds and a building, Charles Parham granted him permission to publish a Los Angeles version of the Apostolic Faith newsletter to assist in the effort to raise funds. Parham was like a doting father toward Seymour's efforts. It was Parham's way toward all those he could help. Parham and Seymour agreed that Los Angeles was an extension of the growing International Apostolic Faith Movement. On the recommendation of Seymour, Parham appointed Florence Crawford first to be the California State Director and then soon organized the Pacific Coast Apostolic Movement with Crawford in the lead.[137] When Seymour left for Los Angeles, Parham moved Anna E. Hall to the lead role, and she often ministered at A.F.M. meetings.

Anna E. Hall

In a time when most white people looked on people of color with suspicion, Charles and Sarah Parham had confidence in "the 35-year-old Seymour who was an unlikely ambassador of the Pentecostal message: he was the son of slaves, not a gifted speaker, lacking in social skills, had almost no formal education, and was blind in one eye. Perhaps his greatest handicap was the fact that he had never spoken in tongues, even though he preached that such a sign should be a part of every believer's experience. He chose Acts 2:4 as the text for his first sermon at the mission on Santa Fe Street in Los Angeles: "And they were all filled with the Holy Ghost, and began to speak with other tongues, as the Spirit gave them utterance."[138]

Those who offer Seymour as the father of all of Pentecost have romantic notions not based in reality. How Seymour was supposed to have accomplished such a feat in just a few weeks surpasses nearly all the miracles in the Bible. What would he have accomplished without the support of a literal army of A.F.M. ministers, the use of the Apostolic Faith name, finances from the A.F.M. and more? If one black man could solve all the nations racial problems, why do we still have racial challenges? Why did Seymour make the Mexicans leave his church? If, as people offer, the rift between Seymour and Parham was racial, why do we assume Parham was racist? For those who want to operate in such a manner, we can easily turn the tables and proclaim Seymour to be racist against Parham because Parham was white and loved Mexicans. Sounds crazy to those who have made this initial offering. Yet, many Hispanics have been told that Seymour was a racist.[139] Florence Crawford's departure from Los Angeles was also not racially motivated and history bears out Crawford's interracial commitment.[140] What needs to happen is to dial down the rhetoric. Claiming that Seymour started the A.F.M. or Pentecostal Movements is like claiming Barack Obama started Harvard College. If we are to ever restore the inclusive multicultural environment that the Parhams created, that set the state for William J. Seymour and his Apostolic Faith Gospel Mission, we must be willing to be honest about the facts. Seymour was not a racist and neither were the Parhams. Nevertheless, both were manipulated by white supremacist for racial reasons.[141] As to origin, Robeck concluded and we concur, that all evidence for origins point to North America, as opposed to multiple, independent, and spontaneous points of origin.[142] Goff echoes these sentiments dismissing the a-historical notions of the fabled "no founder" school, of those content to acknowledge only divine intervention. Goff concludes that the movement originated with Parham.[143]

Seymour wrote to his spiritual father Charles Parham expressing the need for help at the time of the August Camp Meeting at Brunner Tabernacle August 3, 1906, through August 28th. During this Camp Meeting Howard A. Goss, a white minister with no interest in black ministers being his equal, was placed as the A.F.M. State Director of Texas. His predecessor was Warren Fay Carothers, a radically xenophobic man also from Texas.[144] The A.F.M. baptismal service on August 27th drew a crowd of thousands.[145] During this Camp Meeting Charles Parham received a divine call to go to Zion City.[146] Mrs. Anna E. Hall expressed interest to assist Brother Seymour in California. The Parhams provided her car fare to go and she was soon followed by Mr. and Mrs. Oyler and their son Mahlon.[147]

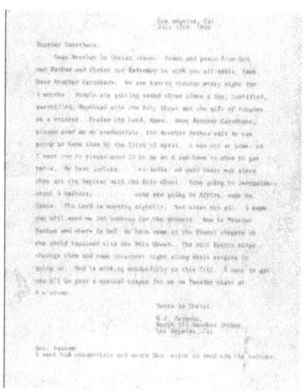

Mrs. Oyler wrote lengthy reports about the Apostolic Faith Gospel Mission in Los Angeles that were printed in periodicals. Oyler wrote, *"... it was plain to me that God was doing a wonderful work and Satan was trying to tear it to pieces. Many things were done that were far from the work of the Holy Spirit. Soon there was bitterness, strife, division and lack of brotherly love."*[148]

A Mr. K Brower wrote, "Seymour introduced Charles F. Parham to the Azusa people as 'his Father in this Gospel of the Kingdom;' all wanted to see the father of the black son. This stirred up the devil in a great shape; Satan's servants who had been at work in the mission in great power, saw their destruction. The next day he closed the door against his 'father.'"[149] It seems evident that the white leadership at the Apostolic Faith Gospel Mission was focused on control. Whether or not that had a racial element is not apparent. The impasse at the Apostolic Faith Gospel Mission did not really hinder the A.F.M. as there were several affiliated A.F.M. churches in Los Angeles.

The rift between Parham and Carothers had quickly come to a head. Carothers possessed radical racial and chauvinistic positions that were contrary to the principles of Charles and Sarah Parham. The Parhams understood that Texas was different than Los Angeles or Kansas but were appalled by Carothers' position on minorities and women. Carothers had been A.F.M. Texas Director, but Parham was the international leader. Unlike Carothers, Parham did not require a fancy title to feel important. In September 1906 Parham dismissed Carothers and replaced him with Howard Goss. Despite the objection of Carothers and Goss, Parham dispatched Anna E. Hall to help Seymour and financed her trip to Los Angeles. Seymour realized that he needed all the help he could get in Los Angeles. Hall was a seasoned minister, and some contend the best of Apostolic Faith preachers.[150] Parham would send her to appointments that he could not fit into his schedule, as in this one to Los Angeles.[151] The Apostolic Faith team sent by Charles Parham helped Seymour form a stable group of ministers to work with him. Some of them were recommended to serve in roles with the international Apostolic Faith Movement; Parham had dismissed Carothers.[152]

"During the Spring and summer of 1906, Parham and Seymour kept up a lively correspondence concerning a visit by Parham to Los Angeles. Their letters were very cordial, and both were anticipating a wonderful reunion. In a letter dated August 27, 1906,[153] Seymour wrote to Parham from the Apostolic Faith Gospel Mission in Los Angeles. A team was appointed to oversee the Apostolic Faith Gospel Mission in Los Angeles and Florence Crawford was appointed State Director of California."[154]

"Both were overly optimistic about the reunion."[155] Charles Parham gave Seymour permission to print some issues of his Apostolic Faith newsletter from Los Angeles. Seymour responded in the very first issue with what functioned as the Apostolic Faith Gospel Mission's Statement of Faith. Seymour was making it certain exactly who oversaw the global outpouring that was called the Apostolic Faith Movement. This was also part of the naming of his church, Apostolic Faith Gospel Mission.

In keeping with the Apostolic Faith Movements revelations Seymour said, *"The Baptism with the Holy Ghost is a gift of power upon the sanctified life; so, when we get it, we have the same evidence as the Disciples received on the Day of Pentecost (Acts 2:3, 4), in speaking in new tongues. See also Acts 10:45, 46; Acts 19:6, I Cor. 14;21. "For I will work in a work in your days which ye will not believe though it be told you. Hab. 1:5. Too many have confused the grace of Sanctification with the enduement of Power, or the Baptism of the Holy Ghost; others have taken the anointing that abideth for the Baptism and failed to reach the glory and power of a true Pentecost."* [156]

This was not some new doctrine being offered by William Seymour. To the contrary, this was the core position of Charles and Sarah Parham's A.F.M. Seymour was a licensed minister of the A.F.M. With Carothers' dismissal by Parham in September of 1907, Seymour's role would have been even more important had his leaders not chosen an independent direction. Seymour's church leadership decision to become independent from the A.F.M. was pivotal. Even while the *Los Angeles Outpouring* and the subsequent revival at the Apostolic Faith Gospel Mission were happening, some ministers in Texas were incensed that their fellow white supremacist Warren Fay Carothers had been dismissed by Parham for opposing what they considered a growing circus headlining blacks and women ministers. We have labeled this opposition group the Texas Syndicate. The Texas Syndicate was displeased with the growing prominent role that Parham was giving to blacks and other minorities. The Texas Syndicates grievances included:

> *August 27, 1906*
> *Dear Brother Parham,*
>
> *Sister Hall has arrived and is planning out a great revival in this city, that shall take place when you come. The revival is still going on here that has been going on since we came to this city. But we are expecting a general one to start again when you come, that these little revivals will all come together and make one great union revival.*
>
> *Yours in Christ,*
>
> *W. J Seymour*
>
> *North 214 Benebra Street*
> *Los Angeles, Cal.*

- The Texas Syndicate opposed blacks, Mexicans, Japanese, Native-Americans and other minorities who were being granted ministerial credentials allowing them equal status with white men.
- Additionally, they opposed women who were being granted credentials and having pastoral roles.
- They were angry that Parham simply ignored the long-established ways these ministers in the South operated. This meaning racist agendas of those who preached a separate but equal Jesus.

- The Texas Syndicate was threatened by Parham's subtle and sometimes not so subtle opposition to the Jim Crow laws. This was putting these ministers in a position where they would have to answer to their constituents about the acceptance of blacks as equals rather than the status quo *separate but equal.*

The vision of the Texas Syndicate for the A.F.M. was of a proper all-white movement of the middle class and upper middle class. Yet, A.F.M. was the ministry of the Parhams. What was happening in Los Angeles was not acceptable to the Texas Syndicate. Their vision did not include blacks, Mexicans, Chinese, Japanese and others they considered lower class. Effectively, the Texas Syndicate saw all non-whites as lower class. The challenge was that the Parhams did not concur. Thus, the Texas Syndicate declared war on the Parham family. Their primary target was Charles Parham, but all the Parhams and their A.F.M. would feel the rage.

With a growing assault on the A.F.M. by Holiness people like the Texas Syndicate, Seymour's Apostolic Faith team printed his doctrinal positions in the Los Angeles version of the Apostolic Faith to be certain that all understood where the Apostolic Faith Gospel Mission stood on the issues at hand. Seymour had met Carothers, Goss and others in person while he pastored in Texas. He knew firsthand how they operated. Seymour signed his name to the declaration in the Apostolic Faith.[157] William J. Seymour, Parham's star pupil from the Houston, Texas Bible School would minister in Los Angeles till his death 16 years later.[158] This Statement of Faith would stand and represent central positions of Seymour's church. It would be eight years before Seymour would address written doctrinal positions. So, much for the denominational surrogates and their printed assumptions of deep racial division between Seymour and Parham. Racial challenges to be sure, but not from Charles and Sarah Parham or their

A.F.M.

As to racial challenges, the first person that opposed Seymour was Warren Fay Carothers. This was racially motivated. The historical record is clear. Carothers was not accepting of black ministers like Seymour as the equal of a Southern white man. Carothers would be a rival for Seymour's position and a manipulator behind the scenes urging the Apostolic Faith Gospel Mission completely away from their spiritual father, Charles Parham. What happened was William Seymour continued as an arm of the A.F.M. This was much in the same manner as the separation of Paul and Barnabas. The division in the A.F.M. only launched the group forward. The failure to divide Seymour from the A.F.M. frustrated the Texas Syndicate. They were ever focused on discrediting Parham, Seymour and other A.F.M. ministers while promoting themselves. "Some of the leaders who attended the services were convinced that they could do a much better job of perpetuating the revival than William Seymour and his team."[159] Later, they supported one of their Texas Syndicate friends, William Durham, attempting a coup against William Seymour. "A tense theological war over the appropriation and experience of sanctification erupted on Azusa Street in 1911. Coming from a Wesleyan-Holiness background, Pastor William Seymour and his associates believed that sanctification, or a "moral cleansing," was a second, instantaneous work of grace. This was the standard view of all holiness leaders. William Durham taught that sanctification was more of a gradual process. While Seymour was away, Durham preached his understanding of the "finished work of Christ" at the Apostolic Faith Mission. When Seymour returned, he was aghast and felt compelled to lock Durham out of the church. This argument created a great schism among the ranks of the congregation that only intensified when Durham proceeded to start a new Pentecostal church nearby.

A significant number of Seymour's congregation joined Durham and a gaping hole was felt in the already troubled congregation. This was truly a terrible wound that the Apostolic Faith Gospel Mission really never recovered."[160] The battle between William Joseph Seymour and the Texas Syndicate was like the one that the biblical patriarch Joseph had with his brothers. Parham favoring Seymour, and treating him like a son was not acceptable. The Texas Syndicate wanted Seymour's place of honor.

Apostolic Faith Camp Meeting. Lucy Farrow Center and Florence Crawford far right.

The second person to oppose Seymour was also racially motivated. Carothers' fellow Independent Holiness comrade Alma White was of the same opinion as Carothers. Blacks needed to keep their place.[161] The third opposition was not racial. It was Mrs. Julia W. Hutchins who disagreed with his doctrine and barred him from her church.[162] In response to Hutchins, a contingent of white Holiness preachers aligned with Phineas Bresse were also racially motivated to reject Seymour's Apostolic Faith teachings. For Seymour's relationship with Parham, race was never the issue. Even when Seymour and Parham had strong disagreement, to his credit Seymour did not evoke the race card. The reason is that everyone knew that this was not the case. Race was only the issue for those who sought to disconnect Charles Parham and black ministers from the rest of the Apostolic Faith Movement. Tragically, they were quite successful in their malevolent endeavors.

~ CHAPTER TWO | WILLIAM JOSEPH SEYMOUR ~
Pastor Lucy F. Farrow (aka Lucy F. Farrar)[163]

Life is often about the moments when God connects one to destiny. For William Seymour that came through his becoming connected to Lucy F. Farrow.[164] Seymour lived in the Houston area for two or three years before his journey to Los Angeles.[165] His Pastor was Mrs. Lucy F. Farrow. [166/167] Pastor Farrow was a widow. As a minister, she was a tent maker,[168] pastoring and making an income as a cook. Her role in the Kingdom of Jesus Christ is significant. Her contribution to the Apostolic Faith Movement is substantial. Lucy Farrow met the Parhams when "Reverend Charles Fox Parham began holding crusades in downtown Houston and preaching about the Baptism of the Holy Spirit with the evidence of speaking in tongues."[169] Farrow became friends with Charles and Sarah Parham. To help the struggling widow financially, the Parhams offered Pastor Lucy Farrow a place to stay in their home. To appease the Jim Crow laws, they publicly presented Lucy Farrow as Governess of their children. However, to the Parhams, Lucy Farrow was family. Denominational proxies and historical revisionist have taken these acts of Christian Charity and made them ugly to fit their bigoted agenda. Lucy Farrow helped as part of the family in the Parham home, but her role as a respected minister of the Apostolic Faith Movement was never questioned. Like other women of color, Apostolic Faith ministers treated her as an equal. There is NO evidence to the contrary. Those who did not see her as an equal were white men like Warren Fay Carothers, Howard Goss, William Durham and their friends.[170]

For Pastor Lucy Farrow, her sabbatical to Kansas with the Parhams was life changing. Free from the horrible Jim Crow laws in Texas, Lucy Farrow was free to worship with her peers of all races and there in Kansas she was baptized with the power of the Holy Ghost evidenced by her speaking in other tongues.[171] It is ironic that the Parhams assisted this "niece of the famous abolitionist journalist Frederick Douglass in receiving perhaps her first real glimpse of natural freedom."[172] Back in Texas, Lucy Farrow was the newest member of the Parham family and beloved "auntie"[173] to the Parham children. This gave her confidence to enlist other black ministers to trust the Apostolic Faith Movement and her family in the persons of Charles and Sarah Parham.

Pastor Lucy F. Farrar (1910)

The invitation for William Seymour to come to Los Angeles was sent to Lucy Farrow from a visitor to her church.[174] The visitor had been a follower of the Apostolic Faith Movement and was friends with **Mrs. Julia W. Hutchins** in Los Angeles. Hutchins was a pastor in Los Angeles and the author of a popular song among the Parhams' students, **Battle Hymn**. The song was printed in the Apostolic Faith in 1905.[175] Lucy Farrow is the most important link in these events. Lucy Farrow is likely the first African-American in Modern History to receive the Holy Ghost evidenced by speaking in other tongues as the Spirit gives utterance. William Seymour was her assistant pastor. Julia Hutchins pastored a church at 9th and Santa Fe in Los Angeles.[176] Mrs. Hutchins was seeking someone to pastor her church in Los Angeles as she felt called to go to Liberia as a missionary. Dispatching William Seymour was in expectation that he would assume the pastorate of Julia Hutchins church. Parham supported the decision. The Texas Syndicate in the Parhams' Movement did not support the decision. Most notably, Warren Fay Carothers and his friends who saw people of color as *less than*. The Parhams held no such limitations over people of color. Seymour was sent, in spite of the objection. The Parhams would feel the wrath of Carothers and his friends in short order, as the Texas Syndicate set out to stop the growing trend of the Apostolic Faith Movement to black and women ministers.

Historian Eddie Hyatt[177] notes, "Parham and Seymour became close friends during this time (in Houston). Seymour introduced Parham to some of the black churches in the Houston area and they ministered together on several occasions."[178] Parham had put his entire ministry at legal risk by opposing the Jim Crow laws in Texas to teach Seymour. Holding nothing back, Parham instructed Seymour because of his spiritual hunger and the strong recommendation of one of Parham's most trusted ministers, the incomparable **Lucy Farrow**. Seymour would lead an important arm of the Apostolic Faith Movement for a short time before they became an independent mission because of pressure placed on Seymour by some in California. Even afterwards Seymour continued to promote the Apostolic Faith from his Apostolic Faith Gospel Mission. In 1906, when Lucy Farrow came through Houston, "Being a dear friend and recognizing the gift of God in her life, Parham did the "unheard of" and invited her to preach in one of the Camp Meeting services. The large tent under which she preached was packed to capacity and the audience listened intently as she told of her experiences in Los Angeles and of her mission to Liberia. At the close of her sermon, she prayed for many to receive the baptism in the Holy Spirit. It was a powerful time. One participant said that she possessed "an unusual power to lay hands on people for the reception of the Holy Spirit."[179] Another point of growing contention for Warren Faye Carothers and friends. Howard Goss testified that when the woman of God laid hands on him there was definite power of God. Yet, the Texas Syndicate would conspire to move the blacks to a segregated status.

Seymour's contribution is deeply respected, but he was not the national leader and certainly not the international leader of the A.F.M. **Lucy Farrow, William Seymour, and Anna Hall** were among the first black ministers in history to be treated as equals in an international ministerial group of the stature of the A.F.M. It is praiseworthy! A surfeit of books has been written about the life and times of Charles and Sarah Parham, it seems most of them have been written in a manner seeking accusation or like a game of "gotcha." These writers portend that readers expect Christian leaders to be without any faults. Our effort is to simply tell the story as truthfully as possible. We do not expect that these are perfect "Holy cherubs;" they are people, much like you and me. We do not propose that Charles and Sarah Parham lived their entire lives fault free. Rather, we understand they had flaws, but were hungry for more of God. As a result of their spiritual hunger, God honored their efforts. They focused on bringing the message of the Gospel of Jesus Christ to a hungry and dying world.

It is our expectation to write this treatise like a letter from Apostle Jude, "Dear friends, although I was very eager to write to you about the salvation we share, I felt I had to write and urge you to contend for the faith that was once for all entrusted to the saints. For certain men whose condemnation was written about long ago have secretly slipped in among you. They are godless men, who change the grace of our God into a license for immorality and deny Jesus Christ our only Sovereign and Lord."[180]

The Legacy Charles and Sarah Parham left to their spiritual posterity, positions them among the most formidable couples in the history of the world. Yet, much of their contribution has been utterly misrepresented by persons seeking personal benefit. Racial hatred has been used as a motive to attempt to rewrite their history. They are easy targets because they were born white. Yet, their enemies were never people of color.

CHAPTER TWO | WILLIAM JOSEPH SEYMOUR

Their enemies were and remain mostly whites Americans. Still, others have re-written the history because the Parhams were so willing to champion women's suffrage teaching and elevating women as ministers. Most who dislike the Parhams because they were anti-segregation believing that racial segregation was merely slavery in a new package. Some haters are agents of hell that endorse Patricide[181] no matter the mayhem it creates.

Our objective is to tell the story of who Charles and Sarah Parham were, what molded them into who they were, their accomplishments, and why we should be interested. It is altogether righteous that we should make such a contribution. It seems fitting and proper that we should remember the good

Robert and Aimee Semple Apostolic Faith Evangelists and Missionaries

these soldiers of the Gospel of Jesus Christ accomplished. Like the lines from Shakespeare's Julius Caesar:

"The evil that men do lives after them. The good is oft interred with their bones;"[182]

> "Some haters are agents of hell that endorse Patricide no matter the mayhem it creates."

It is certainly fair to warn the reader that this book is not going to dance away from the tough questions that have been associated with the Parhams. What the reader will find in the following pages is the Truth. Those that find Truth inconvenient should proceed carefully. Buy the truth, and do not sell it, Also, wisdom and instruction and understanding.[183]

Bishop William Seymour's contribution to the A.F.M. is substantial. Behind Charles Parham, he is at least one of the top four contributors to the Kingdom of Jesus Christ. The other three would be Lilian Thistlethwaite, Florence Crawford, and John G. Lake. Yet, there are so

Brother Dunkelberger baptizing Matt Tatman in the name of Jesus Christ in Mishawaka, Indiana circa 1914.

many others who are worthy of mention. Seymour seems to adopt the expectation that after his church becoming an independent A.F.M. church, that the churches in Los Angeles, Portland, and elsewhere on the west coast are going to see him as the Bishop and overseer. Yet, there are so many forces against him. His primary opposition comes from the New or Neo-Pentecostal. There is little rest for him from within his own church leadership as many of them abandon him in favor of the opposition. The new Pentecostals held no allegiance to Parham so it should come as little surprise that they generally ignored Seymour, disrespected him and sought to seize control of his ministry. Some of this is because of his color, there can be no doubt. However, more of it is just simply ugly church politics and for the most part, Seymour was not good at Church politics.

CHAPTER THREE

INFLUENCERS

"If you don't know where you are going then any road will get you there."

-Harry S. Truman

With the assassination of President McKinley, Theodore Roosevelt, not quite 43, became the youngest President in the Nation's history. He brought new excitement and power to the Presidency, as he vigorously led Congress and the American public toward progressive reforms and a strong foreign policy. During Roosevelt's Presidency there was a great awakening[184] among Christians. This is historically referred to as the Third Great Awakening. [185] People around the world had long sought restoration of the Apostle's doctrine. While many were told that the experiences in the Book of Acts were unique and dispensational and thus no longer available. There were others who did not accept such notions.

This contradiction put the religious world on a collision course with the imprimatur of the Holy Ghost. God would simply not be left without a witness![186] An American revival that began in Topeka, Kansas called the Topeka Outpouring[187] would spawn a global expression of the Holy Spirit. The late 1800's were a time of serious spiritual awakening with noted outpourings of the Holy Spirit in places like the nation of India, Coker Creek, Tennessee[188] the Shearer Schoolhouse Revival, and many more.[189] At the turn of the 20th Century,[190] "on January 1, 1901 the modern Pentecostal movement received its official birth certificate in North America when a student at Bethel Bible School in Topeka, Kansas by the name of Agnes Ozman received the infilling (baptism) of the Holy Spirit and began to speak in the Mandarin Chinese language. Within three days the majority of the 40 regular students, including the school founder Charles Fox[191] Parham had all received the Holy Ghost evidenced by speaking in other tongues as the Spirit of God gave them utterance (see Acts 2:4). This caused quite a stir throughout Christendom as the school seemed to break away from the traditions of mainstream movements within the Christian community.[192]

    Wisely, the Parhams invited not just a plethora of reporters, but experts in foreign languages, Jewish Rabbi, Government interpreters, professors of languages, and foreigners (who spoke other languages).[193] These gave the nascent movement the critical test. The followers of Charles Parham were quickly evaluated by the press as being strange, queer, crazy, holy rollers, and many other superlatives of choice. However, this did not suppress the enthusiasm that was generated by this original group of "tongue speakers" who had a personal encounter with the Holy Spirit."[194] While the Topeka Outpouring began to spread around the World,[195] another revival, this one in Wales starting in 1904 mirrored the Topeka

~ CHAPTER THREE | INFLUENCERS ~

Outpouring and became a move of the Holy Spirit referred to as the Welsh Revival.[196] The commonality of these two outpourings seems to be the Holy Spirit of course, and the sanction of ministers who were encouraging people to seek more from the Holy Spirit. They were expecting a global outpouring from the same.

"Each revival in time past had God's unique signature and outpouring of the Holy Spirit. The Welsh Revival in 1904, had God's special imprint: the spontaneous outbreaks of singing, prayer, open repentance, and confession. Of this revival, **Reverend W. T. Stead**[197] remarked, "Hitherto the revival has not strayed beyond the track of singing people. It has followed the line of song, not of preaching. It has sung its way from one end of South Wales to the other. But then, the Welsh are a nation of singing birds." Here was revival led not so much by the preaching of man, but by the Spirit of God lavishly pouring out on all flesh just like the Prophet Joel forecasted (Joel 2:28). There were also no advertisements, posters, or huge tents, yet throngs of people flocked to church meetings from England, and even America to experience firsthand the mighty outpouring of God's presence."[198]

Joseph Jenkins

Seth Joshua

"The beginnings of the revival could be traced to church services where ministers like Joseph Jenkins[199] and Seth Joshua sought to share their passion and encounters with the Lord. Simultaneously, long meetings were held to seek the Lord's presence and empowerment, and many people were baptized with the Holy Spirit. Over the course of less than a year, the Lord moved in Wales, and the rest of the UK, capturing tens and hundreds of thousands of souls for the Kingdom."[200] Joseph Jenkins pastored the Methodist Church in New Quay. His invitation to Seth Joshua to hold evangelistic services in New Quay was a catalyst for the Welsh Revival. The fact that Seth Joshua was a Presbyterian did not seem to concern Joseph Jenkins. The goal of both was to see souls turn to Jesus Christ. They were much of the mindset of their American counterpart, Charles Parham. They did not expect that one had to join a denomination to get to Jesus Christ. It is said that some in both the American and the Welsh revival were anti-denominational. More fairly it should be said that these outpourings were not controlled by those who led denominations. Whatever the case, they certainly were for Jesus Christ. This departure from man-made denominational control would only be temporary. Men quickly began to devise methods to control the Holy Spirit. "Seth Joshua is best known for his direct influence on a young man who would become the leading face of the Welsh Revival - Evan Roberts. It was at an evangelistic service on September 29, 1904, in Blaenannerch, that Seth Joshua wrote:

"Grand meetings to-day at Blaenannerch and many cried for mercy. It was a remarkable thing to hear one young man, Evan Roberts. He caught at the words and prayed, 'Bend me, 0 Lord,' and this became one of the most frequent petitions of the Revival."

American Revival Of 1905

Some claim that the Welsh Revival was influenced by what was happening in the United States that started with the Topeka Outpouring. Others give the influence to outpourings in India and even others compose that the Welsh Revival was home-grown. Whatever the case there is no doubt that the events led to further flame revival in the United States. While the Topeka Outpouring was being 'noised abroad'[201] by Charles and

~ CHAPTER THREE | INFLUENCERS ~

Sarah Parham and their Apostolic Faith bands, the Wales Revival would reciprocate. Yet, there is evidence that the Topeka Outpouring was the influence for the Wales Revival. "These revivals that started in Orchard, Texas about four months ago and continue with abating have extended to Houston and will reach all over the Southland as it has and is doing in the North, as well as in the East and is doing a great work in Wales."[202]

"What is not as well-known is the fact that the power of revival spread to America as well as many other countries. Welsh immigrants who lived in Pennsylvania were receiving news of the homeland. Suddenly in December 1904 an awakening began in Wilkes-Barre, and the Rev. J.D. Roberts in one month instructed 123 converts. By early spring the Methodists in Philadelphia were claiming ten thousand converts, the greatest ingathering since 1880. In Schenectady, New York, the local Ministerial Association heard reports of the great revival in Wales and united all evangelical denominations in meetings for prayer and evangelistic rallies. By January 22, 1905, all the evangelical congregations in the city were packed with awakened and seeking people. In Troy, New York the awakening began during the January week of prayer held in the Second Presbyterian church and spread to 29 other churches in the city. Throughout New England the revival spread in the spring of 1905. J. Edwin Orr wrote that "the movement was characterized by an intense sensation of the presence of God in the congregations, as in the Welsh Revival... The churches were obviously in the midst of a revival of greater Power and extent than New England had known since 1858."[203]

In Los Angeles, California Pastor Joseph Smale[204] resigned from First Baptist Church and started a new church.[205] They met at Burbank Hall on Main Street in West Los Angeles and called their congregation, New Testament Church. Smale began to teach on the Pentecostal Life.

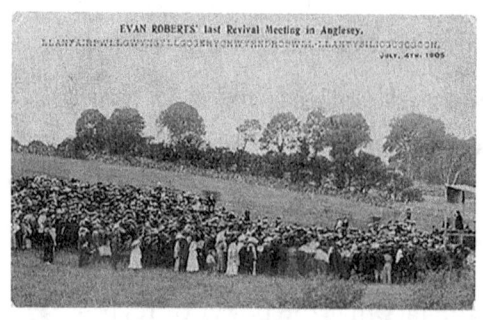

Smale was a convert of the Welsh Revival. Like many others, Smale saw no conflict with denominational barriers. The important thing was the Holy Spirit. Having had his life transformed in Wales, he returned home to Los Angeles, started connecting like-minded churches to pray for an outpouring of the Holy Ghost like the Welsh Revival and the Topeka Outpouring. Here in Los Angeles, they were ready for their own personal Pentecost to come! Frank Bartleman wrote: "Conviction is rapidly spreading among the people, and they are rallying from all over the city to the meetings at Pastor Smale's church. Already, these meetings are beginning to 'run themselves.' Souls are being saved all over the house, while the meeting sweeps on unguided by human hands. The tide is rising rapidly, and we are anticipating wonderful things. Soul travail is becoming an important feature of the work, and we are being swept away beyond sectarian barriers. The fear of God is coming upon the people, a very spirit of burning. Sunday night the meeting ran on until the small hours of the next morning. Pastor Smale is prophesying of wonderful things to come. He prophesies the speedy return of the apostolic 'gifts' to the church. Los Angeles is a veritable Jerusalem. Just the place for a mighty work of God to begin. I have been expecting just such a display of divine power for some time. Have felt it might break out any hour. Also, that it was liable to come where least expected, that God might get the glory. Pray for a 'Pentecost.'"[206]

~ CHAPTER THREE | INFLUENCERS ~

Henry Clay Morrison

The soteriological link between Wesleyan Methodism and the Apostolic Faith Movement is undeniable.²⁰⁷ Late in 1904, the Atlanta newspapers reported that nearly a thousand businessmen united in intercession for an outpouring of the Holy Spirit. On November 2, with unprecedented unanimity, stores, factories, and offices closed in the middle of the day for prayer. Georgia's Supreme Court adjourned."²⁰⁸ In Louisville, Kentucky the press reported "the most remarkable revival ever known in the city is now interesting Louisville... Fifty-eight of the leading business "firms of the city are closed at the noon hour" for prayer meetings. In March 1905 Henry Clay Morrison²⁰⁹ said, "The whole city is breathing a spiritual atmosphere... Everywhere in shop and store, in the mill and on the street, salvation is the one topic of conversation." ²¹⁰ Methodist Henry C. Morrison, was one of the heralds and champions of holiness; with a tongue of fire preached the great Gospel of a Full Redemption. He became its eloquent advocate and propagandist as Preacher, Prophet, Editor, and Educator.²¹¹ Morrison would join those who were seeking their personal Pentecost. He wrote that he received his Pentecost as did many others.²¹² Morrison, a devout Methodist, used the term Pentecost in the same manner and concept as did the founder of the Methodist Church, John Wesley. It was a term widely used by Methodist, Wesleyans, Holiness, and others even before the Topeka Outpouring and other major

revival efforts of the 20th Century. Thus, the idea of a personal Pentecost was not something invented by the Apostolic Faith movement or the subsequent Pentecostal movement to which the Apostolic Faith movement gave birth. However, the manner in which the Apostolic Faith Movement received their Pentecost was different. The difference started at the Topeka Outpouring where receiving one's Pentecost was marked by speaking in other tongues as the Spirit gave utterance. It was a world changing event.

Henry County Kentucky birthplace of H.C. Morrison - Bedford, KY

There is a story told of John Wesley being called to meet Bishop Butler, the high church prelate of Bristol. When Wesley testified to the Bishop the wonderful things of the Spirit, the learned Bishop said: "Sir, the pretending to extraordinary revelations and gifts of the Holy Spirit is a horrid thing, a very horrid thing." It was these extraordinary experiences in the Holy Ghost that produced prophetic men like John Wesley, Henry Clay Morrison, Werter R. Davis and their disciple, Charles Fox Parham.[213] Dr. Morrison as a prophet never played the role of "fore-teller" He was more than that – he was a "forth-teller." He could say: "Thus saith the Lord." He never indulged in fanciful predictions, or in cheap hearsay prophecy. He never sought popular audiences by announcing fantastic subjects. To him, the prophetic office was sacred and he never would lower its standard by commercializing it, or using it for vain purposes. Dr. Morrison looked like a prophet. He was built that way. In the crowded church, auditorium or tabernacle, when he would appear, people would think and say: "Behold the prophet cometh!" When historians look for the inspiration for Charles Fox Parham to come with the imprimatur of Apostolic authority, they need look no further than a Prophet from the same Methodist Episcopal Church as Parham, in the person of Henry Clay Morrison.[214] Of all the ministers influenced by the writing of Henry Clay Morrison, none would become more prolific than his fellow Methodist Episcopal minister, Charles Fox Parham.

> *"To him, the prophetic office was sacred and he never would lower its standard by commercializing it, or using it for vain purposes."*

"It pleased God...to display his free and sovereign mercy in the conversion of a great multitude of souls in a short space of time, turning them from a formal, cold and careless profession of Christianity to the lively exercise of every Christian grace, and the powerful practice of our holy religion."[215]

Before Revival in Wales and before the American Revival of 1905[216] there were many people hungry for God. Most of those who have written Charles and Sarah Parham's history ignore who the Parhams were connected to, influenced by and the fact that both were (first and foremost) devout followers of Jesus Christ. The Parhams were not (as is often presented by self-involved historians) fringe radicals bent on creating some new group for their own enjoyment. What is often overlooked is that the Parhams were not Pentecostals in this modern sense of the word. Charles and Sarah Parham were connected to the Methodist Episcopal Church. They were Pentecostal in the sense that Morrison, Wesley and others described. The vision of Charles and Sarah Parham was much more than Pentecostalism. They dared to dream for a restoration of the Apostles

Doctrine and the New Testament Church. Charles Fox Parham was Methodist and Sarah Eleanor Parham was a birthright Quaker who became a Methodist. Charles was schooled by Methodist ministers, attended a Methodist College, licensed to preach by the Methodists Episcopal Church (M.E.), mentored by the Presiding Elder of the Kansas Conference of the Methodist Episcopal Church (Dr. Werter R. Davis), a Methodist circuit rider, Methodist Evangelist and Revivalist, a Methodist Pastor and fundamentally committed to the Wesleyan-Methodist doctrine. It is the old looks like a duck, walks like a duck, quacks like a duck... Yet, proxies for denominations call it a turkey. The point is that Charles Parham was Methodist.[217] Frankly, it is obvious. Like many who have been part of the Methodist experience, Charles Parham was hungry for God. Sarah and Charles Parham were pious followers of those ministers that dared to believe the Gospel of Jesus Christ held the power to change their world! For Charles that influence would primarily come from ministers in the M.E. Church. Yet, he would ever be a student, praying, fasting and seeking for more from the Holy Spirit.

Sarah Parham was also a disciple of John Wesley,[218] but never professed to being Methodist. For Sarah Thistlethwaite (her Maiden name) Parham the influence from her upbringing in the Quaker movement and subsequent encounters with Jesus Christ placed her on a course to first be a devoted follower of Jesus Christ and then to disciple others. The Quakers, by the time of Sarah Parham, had been championing racial and gender equality for more than 100 years. It was in their DNA. The Quaker movement would prove to be fertile ground for a plethora of Quaker ministers to impact society. No place would Quakers offer a greater contribution than to the equality of people of color.[219] This commitment was not just in the abolition of slavery. This was much, much more. "Neither by word nor deed can the Christian Church give countenance to these intolerable racial disabilities, and it is the duty of the Church to insist upon the full right of the African to rise to the highest plane of industrial efficiency in his own country."[220] It has been postulated that the Apostolic Faith Movement that the Parhams founded was a loosely organized body of Wesleyan-holiness advocates who formulated the theological distinctions of Pentecostal baptism and launched out with a new vision of apostolic purity.[221] Yet, it was more. It was a unique blend of Friend, Methodist, and Wesleyan doctrine.

Charles Parham's influences were strongly inspired by those in his M.E. denomination. After his dramatic conversion, Charles Parham promised God that he would do whatever God asked. This included his stated willingness to go to Africa as a missionary should God so direct. This was not a position that the anti-missionary Baptists of Parham's day would have expressed and subsequently placed him at odds with many of their racially based doctrines and positions. Anti-missioners were the core of the Baptist movement at the time of Charles and Sarah Parham. These Baptists had no interest in missions or helping Africans. Thus, this expression by Parham of a missionary mindset clearly demonstrates the Methodist influence in his world view. The Methodist Episcopal Church was the embodiment of the Wesleyan movement in the United States. The Parhams adhered to the belief of salvation as a second work of Grace. Methodists refer to this as Sanctification. "For Parham, speaking in tongues was the outer evidence of inner Spirit Baptism. It discloses John and Charles Wesley's influence on Parham's philosophy of tongues. He described tongues as the manifest evidence resulting from this Baptism."[222] For Wesley, the Baptism of the Holy Spirit essentially meant inner holiness. Before 1900, Parham had already begun classifying Spirit Baptism into double aspects: the inner one and the outer one, reflected the influence of the Methodist Movement on him."[223] Fellow Methodist, Henry Clay Morrison wrote, "The baptism with the Holy Ghost purifies believers' hearts, and empowers them for service."[224]

While Morrison did not embrace Parham's conclusions on speaking in tongues, the writings of John Wesley lend one to expect Wesley would have agreed. We find several comments that appear to connect Spirit fullness to the sacrament of water baptism in his Journals. On January 25, 1739, Wesley records the baptism of five people, one of whom was born again in a "full sense" of the word; she had experienced a "thorough, inward change, by the love of God filling her heart." Several decades later Wesley shares another example of Spirit fullness, "I baptized two young women; one of whom found a deep sense of the presence of God in his ordinance; the other received a full assurance of his pardoning love and was filled with joy unspeakable."[225] So in the sacrament of water baptism Wesley understood that many were blessed with divine infilling.

In his 1741 sermon, Christian Perfection, Wesley makes a sharp distinction between the privileges of the old and new covenants. Pointing to the words of Jesus in John 7:37-39; Wesley demarcates the new covenant from the old by the gift of the Spirit. This gift, Wesley argues, refers not to the miracle-working power of the Spirit, because the disciples already possessed this power before the day of Pentecost. Instead, what Jesus promised is the Spirit's sanctifying graces, "When the day of Pentecost was fully come...they who 'waited for the promise of the Father,' were made more than conquerors over sin by the Holy Ghost given unto them."[226]

Wesley reflected further, "Many years ago my brother frequently said, "Your day of Pentecost is not fully come; but I doubt not it will: and you will then hear of persons sanctified, as frequently as you do now of persons justified." Any unprejudiced reader may observe that it was now fully come."[227] Here we see that the expectation of a personal Pentecostal type experience was on the mind of both John Wesley and his brother Charles. They understood there was more for them to seek. Which is the primary driving concept behind many of the leading Methodists. It was certainly the thought that drove Charles and Sarah Parham to pursue an understanding of the evidence one would have of receiving their own Pentecost.

People traveled great distances to attend camp meetings, like this one at Witwen around 1900. Photo courtesy Witwen Camp Meeting Association.

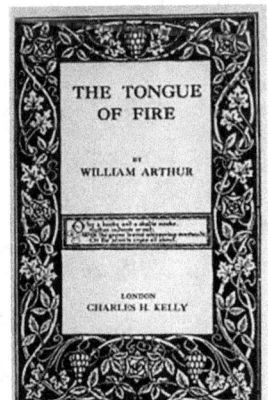

Charles and Sarah Parham were disciples of Wesleyan thought. The men who championed the Methodist movement in the United States were movers and the shakers of not only Parham's M.E. Denomination, but their message also impacted their world. Parham's renowned Pastor was Dr. Werter Renick Davis. Other influences were fellow Methodists Henry Clay Morrison, and William Arthur. Arthur was the author of Tongue of Fire[228] a book that inspired generations to seek the power of the Holy Spirit. These men stirred the hearts and minds of the people of Parham's generation to expect that the Holy Ghost would pour out His power upon His people in a manifestation that proved His occupation of the believer. Arthur subtitled his book, "THE TRUE POWER OF CHRISTIANITY" and instructed his readers to expect the outpouring of the Holy Spirit to impact the whole World![229] Henry Clay Morrison believed those words, as did Charles Parham. These great men of God left no doubt about the need for the believer to receive the Holy Ghost.

Henry Clay Morrison left no doubt about what the believer should expect. It is evident that when Parham wrote his book, Voice in the Wilderness, he was either echoing the words of the powerful evangelist and Prophet Henry Clay Morrison, or the words of the same Holy Spirit. In 1900, Morrison wrote a book titled, Baptism with the Holy Ghost.[230] Morrison explained that the Holy Ghost given on the day of Pentecost was for the Apostles, those who heard their message, and everyone who is called. Morrison quoted, "even as many as the Lord shall regenerate have the promise of the baptism with the Holy Ghost."[231] Morrison pointedly addressed those who were adherents of Cessation doctrine. "Lest someone should say that this baptism of the Holy Ghost was only a temporary gift to the church or a special gift to early Christians. God in His wisdom, put in Peter's mouth words that are plain and unmistakable." "Then Peter said unto them, Repent, and be baptized every one of you in the name of Jesus Christ for the remission of sins, and ye shall receive the gift of the Holy Ghost." For the promise is unto you, and to your children, and to all that are afar off, even as many as the Lord our God shall call.[232] It is evident that these words were an inspiration to the Parhams, as well as many others.

Morrison made it very clear that the message of the New Testament Apostles has not changed, altered, or lessened. Not a marginal participant by any means. Morrison in his day was among the most prolific ministers of the Gospel of Jesus Christ in the World. His periodical, the *Old Methodist* was started in the 1880s, and was published in Louisville, Kentucky. Later, he changed the name to The Pentecostal Herald. If the Parhams are to be termed Pentecostal, it is not merely of their own accord. It is not a word they coined. However, they did put the modern explanation to the concept. Yet, Morrison and other Methodist ministers initiated the call for everyone to seek their own personal Pentecost. Morrison's publications were a major influence in the United States and definitely in the M.E. church where he served as an Evangelist. His publications made their way easily down river from Louisville to Kansas to people hungry for their own Pentecost! No one better accomplished Henry Clay Morrison's moto, "The Whole Bible for the Whole World" than Charles and Sarah Parham.

As President of Asbury College and founder of Asbury Seminary Henry Clay Morrison remains the inspiration for generations of ministers. Morrison was born just a few miles from this author's Kentucky home and a stone memorial marks the place where his mother, Emily Durham-Morrison[233]

dedicated him to the service of the Lord. His name "Henry" is likely in honor of a friend of the Durham family, Henry Bascomb and obviously the famous Senator Henry Clay. Fortunately, both contributed to ending the scourge of slavery. Bishop Henry Bidleman (H. B.) Bascomb,"[234] was often a

 guest at the Durham's as a young man.[235] Bascomb was elected Bishop when some were removed from office because they would not manumit[236] their slaves.[237] The Methodist Episcopal Church made slavery a 'test of fellowship.'

"Emily Durham had met and married William H. English, a member of a prominent Indiana family. After her husband's death, Emily met and married James Morrison. Henry Clay Morrison was born March 10, 1857. The baby son was only three weeks old when he was first left by his mother in the care of a kind neighbor lady in order that she might attend the regular quarterly meeting in the old Hickory Grove Methodist Church near Bedford, KY. A neighbor later related how upon Emily Morrison's return she picked up the baby and while weeping, laughing, and praising God said, "Today while I was at church I gave my little Henry Clay to God to preach the Gospel, and I believe that He accepted the gift and when I am dead and gone this baby boy, grown into manhood, will preach Jesus." Although Morrison was not able to remember his mother, he felt he owed her a debt of gratitude because of her devotion to God. "Through the years," he once said, "I have thanked God that my mother gave me to Him in my boyhood to preach Jesus to a lost world. Two short years of happiness in the Morrison home ended with the death of Henry's mother. God honored her prayers! William Jennings Bryan regarded Morrison to be "the greatest pulpit orator on the American continent."[238]

The reason we are sharing the brief resume of these men of God is to refute the notion that Charles and Sarah Parham were off the reservation when it came to their beliefs about God. The reader should understand that the core doctrines of the Apostolic Faith Movement (A.F.M.) were generally believed among most followers of Jesus Christ. The command of Apostle Peter in Acts Chapter 2 was embraced by nearly all followers of Christ including those in the A.F.M. The Parhams' doctrine was Scriptural. Repentance, water Baptism (by immersion) while invoking the name of Jesus Christ and receiving the gift of the Holy Ghost evidenced by speaking in other tongues are promises to the believer.[239]

Werter Renick Davis, D.D.

When Werter Davis was born Methodism did not have one college.

Dr. Werter R. Davis, First President, Baker University

"The denomination Methodist had 211,000 members, with 701 preachers and two bishops. He lived to see fifty-six colleges, 2,524,053 members, 14,653 ministers, and eighteen bishops. Two-thirds of the continent were practically unoccupied by civilization when this young circuit rider carried his saddle bags into the hill country of Virginia. On June 6, 1835, at Hillsborough Ohio, this lad was licensed to preach by James B. Finley. He was but twenty – a stripling, like young David, strayed from the sheepcote to the field of war."[240] Davis dedicated his entire life to the service of the Lord. Most of that service was in his various capacities within the Methodist church.

When Davis joined the Methodist Episcopal Ohio Conference, it contained such men as Morris, Hamline, Thompson, Finley, Nast, Trimble, Moody, Power, Strickland, of whom it might be said, "There were giants in those days," and among such he soon became a man with a mark.[241] "He received the degree of Doctor of Medicine from a medical college in Cincinnati, and the Doctorate of Divinity from the Indiana Asbury[242] (now

DePauw) University in 1859. Davis served 18 years in the Ohio Conference "old Union Circuit," at Dayton, Sandusky and similar appointments. Davis was known for his oratorical gifts; the people were wanting to speak of his rare combination as logic set on fire. In June of 1858, he accepted the presidency of Baker University. In September of that year moved to Baldwin, Kansas.[243] In 1859, Davis started a publication called the *Kansas Messenger*.[244]

Following John Wesley's lead, M.E. members and clergy championed modeling Christian equality, and were unalterably opposed to slavery. Ministers like Bishop Henry Bascomb, Dr. Werter Renick Davis and Charles Parham represented those who were not satisfied only seeing slavery come to an end, but further they agreed with John Wesley and the visionary words of Thomas Jefferson in the Declaration of Independence that all men are created equal.[245] Like those who signed the Declaration of Independence, these men are not just names on a page. They lived to promote the Gospel of Jesus Christ and pledged their lives, their fortunes and their sacred honor.

Dr. Werter R. Davis was destined to be Charles Parham's Presiding Elder (P.E.) in his district of the M.E. Church. Standing true to his belief system, was once "jailed while in Virginia due to preaching antislavery sentiments."[246] This apparently went against the sensitivities of the people of Virginia. Davis did not seem concerned they opposed his intentions. After the M.E. Church transferred Davis to Kansas, it was noted that "his voice was heard in its halls for freedom and civic righteousness."[247] Davis was willing to literally go to war for the people he served. He was not a sideline observer or promoter. He committed his life to the cause. To that end, he became first a chaplain, then a lieutenant-Colonel in the Union Army during the American Civil War.[248] During the war, Davis was promoted to

~ CHAPTER THREE | INFLUENCERS ~

Colonel.

After the American Civil War, the M.E. church became divided on the subject of racial segregation. Not Davis! Davis was among those Methodist that had dared to dream that the fighting of a horrendous civil war would not only end slavery but would fulfil the dream of the founding fathers of equality for all men. Davis labored to instill his dream in the mind and hearts of his students at his Baker University,[249] in his conference and in the churches he served. Davis was a member of the Methodist General Conferences of 1868, 1872, and 1880, and a delegate to the Ecumenical Methodist conference in London, and to the Centennial conference held in Baltimore, MD in 1884. In 1859, he edited and published "The Kansas Messenger,"[250] the first paper published in Baldwin City, and published several sermons."[251] The Minutes of the M.E. Kansas Conference in 1879[252] list W. R. Davis as the P.E. (Presiding Elder) of the Topeka District with his office in Baldwin City, Kansas.[253]

"When Davis arrived in Kansas as President of Baker University a great struggle was in progress. Kansas was the first battle ground between slavery and freedom. The battle raged both in the general society and in the Church that Davis represented. New England emptied her treasures of money, brain and heart that Kansas might prove a barrier against the encroachment of that devouring power which knew no moderation. In such a crisis this preacher arrived; of all who came, none was better equipped to play a man's great part in the drama. He was by nature chivalrous: no knight had more courtesy. He was the soul of honor, with a poet's temperament. The occasion seized and inspired him. He was the intimate associate of Lane, Robinson, Goodenough, Montgomery and other leading free state men of those tremendous days.

Davis was a chaplain of the Wyandotte convention, rendered

historic as the body of anti-slavery men which drafted the constitution of Kansas and a member of the first legislature. His voice sounded like a prophet's speech. He was in the secret councils of that storied time, a politician as well as an educator and preacher. As president of Baker University, he preached a sermon on the murder of John Brown at Harper's Ferry[254] and the Honorable Everett Dallas declared it the most remarkable effort to which he ever listened. Man, and occasion met his genius for speech was set on fire."[255]

In March of 1892, Dr. Davis became presiding elder of the Baldwin City district of the Kansas Conference. In September he enlisted for the defense of the Union. He was appointed chaplain, was afterward made colonel of the 16th Regiment of Kansas Volunteers and became commandant of Fort Leavenworth. Always a man of military bearing, he looked on his black charger with the trapping of war, every whit a soldier; so long as he lived, he was to the old soldiers always "Colonel Davis,"[256] Davis was not only committed to the equality of all men, but he was also a champion of women's suffrage. Once while preaching in Virginia, he "delivered from jail a young lady imprisoned for the heinous crime of reading the New York Tribune. He was by instinct and grace, a man of peace. When the war was over, he reassumed the presiding eldership and for fourteen consecutive years served the Church in that capacity. He rode districts on which he could reach home only once in six weeks. He had intent like the Asburys of old.[257] Dr. Davis, unostentatiously, kept his line

Depiction of Brown in a mural at the Arkansas State Capitol Building

of march, the goal of which was the seizing of Kansas for God: and it is safe to say, as has been declared by one entirely conversant with the facts, that no one man is Kansas Methodism (the largest denomination within the borders of the state) so greatly indebted as to Werter R. Davis. His life was in the pastorate.[258] Charles Fox Parham inherited this mantle; this is quite evident.

Spirit-Filled Methodists

Wesley was not a cessationist. Over the centuries there have been many spiritually starving people of God who dared to believe that the promise given by Apostle Peter from Acts Chapter 2. Like John Wesley, they hoped they too could have an experience equal to the outpouring of the Holy Ghost on the Day of Pentecost as recorded in the Book of The Acts of the Apostles.[259]

"...For the promise is to you and to your children, and to all who are afar off, as many as the Lord our God will call..."[260]

While John Fletcher[261] is usually credited as the first Methodist to formally link Spirit baptism to entire sanctification, Timothy Smith pointed credit to Charles G. Finney and his Oberlin colleagues for introducing Spirit baptism. In the latter part of the 1830's Finney began proclaiming a second crisis of heart holiness that soon spilled over into Methodism and the burgeoning Holiness Movement.[262] By the end of the 19th century the language of Spirit baptism for entire sanctification was nearly universal.[263] History affirms people being filled with the Holy Spirit in Methodist Camp Meetings in Michigan in the early 1900s, Baptists in Tennessee and thousands in faraway India. None of those were hungrier for a genuine outpouring of the Holy Spirit than a small group in Topeka, Kansas.

Topeka, Kansas at the beginning of the 20th Century boasted such prominent high church[264] preachers as Charles Shelton. Shelton is the famed author of the book, In His Steps. A book that dared to challenge people to live their lives like Jesus Christ by asking the question, "What would Jesus do?" The phrase has become the famous WWJD! Charles Shelton arrived in Topeka, Kansas in 1882. He dared to suggest that white and black people could live, work and serve together. In regard to whether whites and blacks could live together harmoniously Sheldon asked, "Why not? It never has been done. Well let's do it then. Oh! I am tired of hearing it said, 'You can't do it because it never has been done.'"[265]

"And it shall come to pass afterward

That I will pour out My Spirit on all flesh;

Your sons and your daughters shall prophesy ..."[266]

CHAPTER FOUR

THISTLETHWAITE SISTERS

"Charles Fox Parham gave his life to restore the revolutionary truths of healing and the baptism of the Holy Spirit to the Church."

-Roberts Liardon: God's Generals

Prophet Joel said there would not just be sons that would prophesy, but also daughters.[267] The idea that women should have a place in ministry has long been a divisive concept. The notion that women should be seen as equals in ministry has been practiced by only a minority of Christian groups. Charles and Sarah Parham founded a ministry that empowered women in ministry like no Christian effort in history. The record of women ministers who have a connection to the Apostolic Faith Movement fills volumes of books, articles, songs, and more. To God be the Glory!

When Time Magazine printed its list of one hundred top events of the Century; Number 68 *is the Protestant fundamentalist Pentecostal movement, United States, 1906.*[268] This is a significant reference to the ministry of Charles and Sarah Parham.[269] Proxies for various denominations rushed to claim this honor as their own, but it was the Parhams who sacrificed to bring real change. *Render therefore to all their due: taxes to whom taxes are due, customs to whom customs, fear to whom fear, honor to whom honor.*[270] Charles and Sarah Parham and their A.F.M. set the standard that every theologian has had to define, comment, and clarify their position on a number of points that Charles Parham established.[271] These points included:

- "Speaking in tongues was the initial physical evidence of the infilling of the Holy Spirit. In other words, every Spirit-filled believer should speak in tongues.[272]
- It was a working-class movement. It not only attracted the poor and marginalized, but its leaders developed an early theology of poverty, a belief that God had a preference for the poor. As the movement boomed, early Pentecostals interpreted their growth as an example of God's special favor on the poor.
- The Early Pentecostals generally called the Apostolic Faith Movement were known for their commitments to both racial reconciliation and women's rights.[273] William Seymour, the leader of the Apostolic Faith Gospel Mission (aka Azusa Street) Revival was black, and Pentecostal's most famous early leaders, the extraordinary Aimee Semple McPherson, was a white woman. Many early Pentecostal churches were noted for having blacks and whites, and men and women, worshiping and sharing leadership in the church. Abundio and Rosa Lopez were Hispanic.[274]
- A.F.M. ministers were pacifists.[275]

- Racially integrated, affirming of women, opposed to war, on the side of the poor, filled with the Spirit – no one had seen a movement quite like this before. Understandably, they were rebuffed by the other Protestant denominations. Indeed, in some cases they attracted the most vehement attacks from both secular and church voices."[276]

A few years after the high churchman **Charles Shelton** offered his opinion on the vision of multicultural cohesion in Topeka, a young couple would come to Topeka that did much more than imagine. **Charles and Sarah Parham** started Bethel Bible College in October of 1900, with around 34-40 students. They brought with them a vision that was being accomplished by other ministries around the country. Like colleges in Oberlin, Ohio[277] and Berea,[278] Kentucky, Charles and Sarah Parham dared to imagine a college that mirrored the New Testament church and was open to people of all races and both men and women.[279] The Parhams', ministers in their own right, were aided by one of the most capable ministers in the person of Sarah Parham's older blood sister **Lilian Theodora Thistlethwaite**.[280] Though largely ignored by historians, because they were females in a male dominated culture, the contribution to the Kingdom of Jesus Christ by these two siblings (Lilian and Sarah) places them breathing rare air. They wrote books, contributed to many publications, served as editors, preached the gospel, were licensed ministers, served as professors and much more. "Charles Fox Parham trained women for ministry in his Apostolic Faith Movement from 1900 onward. His sister-in-law, Lilian Thistlethwaite, held meetings of her own throughout the Midwest and appeared alongside Parham in extended meetings elsewhere. Parham commissioned a number of women to establish church plants and serve as pastors. The African-American preacher William Joseph Seymour brought the Apostolic Faith Movement to Los Angeles in 1906. His Apostolic Faith

Gospel Mission quickly became known as an interracial congregation led by an African-American pastor, with capable women and men providing leadership and outreach. The Mission was even ridiculed on the front page of the Los Angeles Evening News, July 23, 1906, for violating Paul's command in 1 Corinthians 14:34 regarding the silence of women."[281]

The contribution of Charles Parham's A.F.M. to the inclusion of women ministers is historic as recognized in a plethora of accolades.[282] No ministry, church or denomination of his day could lay claim more inclusive, receptive, and committed to women in ministry than the Apostolic Faith Bands that Charles and Sarah Parham organized as part of their A.F.M. Few groups can point to women in key leadership roles - ever! The A.F.M. accomplished this in 1906 with the incomparable Lilian Thistlethwaite as Secretary General of the A.F.M. The contribution of Charles Fox Parham to women's causes should land his likeness on a coin opposite **Susan B. Anthony.** He should be remembered as **Charles Fox Parham, Civil Rights leader, Champion of Women's Suffrage and Projector of the Modern Pentecostal Movement.** Yet, much of his contribution is never mentioned. Many have attempted to soil his considerable contributions.

"Charles Fox and Sarah Eleanor Parham gave their lives to restore the revolutionary truths of healing and the baptism of the Holy Spirit to the Church. (Note: whenever the "Baptism of the Holy Spirit" is referred to in this treatise, it is inferred that the experience is always accompanied with the "evidence of speaking in tongues"). The first forty years of the twentieth century were powerfully visited by this man's message that changed lives. When he proclaimed to the world in 1901 that, "Speaking in tongues was the evidence of the baptism of the Holy Spirit," the Pentecostal truths of the early church were wonderfully restored to thousands around the world."[283] The teachings of Parham's Methodist Church mentors were going to new dimensions in the Holy Spirit, or at least dimensions that had not been attained in centuries.

Quaker Activism: Sarah Eleanor (Thistlethwaite) Parham[284] And Lilian Theodora Thistlethwaite

The Thistlethwaite Sisters were born to a family of progressive Quakers that encouraged their daughters both to be educated and to be in active ministry. The Quakers were the foremost religious group to take a stance against slavery. The Quaker campaign to end slavery can be traced back to the late 1600s, and many played a pivotal role in the Underground Railroad. In 1776, Quakers were prohibited from owning slaves, and 14 years later they petitioned the U.S. Congress for the abolition of slavery. A primary Quaker belief is that all human beings are equal and worthy of respect. The fight for human rights has also extended to many other areas of society. In the early days Quaker views toward women were remarkably progressive, and by the 19th century many Quakers were active in the movement for women's rights. One of the earliest suffragettes was Quaker minister Lucretia Mott, a fierce abolitionist who refused to use cotton cloth, cane sugar, and other slavery-produced goods. Frustrated by anti-slavery organizations that would not accept female members, Mott set about establishing women's abolitionist societies. When slavery was outlawed in 1865, she didn't stop her activist aims and began to advocate giving black Americans the right to vote.

Another Quaker, Susan B. Anthony, like the Thistlethwaite sisters also dedicated her life to attaining equal voting rights for women in

America. She founded the American Equal Rights Association in 1866. Quaker commitment to bettering the lives of women continued through the 20th century and no group was more committed than the A.F.M. Prominent suffrage leader Alice Paul, widely recognized as helping to deliver the vote for women in the United States in 1920, attributed her Quaker upbringing for her beliefs on rights for women.

Raised in this Quaker mold of expecting societal change and being the agents of the change, the Thistlethwaite sisters were powerful voices for racial and social justice. Historians have often represented the marriage of Sarah Thistlethwaite and Charles Parham as influencing Parham to leave the Methodist Episcopal Church. They present this as though it was some evil manifesto rather than the simple truth that the Parhams were not comfortable with following church leaders that were undecided or wishy-washy in their commitment to racial equality as many M.E. Ministers had become. Further, even though John Wesley had personally embraced women ministers, the church that claimed his legacy discouraged the participation of women preaching. Indeed in 1884 the Methodist Church decided ordaining women was out of order.[285] It would be forty years before Methodism would catch up with the vision of Charles Parham regarding ordaining women.[286]

The American Civil War had divided the United States. Nearly all religious denominations were divided by race and gender. In some cases, such as the Southern Baptist Convention, denominations split and formed new ones that better fit their dogmas. The M.E. Church that Charles Parham was part of was embroiled in a similar fight. While the M.E. Church had helped lead the fight to end slavery, many of the adherents felt like that was enough. They were okay with freeing slaves; for slaves of color, they did not embrace a vision of equality. Some, like self-appointed Bishop,

Alma White, went so far as to expect that people of color 'owed' them for the sacrifice of fighting a civil war primarily on the behalf of people of color.[287] Alma White reasoned, *"We avow the distinction between the races of mankind as decreed by the Creator, and we shall ever be true to the maintenance of White Supremacy and strenuously oppose any compromise thereof."*[288] Pentecostals like Warren Fay Carothers, Howard A. Goss and their friends in the Assemblies of God embraced Alma White's vision of all-white dominance.[289]

While the M.E. Church postured to be a centrist denomination people on both sides of the debate saw the leadership as compromised. The 1896 U. S. Supreme Court upheld segregation, ruling in favor of "separate but equal" facilities for blacks and whites.[290] The war was over, but not the battle.[291] The racial segregationists postured for a *separate but equal* position that many in the M.E. embraced. Misanthropes like **Phineas Bresse, Alma White, W. F. Carothers** and the prejudiced denominations they represented were okay with freeing slaves but certainly did not see Blacks (or Native-Americans and other minorities) as equals. Alma White offered, "Whatever wrong may have been perpetrated against the Negro race by bringing black men to this country...the argument will not hold that they should share equal social or political rights with the white men..." [292] Dear Reader. Pause here. Read the above once more very carefully. Reflect that these people were the primary opponents of Charles and Sarah Parham. To people like this anyone who would dare lift people of color to equal status were the enemy. Charles and Sarah Parham were among the faction of white people who saw this as the time for the Church to lead. Unfortunately, they were generally alone. Even with the Baptism of the Holy Ghost, white people were happy to speak in tongues, but they didn't want Apostolic Revolution. The Parhams' idea of treating Blacks as equals was just too much! This was the driving force behind differentiating between Apostolics and

Pentecostals. The A.F.M. embraced people of all races and elevated women. Pentecostals preferred their women in the kitchen and there was no room for people of color in their all-white groups.²⁹³

The Church of the Nazarene has attempted to portray Phineas Bresse as a Saint, but the stark reality is that Bresse was politically motivated to adopt the status quo. Like Alma White and Warren Carothers, Bresse supported the freeing of slaves but also made alliances with those who fought viciously to keep them enslaved. This is not in keeping with the vision of John Wesley or most of M.E. leaders before the American Civil War. Bresse aligned with southern xenophobes forging a racially bigoted national holiness denomination based on the union of northern and southern churches." Bresse and his Segregationist friends would not leave things to mere change and quickly moved to organize the all-white boys club and called it the Church of the Nazarene in 1895. These preached a gospel not found in Scripture – the separate but equal Jesus.²⁹⁴ Blacks were welcome in a separate group but not in the all-white one.

Pleasant Valley School House in Tonganoxie Kansas where Charles Parham held revival.

Church of the Nazarene first General Assembly, all-white male legislative commission.

Alma White was less subtle about her feelings on black people and since her former associates were forming all-white boys' clubs²⁹⁵ and would not let her in, she decided to start her own all-white hate group. While apologists and proxies writing as historians generally explain away the obvious racial overtones of these and other prominent leaders, the truth remains that all black people were not slaves before the American Civil War, but Segregationists like **Phineas Bresse, Alma White, Warren Fay Carothers** and their friends treated all black people like slaves. Alma White certainly saw all blacks as "less than." Leonard Lovett said, No man can genuinely experience the fullness of the Spirit and remain a bona fide racist. Which begs the question concerning the spiritual condition of so many who aspire to lead others.

For Charles and Sarah Parham, their many enemies were sharpening their proverbial swords. The anti-segregationists in Kansas were led by people like **Werter Renick Davis.** His passing was certainly a blow to the anti-segregationists and directly to Charles Parham as M.E. Church leadership moved more toward the separate but equal, Segregationist view. Other notable anti-segregationists were **Charles G. Finney and John Gregg Fee.** These held commonality in that they realized if men were truly to be free and equal in society, education must be made available to them. To that end Finney led Oberlin College. Fee founded Berea College and Davis founded Baker. Charles and Sarah would join the fight in founding Apostolic Faith College. All of them still exist today!

Rather than feud with the M.E. leadership that devalued people of color and women, the Parhams merely moved onto their mission. Sarah identified the challenge as the non-sectarian spirit of Charles Parham did not please the M.E. Church.[296] Sarah was a major influence in these decisions; this is without doubt. Her serious role in ministry would have been greatly marginalized had she married Charles and he remained tethered to the pastorate of the Methodist church. In Charles, Sarah had found a man who history presents as not being fickle in his commitment to the people of God regardless of their race or gender. For a Quaker lady like Sarah, this was a picture-perfect match. While other Quaker women were impacting the culture with social reforms, Sarah and her sister Lilian were using the Gospel to transform millions.

Historians have primarily acted as proxies for denominations. They often and repeatedly posture that the Parhams were racists using them as scapegoats while virtue signaling each other.[297] This is a tragedy of justice against these good and fair-minded people. The vision of their ministry began in the small town of Tonga-Noxi, Kansas where they first met. "The miracles that occurred in the Parhams' ministry are too numerous to record. Multiplied thousands found salvation, healing, deliverance, and the baptism of the Holy Spirit. Charles Parham started ministry at the young age of 14.[298] Charles helped in several Methodist churches and served as a circuit rider and evangelist. He held his first solo evangelistic meetings at the age of eighteen, in Leavenworth County at the Pleasant Valley School House, near Tonganoxie, Kansas. In the early days, Tonganoxie was a place that most of the "religious people" avoided. All except the Quakers and the occasional Methodist. The locals felt like they were good people and didn't really need or want religious instruction.

Tonganoxie is midway between the cities of Topeka and Kansas City. "Settlement between 1830 and 1890 included thousands of American Indian tribes who were moved to the area from the East and Great Lakes area."[299] "In western Kansas, many early schools were built of sod. In rural communities, the schoolhouse was used for many activities including dances, church services, public meetings, voting, lectures, debates, spelling bees, and arithmetic contests. "Mandatory school attendance was important in the Americanization of immigrants. Public schools required that all students learn English. Instruction was also given in "U.S. history, government, and culture." School-age children, in turn, shared their education at home with younger brothers and sisters and their parents. In this way, the entire family was exposed to the language and customs of their new country. Parochial schools, established by immigrants, often gave instruction in that group's native language. Teachers, however, still taught and stressed the importance of learning English."[300]

Most church denominations avoided places like Tonganoxie preferring areas that were, frankly, more populated by white people. Most white denominations preferred working with immigrants to ministering to blacks and Native-Americans. Religious groups were happy to cater to white communities but places like Tonganoxie were less than desirable. Tonganoxie was named after Chief Tonge-Noxi[301] and held a considerable Native-American population at the time. When Parham ministered there, it was still named Tonge-Noxi. The name was changed to Tonganoxie in 1900 after most of the Native-American population had been forced off their land by the United States government to places further West.[302]
The attitude of Church denominations was a general reflection of the larger society and the society saw little value in the people of that area. "Unionist Robert W. Chester referred to the Kansas immigrants from his district as "Loafers" and "the very scum of creation."[303] Tonge-Noxi was named after the chief of the Turkey Tribe of the Delaware.[304] In addition to Native-Americans, and a growing population of immigrants, Tonge-Noxi was home to many former slaves who sought to restart in and around Tonganoxie. Twenty-five percent of the population was African-American, and legacy names such as Jarrett and Quarles continue that presence."[305]
These were tumultuous times in Kansas. "Westward expansion of the United States eventually reached Kansas. In 1854, the Kansas-Nebraska

Act created the land as a U.S. Territory. In 1861, Kansas became a state. In 1866, the final treaty offered the Delaware two options: live in Kansas as American citizens or move to Oklahoma and merge with the Cherokee. Neither option allowed the Delaware Indians to retain their heritage."[306]

"Despite federal obstruction, popular demands for the land did not end. Captain David L. Payne was one of the main supporters of the opening of Oklahoma to white settlement. Payne traveled to Kansas, where he founded the Boomer "Colonial Association." Payne's organization of 10,000 members hoped to establish a white colony in the Unassigned Lands."[307] Racial tensions ran high in the area. While the American Civil War was over, the issue of race was still raging. Sadly, Most American Church denominations were not willing to treat people of color as equals. Some were okay with what they called, "Separate but Equal," but that was primarily clever branding for those who saw people of color as "less than." Denominations like the Southern Baptist Convention, were very clear about where they stood on the subject. They saw no reason why a white person could not own black slaves. The American Civil War did little to change the mentality of the Southerners.

Chief Tonge-Noxi

The Friends Church (also known as Quakers) had labored for more than 100 years to bring equality. Starting in 1775 the Quaker movement made a strong commitment to ending slavery and bringing equality and justice to all people. The area near Tonge-Noxi became a place that Quakers from Kansas City committed to as a mission. To that end, in 1874 they financed the construction of a brick building to replace the original log cabin schoolhouse. Seven years later they added an addition.[308] In keeping with their spiritual standing, Friends (or Quakers) were more than willing to work with the local population regardless of race or gender. "The first school of higher learning in the area was the Tonganoxie Friends Academy, established in 1882. Friends Academy met in the Pleasant Valley School building. William P. Trueblood was the first principal and served as the superintendent of Schools for many years. Trueblood was a graduate of Tonganoxie Friends Academy.[309] Later principals included Richard Haworth, a member of the Friends and later [310] H. C. Fellow."[311]

"Charles Parham was a stranger to the community when he asked permission to hold a revival in their school building. So, when they gave their approval, Parham went up on a hillside, stretched his hand out over the valley and prayed that the entire community be taken for God.[312] While most felt like a town populated by former black slaves, Native-Americans who had managed to avoid being forced off their land by the government, and immigrants was beneath their dignity, Parham saw the place as a vision of heaven! Parham's willingness to work with people of all races would become his trademark. In the Methodist tradition, Charles Parham arranged a mourner's bench at the schoolhouse for his meetings.[313] "In the Methodist Church, persons are often invited to come forward to the altar and kneel at the chancel railing for prayer. The cushioned comfort of today's altar rails would have been unheard of in the early days of the Methodist Church in America. Early Methodists had a sacred but plain, uncomfortable wooden bench for the purpose of confession and repentance."[314]

At Parham's Revival meetings, "There was little response at first amongst a congregation that was predominantly nominal Friends Church folk. Nevertheless, there were soon many conversions."[315] Parham was following his mentors, **Werter Davis, Henry Clay Morrison,** etc., in preaching the Gospel of Jesus Christ where God directed. As a Methodist minister, he was unfazed by ministering to Quakers and people of other denominations. He was also more than happy to preach to those who had no religious affiliation.

One family of Quakers, by the name of Thistlethwaite, began to attend the meetings led by the young Parham. Anthony Mason Thistlethwaite[316] was from New York and his wife Ann Maria Baker Thistlethwaite was from Durham England.[317] They married November 15, 1871, in Tonge-Noxi, Kansas.[318] Their daughter, Sarah (Thistlethwaite) Parham later wrote that her family were likely the only practicing Christians in the community. Many of the people were what Sarah termed *birthright Quakers*. The meaning of this is that, as Sarah explained, the people of the area felt like they were good moral people and did right by their neighbors. Thus, they equated that because they were born into families that were Quakers, they too were righteous by birth. Some explained that they 'hoped' they would make heaven. Parham presented to these folks that they did not merely have to hope. They could "KNOW." Parham insisted that they should *pray through* with Godly sorrow for sin until they really knew. Despite the self-righteous perspective of some, many others were convicted of their sins, repented and invited the Holy Spirit to take residence in their lives.[319]

> Rev. Charles Parham is advertising to run two excursions to Kansas City for a big rally of the "Apostolic Faith Movement" of which he is the leader. The excursion will be run the 15th, and the place will be the Academy of Music. Mr. Parham is now located in Baxter, Kansas.

Tonganoxie Mirror (Newspaper) 1906

The Thistlethwaites were pillars of the Quaker society in Kansas.[320] This family was intimately involved in teaching and working with the disadvantaged in their communities. The Thistlethwaite family was closely connected to the Baker family. Two of Ann Marie's siblings were also married to Thistlethwaites.[321] Ann Marie had two daughters: Lilian and

Sarah. Her husband, Anthony, was the owner and publisher of the local paper in Tonge-Noxi.[322] The Thistlethwaites wrote of the Parham led meetings to their daughter, Sarah, who had grown up in the community, but was staying with an uncle in Kansas City and attending school.[323] Sarah had previously attended school in the same Pleasant Valley Community School building where Parham was holding his meetings. The school was generally known as Friends Academy.[324] When Sarah returned home, the meeting had closed, but the community had

Pleasant Valley School House in Tonganoxie, KS where Parham held revival. (Front veiw)

arranged for Parham to come back the next Sunday. This Sunday marked Charles Parham's 19th birthday, June 4, 1894. His message was about *Jesus Christ and Him crucified*.[325] At the meeting, the refined Sarah Thistlethwaite was surprised by what she saw. Parham looked much different from the wealthy; cultured preachers she had been used to in Kansas City. When he took the pulpit, he didn't have his sermon written out like the preachers she had seen. In fact, Parham never wrote down what he was going to say. He relied on the Holy Spirit to give him inspiration. Then as Sarah listened to the young evangelist preach, she realized her lack of devotion to the faith. She knew she was following Jesus from "far off," and made the decision to consecrate her life totally to the Lord. She

GOING TO CONFERENCE.

also began to cultivate her friendship with Charles Parham and soon, what began as a simple interest, turned into a union of purpose and destiny.[326]

The Community leaders wrote a letter of gratitude for his revival efforts in Tonge-Noxi. It read in part, *"Charles F. Parham has held nineteen revival services in the Pleasant Valley School House, District 68. The Christians in the district thus unanimously express their thanks to our Heavenly Father for sending him amongst us and for the clear forcible manner in which the gospel has been preached. Many have been brought into the fold. It has been a time of refreshing from the presence of the Lord, like rain upon the mown grass. At the meeting it was unanimously agreed to thus acknowledge our brother's labor among us. The following named persons are authorized to sign this expression of unity on behalf of the meeting."* – *Char W. Hemphill, Lewis H. Peters, Benj. Penfold, T.H. Baker, David Baker, P.W. Goswell, Geo. Mosser, B.F. Haas, Alfred Thistlethwaite."*[327]

In addition to holding meetings like the ones in Tonge-Noxi, Parham labored as a circuit rider filling the pulpit at various M.E. pulpits as needed. One of the places that he assisted was the Eudora Methodist Church where the renowned Dr. Werter R. Davis pastored. As his Presiding

Elder, there is no doubt that Parham was powerfully influenced by Davis. Then, Davis died. At nineteen years of age, Charles Parham was called by the Methodist Episcopal Church to fill the pulpit of the deceased Dr. Davis. Davis was an esteemed minister who founded Baker University. One area where Charles Parham differed from his esteemed pastor was that the Parhams were pacifists.[328] A decade later when the rest of Christendom was seeking to understand what their position would be, the Parhams were already well established in pacifism.³²⁹

Methodist Musical Chairs

LINWOOD (M.E.) CHURCH.

Historians have made much ado about nothing in Charles Parham's departure from his pastorate. Surrogates rail on him that he decided it was not the call for him. They ignore that for two years Parham labored at Eudora, Kansas, also providing Sunday afternoon pulpit ministry and more at the Methodist Episcopal (M.E.) Church at Linwood, Kansas. In today's Methodist culture they would call his labor a 2-charge appointment. Difficult work even under the best conditions. A Methodist pastor moving on or resigning is a regular occurrence. Even more likely is that the Methodist pastor will be moved elsewhere in the Conference, and he will likely have no choice.³³⁰ Many times pastors are appointed by the Methodist Bishop for one year. The decision is seldom left to the pastor prompting many to call the Methodist pastor's appointments *a game of musical chairs.*"³³¹

The primary sickness afflicting the United Methodist Church is its own institutional schizophrenia about just what sort of "good news" it is peddling. Nevertheless, the appointment system is a bit like pneumonia on top of cancer—it is certainly not making the chances of survival any better."³³² The Methodist appointment system was broken then and remains broken. Charles Parham choosing not to stay in such a broken system is congratulatory. Move on, nothing to see here!

During this time Miss Thistlethwaite and her family regularly visited Parham's Methodist Church in Linwood, Kansas. Here she began to cultivate her friendship with Charles."³³³ Sarah wrote that the Methodist

Church in Linwood, Kansas, where Parham had charge, was closer to their family home than the one in Eudora. So, they often attended there. Parham also often returned to hold services in the Pleasant Valley School House. Many others attended these meetings. Even those from other churches. Sarah recalled, "such a spirit of unity prevailed in his meetings that all felt welcome."[334] In horrible weather conditions like drifting snow, Parham would faithfully ride to the locations to minister. Parham preached sanctification as a second definite work of grace as taught by **John Wesley** and the early Methodists. He was a tremendous young example of what the founders of Methodism expected.[335] The first pastor in Linwood was Rev. J. C. Telford. The church was brick. The congregation was described as strong and growing.[336]

In 1913, Parham elaborated on his previous pastoral experiences. "I had the confines of a pastorate, with a lot of theater-going, card-playing, wine-drinking, fashionable, un-converted Methodists; now I have a world-wide parish, with multitudes to preach the gospel message to..."[337] Parham evidently was quite pleased and never considered returning to the pastorate. Not that Charles Parham needed a reason to move from the pastorate to itinerant evangelist but since the surrogates posing as historians like to make it a point, we oblige them. The Eudora area had been the home for Native-Americans for centuries. The Kansa tribe lived there from the 1600s to the 1800s before being forcibly removed from the region by the American Government to satisfy a treaty with the Shawnee tribe.[338] There were a number of Methodist affiliated groups in the area. Dr. Werter Davis had been assigned to Eudora to work with the German population there. The Germans were immigrants who were located there through the efforts of Deutsche-Neuisedlungsverein from Chicago. The group was a German Settlement Company. They chose Eudora, Kansas. White settlers were being welcomed in and non-whites were being forced out.[339]

Davis as a senior minister, former University President and Presiding Elder had considerable influence and sway with the Eudora congregation. Although he was also not there for a long period of time. In contrast, the young Charles Parham, fresh off considerable impact in nearby areas of Kansas, met resistance. The German congregation was not open to Native-Americans and certainly not open to black members from the growing population of former slaves. Like Tongi-noxi, former slaves in Eudora were some twenty-five percent of the population. In the Eudora mindset, multiculturalism and inclusion might be tolerable for places like Tongi-noxi and Linwood, but in Eudora, such ideas as these brought by Charles Parham and his girlfriend, Sarah Thistlethwaite were not welcome. This posture presented to many places in the United States. It was not unique to Eudora. Most Methodist congregations were moving toward a mindset that black people could have their own congregation – Separate from the white people.

"The Parhams, Charles and Sarah, together with Sarah's sister, Lilian, benefited from a unique blend of elements from the Methodist, Quaker, Missionary, and healing movement influences. The Thistlethwaite sisters had experienced "the old-fashioned, mourner's bench conversion experience" through the summer evangelistic ministry of Charles Fox Parham, who at the time was a teenage ministerial student (1889-1893) at Southwest Kansas Methodist Conference College in Winfield, Kansas. From 1893 to 1895, while Parham was pastoring the Methodist Church in Eudora, he also conducted meetings in Tonganoxie on Sunday afternoons. It would appear that he adopted some of the ways of the Friends, for he gave up the opportunity to advance in Methodism when he resigned the Methodist pastorate after much soul-searching, prayer and fasting.[340]

Faced with growing acceptance of racism in the M.E. Church, "Parham began to pray for direction. Many slanderous accusations had been leveled against him, and he was concerned that the rising persecution would forever ruin his work. Then one day while deep in prayer, he heard these words, "I made Myself of no reputation." Immediately, Parham was strengthened and encouraged. As the Spirit of God continued to give him Scripture, he set his course. He would enter the evangelistic field, unassociated with any form of denomination. He would hold his meetings in schools, halls, churches, tabernacles—wherever he could—and believe for the Holy Spirit to manifest Himself in a mighty way.

While holding a meeting in western Kansas, Parham wrote to Sarah Thistlethwaite and proposed marriage. He warned Sarah that his life was totally dedicated to the Lord and that his future was unclear, but if she could trust God with him, they should marry. Charles and Sarah were married six months later, on December 31, 1896, in her grandfather's home. Friends' ministers Jonathan Ballard and his wife officiated. In the Friends tradition, the couple did their own ceremony where they pledged their lives one to the other. 40 years later Sarah Parham wrote, **"I am glad we kept our marriage vows and were true to each other."**[341]

CHAPTER FIVE

SLAVERY

"The anointing of the Holy Spirit is given to illuminate His Word, to open the Scriptures, and to place the spiritual man in direct communication with the mind of God."

-Charles Fox Parham

Methodist's positions on people of color in the time of Charles and Sarah Parham seem quite different from the spirit of the writings of founder, John Wesley. "In 1774, John Wesley published his **"Thoughts Upon Slavery."** Wesley's pamphlet *Thoughts upon Slavery* opens with a definition of slavery. His first note of condemnation appears when he shows that slavery first originated in "barbarous" times and died out with the rise of Christianity in Europe. He proposes that it was only the discovery of America and the need for large amounts of inexpensive labor that brought it back. Wesley then moves on to refute the notion that slavery rescues Africans from the harshest of conditions, quoting from many authorities attesting to the great fertility of Western Africa. He also points out that African nations are highly organized and cultured, using examples from several major tribes and nations to prove his point. Given this evidence, Wesley cannot support the notion that slavery represents an improvement to the Africans.

After revealing the conditions of the slaves, Wesley then questions whether the system is defensible, "on the principles of even heathen honesty?" Human law, in his estimation, was powerless to confer right without consideration of mercy and justice. Wesley denies that slavery is necessary to support the colonial economies, pointing out that no benefit is worth any injustice made to receive it. The penultimate section of the tract is an appeal urging those involved in the slave trade to quit the trade; Wesley uses appeals ranging from fear of God's judgement to pity for the Africans. Finally, Wesley relates unpleasant Dutch and French experiences with slaves. These specific instances and stories further illustrate Wesley's point that the institution is at its core dehumanizing and barbarous."[342]

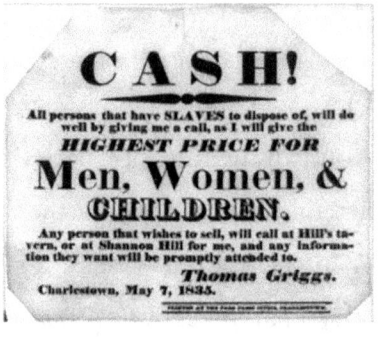

"The founder of the Methodist movement insisted that the concept of enslaving other people was based on "false foundations." For Wesley, merely tolerating the existence of a system of enslavement was an accommodation with evil. American Methodists would agree with Wesley and take even stronger positions against the practice.[343] "In 1780, the American Methodists required preachers to deliver sermons against the evils of slavery. Thereafter, the Methodists in North Carolina and Virginia adopted antislavery statements and insisted that Methodists should free any slaves that they owned. Church leaders declared that the enslavement of other persons is "contrary to the laws of God." In 1785, the first Book of Discipline published by the Methodists included a piece of church legislation that any church member who buys or sells slaves is "immediately to be expelled" from membership, "unless they buy them on purpose to free them." In 1800, the General Conference issued a "Pastoral Letter on Slavery," signed by the three bishops of the church at the time (Coke, Asbury, and Whatcoat). It declared the enslavement of Black people "the great national evil" of the United States. It said, "the whole spirit of the New Testament militates in the strongest manner against the practice of slavery." [344]

The pastoral letter directed annual conferences to appeal to the legislatures in their respective states for the emancipation of slaves. It called for "the universal extirpation of this crying sin." So, the documented history of Methodism makes clear that the founders of the church considered slavery to be "evil." Nothing in the documents indicates that they felt slavery was in any sense "necessary." These documents also make clear that the church leaders expected Methodist preachers and people to take action in the pulpit and also in public to remove the systems of slavery from America. Preachers were to proclaim that slavery is evil. People were to lobby their legislatures for ending enslavement.[345]

Harry Hosier The Greatest Orator

Dr. Benjamin Rush, the founding father and signer of the Declaration of Independence, declared the gentle Harry Hosier,[346] (the little man who can deliver a powerful sermon) one of the greatest orators of all time. Does Harry Hosier mind living out of a saddlebag and traveling the wild, virgin American forests? Does he fear for his life when preaching against slavery in the southern colonies? How did this African preacher become Francis Asbury's traveling companion?

"The Wesleyan movement in America is quick to embrace the Africans. Consistent with the Bible and the teachings of **John Wesley** and **George Whitefield, Francis Asbury**, and his traveling itinerants deliver their life-changing message to all. According to **Booker T. Washington**, "Methodism had started in England among the poor and the outcast; it was natural, therefore, that when its missionaries came to America, they should seek to bring into the Church the outcast and neglected people, especially the slaves." One of these lives invited into the Wesleyan community was **Harry Hosier**."[347] Yes, the gospel message will transform a life, but why choose to become a circuit riding preacher? The life of an 18th-century circuit rider in the American wilderness is a life of arduous effort. In addition to the great exertion required to sustain a life without shelter in the face of an open frontier, the traveling preacher risks physical harm from the wild animals that coexist in these challenging conditions and the unforgiving terrain of a never-ending forest. As with most of the itinerants, Harry Hosier was not an educated man. In fact, he was illiterate. Despite his limitation, he could recite entire portions of the Bible as if reading King James' version word for word. Richard Allen, another African preacher called to the ministry by **Francis Asbury**, attempted to teach Harry Hosier to read. Harry ceased the effort, citing that, "when I try to read, I lose my gift of preaching." The Quakers who know Harry Hosier are convinced that his illiteracy is proof that he preaches from Divine inspiration.

Harry Hosier

Is Harry Hosier a gifted orator? Consider the incident in Wilmington, Delaware at the Old Asbury Chapel. "As the crowd gathers to hear **Bishop Asbury**, many find themselves standing outside the building, straining to hear through the numerous windows of the structure. The sermon begins and continues for a while. During the exhortation, one in the crowd exclaims, 'if all Methodist preachers could preach like the bishop, we should like to be constant hearers.' One inside the building responds, 'that is not the bishop, but the bishop's servant you are hearing.' Unbeknownst to the man outside, Harry Hosier is not the slave of Francis Asbury, nevertheless, the man listening through the window responded, 'if such be the servant, what must the master be?' When he is not preaching to thousands of both black and white, Harry Hosier is the soft-spoken and brilliant companion of Francis Asbury."[348]

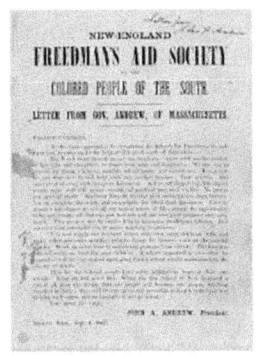

The actions of Methodism's key leaders and original Bishops left us with no doubt about how they felt concerning race. They simply saw no color barrier. In the ensuing years, however, this antislavery dedication faded. The church found ways to dishonor its founders and to ignore the suffering of the enslaved. Forty-four years after the General Conference enacted church laws to demand that Methodists free their slaves or leave the church and to insist that Methodists take public antislavery steps, the denomination decided to divide. Rather than require a slave-owning bishop to emancipate the people whom he considered his property, Methodists split into two denominations. Rather than politically mobilize to end the system of slavery in each state, Methodists split along the boundaries of states that affirmed enslavement. While the debate about the national history continues, it is important for all Methodists with traceable roots in North America to recognize that the founders of Methodism were opposed to slavery, took antislavery actions, and urged the ministers and the people of Methodist churches to become public activists in an effort to end the enslavement of human beings."[349]

"After the Civil War, northern Methodists undertook a successful mission to recruit a biracial membership in the South. Their Freedmen's Aid Society played a key role in outreach to African-Americans, but when the denomination decided to use Society funds in aid of schools for Southern whites, a national controversy erupted over the refusal of Chattanooga University to admit African-Americans. Caught between a principled commitment to racial brotherhood and the pressures of expediency to accommodate a growing white supremacist commitment to segregation, Methodists engaged in an agonized and heated debate over whether schools intended for whites should be allowed to exclude blacks. Divisions within the leadership of the Methodist Episcopal Church caught the attention of the national press and revealed the limits of even the most well-intentioned efforts to advance racial equality in the years after Reconstruction."[350] The church lamented the loss of its African-American members at the start of the war. Whether the concern was genuine certainly may be debated. It was nevertheless, profoundly paternalistic and in no way considered full equality with African-Americans as a possibility in neither the church nor society.

"...while our denomination (Wesleyan Methodist) was born in an antislavery movement, we have sometimes ignored our own heritage and been guilty of both personal racism and prejudice."[351]

Make no mistake, Charles Fox Parham was formidable in his own right as history fairly preserves. He would represent that rare group of Methodist that unalterably opposed segregation. He did not do so with great speeches. Rather, his opposition was of practice and empowerment.

~ CHAPTER FIVE | SLAVERY ~

At the same time, eyewitnesses claim that Sarah Parham was also a powerful preacher and Reverend Lilian Theodora Thistlethwaite was among the greatest spiritual leaders of her generation.[352] Sarah and Lillian were part of the influence for multitudes of women ministers that the Apostolic Faith Movement generated. Powerful, life changing voices that impacted and changed generations. Women like **Mary Arthur, Millicent McClendon, Maria Woodworth-Etter, Aimee Semple McPherson, Florence Crawford, Lucy Farrow, Alma Hall**, and a plethora of

others. Not only were they formidable, but they were also the reason that white male ministers would work diligently in dark places to ban women from leadership and where possible even ban women from ministry. Despite the injustices, Sarah and Lilian labored to impact others for the Kingdom of Jesus Christ. It is tragic that those historians who do bother to mention Sarah and Lilian, generally do not even spell their names correctly. We made the point of including Lilian's tombstone to emphasize the point of the correct spelling of her name.

Those with a xenophobic agenda often postulate that William J. Seymour is the father of the Apostolic Faith Movement. Kind of like he was his own spiritual father! Not sure how that works, but they have sold books claiming such nonsense. If a case were to be made for someone other than Charles Fox Parham as the father of the Apostolic Faith Movement, Lilian Thistlethwaite should be first in line. The same self-aggrandizing proxies posing as historians that postulate other theories ignore Lilian, because she was a woman.

The Statesman Thaddeus Stevens said, *"There can be no fanatics in the cause of genuine liberty. Fanaticism is excessive zeal. There may be and have been fanatics in false religion – in the bloody religions of the heathen. There are fanatics in superstition. But there can be no fanatic, however warm their zeal, in the true religion, even although you sell your goods and bestow your money on the poor and go on and follow your Master. There may, and every hour shows around me, fanatics in the cause of false liberty – that infamous liberty which justifies human bondage, that liberty whose 'corner-stone is slavery.' But there can be no fanaticism however high the enthusiasm, in the cause of rational, universal liberty – the liberty of the Declaration of Independence."* – June 10, 1850.[353]

Bishop William Seymour (center with some saints, worshiping at the Apostolic Faith Gospel Mission in Los Angeles (circa 1920).

CHAPTER SIX

RACIAL SEGREGATION THE NEW SLAVERY

"Give me one hundred preachers who fear nothing but sin and desire nothing but God, and I care not whether they be clergymen or laymen, they alone will shake the gates of hell and set up the kingdom of heaven upon earth."

-John Wesley

After the American Civil War, a stark reality came to the American people. They had ended the terrible scourge of slavery by law, but in the minds and hearts of the American people, little, perhaps even nothing had changed. Perhaps in some ways it was even a little worse. Before the war people were generally divided as slave or free. After the war, a new American caste system began. Those who before the war saw slaves (both those of color and white slaves) as less than people, or at least people that were *beneath* their social status, continued to live their lives in that manner. These found freed black slaves as a whole new labor force to exploit. These continue today, generally treating people like they do their waste.

Those who thought that the Civil War would usher in a new age or as some religious affiliated people believed, the **Kingdom of Heaven**,[354] were generally quite dismayed by the outcome. The expectation that after the Civil War would be a time of equality and brotherhood is a vision, we as the American People have yet to achieve. The words, *"We hold these truths to be self-evident that all men are created equal…"* are genuine, but represent more of a goal than the existing reality. Those that expected the Civil War to end racial equality issues largely underestimated the will of evil men. Abraham Lincoln's Republican Party, in passing the 13th Amendment, certainly brought an end to the buying and selling of people in the open market, but it also opened a Pandora's box of other challenges. Among these challenges they found that those who had previously enslaved or were in favor of the enslavement of others changed their tactics. Slavery was merely repackaged as racial **SEGREGATION**.[355]

"Douglas is a cunning dog & the devil is on his side," wrote Abraham Smith to Abraham Lincoln in the summer of 1858. One month earlier, the Republican Party of Illinois had decided to run Lincoln for the Senate against Stephen A. Douglas, the incumbent Democrat. Smith, an Illinois farmer, encouraged Lincoln to take "the high ground" during the campaign. He called upon Lincoln to remind all who would hear that "the bible teaches the same that is taught by the declaration of Independence—by the Constitution of the U.S. and by the fathers of the republic." What others might view as separate strands of "religion" and "politics," or "church" and "state," Smith wove together tightly. For him, the Bible, the Declaration of Independence, the Constitution, and the Founding Fathers constituted one holy garment.

~ CHAPTER SIX | RACIAL SEGREGATION, THE NEW SLAVERY ~

The Lincoln-Douglas struggle, moreover, was much more than just another political event that pitted two men against one another for a legislative position. The race signaled forces higher and lower, lighter and darker. "As I view the contest (tho we say it is between Douglass & Lincoln—) it is no less than a contest for the advancement of the kingdom of Heaven or the kingdom of Satan."[356]

Thaddeus Stevens said, *"In my youth, in my manhood, in my old age, I had fondly dreamed that when any fortunate chance should have broken up for a while the foundation of our institutions, and released us from obligations the most tyrannical that ever man imposed in the name of freedom, that the intelligent pure and just men of this Republic, true to their professions and their consciences, would have so remodeled all our institutions as to have rid them from every vestige of human oppression, of the inequity of rights, of the recognized degradation of the poor, and the superior caste of the rich. In short, that no distinction would be tolerated in this purified Republic but what arose from merit and conduct. This bright dream has vanished 'like the baseless fabric of a vision.' I find that we shall be obliged to be content with patching up the worst portions of the ancient edifice, and leaving it, in many of its parts, to be swept through by the tempests, the frosts, and the storms of despotism. Do you inquire why, holding these views and possessing some will of my own, I accept so imperfect a proposition? I answer, because I live among men and not among angels; among men as intelligent, as determined, and as independent as myself, who not agreeing with me, do not choose to yield their opinions to mine. Mutual concession, therefore, is our only resort, or mutual hostilities."*[357]

In the South, church leaders developed an elaborate system of scriptural justifications for slavery. A Baptist pastor in Alabama, the Reverend Dr. Basil Manly, Sr.,[358] became the country's leading religious voice in support of the institution, playing a central role in the establishment of the Southern Baptist Convention—formed in the aftermath of the Baptists' schism over slavery—and delivering the invocation when Jefferson Davis was inaugurated as President of the Confederacy.[359] In the rank and file of the M.E. Church in America, the call to join Abraham Lincoln's Union Army and vanquish the enemies in the South was a rallying cry that spurred tens of thousands of Methodist Episcopal clergy and layman to pick up weapons and fight to end the scourge of slavery. John Wesley's imprimatur from 1776 to end slavery would come to pass. However, when the mission was accomplished the voice of John Wesley seemed somehow dim. Lost in the tumult was the voice of Methodism's First American Bishop, Francis Asbury. "One of the first major white religious voices against slavery, Asbury petitioned George Washington to enact anti-slavery legislation. The bishop wrote, *"My spirit was grieved at the conduct of some Methodists, that hire slaves at public places to the highest bidder, to cut skin, and starve them."*[360]

The post American Civil War Methodist Church leadership was intensely divided. "From the outset, the motto of colonial American Methodism was 'to spread Christian holiness over these lands.' Yet, in practice, the doctrines of holiness and perfectionism were largely ignored by American Methodists during the early decades of the 19th century. In 1843, about two dozen ministers withdrew from the Methodist Episcopal Church to establish the Wesleyan Methodist Church of America, establishing a pattern of defections or looser ties. Sizable numbers of Protestants from the rural areas of the Midwest and South were joining the Holiness movement. These people had a penchant for strict codes of dress and behavior. Most of them had little sympathy for the 'superficial, false, and fashionable' Christians allegedly preoccupied with wealth, social prestige, and religious formalism."[361] All of these efforts to achieve holiness created racially segregated movements, denominations and congregations.

The same Methodists that had fought valiantly to end the

~ CHAPTER SIX | RACIAL SEGREGATION, THE NEW SLAVERY ~

institution of slavery in the United States now were faced with a decision. They must decide if they wanted their brothers and sisters who were formally slaves to join them in society or if they preferred to keep the status quo, they were divided. Some Methodists, like the infamous Alma White were quite willing to speak on behalf of all Methodist and Independent Holiness people. White said that the Blacks needed to learn their place and they "owed" white people for freeing them from slavery.[362] Men like Warren Fay Carothers and A. P. Collins adamantly agreed. White, a hero of the Holiness movement never left doubt where she and her friends stood on the issue. She would take her utopian dream so far as to fashion her church as an arm for the **Ku Klux Klan (KKK)** for men and women. While Sarah Parham was standing with her husband for the rights of all people to worship Jesus Christ, Alma White was moving her followers toward a racial frenzy against all people of color. This is not what Methodist leaders like **Asbury, Davis**, and Wesley envisioned. To equate such drivel with John Wesley and his followers is heresy. Yet, this was the world that Charles and Sarah Parham faced.

There is wild conjecture from historians about Parham's decision to leave the Methodist church. It really is not that complicated. These historians say, Parham was not ordained in the Methodist church; this is true.

Alma White's utopia offered white women the opportunity to be Klanswomen

He also was not ordained in the Baptist Church or Apostolic Church. Like Dwight Moody, Parham was apparently not ordained by anyone! Proxies posing as historians offer not being ordained by the Methodist church as though Parham committed a crime. Parham's decision to not be ordained as part of the Methodist church was a personal one and in no way diminished his ability or capacity as a minister. Like most denominations, Methodist have expectations that a minister must complete to be recommended for ordination.[363] What really happened was that Parham, who held a license as a Methodist minister, chose not to renew his license. Sarah Parham's influence is evident here. The Methodist had decided to stand against women ministers which was problematic for the Parhams. Further, Quakers do not ordain ministers.[364] Quakers consider every man and woman to be a minister (regardless of race). This Quaker method became the culture of the Apostolic Faith Movement. George Fox (the "founder" of Quakerism) believed that all could have access to God without the necessity of clergy.[365] It is evident that Charles Fox and Sarah Eleanor Parham chose to develop their Apostolic Faith ministry structure in a manner similar to the original Quaker concept. Everyone, men, women, white, Black, Hispanic, etc., was a minister in the Parham's Apostolic Faith Movement. It is understandable that this made them enemies in other religious circles. The proxies of these enemies continue their slander to this very day.

"In order for long-term systematic change to occur collectively, we must be disturbed deeply. The truth operates like laser surgery. Are we to anesthetize the patient properly? Are we to engage in painless surgery? Are we to treat the manifest symptoms, or are we to strike deep through radical surgery to annihilate the root cause of

A meeting of the Quakers, or Religious Society of Friends (1725). Public Domain

the disease and be healed for a lifetime? The time has come that the axe must be laid to the root of the tree. Over three decades ago, the late Kyle Haselden, Baptist pastor and columnist, admonished us about the church not only being the mother of racial pattern and the purveyor of arrant sedatives, but that the countenance of the church is often viewed clearly in the mirror of race.[366] Says the writer of 1 Peter 4:17, "The time is come that judgement must begin at the house of God."[367] *"I will be satisfied if my epitaph shall be written thus: 'Here lies one who never rose to any eminence, who only courted the low ambition to have it said that he striven to ameliorate the condition of the poor, the lowly, the downtrodden of every race and language and color.'"*[368]

CHAPTER ~~SEVEN~~

RELIGIOUS EXCUSES FOR WHITE SUPREMECY

"Like I said, this Martin Luther King is leading his people to a crucifixion. It's communistic."

-William Branham[369]

The casual reader may miss what was really happening in the societal conflicts of the United States. Most historians present the facts of the Parhams lives as though they lived in some other place and not in the rough and tumble Midwest State of Kansas in the United States of America. In the big picture the Nation had just fought a Civil War over the right of one man or woman to own another. When this 'right' was stripped away by the victors of the war, the autocratic class reorganized and put the nation back on a course to re-create a predominately white class of people as the first tier of a caste system under the ruling class. Although they dare not call it a caste system. In simple terms, the first tier would consist of the ruling class which was already all-white. This would be followed by the all-white political class. Then would come the white collar or upper middle class. These would be above the subservient predominately white, blue-collar class. The blue-collar workers would also have some people of color, but most of them as well as nearly all others were to be the poor class of this new world order. Later, labor unions were formed to further ensure the superiority of white men in society.[370] The primary driver behind the concept was of course money, but race was the dividing line. If everyone stayed 'in their place,' the autocrats would be appeased.

This conflict over racial equality pitted the segregationist (proponents of slavery) against those who saw all men as equal. Slavery was repackaged in a "New and Improved Box" and sold to society as "Separate but Equal." It really was an old concept, especially in religious circles. The Southern Baptists were selling this version long before the American Civil War and afterwards found a growing population (predominately white but many blacks signed on) welcoming of their dogma*. This spawned a new age where Southern Baptists would become the largest Protestant denomination in the United States. The attitudes of this generation would set the table for the rise of the **Ku Klux Klan**[371] as the Invisible Empire in the next generation.[372]

Most may not have realized that the idea of racial segregation for those who claim Christ Jesus was conceived in Kentucky (USA) by the leaders of the Baptist church.[373] True, it was a much older heresy brought by Mani,[374] but the Baptists leaders in the early 1800s reworked it for their own diabolical purposes. The Baptist call it **"Two Seeds Doctrine."** [375] Essentially, the Baptists believe there is one group of people who are the seed of Adam and Eve, and they are **Predestined**[376] for heaven.[377] There is a second group that Baptists teach: the seed of Satan and Eve.[378] Predestination is a core tenet of the Southern Baptist religion. Predestinationist hold that all of these "undesirables" are predestined for eternal damnation based on the conditions of their birth. Daniel Parker was one of the three primary leaders of the Baptist movement and one of their heroes.[379] *"Daniel Parker taught that part of Eve's offspring were the seed of God and elect to eternal life; part were the seed of Satan and foreordained to the kingdom of eternal darkness. By the divine decree all events whatever, from the creation to the final consummation, were foreordained, so that nothing can interfere with or change his plans."*[380]

This is presented as doctrine, but it is merely classism.[381] No Bible is needed to understand this one. Ironically, even Islam has a version of two seeds doctrine. In the Islam version, Blacks are also predestined for hell. This likely made it easier for the Muslims to begin the slave trade.[382] صلى الله عليه وسلم - قال: (خلق الله آدم حين خلقه ، فضرب كتفه اليمنى ، فأخرج ذرية بيضاء كأنهم الذر ، وضرب كتفه اليسرى فأخرج ذرية سوداء كأنهم الحمم ، فقال للذي في يمينه : إلى الجنة ، ولا أبالي ، وقال للذي في كتفه اليسرى : إلى النار ، ولا أبالي) . رواه أحمد "Abu Darda reported that the Holy Prophet said: Allah created Adam when he created him. Then He stroke his right shoulder and took out a white (bright/good) offspring as if they were seeds, and He stroke his left shoulder and took out a black (gloomy/sinning) offspring as if they were coals. Then He said to those who were in his right side: Towards paradise and I don't care. He said to those who were on his left shoulder: Towards Hell and I don't care."[383]

Charles Parham as a Methodist in spirit of Asbury, Wesley, and other key founders harbored no such illusions as the Predestination of the wicked. Parham taught eternal destiny was a choice offered to every man and woman regardless of color or gender. Parham expected that to gain Eternal Life one must be born of the water and of the Spirit. He further expected that no man-made organization could deny someone their salvation based on some predestined idea. This is just as Jesus Christ said to Nicodemus in John Chapter 3. *"He who believes in Him is not condemned; but he* *who does not believe is condemned already, because he has not believed in the name of the only begotten Son of God." John 3:18 NKJV*

In churches that offer Predestination one generally joins the church, much like joining a social club. In the M.E. Church, one became part of the Body of Jesus Christ through a personal experience of salvation and holiness. Parham was certainly facing changing times. Rather than engage in a war of wills or words, Parham opted to decline further invitation to serve as a charge Pastor to any congregation, preferring the role of itinerant evangelist. A role he was not only well suited for, but had already demonstrated tremendous success.

For Parham's adversaries, their two seeds doctrine remains a core doctrine of the Baptist Church. This is one of the reasons Baptist adherents cling to the Predestination dogma of their forefathers. The conflict with racial Segregationists led to all not being well between Charles Parham and the Methodist denomination leadership in Kansas. The denomination's leadership saw a great future for Parham, and they would have given him most any pastorate or assignment.[384] With Parham's mentor, Werter Davis, deceased, Parham's connection to Methodist leadership in Kansas was less important. Just as in the challenges before the American Civil War, the Parhams would leave this conflicted M.E. Church only to later faceoff with those same bigoted ideas from Independent Holiness ministers who judged their fellow man based on the color of their skin.

What some historians postulate as his unwillingness to submit to their authority was a continuation of the conflict of race and other indifference that plagued the M.E. Church. Before the American Civil War, the M.E. Church was motivated and mobilized to end the scourge of slavery. After the war, there was serious division in their mindsets. Some like the Quaker people in Tonganoxie welcomed people of all races as brothers. The Methodists at Eudora saw Parham's willingness to work with blacks and Native-Americans in a free Kansas as unacceptable. They quickly sought to seek some doctrinal point with which to claim disagreement. They decided his position on God's judgement upon the wicked would be a "hill worth dying on."[385] Much has been made about Parham's departure from higher education. However, one of his mentors is never mentioned in the descent. "Morrison himself became an embodiment of this phenomenon when he left Kentucky to attend Vanderbilt University in 1884. Even though Vanderbilt Divinity School in 1884 was awash in Southern evangelical piety, Morrison was uncertain about the appropriateness of his matriculation, and he spent only one year there. Morrison's ambivalence toward his enrollment at Vanderbilt is indicative of his ambivalence toward higher education in general. He appreciated the erudition (and the piety) of his professors, but his single-minded commitment to evangelism compelled him to withdraw from academic pursuits."[386] Like Morrison, Parham would establish a Bible College that still exists today.

The Parhams Understood The Times.[387]

Charles and Sarah Parham's unwillingness to see people of color as less than themselves would be a challenge that their enemies would exploit throughout their lifetimes. Parham had vowed to follow the leading of the Holy Spirit. This had been the modus operandi of Parham's pastor and mentor Werter Davis. Davis was a man who throughout his lifetime followed the leading of the Lord regardless of personal sacrifice. The times had changed. Parham was following the excellent training from his pastor, but the predominately white congregation was not receptive to the idea of welcoming people who were *not like them*.

Charles and Sarah Parham, "lived and ministered during a time when racial segregation was accepted and practiced throughout America. The 14th amendment to the constitution had included a 'Separate but Equa' clause, recognizing segregation but requiring that all citizens be treated equal under the law. In the 1896 case, 'Plessy vs. Ferguson,' the United States Supreme Court upheld the 'separate' part of this clause when it ruled that a law in Louisiana requiring blacks and whites to ride in separate railroad cars did not violate the constitution."[388] Charles and Sarah Parham were guilty of ignoring these laws and seeing all people as part of one race. This made them considerable enemies to established religions and those who desired to keep the status quo. It was obvious that the "separate" part of the clause was upheld far more vigorously than the "equal" part. Public facilities for Blacks were inferior and fewer in number than those for whites. Blacks were commonly required to sit on the back seats in trains and buses and to eat in dilapidated, back rooms in restaurants. The best hotels were for whites only and even professional sports was for whites only."[389]

"And the Church? Decades later, in the 1960s Dr. Martin Luther King Jr. declared 11 a.m. on Sunday morning to be the most segregated time in America. It was even more so fifty years earlier. There is little improvement in 2022. A black person in a white church or a white person in black church was considered strange and even inappropriate. Most professing white Christians believed the white race to be superior and that racial segregation could be defended with Scripture."[390] Charles and Sarah Parham dared to question such notions, which made them a scourge of white Pentecostals, and patsies to be gaslighted as racists.

Another challenge is that Parham was not about building a denomination. This position would also bring him formidable enemies.

CHAPTER SEVEN | RELIGIOUS EXCUSES FOR WHITE SUPREMACY

In advising new converts, he would exhort them to find any church home, even if it wasn't the Methodist church. He explained that joining a denomination was not a prerequisite for heaven, and that denominations spent more time preaching on their particular church and its leaders than they did on Jesus Christ and His covenant. While many historians present this as some kind of rebellion, they ignore the simple honesty that what Parham presented is fact.

It is interesting how surrogates of various denominations have written about Charles and Sarah Parham. The denominations that have often seen women as "less than" generally have ignored Sarah Parham even though she was perhaps the best historian who ever wrote on the subject of Charles Parham, the Apostolic Faith Movement and the Topeka Outpouring. No one knew the subject better. Ironically, proxies also attempted to castrate Parham for statements like this, *"Finding the confines of a pastorate, and feeling the narrowness of sectarian churchism, I was often in conflict with the higher authorities, which eventually resulted in open rupture; and I left denominationalism forever, though suffering bitter persecution at the hands of the church.... Oh, the narrowness of many who call themselves the Lord's own!"* In reality, likely most and perhaps all pastors have felt something like these sentiments at one time or another. I am reminded of accomplished ministers who say things like, *"My pastor did not understand me..."*

The purposeful effort by historians to separate Parham from Methodism is in and of itself an attempt to discredit him. No offence intended to my Holiness friends, but historians generally equate Holiness people with being half-baked, uneducated, bigoted, racist, etc. In fairness, most holiness groups represent in such a manner. The Holiness movement has a horrible track record in the areas of gender equality and racial equality. To equate the same with Charles and Sarah Parham is part of the strategy of denominational proxies.

We used the comparison of Charles Parham to Henry Morrison because there is not nearly as much hyper critical writing about Morrison as Parham. Morrison held the successful pastorate of a prosperous congregation. Soon thereafter, he left his appointment as a local Pastor, began an itinerant evangelistic ministry, and started his newspaper (The Old Methodist, later the Pentecostal Herald). Then, Morrison started a Bible college. Parham did the exact same thing. The critics of Parham in this area exaggerate their contempt revealing their own nature. The ministries of Morrison and Parham are amazingly similar. Both were very impactful for the Kingdom of Jesus Christ in their own right. Historians and their proxies need to give both the benefit of the doubt. The real deal is that men who are organizational minded cannot fathom a man of God who does not need their denomination to direct him. Men and women that can hear from God scare them. This is very well. Yet, we all need someone to speak into our lives. Parham had such ministers, and the best historians can confirm that Parham never felt the need to start a denomination.

Parham was not alone concerning those who were troubled by the direction of the Methodist Episcopal (M.E.) leadership. Among those who were concerned about the direction of Methodism was a group that left the M.E. to form the Free Methodist Church in 1860. "The Free Methodist understanding of the pertinent issues surrounding the preaching of entire sanctification presaged late nineteenth-century developments within the Holiness wing of Methodism. Free Methodists saw themselves simply as holding on to the original vision of Methodism: "to reform the nation, especially the church, and to spread Scriptural holiness throughout the land," which, for them, was a summons to preach the experience of entire sanctification and to condemn any moral compromise with the 'world.'"[391]

~ CHAPTER SEVEN | RELIGIOUS EXCUSES FOR WHITE SUPREMACY ~

"The Free Methodist's commitment to moral purity meant a repudiation of the surrounding culture's acceptance of slavery, personal adornment, status distinctions, and petty vices.[392] It also meant a repulsion of typical urban Methodist Episcopal (M.E.) congregations, with their expensive neo-Romanesque auditoriums."[393]

Parham's desire to follow the example of his pastor and others who saw no color in the application of the Gospel of Jesus Christ was met with great opposition. The M.E. church was in competition with their Baptist counterparts and others. At the time, the M.E. was the largest and fastest growing denomination in the United States. At one time boasting a church in every zip code in the United States.[394] The shift toward Baptist heresy would not help them retain the pre-eminence. The Baptist had long before adopted a whites-only position both corporately and doctrinally and the Methodist were decidedly following their lead.

Corporately, the Southern Baptist Convention, the largest Baptist group in the United States, organized at Augusta, Georgia, in 1845 by Southern Baptists who disagreed with the antislavery attitudes and activities of Northern Baptists.[395] Key Baptist leaders of the 1800s: Alexander Campbell, John Taylor, and Daniel Parker developed the concept of anti-missionary.[396] The concept was simply a method to keep non-whites out of their group. These key Baptist leaders did not want people from other countries (especially Africa) in their all-white group. Parham had vowed to God his willingness to go to Africa as a missionary; this was not of interest to anti-missioners.

The concept of some being predestined was conceived in the struggle by white immigrants in the United States with the Native-Americans for the control of their land. However, the dogma was easily adaptable to others deemed undesirable by these same white adherents. So, Black slaves and others were added to the growing list that later included Jews, Mexicans, Catholics, etc. While the dogma was presented as doctrinal, it was merely a clever ruse for racism and classism. This doctrine in some form still exists in nearly every denomination in the United States. Later, the KKK under the guise of the Invisible Empire would spread this core Baptist dogma to any denomination that would adapt. Most, if not all, acquiesced.[397] Predestination is much like a line from George Orwell's Animal Farm, "Some of us are more equal than others."[398]

"The Anti-missionary spirit owes its modern origin to the notorious Daniel Parker. He was the first person called Baptist that lent a hand to the Infidel, and Papist in opposing the proclamation of the gospel to every creature, and the translation and circulation of the Scriptures in all languages and among all people. Possessing a strong native intellect, and a bold adventurous imagination - with a mind cast in nature's most capacious mold, but for want of cultivation admirably calculated to be the receptacle of notions, the most crude, extravagant, and chimerical, he generated a Utopian scheme of theology, the tendency of which was to subvert all practical religion. The grounds of his opposition to missions were that the devil was an eternal 'self-subsistent being' (to use his own phrase); that though God created all, yet the devil begat a part of mankind; that those begotten of the devil were his bona fide children, and to their father they would and ought to go; of course sending them the gospel and giving them the Bible were acts of such gross and supreme folly that no Christian should be engaged in them."[399]
"On the other hand he taught that the remaining portion of the human family were the actual sons of God from eternity, and being allied to Jesus Christ ere 'the morning stars sang together and all the sons of God shouted for joy'[400] by the nearest and dearest ties of consanguinity, being no less

CHAPTER SEVEN | RELIGIOUS EXCUSES FOR WHITE SUPREMACY

than 'particles' of his body - bone of his bone and flesh of his flesh, the Redeemer *nolens volens*, take them to mansions prepared for them in bliss; hence Mr. Parker very wisely concluded, that if such were the case, the Lord had very little use for the Bible or Missionary Societies..."[401]

"There were many who embraced only half the doctrine of Mr. Parker and though they manifested no great apprehension for the liege subjects of the Prince of Darkness, yet they expressed great alarm lest the missionaries should help the Lord to perform his work and convert the souls of some in a way God never intended they should be. They were such staunch friends of the Lord's doing all his work, that they set upon and terribly assailed their missionary brethren, for fear they should by some means assist the Lord in the salvation of his elect. In their zeal against these ambitious strides of the missionaries, they have occasioned great disturbance and distress - and destroying the Peace of Zion, the progress of religion has been greatly retarded, and the influence and usefulness of many ministers and churches utterly paralyzed."[402][403]

"Mr. Parker is one of those singular and rather extraordinary beings whom Divine Providence permits to arise as a scourge to his church, and as a stumbling block in the way of religious effort. Raised on the frontiers of Georgia, without education, uncouth in manners, slovenly in dress, diminutive in person, unprepossessing in appearance, with shriveled features and a small piercing eye, few men, for a series of years, have exerted a wider influence on the lower and less educated class of frontier people. With a zeal and enthusiasm bordering on insanity, firmness that amounted to obstinacy, and perseverance that would have done honor to a good cause, Daniel Parker exerted himself to the utmost to induce the churches within his range to declare non-fellowship with all Baptists who united with any missionary or benevolent (or as he called them, new-fangled) societies. He possessed a mind of singular and original cast. In doctrine he was an Antinomian[404] from the first, but he could describe the process of conviction, and the joys of conversion, and of dependence on God with peculiar feeling and effect. This kind of preaching was calculated to take a stronghold on the hearts and gain the confidence of a class of pious, simple-hearted Christians, of but little religious intelligence and reading. He fully believed, and produced the impression on others, that he spoke by immediate inspiration. Repeatedly have we heard him when his mind seemed to rise above its own powers, and he would discourse for a few moments on the divine attributes or some doctrinal subject with such brilliancy of thought and force of correctness of language, as would astonish men of education and talents. Then, again, it would seem as though he was perfectly bewildered in a mist of abstruse subtleties.[405] "Parker is as well-known for his two-seed views as for his anti-missionism. He published *Views on the Two Seeds* in 1826. The following year he published the *Second Dose of Doctrine on the Two Seeds.* Described as a modification of ancient Manichaeism,[406] these two works attempted to prove that the two existing spiritual principles of good and evil were eternal and self-existing.[407] While Daniel Parker is long dead his dogma continues to be espoused by many.

Although they do not always claim it as two-seeds doctrine, nearly all Baptist, Holiness and Pentecostal denominations practice this cleverly disguised motif that presents white people as superior by birth and all others as inferior. The only difference between the version offered by these groups and the one offered by Daniel Parker is that Parker's version was much more thought out. Recently, I had lunch with a powerful man of God. It turns out that he was born African-American. He related to me how he was raised in a Pentecostal Church that was predominately people of color. When they asked the neighboring white pastor from their denomination why they did not just worship together, they were told it was because they could not be ***unequally yoked together***. Yes, horribly, the imprimatur of the Texas Syndicate lives on in the United States of America. There are United Pentecostal churches in the South that have it written into their charter that black people cannot become members. The legacy of the Texas Syndicate is horrendous.[408]

CHAPTER EIGHT

BETHEL

"The past is never dead. It's not even past."

-William Faulkner

In Topeka, Kansas USA, Charles and Sarah Parham opened a healing home at 335 SW Jackson Street. The building continues to be used for ministry and is now, Tree of Life Church.[409] Sarah's influence was apparent from the start. She named the home, *Bethel Divine Healing Home*. The purpose was to provide "home-like comforts for those who were seeking healing." The ground floor housed a chapel, a public reading room and a printing office. The second floor had fourteen rooms with large windows, which were always filled with fresh flowers, adding to the peace and cheer of the home. The third floor was an attic which doubled as a bedroom when all others were full. Each day the Word of God was taught, and prayer was offered individually whenever it was necessary. Bethel also offered special studies for ministers and evangelists which prepared and trained them for Gospel work. This would be the first step in the Parhams later establishing a Bible college. Charles and Sarah also found Christian homes for orphans, and work for the unemployed. Using the skills that Sarah and her sister Lilian learned from their father, Anthony Thistlethwaite, at his newspaper in Tonganoxie, they created a publication. In 1897, the Parhams had first established their ministry newsletter.[410] They named their newsletter, ***Apostolic Faith***. It was published bi-weekly, and initially had a subscription price. Charles Parham changed this by referring readers to read Isaiah 55:1, then give accordingly.

"Parham taught second work of grace as taught by Rev. A. B. Simpson."[411] The Lord wonderfully provided. Each edition published wonderful testimonies of healing and many of the sermons that were taught at Bethel. As well as conversions and powerful healings the Parhams experienced miraculous provision of finances on several occasions. The first larger multicultural gathering for Bethel would set the tone and establish the culture of the Parhams' ministry. New Year's Day brought 300 people from all over the Topeka region together for a meal: red, yellow, black, and white.[412]

The Bethel building in Topeka Kansas as it looks today

One must realize that people of different racial backgrounds never went to the same church as equals. Charles Sheldon well known author of the book, In His Steps,[413] dared to dream of the possibility of white and black people worshiping together. Likely, few thought that anyone would attempt such a feat, especially in the South where they were plagued by Jim Crow laws. Charles Shelton dared to suggest that white and black people could live, work, and serve together. In regard to whether whites and blacks could live together harmoniously Sheldon asked, "Why not? It never has been done. Well, let's do it then. Oh! I am tired of hearing it said, 'You can't do it because it never has been done.'"[414] While Charles Shelton gave lip service to the idea of such racial harmony, a decade later Charles and Sarah Parham would arrive in the same town (Topeka, Kansas) and do more than dream—they acted. Moreover, in one of his printed sermons, he encouraged the readers to let nothing keep them "from loving every true child of God of whatsoever name, sect, or order they may be."[415]

The Apostolic Faith Movment

In 1897, Charles and Sarah Parham began what they called the Apostolic Faith. This started in the form of a periodical of the same name, Apostolic Faith. This group would become the Apostolic Faith Movement and would spark an outpouring of the Holy Ghost in Topeka, Kansas. The spark spread throughout the United States (including Los Angeles) and to the whole world. The key leaders in this effort were primarily women and people of color. In 1905, and perhaps even before, white ministers began distancing themselves from Charles Fox and Sarah Eleanor Parham because the Parhams were too quick to ignore Jim Crow laws. They embraced Hispanics, African-Americans, as well as women to work in Apostolic Faith Bands as ministers of the Gospel - not just ministers - equals.[416] Vinson Synan, a Pentecostal scholar in history, recognizes that Charles Fox Parham is the one "who subsequently formulated the 'initial evidence' teaching that is central to the theology of most of the classical Pentecostal churches of the world. This teaching holds that speaking in tongues unknown to the speaker is the necessary first sign that one has received the Pentecostal experience. This teaching was based on the fact that tongues appeared as the Spirit was poured out in the primitive church in Acts 2, 10, and, 19 and were implicit in Acts 8 and 9."[417]

After Bethel was well established, Parham left two ministers in charge and set out to visit several different ministries in Chicago, Boston, New York, and Maine. Historians have made much ado about this trip. They present the journey like Parham didn't know what he believed, but was searching for what he should believe. This presentation was insulting to Charles and Sarah Parham and to those who were their mentors. According to Charles Parham what came from the trip was more hunger for the things of God.

Because of his tremendous success at Bethel, many began to urge Parham to open a Bible school. Parham invested time fasting and praying while he ventured on his journey. Among the stops on Parham's journey was a visit to the shaman Alexander Dowie at *Zion City*, Illinois, the revivalist A.B. Simpson in New York and the cult called the *Holy Ghost and Us* led by spiritualist Frank Sandford at a place they called Shiloh in Durham, Maine. Denominational proxies have long referenced only these three stops to make it seem like Parham was searching for something strange or at least abnormal. It fits the narrative they wish to portray. Parham visited these places because of their proximity to his other stops. Parham explained that he had heard rumors of Sandford in faraway Kansas City. The rumors claimed that Sandford was raising the dead.[418] Parham wanted to meet such a man and judge for himself if there was substance to

Shiloh

~ CHAPTER EIGHT | BETHEL ~

Hospice as some attempt by Parham to be Elijah. Elijah Hospice was a hotel in Zion City.[440] Dowie was the one fixated on Elijah in Zion City. Parham never shared his delusions.

G. There was yet another Elijah. This one was a food called Elijah's Manna. Popular in 1906. Today we call it Post Corn Flakes.[441]

Just because it is on the internet does not mean it is true. Before the internet, we had the National Enquirer;[442] it was like the internet, but in print. The story as published is either propaganda or paranoia, maybe both! Voliva was paranoid and those who repeat his delusions buy into his paranoia. This was more of the campaign that Wilbur Voliva directed after the death of his mentor and fellow fraud, Dowie. Voliva, who had a front row seat to the shaman Dowie's reign as a self-appointed Elijah, understood better than most the horror of the error. In one of his many demented illusions, he attempted to connect Parham to the fallen Dowie. Voliva used fear tactics and the people feared Dowie. Voliva's reign of terror on the people of Zion was yet in the future. It would make the tactics of organized crime seem tame in comparison.[443]

Elijah's Manna

Dowie, Voliva, and their leaders were not at all receptive to the Apostolic Faith message. This is further evidenced in the ministry of Mrs. Waldron. "Waldron received her spirit-baptism under Parham in Kansas and relocated to Zion City around 1904. Lilian Thistlethwaite, a leading minister in the Apostolic Faith Movement, was conducting meetings in the Zion at the invitation of Mrs. Waldron. Waldron attempted to spread Parham's teaching in Zion City, believing Parham's message compatible

> **Three New Elijahs.**
> (Public Opinion.)
> There are no less than three Elijahs now posing before the people in various parts of the country. John Alexander Dowie, Elijah III., is fighting with the rest of his Christian Catholic church for the possession of Zion City, on the shore of Lake Michigan; Sandford, the Elijah at the head of the "Holy Ghost and Us," of Shiloh, Me., has just returned, after an extended yachting trip in Mediterranean waters, to be tried for manslaughter; and now a negro Elijah has arisen in Plainfield, N. J., a paralytic prophet, William S. Crowdy, head of the Church of God and Saints of Christ.

with Dowie's."[444] Dowie and his officers did not agree. Like Sandford they were not interested in the notion of anyone speaking in tongues. These cults were only "Pentecostal" in the sense it was a popular word of the time, and fit their modus operandi for attracting marks. The Church of the Nazarene, The Pentecostal Union, and other Holiness groups used the term Pentecostal, but distanced themselves from the term when it became the designation of choice for the Assemblies of God.

Waldron was pressured to leave Zion City.[445] The welcome mat was not available to the A.F.M. "John G. Lake records that Lilian Thistlethwaite preached in F. F. Bosworth's home[446] during her 1904 evangelist trip to Zion.[447] Critics who despise the A.F.M. pose as historians and mention these cults as part of an effort to connect them to the A.F.M. in particular and Pentecostals in general. They seek to connect this mess to Parham, pretending that he was like these messengers of hell, Dowie and Sandford. Fortunately, for all of us, Charles and Sarah Parham were something much different.

In A. B. Simpson, Parham did find commonality.[448] They were both filled with a desire for more of God. Simpson was Presbyterian and Parham was Methodist, but like many others they were not concerned about denominational barriers. Parham was motivated to include Simpson in his trip because of Simpson's position on the topic most on Parham's mind- the evidence of one receiving the Holy Ghost. In 1893, Simpson advocated seeking gifts of the Spirit, but had not embraced speaking in tongues. Nevertheless, Simpson writes of 1 Corinthians 12 that all the charismata may be expected throughout the entire church age and are "designed to be zealously sought, cherished, and cultivated"⁴⁴⁹ There is no doubt that Parham and Simpson conversed about his thoughts in this arena.

While historians search for outrageous conclusions from Parhams' 1900 journey, one thing that became an ear mark of their movement and that it was influenced in some measure by A. B. Simpson seems evident. A.F.M. became a strong missionary sending group like Simpson's Christian Missionary Alliance. Later, A. B. Simpson and most of his leaders would be converted to Parham's way of receiving the Holy Spirit – evidenced by speaking in other tongues. "Citing Simpson's diary and some of Simpson's comments to Pentecostal leaders, Charles Nienkirchen demonstrates that Simpson was, in fact, a seeker of tongues. Further, he claims that Tozier's previous account of the writing is revisionist. Tozier changed the narrative to fit his agenda."⁴⁵⁰ Grant Wacker responded to Simpson with this, "there can be little doubt that he sought all the gifts of the Spirit, including tongues if the Lord willed it."⁴⁵¹

> *"Parham was motivated to include Simpson in his trip because of Simpson's position on the topic most on Parham's mind—the evidence of one receiving the Holy Ghost."*

A. B. Simpson is not alone in facing history revision by enemies of the Cross. This same tactic has often been the case in the history of Charles and Sarah Parham. It is criminal what is done to harm people's reputations.⁴⁵² Historians and their proxies conveniently ignore that Parham went to Chicago to visit Moody, and to Boston to visit A. J. Gordon as this did not fit their narrative which they present as a trip to learn how to become a shaman.⁴⁵³ It is evident from the nature of Parham's journey that the primary mandate was direction on his decision to start a Bible College. Dwight Lyman Moody had passed away in the December before Parham's arrival. Already installed by Moody as leader of his Chicago Evangelization Society, R. A. Torrey succeeded Moody as its president. In a meeting with Torrey, Parham was "taking notes" on how Moody had established his ministry and college. Torrey and Parham would later disagree on speaking in other tongues. Despite that, in many ways the ministry that Charles and Sarah Parham established was a reflection of that great revivalist Moody, who is credited with beginning the Great Awakening.[454] Historiographers seem to develop amnesia about Parham's visit to Moody, opting instead to promote their perverted fantasies about Parham's visit to Sandford's delusion.

Fortunately, beyond all the speculation of denominationally financed proxies, we know what Parham thought of his journey, *"I returned home fully convinced that while many had obtained real experience in sanctification and the anointing that abideth, there still remained a great outpouring of power for the Christians who were close to this age."* "Parham criticized those centers of holiness and healing spirituality on two counts. Not only did they fall short of "the account in Acts" in Parham's estimation, but they also spawned an offensive sectarian spirit. He censured those "Bible Schools" "Zions," (and) "colonies" (Shiloh) he had toured because they adhered to the doctrines "of one man," which caused them to "become narrow, selfish... self-advancing; until denouncing and un-Christianizing all others, they [came] to

> **IMMERSED 250 CONVERTS.**
>
> **Rev. Charles F. Parham, Formerly of Kansas City, Makes a Record.**
>
> GALENA.— (Special.) Notwithstanding the inclemency of the weather, Rev. Charles F. Parham, formerly of Kansas City, baptized 250 converts in Spring river, at Lowell, three miles southwest of here, Sunday afternoon. The Rev. Parham went from this place to Baxter Springs about three weeks ago, and since that time has been holding a series of meetings at that place. Many of the Baxterites are now firm believers in Parhamism, and the candidates immersed Sunday afternoon were from Galena, Baxter, Cave Springs and Garden Hollow, including, like the Salvation Army, a class that is not reached by the local clergy.
>
> This is Rev. Mr. Parham's third baptizing in Spring river, the two former being in midwinter. Since coming to this vicinity, in August, he has held his services in divers places, beginning in a large tent, but cold weather drove them to a large empty business building in Galena, which was inadequate for the crowds. In Baxter the city hall was rented, after Mr. Parham was refused admittance to the churches. But after three nights' meeting the electric light wires were cut to force a close of the services. Then a billiard hall was tendered for his use. Through it all Mr. Parham has achieved the greatest religious success ever known here. This closes his work here for the present.
>
> **BIDS OPENED AT FORT RILEY.**

believe they [were] the only people."⁴⁵⁵ It is also likely that one of his future students, Agnes Osman, became acquainted with Parham because of his visit to Simpson, as Osman was a student there.

CHAPTER NINE

TOPEKA OUTPOURING

"God had honored Charles Parham as no man of God in modern days has been honored!"[456]

-John G. Lake

When Charles returned to Topeka, he and Sarah (whom he affectionately called "Nellie"[457] and her sister Lilian began to put the vision of a Bible college in motion.[458] In October of 1900, Charles and Sarah Parham obtained a beautiful structure in Topeka, Kansas, for the purpose of beginning a Bible school. Locals called the building, "Stone's Folly." Lilian Thistlethwaite wrote about the structure, "The building was patterned

Stone's Folly

after an English castle. The builder ran out of money before the structure could be completed in style. The staircase that joined the first and second floor was carved with finished woodwork of cedar, cherrywood, maple, and pine. The third floor was finished in common wood and paint."[459]

The outside of Stone's Folly[460] was laid in red brick and white stone, with a winding stairway leading to an observatory. Another doorway led from there to a small room known as the Prayer Tower. Students took turns to pray three hours each day in this special tower. When Stone's Folly was dedicated, a man looked out from the Prayer Tower and saw a vision above Stone's Folly of a "vast lake of fresh water about to overflow, containing enough to satisfy every thirsty need." It would prove to be a sign of things to come. The outside of Stone's Folly was laid in red brick and white stone, with a winding stairway leading to an observatory.[461]

Like Gordon's college, Oberlin College, Berea College and others, Parham's Bible school was open to every Christian minister and believer, who was willing to "forsake all." The Parhams were committed to Charles Finney's vision. Charles Parham quoted Finney, "Until we can remove from the minds of the people the impression that the current Christianity of the age is true Christianity nothing, nothing can be done for the salvation of the world."[462] They were to arrive willing to study the Word deeply and believe God for all their personal needs. The student's faith was their only tuition; everyone was to believe that God would supply their needs.[463]

Examinations were given that December on the subjects of repentance, conversion, consecration, sanctification, healing, and the future coming

Apostolic Faith Movement - 1905

of the Lord. When the book of Acts was included for the study of these subjects, Parham gave his students a historical assignment. They were to diligently study the Bible's evidence of the baptism in the Holy Spirit and report on their findings in three days. This was a recurring theme among Methodist people. There was a spiritual hunger they sought to satisfy. After assigning this homework, Parham left his students for a meeting in Kansas City. Then he returned to Stone's Folly for the annual Watch Night Service.[464]

On the morning that the assignments were due, Parham listened to the reports of forty students, and was astonished by what he heard. While different manifestations of the Spirit occurred during the outpouring of Pentecost in Acts, every student had arrived at the same general conclusion: Every recipient baptized by the Holy Spirit spoke in other tongues! While this is indeed the Scriptural conclusion, the general position of Religious Denominations of the day, was that speaking in other tongues while the Spirit gave utterance was something that only happened at the time of the Apostles. Yet, Methodist ministers like Henry Clay Morrison had denied the argument that these things ended with the New Testament Church.

Now there was a great excitement and new interest at Stone's Folly surrounding the book of Acts. Anticipation filled the atmosphere as seventy-five people crowded around one another at the school for the evening Watch Night Service. The Apostolic Faith Movement held Watch Night services; this was significant. "John Wesley adopted the practice for his Methodist followers, who held similar vigils. It was given new significance among African-Americans on December 31, 1862, when, according to tradition, slaves in the Confederate states gathered in churches and private homes on the night before U.S. Pres. Abraham Lincoln's Emancipation Proclamation was expected to go into effect, pending his signing of the document. The soon-to-be-free slaves stayed awake all night and watched the night turn into a new dawn while waiting for news that the Emancipation Proclamation had been issued, thus making all the slaves legally free. Church services on Watch Night generally began sometime between 7:00 and 10:00 PM and end at midnight."[465]

Charles Parham (center) with Apostolic Faith students

Thomas Fudge wrote on the eerie similarities of the Topeka Outpouring to the Day of Pentecost. Topeka was Pentecost in almost every detail transplanted from Jerusalem to Kansas.[466] "An examination of the principal text in the Acts of the Apostles reveal eight conspicuous features of the original Pentecostal event; they were gathered in an upper room, prayer was the main activity, about one hundred and twenty persons were present, there was wind, visible tongues of fire, those flames sat on each person's head, they spoke in tongues and this speaking in tongues was in the form of known, identifiable world languages. The accounts of the Topeka scenario of 1900/1 betray an uncanny similarity to the event surrounding the Day of Pentecost in the upper room in Jerusalem. Gathered in an 'upper room' in Stone's Folly that New Years Eve and following days were the forty students and about seventy-five others, close to one hundred and twenty souls."[467]

During the service, a spiritual freshness seemed to blanket the meeting. Then a student, Agnes Ozman, approached Parham and asked him to lay his hands on her so she would receive the baptism of the Holy Spirit. Ozman believed she was called to the mission field and wanted to be equipped with spiritual power. At first Parham hesitated, telling her that he himself didn't speak in other tongues. However, she persisted, and Parham humbly laid his hands upon her head. Parham would later write of the incident, explaining it like this:[468]

"I had scarcely repeated three dozen sentences when a glory fell upon her, a halo seemed to surround her head and face, and she began speaking in the Chinese language, and was unable to speak English for three days."[469] Ozman later testified that she had already received a few of these same words while in the Prayer Tower. After Parham laid hands on her, she completely overflowed with the supernatural power of God.[470] Parham soon followed with a similar experience, "Right then and there came a slight twist in my throat, a glory fell over me and I began to worship God in a Swedish tongue, which later changed to other languages and continued..."[471]

God rewarded the spiritual hunger. *"Charles Parham's doctrine of the Holy Spirit baptism—and the corresponding Azusa Street revival that made both the doctrine and experience available to thousands of people, of all races, worldwide—defined the Pentecostal experience, the notion of a post conversion experience or even the spiritual phenomenon of speaking fluently in an unknown language.*[472] *The hunger was rewarded with an outpouring of the Holy Spirit that would sweep throughout the entire world.*[473]

Soon the news of what God was doing had Stone's Folly besieged by newspaper reporters, language professors, and government interpreters. They sat in on the services to tell the whole world of this incredible phenomenon. They had come to the consensus that Stone's Folly's students were speaking in the languages of the world. Their newspapers screamed with the headlines "Pentecost! Pentecost!" Newsboys shouted, "Read about the

Pentecost!"[474]

On January 21, 1901, Parham preached the first sermon dedicated to the sole experience of the baptism of the Holy Spirit with the evidence of speaking in other tongues. It sounded much like pages from Henry Clay Morrison's book, Baptism with the Holy Ghost. Parham said, "Some say today that "tongues have passed away." My friend, when miracles pass away, when signs and wonders pass away, when the manifestations of the Holy Spirit pass away, tongues will pass away too. Then we will have no need for other tongues. As long as we are on planet Earth, these things shall remain. The book of Acts continues to be lived out in the life of the Church today. The only thing that has passed away is the sacrificing of lambs, because Jesus fulfilled the sacrifice system of shedding of blood and removed the veil separating God and man." Parham went throughout the country, preaching the truths of the baptism of the Holy Spirit in wonderful demonstration. Once in a service, he began to speak in other tongues, then when he had finished, a man in the congregation stood up

Charles Parham (Center) with 17 students and The College of Bethel faculty. Sarah Parham 2nd from left, Lilian Thistlethwaite 8th from left, Agnes Osman 5th from right. Circa 1901. Photo at the Kansas City Academy of Music.

and said, "I am healed of my infidelity; I have heard in my own tongue the 23rd Psalm that I learned at my mother's knee." This was only one of the countless testimonies regarding the gift of other tongues that came out of Parham's ministry. Soon, hundreds upon hundreds began to receive this manifestation. Along with this mighty outpouring came a slanderous persecution of those who despised it.

While there were initially no black students at Bethel there were three who received the baptism of the Holy Spirit during the February 1901 Lawrence Campaign. This propelled the Apostolic Faith movement into the arena of multicultural. Something quite rare at that time.[475] In the fall of 1901, the Bible school in Topeka was unexpectedly sold out from under Parham. It was then that Parham began to hold meetings around the country. Hundreds of people, from every denomination, received the baptism of the Holy Spirit and divine healing. As is true with every pioneering revivalist, Parham was either greatly loved or hated by the public, but his colorful personality and warm heart were recognized by all. One Kansas newspaper wrote: *"Whatever may be said about him, he has attracted more attention to religion than any other religious worker in years."*

CHAPTER TEN

EVIDENCE OF SPIRIT BAPTISM GOES GLOBAL

"Men will never fly, because flying is reserved for the angels."

-Bishop Milton Wright (Father of Orville and Wilbur)

While men of the faith like Moody, Wesley, Gordon, Asbury, Morrison and a host of others, believed in the necessity of receiving the Holy Ghost, they stopped short of offering that there was audible evidence of the same. It may well be that like those at the time of the coming of Christ Jesus, they did not expect the manner in which He arrived. The way the Holy Spirit was perceived verses how it arrived brings to mind a Church convention. One leader stood up and shared his vision both for the church and society at large. He told the ministers and evangelists how he believed someday men would fly from place to place instead of merely traveling on horseback. It was a concept too outlandish for many members to handle. One minister, Bishop Wright, stood up and angrily protested, "Heresy!" he shouted. "Flight is reserved for the angels!"⁴⁷⁶

He went on to elaborate that if God had intended for man to fly, He would have given him wings. Clearly, the bishop was unable to envision what the speaker was predicting. When Bishop Wright finished his brief protest, he gathered up his two sons, Orville and Wilbur, and left the auditorium. That's right. His sons were Orville and Wilbur Wright. Several years later, on December 17, 1903, those two sons did what their father called impossible. They made four flights that day. The first lasted only 12 seconds, but the fourth lasted 59 seconds and took them 852 feet. The two brothers partnered together to accomplish the impossible – and in the process, they changed the world. They discovered the power of partnership.'⁴⁷⁷

While Bishop Wright's sons were proving his opinions to be incorrect, Charles and Sarah Parham were using the imprimatur of the Holy Spirit to prove numerous well-intentioned ministers to have misjudged the situation. The consensus belief: receiving the Holy Spirit was an act of faith that occurred sometime after your coming to belief in Christ. For some the idea that speaking in other tongues as the Spirit gives the utterance was not a serious thought. Yes, they understood that those in the Book of Acts and the adherents of the New Testament manifested such gifting as speaking in other tongues, but they had generally been taught that such things had ended or ceased after the days of the Apostles. Cessation is a doctrine that spiritual gifts such as speaking in tongues, prophecy, and healing ceased with the Apostolic Age. Reformers such as John Calvin originated this view. ⁴⁷⁸

Henry Clay Morrison, founder of Asbury Seminary, his story of his receiving his own Pentecostal blessing is amazing and an experience that covered more than fifteen days. He did not say that he spoke in other tongues. What he did say was that the Pentecostal Blessing is for everyone.[479] He makes the point by evoking the imprimatur of Apostle Peter. *"Then Peter said to them, "Repent, and let every one of you be baptized in the name of Jesus Christ for the remission of sins; and you shall receive the gift of the Holy Spirit. For the promise is to you and to your children, and to all who are afar off, as many as the Lord our God will call."*[480]

"I come from a Holiness Wesleyan group, where there are three events: being born again, receiving entire sanctification, and receiving the holy ghost (with some kind of 'sign following' but not necessarily tongues). We can understand Morrison's goal for the founding of a new Holiness seminary on the campus of Asbury College. In the midst of religious insecurity, when 'large numbers of preachers ...have ceased to believe the plain work of the Bible...[and] are preaching their unbelief, 'the new seminary would 'stand true to the Bible from first to last.' As a Methodist who supported academic training but who was also wary of it, Morrison intended that his seminary would fulfill America's need for a 'well-educated, Spirit-filled, evangelistic ministry who are loyal to the Word of God and the Son of God.'" "Camp meetings led by Morrison were characterized by jumping, clapping, shouting, and "frequent prostrations or trances" in which numbers of people "lay prone on the straw, seemingly dead for hours." If you were to witness one you would expect it was a Pentecostal meeting. Nonetheless, Morrison regularly condemned "fanaticism" [481]

Parham had his first experience with fanaticism in 1903. He preached at a church where wild and fleshly manifestations took place. The experience would add a dimension to his teaching. Though he never allowed himself to be called the leader in this Pentecostal Movement, Parham felt personally responsible in seeing that the baptism of the Holy Spirit was manifested according to the Word. Apparently, his students also were taught these lessons as it was William J. Seymour (not Parham) who first recognized this problem at the Apostolic Faith Gospel Mission in Los Angeles (aka Azusa Street Revival). Parham wrote of fanaticism, *"Those who have had experience of fanaticism know that there goes with it an unteachable spirit and spiritual pride which makes those under the influences of these false spirits feel exalted and think that they have a greater experience than anyone else, and do not need instruction or advice."*

In the Galena, Kansas meetings, two newspapers, the Joplin Herald and the Cincinnati Enquirer, declared Parham's Galena meetings to be the greatest demonstration of power and miracles since the time of the Apostles, writing, "Many...came to scoff but remained to pray." The Galena "embraced all social classes throughout the region, and in a three-month period more than 800 people were saved. The Apostolic Faith bands were composed of men and women alike. They were co-laborers with no sense of women being secondary or subordinate. The names of two women were recorded again and again, Mable Smith and Lucy Farrow. Both women were later sent in response to William J. Seymour's pleas for help in the opening days of Apostolic Faith Gospel Mission. A.F.M. was going global. Inquiries came from all over the World. A.F.M. ministers held meetings all over the nation – Illinois, Ohio, California, New York, Alabama, and all points in between. If the train went there, so did Apostolic Faith ministers. It was said, "people come to scoff, remain to pray, seek and find to their great joy the baptism of the Holy Ghost."[482]

B. F. Lawrence considered the[483] Apostolic Faith Movement[484] as a direct reversion to New Testament life and practice.[485] "Parham arrived in Houston with about twenty-five workers in July of 1905. For the first time he encountered a large black populace and an intense racial prejudice he had not known in his home state of Kansas. He conducted a very successful meeting in Bryan Hall which was attended by many Blacks and Mexicans. Parham reached out to the underserved communities. He made friends with black leaders such as Lucy Farrow and William Seymour. In fact, his racial openness made some white Christians in Houston very uncomfortable. A white pastor, Warren Fay Carothers, referring to the Parhams and their Kansas workers, wrote the following rebuke in December of 1905."[486]

"I trust, therefore, that our evangelists and workers from the North will not forget this condition of affairs [racial segregation] and embarrass the work South by well-meaning but mistaken efforts to disregard them. Let the race question alone until you have been South long enough to know by experience what it seems impossible for our Northern brethren to learn through other sources.[487] This was the beginning of a terrible fight for his life for Charles Fox Parham.

While Mr. Carothers concerned himself with controlling the gender and the color of the Revival, the outpouring of the Holy Spirit was going global. Encouraged by the boldness of the A.F.M., Rev. A. A. Boddy Vicar at All Saints with his wife Mary Broddy received their own personal "Pentecost." The Broddy's brought the A.F.M. to England and stayed in contact with A.F.M. ministers around the world.[488] The Boddy's in England started a conference and a publication, Confidence. A.F.M. ministers, like George Studd kept the European branch of the Movement abreast of how things were progressing in the United States.[489] The Boddy's promoted their Whitsuntide at Sunderland to be the INTERNATIONAL CONFERENCE.[490] Confidence attempted to bring updated information about the A.F.M. and the Pentecostal Outpourings around the world with reports from A.F.M. Missions as far away as Egypt,[491] China, and Australia.[492]

Parham's First Serious Encounter With The Race Issue

The A.F.M. did not limit outreach to the white neighborhoods. They made a serious effort to evangelize even the "Red Light District" where people of all nationalities were present.[493] The A.F.M. also began to evangelize Jewish people, especially those with Zionist expectations.[494] Parham began preaching to Jewish audiences and authored pro-Jewish sermons railing against societal stereotypes of Jewish people."[495] "During the summer of 1905, Parham, for the first time, ventured south across the Mason-Dixon line into Texas. He went there to declare his newly discovered message of the baptism in the Holy Spirit evidenced by speaking in tongues. Five years earlier, the students in his Bible school in Topeka had identified speaking in tongues as the "Bible evidence" of Spirit baptism. Almost immediately the entire school experienced a mighty outpouring of the Holy Spirit with virtually everyone present, including Parham, speaking in tongues. Parham believed that their experience signaled the beginning of the world-wide, last-days effusion of the Spirit promised in Acts 2:17, and he had come South to declare this newly discovered truth."[496]

Parham met a new adversary in Texas. This demon had a name. His name was Jim Crow. Jim Crow did the work of Satan and Parham would fight numerous battles with him. "Jim Crow was the name of the racial caste system which operated primarily, but not exclusively in southern and border states, between 1877 and the mid-1960s. Jim Crow was more than a series of rigid anti-black laws. It was a way of life. Under Jim Crow, African-Americans were relegated to the status of second-class citizens. Jim Crow represented the legitimization of anti-black racism. Many Christian ministers and theologians taught that whites were the Chosen people, blacks were cursed to be servants, and God supported racial segregation."[497] Jim Crow would do horrible things to Charles and Sarah Parham, and he would have lots of helpers.

CHAPTER TEN | EVIDENCE OF SPIRIT BAPTISM GOES GLOBAL

Due to high public demand, the team returned to Houston once more, but this time, heavy persecution came their way. Several of Parham's workers were poisoned during one meeting. Undaunted by the persecution, Parham announced the opening of a new Bible school in Houston, then moved his headquarters there in the winter of 1905. The school was supported like the one in Topeka, through freewill offerings. There was no tuition. Each student had to live by faith. It was said that a military style of order was practiced at the school and that each person understood how to work in harmony. Parham's schools were never meant to be theological seminaries. They were training centers where the truths of God were taught in the most practical manner—with prayer as a key ingredient. Thousands of ministers left the Parhams' schools to serve God throughout the world.

"In the South, the racial apartheid was even more pronounced. Jim Crow laws designed to marginalize the black populace were in place. Blacks were required to use separate public restrooms and drinking fountains. They were required to sit in separate sections on trains, buses, in restaurants and in all public facilities. All public education was segregated according to race. Blacks lived in separate neighborhoods and both overt and subtle forms of intimidation were used to keep them "in their place."[498]
The Jim Crow laws required meetings to be racially segregated. This created new challenges for the Parhams and their multicultural Apostolic Faith Movement. This forced Charles Parham to have separate revival meetings for blacks in the Houston area. The Jim Crow Laws forbid blacks and whites from attending school together. One of the ways Parham had worked around the Jim Crow laws was claiming Lucy Farrow was the family's Governess. Under Jim Crow, white families could not have black people living in their home unless they were domestic servants. So, the Parhams presented Lucy Farrow as the Governess. However, in practical

application Lucy Farrow was a powerful minister in her own right. She was the catalyst for the Apostolic Faith making serious in roads in black communities in Houston and beyond. Lucy Farrow was the speaker at many Apostolic Faith Movement meetings, camp meetings, etc.

William Seymour was given a place in Parham's Houston, Texas school where he experienced revolutionary truths on the baptism of the Holy Spirit. William Seymour would later become the leader of the Apostolic Faith Gospel Mission in Los Angeles, California. "Both Parham and Seymour preached to Houston's African-Americans, and Parham planned to send Seymour out to preach to the black communities throughout Texas."[499] At this time, Parham wrote specifically about also reaching out to Japanese people, marking even further racial diversity in the A.F.M.[500] After Parham's historical Houston school ended, he moved his family back to Kansas. It was at this time that he received letters from Seymour, asking him to come to the Mission in Los Angeles at Azusa Street. It was said that Seymour wrote "urgent letters appealing for help, as spiritualistic manifestations, hypnotic forces and fleshly contortions...had broken loose in the meeting. He wanted Mr. Parham to come quickly and help him discern between that which was real and that which was false." Despite the plea, Parham felt led by God to hold a rally in Zion City, Illinois, instead.

Zion City Outpouring

When Parham arrived in Zion, he met with great opposition, and was unable to secure a building for the meetings. So, all doors of opportunity seemed to close. Finally, at the invitation of a hotel manager, he was able to set up a meeting in a private room. The next night, two rooms and the hallway were crowded, and attendance grew steadily from there. Soon Parham began cottage meetings in the best homes of the city.

CHAPTER TEN | EVIDENCE OF SPIRIT BAPTISM GOES GLOBAL

One of these homes belonged to the great healing evangelist and author, F. F. Bosworth. Bosworth's home was literally turned into a meeting house during Parham's stay. Every night, Parham led five different meetings in five different homes, all beginning at 7:00 P.M. When his workers would arrive, he would go preaching from meeting to meeting, driving rapidly to make sure he reached each one. As a result, hundreds of ministers and evangelists went out from Zion filled with the power of the Spirit to preach God's Word with signs.

Though Zion was a Christian community, it seemed the persecution against Parham was the greatest ever there. The wild claims that were presented as Carothers' kangaroo court in Texas likely originated in Zion or through the Zion publications. Secular newspapers had a media blitz, citing the "Prophet Parham" as taking the ground of the "Prophet Dowie."[501] Dowie himself went on public record to criticize Parham's message and actions. The new Overseer of Zion, Wilbur Voliva, was eager to see Parham leave the city. Voliva wrote Parham to ask how long he intended to stay in Zion. Parham replied, "As long as the Lord wants me here."

In October of 1906, Parham felt released from Zion and hurried to Los Angeles to answer Seymour's call. Lilian Thistlethwaite stayed and led the Apostolic Faith Movement in Zion. The results were astonishing. Among those who found their Pentecost in this Revival were John Graham Lake and many others.[502] Certainly volumes could be written about the subject of this chapter. We have only mentioned the highlights.

CHAPTER ELEVEN

LOS ANGELES OUTPOURING

So, beloved, when you get your personal Pentecost, the signs will follow" [503]*":in speaking with tongues as the Spirit gives utterance*

-William J. Seymour

For the Parhams and practically every other early Pentecostal leader, the principle of *sola scriptura* was an unassailable and incontestable fact.[504] The candles God lit at Stone's Folly in January 1901 began igniting others including: Topeka, Baxter Springs, Kansas; Houston, Texas; Zion, Illinois; New York, New York; and Los Angeles, California. In addition, it spread to other parts of the world, such as Wales,

Parham Family: Charles F. Parham top left. Top right, Parham's sister-in-law, Lilian Thistlethwaite. Seated, Parham's wife, Sarah.

South Africa, China, Japan, Korea, and Australia; this was even before Azusa Street (1906-1909)."[505] The Apostolic Faith welcomed people into their ranks from all races. They welcomed women ministers and openly promoted women as ministers into the ministry.

Joe Creech refers to the "central myth of origin for almost every Pentecostal denomination" that placed Azusa Street in the middle of American Pentecostal historiography and overlooked or minimized other important centers of Pentecostal expansion.[506] "Since every Pentecostal group in existence today can trace its roots back to (Charles and Sarah) Parham, it can be stated that no other person has made a greater impact on the growth of Pentecostalism around the world than Charles Parham. Parham held the candle ignited at the first Holy Spirit fire fall and he carried it to thousands, who then carried it to thousands more. Today, one-quarter of all Christians and nearly ten percent of all people on Earth are holding lit candles of the Spirit.[507] In just a few years *"... the Apostolic Faith movement circled the globe; so that millions would receive the baptism of the Holy Spirit with the accompanying evidence of speaking in other tongues and the coordinate gifts of healing the sick and the casting out of devils in Jesus' name..."*[508]

The Los Angeles Outpouring "added fuel to the substantial fire of a revival movement that was already making it appearance throughout the world. Widespread circulation of literature...quickly carried the message overseas."[509] "There is a mistaken impression that this Movement is a mushroom growth, originating in California in 1906. This is not the case. God, who in sundry places, at diverse times poured out His Spirit with the sign of tongues, sent the outpourings to Zion City and Los Angeles after He had prepared for it by smaller, but by no means less genuine, works in other places. Observe, also, how many of our present ministry received

~ CHAPTER ELEVEN | LOS ANGELES OUTPOURING ~

the baptism prior to that outpouring."[510] "The direct line from Topeka Outpouring to the Los Angeles Outpouring has already been noted and the documentation regarding those developments includes newspaper reports concurrent to the events, early written accounts by those who were involved, and a reasonable number of reliable sources."[511]

Following a successful Los Angeles tent meeting conducted by A.F.M. Minister William Francis Manley beginning January 1905, religious meetings were convened in a private home at 214 N. Bonnie Brae Street. While those meetings were in progress one of Charles and Sarah Parham's students, William Joseph Seymour, was making his way to Los Angeles.[512] **The Los Angeles Outpouring** started after **The Topeka Outpouring**, but had started before the revival meetings at the Apostolic Faith Gospel Mission at 312 Azusa Street. The revival meetings at the Apostolic Faith Gospel Mission became part of the larger Los Angeles Outpouring. The revival at Apostolic Faith Gospel Mission was a direct descendant of The Topeka Outpouring. On the other hand, the Los Angeles Outpouring seems to have initially stemmed from the Welsh Revival then later The Topeka Outpouring. It may well be that the Welsh Revival was itself impacted by the Topeka Outpouring. Whatever the chronological order, The Topeka Outpouring remains the catalyst. B.H. Irwin's multiple Spirit reception does not appear compatible with traditional American Pentecostal pneumatology. This ended the debate about his pre-Topeka honors. This was demonstrated in that it was only after Topeka and thus after the Los Angeles Outpouring that the Fire-Baptized Holiness Church officially adopted the Apostolic Faith doctrine of Spirit-baptism.[513] This does not diminish the importance of any move of the Holy Spirit.

Charles Parham – Applecart Pusher

A plethora of self-appointed historians have maligned the Parham family in every way possible, painting the canvas of Charles' life as though he was a wild-eyed narcissist. In contrast, the real Charles F. Parham considered himself an apple cart pusher. *"The Lord used the Apostolic Faith Movement as an applecart to push the truth of Pentecost along, until it became a world-*

wide blessing. It had fulfilled its mission, and now fades in the light of recognition of a general world-wide fellowship in extending the hand of love to all Full Gospel Movements and Churches. The heritage of this truth is the divine right of all the children of God, and the result cannot be harvested by one man or one movement."[514] Although Charles Parham was correct in his assessment, there was no shortage of groups or individuals that sought credit for the results of the global outpouring of the Holy Spirit. The popular song, "We are Children of Azusa Street" makes a good tune but it is not true. Most of us are not Children of Azusa Street. More of us are possibly children of The Los Angeles Outpouring. However, nearly all of us are the spiritual children of Charles and Sarah Parham and their Topeka Outpouring.

The Topeka Outpouring fed a spiritual hunger across America and around the World. People came to meetings led by Apostolic Faith ministers, read their books and publications. In the end, people from every nation under heaven would be impacted by this outpouring. In 1905, as part of the American Revival, hungry people in Los Angeles began a similar quest as those in Topeka, Kansas a few years earlier. Hundreds of Los Angeles churches united in prayer expecting an outpouring of the Holy Spirit. Contrary to published opinions, the Apostolic Faith Movement's influence in the Los Angeles area began before the arrival of William J. Seymour. Before the Parhams even went to Houston the Apostolic Faith

~ CHAPTER ELEVEN | LOS ANGELES OUTPOURING ~

message arrived in Los Angeles. In January of 1905, **William F. Manley** an Apostolic Faith Movement minister from the Dayton, Ohio area, temporarily relocated his ministry and set up a tent in Los Angeles and began ministering to the Spiritual hunger.[515] Thus Manley would fairly be the first to preach the A.F.M. message in the Los Angeles Outpouring.

The next key leader in the Los Angeles Outpouring was Joseph Smale, Pastor of First Baptist Church in Los Angeles. "In 1902 Smale resigned at First Baptist. The leaders called for a vote of confidence. The vote was 226 to 30 in his favor; so, he stayed.[516] The pressure on Smale was unrelenting, and by 1904 he was exhausted and demoralized, and much in need of a break. The deacons gave him leave of absence and provided funds for him to visit England and to go on a tour of the Holy Land with his mother, Ann. The two of them left for Europe on 24th August 1904. The timing would prove to be very significant, for revival was already brewing in Wales, and would burst forth fully and simultaneously under the ministry of Evan Roberts at Loughor in the south of the country, and R B Jones in Rhosllanerchrugog in the north, just two months later. Smale was unaware that though things had seemed to be going wrong for him, God was about to use his circumstances to position him to be the carrier of some of the Welsh fire back to California to help start an inextinguishable blaze. The Revival there represented the kind of experience of God that he had himself longed to see in his own church. He took the opportunity of traveling from Liverpool to experience the Revival in North Wales for himself while waiting for passage to America."[517] Smale was the spark that launched the Los Angeles Outpouring. It appears that Smale had packed the Welsh Revival in his luggage and brought it to Los Angeles.[518]

"The Rev. E. Williams, Baptist minister, Rhos, has just received the following letter from the Rev. Joseph Smale, pastor of the First Baptist

Church of Los Angeles, California.

My dear Brother, you will doubtless recall my visit to you back in April. I left the old country the 10th of May, for home, arriving here the 25th of the same month, and am glad to tell you that a wonderful work of grace commenced immediately I resumed my ministry. While I was recounting the Lord's doings in your country the Holy Ghost fell upon the people, and fully two hundred of them came out of their seats and wept in penitence before the Lord. This was the first Sunday morning after I returned home, and similar scenes have greeted us every now and again in our meetings. This is the eighth week of special gatherings for prayer. We are coming together every day in the afternoon and evening meeting with glorious results, principally in sanctification of the lives of believers. Conversions are not as yet very numerous, but we are looking for a great awakening. The glory of the Lord has indeed settled among us, and people from all over Southern California are coming and feeling the power divine. May I ask of you and your Church an interest in the Lord's work here. Will you pray for us and that the Lord will grant us to see greater things for His Glory."[519]

"In the fall of 1905, Smale preached a series of sermons titled "The Pentecostal Blessing."[520] He encouraged believers to seek a restoration of the spiritual blessings described in the New Testament. Under Smale's ministry, countless people developed a great hunger for God and engaged in deep prayer and Bible study. Smale would be the catalyst to the upcoming revival."[521] In a tactic that **Charles Parham** had experienced, Smale's enemies began to cite his lack of an earned degree, and claimed he "has always been out of harmony with the State and District Conventions."[522] In 1905, Smale resigned from First Baptist and started a new ministry, New Testament, with 163 of the members from his former church.[523] Smale became receptive to speaking in other tongues as the Spirit gives utterance. This may be the single most important reason why the Los Angeles Outpouring transpired. Pentecostals were quick to

~ CHAPTER ELEVEN | LOS ANGELES OUTPOURING ~

take credit for the events.[524] Often this leads to the alienation of their denominationally connected brethren and then Pentecostals gaslight the same denominations claiming they disliked Pentecostals. In reality, there were no Pentecostals involved in The Los Angeles Outpouring. The Apostolic Faith Movement was intimately involved and most of the names associated with the outpouring were connected or would be connected to the A.F.M. The new Pentecostals would come later attempting to claim the Outpouring as their own.

1905 Los Angeles

"**Florence Crawford**, a member of First Methodist Church in Los Angeles, reported that the young men in her church were holding all night prayer meetings. "This was an unprecedented activity in Los Angeles; to Crawford, it illustrated how deeply the city's people were sensing their own spiritual need. 'God was laying it on the hearts of the people to pray for the outpouring of the Spirit.'"[525] For some years the ground had been prepared for the revival at Azusa Street, as a "spirit of expectancy" had gripped the evangelical world for a seismic event of this nature.[526] Into this fertile environment came more ministers from the Apostolic Faith Movement. Florence Crawford received her Pentecost in the Los Angeles Outpouring, and she became a leader working with the Parhams to lead the Pacific Coast A.F.M.[527]

The A.F.M. was different than anything Los Angeles had witnessed. Among their peculiar traits, they expected those who received the Holy Spirit would speak in other tongues as the Spirit gave utterance. This was just like the Apostles in the Book of the Acts of the Apostles. Their leader,

Charles Fox Parham had authored a book, *A Voice Crying in the Wilderness* in 1902. In his book he made it very clear that the Holy Spirit is evidenced by speaking in other tongues. *"...no one has received Baptism of the Holy Spirit who has not a Bible evidence to show for it. As pardon is received as a result of sincere repentance, restitution and surrender; sanctification received as a result of entire consecration; so the speaking in other tongues is received as the result of this Baptism. The Holy Spirit, thru witnessing to the work of Calvary wrought in our lives, in justification and sanctification, reserves the speaking in other tongues as the evidence of His own incoming.*[528] Perhaps this was not a direct reflection of the writing of Henry Clay Morrison, but the words of Parham's book sincerely repeat similar words in Morrison's book from just two years earlier in 1900. It shows the continuity of belief from those with denominational background which is usually surprising to those with roots in the Apostolic Faith or Pentecostal movement.

Charles Parham preaching on the street to a multicultural crowd. Whosoever will, let him come!

An exceptional characteristic of the A.F.M. was Parham's perseverance that women and persons of color were to have equal status with their white and male peers. It was not an edict; it was just the culture that the Parhams developed. Anyone doubting this commitment should make note of three major appointments:

- **William Seymour** (black man) to lead the Los Angeles branch of the Apostolic Faith.

- **Lillian Thistlethwaite** (white woman) as Secretary General of the Apostolic Faith.
- **Florence Crawford** (white woman) as Director of the Apostolic Faith Movement in California and then Pacific Coast.

  This appointment made her overseer of the entire West Coast area of the United States for the A.F.M.

These moves and others were unprecedented and were not well received by some white male ministers in the Texas branch of the A.F.M. led by Howard A. Goss and previously by Warren Faye Carothers who was not in favor of Seymour in leadership.[529] The latter who continued to function as sort of a black pope.[530]

While the A.F.M. had been developing their multicultural approach for more than a decade, California was a brand-new challenge. Yet, the larger challenge was not external. This challenge was within the A.F.M. In Los Angeles, as in other places, the A.F.M. became front page news.[531] Like Oberlin College, Charles and Sarah Parham's Bible College welcomed people of all races and both men and women. "The early causes of Oberlin College were emancipation and commitment to full societal rights of African-Americans and women. Oberlin was unique among liberal arts colleges in that its first college charter stated that the college would enroll both women and blacks—a first for any educational institution in the country. This came in direct defiance of societal norms and, at that time, regional laws that restricted the formal education of blacks and women. As a result, the college has retained a "radical" image and ethos ever since its founding." [532]

The Apostolic Faith's multicultural membership was unprecedented in Los Angeles and area newspapers took notice. They especially made mention of the fact that blacks and whites freely interacted with each other. The mentions were not intended by the press to be complimentary.

Many would take advantage of this to malign the Apostolic Faith. Charles and Sarah Parham had been preparing all their lives to influence others for the cause of Christ. They did so without regard to the person's  color or gender. Charles Parham had long expected that he needed to reach other ethnicities to be effective in his Kingdom mission. To that end he had trained Mexican and Black ministers even in the face of Jim Crow laws in his Houston, Texas Bible School. Now, the time had come to utilize the gifting of these Black ministers. **William J. Seymour** was the first to arrive in Los Angeles. **Lucy Farrow, Anna Hall**, and others soon followed. All three had been students at Parham's Bible School. These Apostolic Faith ministers were a powerhouse of evangelism. The whole world would soon be impacted by the Holy Ghost working in their lives.

These three were like Parham's version of Peter, James, and John: William J. Seymour would emerge as the lead pastor of the most notable of the Apostolic Faith Mission works; Apostolic Faith Gospel Mission in Los Angeles. Anna Hall was the minister who was sent to speaking engagements in Parham's stead. Her ministry produced notables like Robert Semple who became husband and missionary partner to Aimee Semple (McPherson). Lucy Farrow was the trigger that set events in motion that spawned the revival at the Los Angeles Apostolic Faith Gospel Mission. When Lucy Farrow laid hands on Edward Lee and he was filled with the Holy Ghost speaking in other tongues, the long prayed for Los Angeles Pentecost had come! The elevation of women and persons of color led the efforts of the

A.F.M. in Los Angeles. This prompted Warren Fay Carothers and his Texas Syndicate to lead the charge against their efforts, and their subsequent new Pentecostal movement.

Detractors would often mention blacks laying hands on whites as though it was evil. Of course, this was about racism on the part of the detractors.[533] It was also about Cessationism; the unbiblical doctrinal position that the *laying on of hands* by the Apostles and New Testament Church had ceased or died out with the Apostles.[534] Parham was looking outside his A.F.M. for those disparaging him. Like the Prophet Daniel,[535] There were certainly plenty of haters inside of the A.F.M. The main source of detestation toward the Parhams was from white men in leadership within the Movement.[536] Black ministers laying hands on white people was more than religious people like Warren F. Carothers, Howard Goss (and his Southern friends) were willing to tolerate.[537] From their lofty places, they judged Parham, and felt he must be stopped!

These evangelists from the Apostolic Faith Movement brought the message of Holy Ghost baptism evidenced by speaking in other tongues, just like the Bible says, to a hungry audience. Eager people from all over the city had been rallying to meetings led by Joseph Smale. The media had created a frenzy and even used the tactic of painting Pastor Smale as a racist. This was prompted by his willingness to include people of color.[538] All this attention sparked overflow crowds to flock to an old church building, in the heart of Los Angeles on Azusa Street. What became known as the Apostolic Faith Gospel Mission was secured with funds from the A.F.M. and Charles F. Parham in support of William J Seymour. Everything in Los Angeles did not happen on Azusa Street, that is a myth propagated by the new Pentecostals who wanted to take the credit and control the narrative. There were several other Churches and places that became an

integral part of the **Los Angeles Outpouring.**
539

One of Parham's disciples, licensed A.F.M. minister William Joseph Seymour, was reviled by the local clergy, especially those who were followers of **Phineas Bresse and Alma White.** While Bresse claimed to be opposed to the A.F.M. because of their speaking in

> *"Everything in Los Angeles did not happen on Azusa Street. That is a myth propagated by the new Pentecostals who wanted to take the credit and control the narrative."*

other tongues, Bresse offered much stranger explanations of his own faith.[540] Based on his own testimony, Bresse was more than willing to accept mysticism.[541] Bresse rejecting the Apostolic Faith message of the Holy Spirit being evidenced by speaking in other tongues was more about race than doctrine. Bresse did not see blacks as his equals. By Parham allowing blacks to minister to whites in his A.F.M. made Parham a linker meaning; Parham was persona non grata to Bresse. Bresse considered all non-whites inferior beings who must stay *in their place*. Bresse's connection to mysticism hardly makes him an expert and certainly does not place him in position to judge the A.F.M. He is only mentioned in this narrative because his hatred was pointed toward Charles Parham and the A.F.M. Yet, Bresse, Alma White and their strange bedfellows in the Texas Syndicate expected that the only thing as low as non-white people were white people that would consider or promote those, Bresse and his racist friends considered undesirable. To these people, the American Civil War was still unfinished business. Charles Parham's A.F.M. ministry openly interacted with blacks and others; this was taboo. Bresse and his Texas Syndicate comrades were strong proponents of the racially motivated *Separate but Equal* standing.

After Independent Holiness people like Bresse dismissed Seymour, he was invited to join the prayer meetings that were taking place in the

~ CHAPTER ELEVEN | LOS ANGELES OUTPOURING ~

home on Bonnie Brae Street. It was in this home people began to receive the baptism of the Holy Spirit, or as the A.F.M. called it, "their Pentecost."[542] Bresse was opposed to both the A.F.M. message and the black A.F.M. ministers. More so the vessels than the message.

Phineas Bresee (l.) and C. B. Jernigan, the son of a Confederate captain, set aside political and social differences to help found the Church of the Nazarene.

The Parhams were pleased with the reports they received from their A.F.M. disciples (workers) in Los Angeles. Charles Parham wrote to William Seymour, and it was published in the Los Angeles edition of the Apostolic Faith. *"Bro. Chas. Parham, who is God's leader in the Apostolic Faith Movement, writes from Tonganoxie, Kansas, that he expects to be in Los Angeles September 15. Hearing that Pentecost had come to Los Angeles, he writes, 'I rejoice in God over you all, my children, though I have never seen you; but since you know the Holy Spirit's power, we are baptized by one Spirit into one body. Keep together in unity till I come, then in a grand meeting let all prepare for the outside fields I desire, unless God directs to the contrary, to meet and see all who have the full Gospel when I come."*[543] Externally the Apostolic Faith was growing exponentially despite the many detractors. The foremost detractor was former A.F.M. Texas State Director and the leader of the Texas Syndicate, Warren Fay Carothers. Carothers' xenophobic positions were raging.[544] This caused Parham to first dismiss him from his position in the fall of 1906 and then just simply dissolve all the positions in the A.F.M., but Carothers was plotting to even the score and turn the A.F.M. into an all-white group like his friends Phineas Bresse an Alma White and other Independent Holiness denominations.

The Texas Syndicate's opposition to Seymore was not just because

Seymour was black. The Texas Syndicate would tolerate black people preaching to black people. However, when Parham promoted black ministers to minister to white people it was more than the Texas Syndicate was willing to tolerate.[545] The core of the challenge was that Parham treated Seymour like a white person. It is ironic that Seymour's middle name was Joseph. Carothers and his Texas Syndicate plotted against William Joseph Seymour to the dismay of their spiritual father, Charles Parham. The Texas Syndicate attributed Seymour's race and thus lack of social standing as making him inferior to them. Carothers and his friends did not see black people as equals. The Los Angeles Outpouring at the Apostolic Faith Gospel Mission was a wonderful multicultural meeting like nearly all A.F.M. meetings. Those in the A.F.M. around the world were excited about the reports coming out of Los Angeles. Everyone, except Warren Faye Carothers and his friends in the Texas Syndicate were pleased. Carothers was unhappy that blacks and women had a growing role in the A.F.M.

"An occasional visitor to the New Testament church was Frank Bartleman. He was an unusual person. He was a preacher but would not accept a pastorate. He also would not affiliate with any denomination. He did go around among all the churches where he was allowed to participate to any degree. For instance, he would go to the New Testament church before time for the church service to begin and urge all those who had come early that they should not depend on the pastor to start the prayer meeting. He would try to get them to begin a prayer meeting on the church steps before the pastor arrived. A name is painted on the Azusa Street church. It was "Apostolic Faith Gospel Mission." This greatly offended Frank Bartleman. He said they had failed God, and he left. Although he considered himself rather important there, (often saying "at Azusa we did this" or "we did that") he left without claiming to have received the baptism. He did claim to have the gift of music, but not of words. When the 'Heavenly Choir' would sing in tongues, he would join in making guttural sounds that he said were beautiful. They were all singing the same verse of the same song at the same time so he could only 'sing' along without words.

Frank Bartleman was so taken up with himself that he wholly misunderstood what was going on. He had a feeling that since he had written four letters to Evan Roberts and had urged people at the New Testament Church to begin prayer meetings on the front steps of the church while waiting for the pastor to arrive, that he had been a major cause in what happened on Azusa Street. In reality, what was happening in the Azusa Street Mission was a continuation of what had happened earlier in the home of Richard and Ruth Asbery on Bonnie Brae Street. What happened there was related to something that had happened more than five years earlier. Something Frank Bartleman had nothing to do with. His book, How Pentecost came to Los Angeles, has an accurate timeline; he was there for almost four months, but his basic premise is in error. We do not think Pentecost came to Los Angeles as told in his book. The book has now been revised and reprinted under the name AZUSA STREET.
Frank Bartleman helped find a temporary place for Durham to preach and sat on the platform with him. The easier way was a smashing hit. Great crowds came to hear and join him. Not long afterward, (1912) Durham died, but his easier way is still popular today. His teachings were incorporated into quite a number of existing churches, but was denounced by Sis. Crawford, Seymour, Parham, Mason, and Fisher."[546]

Much attention was given by proxies to the events at the Apostolic Faith Gospel Mission in Los Angeles. Meanwhile, a more important development was spawning. Warren Fay Carothers, weary of Parham's insistence on inclusion, decided to take the opportunity of Parham being in California to blackmail Charles Parham. While Parham was in Los Angeles, Carothers telegraphed Parham demanding that he resign from the Apostolic Faith Movement leadership or Carothers would reveal some dark secrets "known only to him."[547] Carothers never proved any of the accusations, and as late as 1908 was making desperate attempts to get Parham "in front of him." He offered Brunner Tabernacle as a place to hold another "trial" so that Carothers could preside as Judge over some error that Carothers expected was there.[548] Carothers and his Texas Syndicate failed at least twice to get anything substantial from their witch hunts, but would tell everyone who would listen that they had confessions. Yet, their desperation spoke for itself. The A.G. would continue the same witch hunt for...the A.G. is still witch hunting in the case of Charles Parham.

CHAPTER TWELVE

ZION CITY

"Discernment is being able to tell the difference between a man and a scarecrow."

-Charles F. Parham

From the Los Angeles Outpouring, at the **Apostolic Faith Gospel Mission**, the whole world received the news of this multicultural group, The Apostolic Faith. According to Frank Bartleman, the Apostolic Faith through the Apostolic Faith Gospel Mission had "washed the color line away."[549] At this point, washing the color line away had been true of the Parhams A.F.M. for more than a decade. It was wonderful that Los Angeles understood the culture of the A.F.M. While most of the world celebrated such a rare and historic accomplishment, the Texas Syndicate saw this as a terrible challenge and problem that needed to be abolished.

For the record, Bartleman made the exact same claim about the color line when he was writing about New Testament Church, pastored by Joseph Smale some months before. His writing is a quote from W. E. Dubois.[550] Both times there is truth to the statement; in the case of the Apostolic Faith Gospel Mission, it is presented as new. "The 'newest religious sect' had, in fact, been around for a few years. Beginning in the late nineteenth century, Midwestern Methodists and other Christians had become fascinated with divine healing and the possibility of speaking in tongues—doctrines and practices dispensationalists argued ended with the apostolic age. One of these Christians was an 18-year-old Kansas collegian named Charles Fox Parham."[551] A long list of haters developed for Charles Parham over the next decade. Parham had made the most impact on Christianity in centuries.[552] The impact was so profound it forced all religious people, (either for or against) to address the matter. In addition to creating enemies of religious and denominationally affiliated people, Parham's doctrines irritated racists, segregationist, and nearly all denomination leaders (even some who were of color).

> "...Parham's doctrines irritated racists, segregationist, and nearly all denomination leaders (even some who were of color)."

The Apostolic Faith Movement worked diligently to accomplish having a group that saw no color, allowed women to minister, and saw all mankind as equals. Headlines in Chicago, Houston, Los Angeles and other places were typical of the media. Sensational headlines sell newspapers. The stories about the Apostolic Faith movement varied from promoting **Wild Weird Babbling** to people claiming the Apostolic Faith was a sex cult. In this media frenzy, Pastor Seymour wrote to his leader, Charles Parham, asking for help. Charles Parham as the leader of the A.F.M. was the target of most of the assault, ridicule, slander, etc. Parham dispatched the quite capable Lucy Farrow and a team, soon followed by the most capable preacher *Anna E. Hall* to Los Angeles while he made his way to Zion, Illinois. Other capable Apostolic Faith ministers also went to help William Seymour including the seasoned minister, Mabel Smith. The level of attack against the Apostolic Faith was about to increase exponentially.

The Revival at the Apostolic Faith Gospel Mission was led by A.F.M. ministers **William J. Seymour, Lucy Farrow, Mabel Smith, Alma E. Hall** and others. At the same time Charles Parham and another part of his Apostolic Faith Movement team

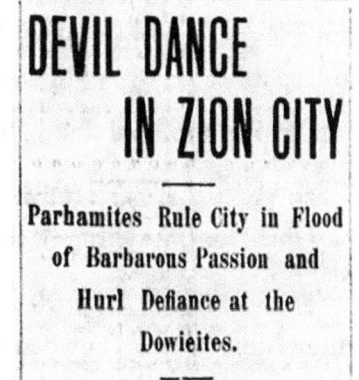

(which included the powerful evangelist **Lillian Thistlethwaite** and others), were in Zion, Illinois where the followers of Alexander Dowie brought the wildest of unfounded allegations. A.F.M. ministers were barred from having church services in any public building in the city of Zion by Wilbur Voliva, the tyrant of Zion. Reportedly, he spent some $10,000 renting every available hall to keep the Apostolic Faith Movement from having a place to hold services. Voliva was a sick man who believed a surfeit of strange dogmas including that the Earth was flat. Because of the latter heretical position, he did not allow World Globes to be in possession by anyone in Zion City (including at the schools). "Being a true believer in his own rip on reality, Voliva told his followers that the sun was a mere 3,000 miles from Earth. He made the following statement: "God made the sun to light the Earth, and therefore must have placed it close to the task it was designed to do." This messiah of misinformation managed to draw a lot of attention and accumulate a small fortune.[553]

"Voliva's Theocratic Party gained political power by election fraud and then maintained it by further fraud, perjury, intimidation, and violence. Once in power, Voliva's hand-picked officials sometimes refused to put rival slates of candidates on the election ballot. On at least one occasion, Voliva associates met in his offices, selected a "Republican" ticket, ratified it, and put it on the ballot without the knowledge of local Republicans."[554] "Voliva's takeover of the bankrupt city was almost complete. He implored and browbeat loyal church members into mortgaging their property and giving the money to him. He used the cash to buy the Zion properties back from the receiver piece by piece. When he redeemed the last piece early in 1910, "Zion Industries and Institutions (Wilbur Glenn Voliva)" owned the major businesses in town. Note the personal name in parenthesis; it was usually printed that way as part of the company name. Ads in Leaves of Healing advised mail order purchasers of Zion products to make their checks payable to Wilbur Glenn Voliva. Though he bought everything with the church's money, Voliva put every title in his own name, and he owned Zion Industries and Institutions outright!

"Under Voliva, Zion saw tremendous political, financial, and religious strife. Some Methodists whose ancestors settled in the area long before Zion was founded resisted Voliva's control. In 1908, the little Methodist church, built 70 years earlier, burned under mysterious circumstances. Voliva's takeover caused much dissension. The anti-Voliva factions organized as the Independent Party, and Voliva openly boasted that he would drive them out of town. Billboards appeared at various locations around town with messages like the following: ZION'S SLOGAN: This City for Zion People and for Zion People Only!!! The Zion Flag

~ CHAPTER TWELVE | ZION CITY ~

Floating Over Every Building—Over Every Foot, Inch and Pinch of the Original City Site. Traitors, Thieves and Thugs Will Find This City HOTTER THAN HELL."555

Despite the prohibition for having church services in Zion's public buildings, one of the greatest modern-day revivals began in Zion. While Zion would not be as publicized as events in Los Angeles, the numbers were much larger. While Charles Parham departed to see what he might do to help the Apostolic Faith band in Los Angeles, **Lillian Thistlethwaite** stayed and led thousands to Christ.556

"Lilian worked closely with her sister, Sarah, and brother-in-law, Charles Parham, in the birthing of the Pentecostal movement at the turn of the 20th century. She was one of those who was baptized in the Holy Spirit and spoke in tongues in the Watchnight Service January 1, 1901 at **Bethel Bible College** in Topeka, Kansas. She continued to play a major role as a teacher and minister in the early Apostolic Faith Movement. In March 1906, Parham named Lilian the first "General Secretary of the Apostolic Faith Movement." As a result, she became the first woman to serve in an official leadership position in a Pentecostal organization.

Lillian Thistlethwaite, General Secretary of the Apostolic Faith Movement at Headquarters building. Sarah Parham and children also in the photo.

In September 1906, Lilian was part of the ministry team that accompanied Parham to Zion City, IL. As a result of their ministry in that city, a great revival erupted that rivaled the Los Angeles Revival in its scope and influence on the burgeoning Pentecostal movement. According to Gordon

Gardiner, editor of Bread of Life, an early Pentecostal magazine, this revival resulted in at least 500 missionaries and workers going "out of Zion into all the world" preaching a message that included the Biblical doctrines of Divine Healing and the Baptism of the Holy Spirit."[557] "Many of the meetings took place in homes throughout the city. Among those impacted in this revival were John G. Lake, Marie Burgess Brown, Martha Wing Robinson and F. F. Bosworth, who were residents of Zion City at the time.

Lake spoke specifically of the impression Lilian made on his life. He wrote, *I sat in Fred Bosworth's home one night before Fred thought of preaching the gospel. I listened to that woman [Lilian Thistlethwaite] telling of the Lord's love and sanctifying grace and power; and what real holiness was. It was not her arguments or logic. It was herself. It was the holiness that came from her soul. It was the living Spirit of God that came out of the woman's life. That night my heart got so hungry that I fell on my knees and those who were present will tell you yet that they had never heard anyone pray as I prayed. As I talked with Lilian, I observed that the one supreme thing in that woman's soul was the consciousness of holiness.* She said, *"Brother that is what we prayed for; that is what the baptism brought to us. That's what we coveted from God."* Dr. Susan Hyatt notes Lilian's major contribution to the spread of the truth of divine healing. She points out that according to Dr. Paul Chappell, former Dean of the Oral Roberts Graduate School of Theology and Missions, it was Charles Parham's and Lilian Thistlethwaite's ministry in Zion City that embedded the doctrine of "Healing in the Atonement" in the Pentecostal Revival. Another person greatly affected by Lilian's ministry was F. F. Bosworth, in whose home she taught the Word of God in Zion City."[558] "Parham says that he has taken a deep interest in the Zionist (referencing his concern for those who were decimated by Dowie) movement since its inception, He asserts that God appeared to him in a dream two weeks ago and told him that Voliva was a false prophet and would lead the people of

~ CHAPTER TWELVE | ZION CITY ~

Zion into ruin.[559] Ten days ago Parham says that "the spirit" again appeared to him at Topeka and commanded him at once to go to Zion and combat the evil influences of Voliva."[560] Those who interpreted Parham's motives as an interest in leading Zion City were misinformed. Zion City's challenges were legal, and Parham only showed interest in Zion into Spiritual matters. Even in Spiritual matters, Parham was happy to minister to the people but had no interest in being their local pastor. True to his word, when he left the pastorate in Eudora, Kansas because of a calling to evangelize, he remained on that path till his death.

In contrast, it does present that Warren Faye Carothers had grandiose visions of Zion City and apparently became obsessed with the idea to the point that he began spending considerable amounts of time in Chicago. Carothers was concerned over the wild headlines that were primarily propaganda pieces written by Wilbur Voliva and his friends.[561] The articles were wild sensationalized allegations ranging from murder to smoking cigarettes. The articles are so transparent that from an historical viewpoint it is easy to discern. Many of the articles would make even the National Enquirer blush.[562] Yet, people of the time may have thought it real. Afterall, many thought aliens were invading![563] To be fair, Chicken Little really thought the sky was falling![564]

Apostolic Faith Orchard, Texas

It is also feasible that some of the information was coming from Carothers as he is obviously conflicted on the subject. Unfortunately for Carothers and his Texas Syndicate, God had not given him a dream, a vision or apparently anything related to Zion City. In place of spiritual revelation, Carothers would turn to fleshly ambitions. From Chicago, Carothers sent a telegram to Charles Parham who was ministering in California. Carothers' telegraph demanded Parham resign because his activities were going to impede the possibility of Zion City being merged with the Apostolic Faith Movement.[565] How Zion City would fit with Carothers' warped sense of people and as he expressed, Southern ideas, was something only Carothers understood. In spite of his selling out Parham for a few pieces of silver and using Voliva's friends in the ruse, Carothers never made any tangible progress in taking over Zion City.

As to his prophecy against Wilbur Voliva, for a time it likely seemed to everyone that Parham as a prophet had "missed the mark" on this one. Although he rarely prophesied, Parham as a Prophet, was hitherto very accurate. As is usual, people are swayed by what they see. When the wicked prosper they expect the Prophet was wrong. Voliva seemed to flourish. Not so fast! Ultimately, the New York Times would announce the decision of Federal Judge Charles G. Briggle declaring Voliva "Flat Broke." Voliva ended in bankruptcy.[566] Ironic that Voliva was flat broke since he thought the whole earth was flat.[567]

It was told to Parham that Seymour had gone to Los Angeles with a humble spirit. This report apparently came from Carothers. He was obsessed with all non-whites showing proper humility to their betters. Those from Texas who moved to Los Angeles with Seymour were impressed with his ability. It was clear that God was doing a wonderful work in Seymour's life. It was also clear that Satan was trying to "tear it to pieces." Los Angeles was (and remains) a city filled with fanatics. Pastor Joseph Smale had a number of episodes dealing with the challenges of fanaticism.[568] Smale experienced members barking like dogs and other manifestations.

Smale responded, "I do not condemn all of what purports to be the gift of tongues." Seasoned ministers like Smale and Parham were keen to discern the difference.[569] Smale said, "much of this so-called gift of tongues, I believe, is more than mere fanaticism; it is spiritualism, and the people are in great danger from permitting evil spirits to possess them."[570] William Seymour would also have great difficulties. Seymour had been a student at Parham's school and was in Los Angeles representing the Apostolic Faith Movement so, Parham felt responsible for what was happening at the Apostolic Faith Gospel Mission.

Before Parham arrived in Los Angeles the A.F.M. had become a global force. The Apostolic Faith Gospel Mission on Azusa Street. was enjoying the limelight of the internationally recognized Apostolic Faith Movement's global attention. Attention, preeminence and money flowed to the Mission because of the world-wide success of the A.F.M. Having someone of Parham's stature, leader of an international movement, come to the Apostolic Faith Gospel Mission was historic. Most of the leaders at the Apostolic Faith Gospel Mission were white and had a plethora of religious backgrounds. None of them had much experience as a leader of a local body of believers and none as a leader of a national or international movement. Parham was attracted t California because of the masses o people hungry for the Holy Ghost "California had by far the most diverse population of any state in the United States and had no

apartheid laws requiring racial segregation of public meetings."[571] Parham would invest much of the rest of his life ministering in California.

Parham's experiences added to his understanding of fanaticism.

According to Parham, there were many genuine experiences of receiving the true baptism at the Apostolic Faith Gospel Mission in Los Angeles, but there were also many false manifestations. This is certainly not unusual in any genuine move of the Holy Ghost. The counterfeit is almost always present as well as the genuine. Seasoned ministers can discern the difference. Historian Frank Bartleman confirmed that he had dealt with fanaticism long before either Seymour or Parham arrived in Los Angeles. Bartleman said, *"I preached at Fifth Street Mission, where the "Burning Bush" had gotten control. God preciously anointed me as I exhorted to a middle-ground between formalism and fanaticism. They were going wild. Jesus was crucified between two thieves. The devil splits a work in the middle, runs away with the heart, leaving the shell, thus driving the saints to both extremes, and destroys the whole. We are creatures of extremes."*[572]

Parham held services at Apostolic Faith Gospel Mission in Los Angeles. "I hurried to Los Angeles, and to my utter surprise and astonishment I found conditions even worse than I had anticipated. Brother Seymour had come to me helpless, he said he could not stem the tide that had arisen. I sat on the platform in Azusa Street Mission, and saw the manifestations of the flesh, spiritualistic controls, saw people practicing hypnotism at the altar over candidates seeking baptism, though many were receiving the real baptism of the Holy Ghost. After preaching two or three times, I was informed by two of the elders, one who was a hypnotist (I had seen him lay his hands on many who came through chattering, jabbering and sputtering, speaking in no language at all) that I was not wanted in that place."[573] Parham was unable to convince Seymour's leaders to make some adjustments. The door to the mission was padlocked. While his detractors falsely claim this was racially motivated. They ignore that William Seymour made the same assessment as Parham. How Seymour could have been racist against himself is never explained. There are several third-party confirmations. It all make sense if you didn't think about it!

The Apostolic Faith Gospel Mission (aka Azusa Street Revival) was noticeably free of all nationalist feeling, according to one observer. "If a Mexican or a German cannot speak English, he gets up and speaks in his own native tongue and feels quite at home, for the Spirit interprets through his face, and the people say 'Amen.' No instrument that God can use is rejected on account of color or dress or education." It was no accident that this observer's first example of varied ethnicity was "a Mexican," for since the beginning of the Apostolic Faith Movement, Latinos have played an important role. Abundio and Rosa López were among the first to be baptized with "Holy Ghost and fire," at the Apostolic Faith Gospel Mission in Los Angeles. *"Thanks be to God for the Spirit which brought us to the Apostolic Faith Gospel Mission (Azusa Street), the Apostolic Faith, old-time religion,"* they exclaimed. *"We cannot express our gratitude and thanksgiving which we feel moment by moment for what He has done for us, so we want to be used for the healing of both soul and body." From the very beginning, Latinos flocked to the Mission in search of a transcendent God and a better life.*[574]

For reasons that are not entirely clear, their unbridled enthusiasm and desire to testify prompted the leader of the mission to "ruthlessly crush" the Latino contingent in 1909.[575] Seymour jettisoned the Hispanics from his church. Scores left the mission and began preaching the A.F.M. message throughout barrios and migrant farm labor camps in the U.S., Mexico, and Puerto Rico. As early as 1912, Latinos organized their own completely autonomous and independent A.F.M. churches in California, Texas, and Hawaii.[576] In fairness, Seymour drove the Mexicans out of his Apostolic Faith Gospel Mission in 1908 and in 1914 banned all whites from leadership. These certainly could be parlayed as acts of racism and in fact they are. In fairness, like Charles and Sarah Parham, there is no real evidence that William Seymour was racially oriented in either his expulsion of Mexicans or his changing the by-laws to exclude white leadership. For both Seymour and Parham there were many other forces at play.[577]

Parham was in the unique position of understanding that the A.F.M. was facing a global battle. Not only for souls, but also a media battle for perception of the movement. Most of the inexperienced leaders in Los Angeles had no interest in Parham fixing the media battle they were facing. As a result, the predominately white leadership team disfellowshipped Parham. The multicultural flavor diminished somewhat over the next couple of years, but it did continue. The Los Angeles Apostolic Faith Gospel Mission initially received a lot of help from those in Zion, Illinois because of the difficulty imposed by Voliva on having a place of worship. Some of that waned after the Los Angeles group became an independent church in the tradition of the A.F.M. There is no evidence that the Mission separating from the Apostolic Faith movement removed them from fellowship of other ministers in the Apostolic Faith. The only change was that Parham did not minister at the Los Angeles Apostolic Faith Gospel Mission.

There were concerns about the Los Angeles Apostolic Faith Gospel Mission. Parham's reference to concerns about the Apostolic Faith Gospel Mission being perceived like a "Darky Camp meeting in the South" were not something that he made up. There were some evil things that were associated with some odd meetings in the South.[578] Walt Whitman, a popular author of the time, had referenced them just like Parham quoted.⁵⁷⁹ Parham was merely quoting understood literature of his day. It may not have been the best choice of words, but it reflected Parham's serious concerns in a manner people understood. Certainly, if it was said by someone with a racial agenda it would be racist. For Charles Parham, who is not on record anywhere intentionally making racist comments, it is a stretch, considering the plethora of xenophobes that were readily available.

Parham did minister in many other places in Los Angeles. Seymour and Parham were not in disagreement about the challenges of leading a church or that the Gospel was for all people regardless of race. Neither ever faltered on the subject. Despite areas where they may or may not have agreed, they remained colleagues until Seymour's death. Both would continue to promote the outpouring of the Holy Ghost evidenced by speaking in other tongues. In 1911 when Durham attempted a coup on Seymour, Parham was in Oakland, California having meetings. He sprang to Seymour's defense.

Frank Bartleman, the famed author of *"How Pentecost Came to Los Angeles."* confirmed, *"The Devil overdid himself again. Outside persecution never hurt the work. We had the most to fear from the working of evil spirits within. Even spiritualists and hypnotists came to investigate and to try their influence. Then all the religious soreheads, crooks, and cranks came, seeking a place in the work. We had the most to fear from these. But this is always the danger to every new work; they had no place elsewhere. This condition cast a fear over many that was hard to overcome. It hindered the Spirit much. Many were afraid to seek God for fear the Devil might get them. We found early in the Azusa work that when we attempted to steady the ark, the Lord stopped working. We dared not call the attention of the people too much to the working of the Evil One. Fear would follow. We could only pray—then God gave victory. There was a presence of God with us that, through prayer, we could depend on."*⁵⁸⁰

The Parhams had many enemies. There were evil men and women that could not fathom that Parham and his Apostolic Faith followers would see blacks, Mexicans, Chinese, Native-Americans, and others as equals. They desired to control the outpouring at Los Angeles. They could not allow Parham's group to take control of their coveted religious strongholds. To that end, they began propaganda toward their agenda. First, they claimed the Apostolic Faith Gospel Mission was all of the Los Angeles Outpouring, as though hundreds of thousands came to an old church building that would only seat a few hundred people. Second, they ignored the meetings at the Apostolic Faith Gospel Mission that were part of the Los Angeles Outpouring. Later, they began calling the meetings the" *Azusa Street Revival"* (the Apostolic Faith Gospel Mission was on Azusa Street). This propaganda went so far that when they published information, they rebranded the same. Third, the *new* Pentecostals began to claim that the Azusa Street Revival was a black group to both grow their all-white base and to pull whites away from the Apostolic Faith Gospel Mission.

Fourth, depending on what benefited them they would alternately claim it was an unorganized group of Negroes or they would claim the Mission as the beginning of their particular branch, cult or movement. Fifth, they claimed that those who opposed Seymour, or the leadership of Azusa did so because of their race. Of course, these are lies. These men vowed to do whatever it took to discredit Parham and by default the Apostolic Faith Movement in their bid for a hostile takeover, so that they could elevate themselves as the new leaders of the movement. Somewhat in the manner of Charles Manson, they felt these people needed their leadership as opposed to Charles Parham.

The meetings at the Apostolic Faith Gospel Mission included a plethora of nationalities. The Topeka Outpouring became the seed for a number of even larger moves of the Holy Ghost. The Los Angeles Outpouring was a vision of what John the Apostle spoke of in Revelation 7:9 - A people out of every Tribe, Kindred, and Nation! The Los Angeles Outpouring would benefit every nation under heaven. The Los Angeles Outpouring was perhaps the most multicultural outpouring in history. It was like the Day of Pentecost as captured in the Book of the Acts of the Apostles. "...There were gathered in Jerusalem people out of every nation under heaven..."[581]

Parham's departure from the Apostolic Faith Gospel Mission in Los Angeles was never about race. White Supremacists, especially those with the Texas Syndicate, used racial propaganda to divide the people to move their all-white scheme forward. Those who repeat the false charge of racism against Parham or Seymour have merely fallen prey to the deception set by racists. "The evidence indicates that it (division between Parham and the leadership of the Apostolic Faith Gospel Mission in Los Angeles) was over differences and questions concerning order, worship style and the genuineness of certain spiritual manifestations. Interestingly, the 'racist' accusation was never made by Seymour, Farrow nor by any of the Parhams' friends or enemies while they were alive. Although Parham criticized the Azusa Street revival because of its alleged excesses, he did not blame Seymour or the black participants. Instead, he pointed the finger at the Holy Rollers of Los Angeles whom he said invaded the meetings. He later wrote, [582] When Parham spoke of Holy Rollers it was generally a shot at the conspirators that formed what we have called the Texas Syndicate and later formed the *all-white Assemblies of God.*

"There was a beautiful outpouring of the Holy Spirit in Los Angeles. Then all of a sudden, a *Holy Roller* religious meeting in the city dismissed and came down to Azusa Street, and everything that was prevalent in their meeting was turned loose into the Azusa Street Meeting.[583] Seymour and Parham were never adversaries. There were strong feelings on both sides, but they were tempered by their love of each other in Christ. Like Paul and Barnabas,"[584] they both labored in the Kingdom of Jesus Christ until their death.

After the 1906 Earthquake, thousands surged to the **Apostolic Faith Gospel Mission**. "The gathered crowds shouted, cried, danced, were 'slain in the Spirit,' spoke in tongues while sermons and exhortations were given by practically whoever wished.[585] Seymour rarely preached.[586] Supposedly, the Spirit was in control. The 'apostle of Pentecost' sat behind the pulpit with his head in a shoe box. Emotionalism and physical demonstration of the Spirit prevailed.[587] "The descriptions and reports of the events on Azusa Street in those early days, are problematic. In the early days of the revival there may have only been a dozen or so in attendance. These contradict claims of multitudes."[588] Parham does not seem much affected by being dismissed by the Azusa Street leaders. Perhaps he was relieved not to have to have the task of righting the situation. Yet, his burden for souls being great; it is evident he grieved at the schism.[589] Los Angeles leadership reflected other leadership groups associated with Charles and Sarah Parham's A.F.M. as multicultural. The racial problem did not really manifest until 1914 in response to the formation of the all-white Assemblies of God – as Parham called them, the new Pentecostals or *Holy Rollers.*

After the passing of both William and Charles, their widows had a meeting. Pauline Parham wrote, *"When Dad Parham died in February of 1929, my husband, Robert, Mother Parham and I picked up the mantle and fulfilled his itinerant schedule of ministry. Later that same year, his schedule took us to the Los Angeles area. While there we visited the Azusa Street Mission and Jenny Seymour, who had pastored the mission since her husband's death in 1925. We had a very friendly* visit with Mrs. Seymour and then proceeded on our way. Being a young twenty-year-old, I did not realize the significance of this visit and did not know the details of the earlier rift between Dad Parham and the Azusa Street Mission. Actually, Dad Parham never blamed Seymour for the rift but, rather, some of the elders at the Azusa Mission. I now realize that Mother Parham was going out of her way to reach out to Mrs. Seymour." Pauline Parham also wrote, "Dad Parham was loved by the black people in our hometown of Baxter Springs, Kansas. He often preached in the black Pentecostal church there and even encouraged the whites to attend services at the black church. The black people loved him because he treated them right. The yearly Camp Meetings he conducted in Baxter Springs were attended by all races. He was not a racist!" The latter point, He was not a racist! He could have been written in response to accusation or it could be interpreted as pointing that there were racists in the A.F.M. at one point, but the Parhams were not among them.

Parham haters tell a tale of his departure from the Apostolic Faith Gospel Mission being the end of his ministry. The truth is that instead of leaving Los Angeles, Parham rented a large building and held great services three times a day that ministered deliverance from evil spirits to the crowds who had previously attended the meetings.[590] "With workers from the Texas field we opened a great revival in the W. C. T. U. (Women's Christian Temperance Union) Building on Broadway and Temple Streets in Los Angeles. Great numbers were saved, marvelous healings took place, and between two and three hundred who had been possessed of awful fits and spasms and controls in the Azusa Street work were delivered and received the real Pentecost teachings and many spoke with other tongues."[591] Parham would retain a presence with meetings in the Los Angeles area for the next twenty years. There are notable meetings in the Los Angeles area led by Parham 1906 through 1912 and beyond. For example, he held a notable "Pentecostal Revival" starting January 12, 1908, and apparently was repeated numerous times through the ensuing years.[592] It may be that Parham invested more time in Los Angeles than anywhere else.

Parham's Hometown Race Relations

Parham conducted an annual Camp Meeting in his hometown of Baxter Springs, Kansas right up to the time of his death in 1929. Several thousand people from throughout the nation attended each year. One person, impressed with the interracial character of the Baxter Springs Camp Meeting, wrote, "People of all creeds and colors were made to feel at home in the meeting and they certainly used their liberty in the Lord."[593] Even non-Pentecostal scholars have noted the inter-racial character of Parham's ministry and meetings. Robert Mapes Anderson wrote,

"Even before the Los Angeles revival, Parham had tapped this new ethnically heterogeneous constituency in Houston, where he garnered black converts like Seymour, Miss Farrow, and "Brother" Johnson, and some Mexican-Americans. At the 1913 summer encampment of Parham's group in Baxter Springs, Kansas, "White people, colored people and Indians all took part in the meeting" and as Brother Parham remarked, "We had the Gospel in black and white and red all over." "For years, Parham held integrated meetings throughout the lower Midwest."[594] Parham regarded the Seymour conflict as an example of spiritual pride. He wrote about it in his newsletter and noted that fanaticism always produces an unteachable spirit in those given over to it. He explained that those under the influence of these false spirits: "...feel exalted, thinking they have a greater experience than anyone else, not needing instruction or advice...placing them out of reach from those who can help." He ended his newsletter with hope and expectation that Seymour would recover: "...although many forms of fanaticism have crept in, I believe every true child of God will come out of this mist and shadow stronger and better equipped against all extremes that are liable to present themselves at any time in meetings of this kind."[595] Parham continued, "I have witnessed great dangers in the work here in Los Angeles, and in pointing them out I shall not refer to individuals, but to the work itself as a whole, that we all may see the error of our way and get back to God."[596] This impasse contributed to Parham's resolve to dissolve the newly created leadership system devised by Carothers.

Parham returned to Zion from Los Angeles in December of 1906. Unable to obtain a building, he pitched a large tent in a vacant lot. Parham's tent meetings were well attended by some two thousand people. On New Year's Eve, he preached for two hours on the baptism in the Holy Spirit and produced such an intense excitement that several men approached Parham with the idea of beginning a "movement" and a large church, but Parham was against the idea. He told the men that he was not there for personal gain and that his idea of coming to Zion was to bring the peace of God to replace its oppression. Parham believed America had enough churches and said that what Zion needed was more spirituality in the churches they already had. Parham felt that if his message had value, then the people would support it without an organization. He was concerned that groups who gathered around the truth of the "baptism of the Holy Spirit" would eventually develop a worldly, secular objective.[597]

Apostolic Faith Gospel Mission

The Azusa Street Revival is a well-known event, but what most people think they know about the event is incorrect. First, it was NOT a black revival. This is perhaps the most insulting misnomer. Xenophobic surrogates who have attempted to control the narrative, want readers to believe that William Joseph Seymour was only ministering to blacks. This is offered in a narrative that would make the reader think that Seymour was incapable of ministering to white people. Nearly every picture taken at the Los Angeles Apostolic Faith Gospel Mission, especially the ones with William Seymour show him surrounded with white ministers. Many of these came from other places where Charles Parham and his A.F.M. teams were ministering.

Remember, this revival started at an Apostolic Faith Movement Mission. Frank Bartleman wrote about Seymour putting the Mission's

name Apostolic Faith Gospel Mission[598] on the side of the building because he, Bartleman, was opposed to all organization. Yet, Bartleman only stayed at the Mission a couple of months, and he splintered off and started his own church. From the Mission's inception late in the Summer of 1906, **Apostolic Faith Gospel Mission** was the name. There was on the ground in Los Angeles a team of Apostolic Faith ministers to help set the nascent Mission in order. Today, we would refer to them as the advance team. They helped Seymour organize the Apostolic Faith's Credentialling Committee. They helped not only Seymour, but initially helped expand the larger Apostolic Faith Movement.[599] They did an amazing task. In short order, they were raising funds, printing publications, and being visited by both locals and people from afar. This resulted from the worldwide recognition of the A.F.M. and Charles & Sarah Parham. Many people also came to Los

Angeles from the burgeoning Zion Outpouring. Being prohibited by law to hold meetings in Zion, far away though it was, Los Angeles became a gathering place. Most of the prominent people that came were well acquainted with the Apostolic Faith Movement and the opportunity to go to Los Angeles was convenient for travel. Most of these had either met Charles Parham or had heard about his ministry. Most came to receive the baptism of the Holy Ghost.

The initial attacks on the Apostolic Faith Gospel Mission had nothing to do with Seymour or his race. Frankly, Seymour was unknown. Everyone understood that the leader was Charles Parham. Charles Parham and a very effective Apostolic Faith team were at the time of

The multi-cultural and multi-congregational credentialling committed of the Apostolic Faith movement in Los Angeles.

the beginning of the Los Angeles meeting having tremendous success in Zion City and a plethora of those who came to Los Angeles were converts from those meetings that the capable Lilian Thistlethwaite continued even after Parham left and had arrived in Los Angeles. Because of the culture of the Apostolic Faith Movement, there were few in Los Angeles that questioned William Seymour as the lead. Parham had put the trust in Seymour and the Apostolic Faith team worked diligently to put structure around the burgeoning outpouring.

The reality is that Parham was the only one who ever successfully led the unified Apostolic Faith movement. Nearly all those who wrested factions of the movement away were white and established all-white ministries. Seymour was a good man but "only for a brief moment did he enjoy widespread influence."[600] His leaders' decision to become an independent mission and leave the larger Apostolic Faith was a tragedy for Seymour and his ministry. Parham's enemies used the impasse to alienate Seymour while at the same time paying lip service to what they named the Azusa Street Revival.

Surrogates have generally painted the Apostolic Faith Gospel Mission (aka Azusa Street Mission) Revival as a black revival. This is simply not the case. The church and the leaders were predominately white until 1914 when in response to the forming of the all-white Assemblies of God, Seymour responded by banning all whites from leadership. Until 1914 the congregation was about 300 whites and 25 blacks. Many historians have misrepresented the make-up of the Azusa Street Mission as part of a hidden agenda to give the impression it was a black revival. The Apostolic Faith Gospel Mission was very multicultural in the beginning. The Mission was an outreach of the much larger Apostolic Faith Movement led by Charles Parham and the funding for Azusa was primarily from the Apostolic Faith movement followers.

When the Assemblies of God organized as an all-white group in 1914, William Seymour responded by barring white people from leadership. Clearly, this was an effort to keep the racially oriented leaders in the all-white Assemblies of God from trying to control the Azusa Street Gospel Mission. Seymour's response is understandable. The Assemblies of God claimed genesis from Seymour's church yet, they barred him from membership in their all-white group. Seymour had personal experience with the Texas Syndicate.

The Texas Syndicate opposed Seymour's appointment by Parham to Los Angeles. The Texas Syndicate tried unsuccessfully to oust Seymour through the person of William Durham. Time and maturity had taught Seymour that the all-white Assemblies of God was merely the organized and public version of the Texas Syndicate. Seymour acted swiftly to protect his congregation from these new Pentecostals who spoke with flattering words but secretly plotted against all non-whites, especially those connected in any way to Charles Fox Parham and the A.F.M.

William Seymour made changes at the Apostolic Faith Gospel Mission in Los Angeles. Seymour instituted a provision in his doctrinal statement that limited women's functionality. It stated, "All ordination must be done by men, not women. Women may be ministers, but not to baptize and ordain in this work."[601] What began as a beautiful multiracial, egalitarian movement that crossed class barriers and was birthed out of a multi-denominational worldview of unity was "marred by racism and exclusion."[602] This was indeed a departure from the original vision of Charles and Sarah Parham's Apostolic Faith Movement.

CHAPTER THIRTEEN

WHITES ONLY

"Give liberty to whom liberty is due, that is to every child of man, to every partaker of human nature."

-John Wesley

To read the denominational proxies reports on the history of the Apostolic Faith Movement one would think that there was only one racist in the whole world, and he had nothing better to do than to discriminate against the very black ministers he had empowered to lead in his **Apostolic Faith Movement.** Everything about their version of the events is backwards. Dr. Eddie Hyatt wrote, *"Parham's falling out with Seymour has often been ascribed to racism. William Seymour never made this accusation, nor did even his enemies accuse him of racism while he was alive."*[603] Among the reasons that Parham was never charged with racism by his enemies, is because his primary enemies were white supremacists. A charge of racism against the Parhams is ludicrous. A.F.M., by the time of the Los Angeles Outpouring, could draw a crowd of thousands for just a baptism. There were hundreds of A.F.M. works across the nation, and followers all over the world. There were many Black, Native-American and other ministers of color in the movement. It should be noted that the Parham family was not just Charles. Sarah Parham and her sister Lilian Thistlethwaite were part of the leadership of A.F.M. Such broad-brush positions as claiming that the Parhams were racist are ridiculous and unfounded.

> "Such broad-brush positions as claiming that the Parhams were racist are ridiculous and unfounded."

Dr. Gary Garrett[604] points out that after Seymour died Sarah Parham visited his wife **Pastor Jeannie Seymour.** This was important for Sister Seymour as she was facing challenges for leadership of the church and Sarah Parham's visit served to affirm her role not just as Seymour's wife, but as the legitimate successor. The endorsement of the Parhams in that manner showed their long-standing friendship and respect despite some of the church leadership challenges.[605] The challenger to Sister Seymour was another of the all-white new Pentecostal's efforts to disrespect the A.F.M. in general and black leadership in particular, as well as women of faith. Although it is fair to note that William Seymour's 1914 changes may have been counterproductive for Sister Seymour.

"Although the movement was racially integrated in its early years, racial divisions soon developed. Many white clergy would not accept the presence of both blacks and whites in the congregation; the clergy subsequently left to form the Assemblies of God where blacks could be excluded."[606] It is notable that as an independent church the Seymours were repeatedly disrespected by white leaders, especially the group of white ministers that formed the initial leadership of the Assemblies of God. These white men loved to give lip service to Azusa Street, but in practical

~ CHAPTER THIRTEEN | WHITE'S ONLY ~

application saw the Seymours and other leaders as beneath them. While leaders like Howard Goss made spurious claims of working closely with black ministers there was never a real attempt to include black ministers. Goss's work with black ministers is primarily hearsay. The organizing of the all-white Assemblies of God in 1914 made the bigotry of white ministers all too real to the Seymours. "Even as white Pentecostals spread their religious doctrines across the world through missionary activities, at home they refused to engage their neighbors of a different race who were only blocks away."[607]

Charles and Sarah Parham were separated from the Seymours making Apostolic Faith Gospel Mission independent of the A.F.M. To be certain, there were strong feelings on both sides of the division. Nevertheless, the Parhams never challenged the Seymours use of their ministry name, *Apostolic Faith*. The Parhams had developed a culture where those connected to them were family. They never attempted to lord over others. In fact, they publicly proclaimed that all those who were born of the water and the Spirit speaking in other tongues were part of the A.F.M. global family.

In contrast, **William Howard Durham,** who was aligned with Howard Goss, Warren Carothers and others who comprised the Texas Syndicate made no pretense that he thought Seymour was inferior, illiterate, in false doctrine and more. He and his Texas Syndicate allies tried a hostile takeover of Seymour's church. Sadly, it was an oft repeated method of Durham, Carothers, Goss, Bell, Flowers, and their growing network of like-minded colleagues.[608] It was Charles Parham who used his substantial influence to stand up for William and Jeannie Seymour and challenge Durham's abuse of the Seymours.

"In my analysis of the Life of Minister Charles F. Parham, I ran upon information that finally added up to the Truth. If you read many accounts of the Azusa Street Revival, you will come to believe Parham was a racist whom everyone hated. On the contrary, that is as far away from the truth as the east is from the west. Charles loved people, black and white. During his time on earth, the United States had a list of laws adopted by white Democrat politicians in the Southern United States. These laws were particularly designed to keep black people in their place. These were called Jim Crow Laws. Jim Crow Laws would forbid whites and colored people from sitting together and a host of other regulations. If you studied His (Parham's) Ministry as close as I have, you'll learn he often ignored these laws and accepted Black Men and Women to preach in his Ministry and supported them financially as well, in the case especially of William J. Seymour."[609] The Parhams came from a lineage of those who sought equality and justice; Sarah and her Sister Lillian were raised Quaker. As such they were encouraged (even as girls) to study and learn in their father's library.

Those who do not believe fairy tales understand that there is much more to the story, like the Truth. Racism is real. Then as now, racism is rampant. While Parham was unhurried in realizing the challenges, some of the worst racist in all human history were leaders in his group masquerading as preachers. Their departure from the A.F.M. would be messy. The Assemblies of God and other all-white racist groups would not only welcome them, but put them in the highest places of leadership.

"The African Methodist Episcopal and other black churches were born partly as a result of revival preaching, partly because of white segregation."[610] "A giant gorilla in the room, is racism. The Wesley brothers were both abolitionists, and their movement produced some of the great abolitionist leaders in both Britain and the U.S.A., including

~ CHAPTER THIRTEEN | WHITE'S ONLY ~

William Wilberforce, Gilbert Haven, LaRay Sunderland and Anthony Bewley. Indeed, Charles Finney, a revivalist of much renown, arose within Wesleyan tradition, opposed slavery, and wrote a very powerful argument that regeneration and the decision to oppress one's brothers cannot coexist. Churches within these groups regularly restricted black worshippers to the balcony or some other carefully segregated area, where they could watch white people worship but not participate. The formation of separate churches and denominations, was undoubtedly the best solution available in some places and times, given the militant hatred of many white church leaders and state legislators; this is what occurred."[611]

The Wesleyan Methodists (today called just "Wesleyans") in 1843, and the Free Methodists in 1860, separated from the white Methodist mainstream in large part because leadership within the larger denomination either tolerated or actively defended slavery. An irony in all of this, is the fact that while the holiness groups were initially composed of abolitionists who separated from the Methodist mainstream over the slavery issue, for the most part they all — the Wesleyans and Free Methodists included — formed segregated churches. In some cases, the result was the formation of separate black denominational groups, like the original (1893) Church of God in Christ. In others, such as the Church of the Nazarene and the Church of God / Anderson (now "Church of God Ministries"), the result was separate black congregations within the denomination. Very seldom did the teaching of the holiness movement lead to the formation of integrated congregations.[612]

The Apostolic Faith movement of Charles and Sarah Parham was an exception. Generally whitewashed off the list of those who brought racial reform is Charles and Sarah Parham. While the Baptists had made their position clear that black people were inferior and were better off enslaved,

Methodist squabbled over Segregation, Holiness groups formed all-white and some even radically anti-black denominations, Charles and Sarah Parham used their A.F.M. to give African-Americans a voice, a platform, and both equality and dignity. This platform offered by the Apostolic Faith Movement was an exception that did not garner the appreciation of most of their counterparts in denominations.

RACISM

"What is racism? From a socio-political perspective, racism exists when one group intentionally refuses to share power and resources, maintain inflexible institutionally practices, procedures, policies, justifies its actions by blaming the victim and subjugating persons on the basis of the pigmentation of their skin."[613] "The tacit decision to excuse racism, and similar decisions about other sins, led to an absurd result. Many began to abandon a growing closeness to God as evidenced by obedience to His will in love of God and neighbor and enemy, and instead, began to

emphasize church-attendance, church-money, instant 'entire sanctification' experiences, and various (very) physical behaviors regardless of state of being. Many in the holiness movement appeared to take the attitude, essentially, that 'As long as I don't drink, smoke, cuss or chew, and I've had the defining sanctification 'experience,' it's okay if I'm still a racist!'"[614]

Parham began the struggle with Warren Fay Carothers' radical hatred at least by May of 1906. In contrast to Carothers' bigoted racial hatred, Parham presents that the Church is like a family. Parham presents that family is not segregated.[615] It was a consistent position for both Charles and Sarah Parham. The story of the Los Angeles Outpouring has been

CHAPTER THIRTEEN | WHITE'S ONLY

manipulated to please a predominately white audience. Most White people were happy to have the attention being brought to the new fad of speaking in other tongues, but they did not want to have what was considered by most to be the social stigma of close association with people of color. Religious people were no different. In reality, religious people were worse.

In the fall of 1906, Charles Parham prophesied against the new leader of the Zion, Illinois cult, Walter Voliva. Most of the Zion, Illinois allegations against the Apostolic Faith movement, while horrible, were not racially associated since Parham was the main target and he was white and most of his detractors were also white. Even though Charles and Sarah Parham were open to and included black ministers it took some time before their inclusion was noticed by outsiders. However, when word got out that the Apostolic Faith team leading the Los Angeles Outpouring, was populated by key ministers, William Seymour, Lucy Farrow, and Anna Hall who were black (two of them women), the attacks took on a new dimension. Charles Parham's followers in Los Angeles were a different story than other places where key revival and outpourings had happened. Hate was rampant in Los Angeles and racial hatred spilled over in the media there.

Religious white people of that time period were similar to those today. They are okay with blacks and other minorities being ministered to, but they did not see them as equals. Today's version is happy to send missionaries to places like Africa, but they don't want them to be part of their church, community, and certainly not their family! Religious people, especially those who led all-white denominations, generally agreed that Charles & Sarah Parham and their Apostolic Faith movement were malevolent. The attacks on the Parhams from these, were vicious. They were predictable and subsequently, knew no boundaries. They intended to cause damage to the body of Christ. These religious leaders especially despised black people and the fact that Charles and Sarah Parham elevated blacks simply was not acceptable in their sanctimonious eyes.

Modern apologists have made a plethora of excuses for the unwillingness of church leaders to stand against hatred and ignorance against their fellow man based merely one the color of one's skin. These generally explain that "was the culture or the times." Dreadful reason to hate someone; this was an atrocious for those who claim Christ! Religious people have sought to be clever and hide their hatred in religious rhetoric. The considerable contribution by people of color to the global outpouring of the Holy Ghost is immeasurable.

> *"Parham's most notable disciples were blacks and women."*

The inclusion of blacks was primarily the work of Charles Fox Parham until Tomlinson, and his Church of God joined the fray with robust conviction. Parham's most notable disciples were blacks and women. Key ensembles were women like Lucy Farrow, Lillian Thistlethwaite, Maria Woodworth-Etter, Mary Arthur, Aimee Semple McPherson, Florence Crawford, Maggie Bowdan, Millicent McClendon, Anna E. Hall, Hattie Allen, Sarah Parham and a plethora more (both white and black ladies are included in this partial list). Important black men in the movement were Charles H. Mason, Earnest Lloyd, Henry Prentiss, William J. Seymour, Garfield Thomas Haywood, William Bowdan, Frank W. Williams, R. C. Lawson, and many others.

Church of God General Overseer Ambrose Jessup (A.J.) Tomlinson & Mary Jane (Taylor) on their wedding day, April 24, 1889. A.J. born Sept 22, 1865, near Westfield, Indiana.

Charles and Sarah Parham And Their Racially

~ CHAPTER THIRTEEN | WHITE'S ONLY ~
Vindictive

Detractors **Phineas Bresse**, and **Alma White** fired the initial salvos against the Apostolic Faith Movement. These were not really about the black ministers the Parhams promoted; it was about the Parhams for making such allowances. Racially biased accomplices, proxies and surrogates, portrayed the Apostolic Faith Gospel Mission meetings as a "bunch of Negroes" who were having orgies.[616] There is no doubt these people, who saw the world through white-colored glasses, were well informed. They knew that the A.F.M. had made serious inroads in black communities and were actively recruiting, licensing and ordaining black ministers. The Independent Holiness, Baptists, and others, responded with a volume of verbal assaults. Yes, it is demented, but that is only part of the message. Previous to Los Angeles, the racially oriented attacks on the Apostolic Faith Movement had been minimal. William Seymour and several other black ministers had operated fairly well as Apostolic Faith ministers even in Jim Crow dominated Houston, Texas. One of these ministers even served as a local director in the Apostolic Faith Movement in Texas. The Texas Syndicate was okay with blacks as long as they stayed in their place. They were not going to tolerate "these uppity blacks" leading white people. The arrival of the A.F.M. in Los Angeles (which began in 1905) made them fair game for horrible racist attacks.

Phineas Bresse was a former Methodist. He was exactly the opposite of the Parham family and the A.F.M. about black ministers. Bresse was a religious politician. He said all the right things, but was more worried about his persona than anything else. Bresse was one of that kind who was fine with black people if they stayed in their place. He was a "law and order" preacher who demanded worship to be conducted in a certain manner.[617] Certainly not in a manner like the Apostolic Faith people in Los Angeles were behaving.[618] "Bresee condemned the Azusa Street revival.

Speaking in tongues was 'a senseless mumble,' Bresee was happy to write or tell lies if it (the propaganda) benefited him. He wrote in an article for a national Nazarene magazine, that the Pentecostal revival had an insignificant influence on the religious life of Los Angeles...he maintained, 'about as much influence as a pebble thrown into the sea.'"[619]

The connection of speaking in tongues to the Apostolic Faith movement that was so open with blacks and their unsanctimonious worship was not acceptable to Bresse and certainly not acceptable to his friends in the former Confederacy who openly sought to murder blacks and then joined with Bresse to form the Church of the Nazarene. Black people would be rewarded by their new white masters in the Church of the Nazarene. They were allowed to join the Church of the Nazarene if they organized their own congregations. Like most groups of this type, the Church of the Nazarene believe in the 'separate but equal' Jesus.

Alma White was the leader and self-appointed "bishop" of Pillar of Fire. One of her disciples, Nettie Harwood, reported people at the Apostolic Faith Gospel Mission were singing songs "in a faraway tune that sounded very unnatural and repulsive."[620] Alma White was not only against speaking in tongues, but she was also obsessed with the subject to the point she wrote a book titled, **Demons and Tongues** (1910). Charles and Sarah Parham and anyone associated with them was her sworn enemy. She even changed the name of her denomination to make certain that no one confused her racially driven cult with the Parhams. White despised the Parhams to the point she fantasized they would be stricken with blindness.[621] She avowed that hating people because of their skin color was righteous, but speaking in tongues was of the devil.[622] She wrote, "It is within the rights of civilization for the white race to hold the supremacy; it is no injustice to the colored man. The white men of this country poured out their blood to liberate the colored people from the chains of slavery, and the sacrifice should be appreciated."[623] White held that blacks "must keep in their places and appointed sphere."[624] Mongrelization has been proven bad.[625]

Alma White was a racial bigot. She organized her church like a hate group. It is sacrilege that she is even mentioned as an opponent of Charles Parham or his Apostolic Faith Movement.

> *"She avowed that hating people because of their skin color was righteous, but speaking in tongues was of the devil."*

Her opinion is so obvious that it is like saying that cats hate mice. White's disapproval is unimportant considering she and her denomination became an arm of the Ku Klux Klan. She served as a promoter for the Klan. Helped the Klan reorganize in 1915 and she later wrote the first of several books venerating the Klan. The first was **"The Ku Klux Klan in Prophecy** (1925), in which she outlined biblical sanctions for the Klan."[626] Likely, Charles Parham considered it somewhat of a compliment that racially bigoted Alma White and her friends would oppose the Apostolic Faith Movement in general and Apostolic Faith ministers at the Apostolic Faith Gospel Mission on Azusa Street in particular. White was not just opposed to those who were black. White people who cavorted with blacks were considered just as horrible, perhaps considered worse. *Sodomites* was a favorite word used to describe those whites who embraced non-whites.[627] Like Phineas Bresse and those in the Texas Syndicate, Alma White opposed the Apostolic Faith primarily because it was inclusive of persons of color and their worship traditions which she considered 'primitive.'"[628] "Native, white, Protestant supremacy."[629]

On his way to Los Angeles William J. Seymour stopped in Denver, Colorado, and visited Alma White's Pillar of Fire movement. Alma White was not impressed with Seymour. She later said, "I had met all kinds of religious fakers and tramps, but I felt he excelled them all."[630] At this point, William Seymour was unknown. The larger target of nearly all the attacks in Los Angeles would be Charles Parham. Most of the negative remarks about the Azusa Street Revival came after they had decided to be an independent church. However, once Parham was disconnected from the Azusa Street Mission it was important to his detractors to keep him in the narrative. Thus, this Charles and Sarah Parham who dared stand up to Jim Crow laws in Texas, who taught black students in their schools and without charge, who opened their home to blacks, trained black ministers, promoted black ministers, had black ministers like Lucy Farrow as keynote speakers in their camp meetings[631], licensed black ministers and much more, were suddenly called racists. Only their political enemies and their proxies could have accomplished such a scheme. White ministers in the Apostolic Faith Movement did not want the black ministers so the division at Azusa would work better than they could imagine. They could still claim it as a great revival, they could give lip service to the black ministers there, but they were never connected to them in any formal way and any problems or concerns they could blame on the Parhams. Today, they are still blaming the Parhams.

Independent Holiness Choir

Other racist white ministers joined the din. The new Pentecostal surrogates who had written the history to their liking had been consistent in presenting those who they deemed "relevant." We are working with this list not because we agree, but to reveal the character of those who the new Pentecostals offer to us as relevant. "G. **Campbell Morgan** who was involved in the racially based Christian Identity[632] movement described the activities on Azusa Street as "the last vomit of Satan." R. A. Torrey declared that this movement was "emphatically not of God."[633] A careful read of Torrey's thoughts on some of the displays in Los Angeles make even this author, with an extensive Apostolic Faith background, cringe. We would not tolerate some of the demonstrations Torrey exposes.

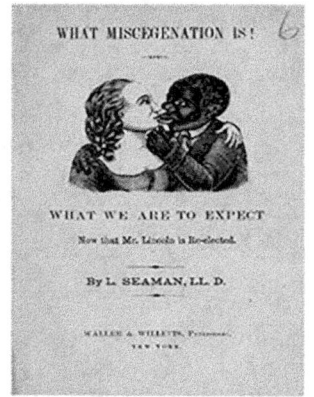

Yet, it could be asserted that Torrey was emphatically for the Baptism of the Holy Ghost. In *The Baptism with the Holy Spirit,* Torrey testifies, "It was a great turning point in my ministry when...I became satisfied that the Baptism with the Holy Spirit was an experience for today, and for me, and set myself about obtaining it. Such blessing came to me personally."[634] He was emphatic that "The Baptism with the Holy Spirit is a necessary preparation for effective service for Christ along every line of service. The A.F.M. concurs with Torreys statement on the Baptism with the Holy Spirit."

Another favorite hater of the Apostolic Faith Movement is H. A. Ironside. He said in 1912 that the movement was "disgusting...delusions and insanities...pandemonium's were exhibitions worthy of a madhouse or a collection of howling dervishes," causing a "heavy toll of lunacy and infidelity."[635] While it is obvious that both Torrey and Ironside were in opposition to the happenings in Los Angeles. We do not have them on record being opposed with any other Apostolic Faith groups. It is also not fair to lump Torrey in with the racially motivated haters. Torrey presents legitimate reasons for his opposition and despite what has been added to his statements, it does not seem that he held ill will or animosity.

However, Ironside is in good company. Right in goose-step with his racist friends. Among his other racially oriented activities was his active participation on the Board of the Racially prejudiced **Bob Jones University.**[636] This group of haters has direct connections to the Ku Klux Klan. Ironside's friend Bob "Jones Sr. was of the view that twentieth-century blacks should be grateful to whites for bringing their ancestors to this country as slaves. If this had not happened, Jones wrote in 1960, "they might still be over there in the jungles of Africa, unconverted."[637] Integrationists, according to Jones, were wrongfully trying to eradicate natural boundaries that God himself had established."[638] Like Warren Faye Carothers and his Texas Syndicate friends, Ironside did not see black ministers as anything close to his equal.

W. B. Godbey saw the movement as a result of spiritualism and that the participants were "Satan's preachers, jugglers, necromancers, enchanters, magicians, and all sorts of mendicants."[639] Well, of course. W. B. Godfrey, evangelist to the all-white Wesleyan Church, was a close personal friend of white supremacist Alma White. He even advised her about marriage and was the minister who officiated her marriage to Kent White.[640] Alma White who reveals that even as a young woman, she held clearly formed beliefs about how society was supposed to be structured.[641] Godfrey advised his racist friend Alma White that no person but a preacher had a chance of winning her favor.[642] While Alma White projected in her white supremacist persona that all blacks were inferior to whites, she did concede that a colored preacher named Rebecca Grant was the inspiration for her understanding *there is neither male nor female; for you are all one in Jesus Christ.*[643] Alma White came to understand that God does not make distinctions between men and women, but could not separate Jew

~ CHAPTER THIRTEEN | WHITE'S ONLY ~

from Greek and bond from free.⁶⁴⁴ White clung her entire life to a society that taught her she was somehow superior because she was born white. Equally, she clawed her way to the forefront against white men who treated her as subservient because she was a woman.⁶⁴⁵

While White had some understandable grievances with the all-white male leadership of her Methodist Episcopal church regarding the sexual abuse of women and cover up of the same, serious chauvinism to the point that some Methodist ministers expected a woman's only purpose is serving men. Extreme legalism especially in ideas like women are not to speak in the Church, etc.⁶⁴⁶ The environment of her circumstances, marriage, the Methodist church formed her life view. Whether her view was correct or imagined it was hers none the less and she was very vocal about her opinions. Her life view affected Alma White to the point that she obviously despised men but not all men. She just despised the men who disagreed with her opinions and views. Her own husband, Kent, was likely her model of male ministry. He opposed her in nearly everything she attempted. Perhaps he knew more than the public realized. She started her movement with just her two sons as followers, but grew the movement by attracting other deeply wounded persons, especially women and those who found fault with the Methodist movement.⁶⁴⁷ Alma Whites sons both became leaders in her new cult.

Like Warren Fay Carothers and his friends in the Texas Syndicate, Alma White not only hated black people, she hated, Jews, Mexicans, Catholics, and others.⁶⁴⁸ She especially hated the Knights of Columbus, imagining that they saw her as the enemy.⁶⁴⁹ Alma developed more reasons for hating those who spoke in other tongues when her husband Kent White left her organization, separated from her (although they stayed legally married), and joined with a group that believed in speaking in other tongues.[650] On July 7th, 1910, Kent White was baptized with the Holy Spirit.[651] The same year, Alma White released her book, Demons and Tongues.[652] A book written primarily about the Apostolic Faith Movement's call to receive the Holy Ghost evidenced by speaking in other tongues.

Phineas Bresse and Alma White's fellow Independent Holiness leader, **Warren Fay Carothers** joined the Apostolic Faith Movement in a brash plan to become the leader and infuse his own white supremacist strategy. "After the South's defeat in the Civil War, Southern church leaders struggled to help their congregants make sense of their loss. The result was the religion of the Lost Cause, a mythology that ennobled the Confederacy and idealized the antebellum South as a bastion of Christian piety and morals. This fusion of religious and cultural values, delivered from the pulpit, helped to legitimize a social order that continued to subjugate Black people. Later, as evangelical Christianity, anchored in the South, grew to become the dominant expression of Christianity in America, its cultural scaffolding, rooted in white supremacy, spread as well. During the era of Jim Crow, when Southern statutes enforced the strict separation of races and restricted the rights of Black people, Northern Protestant churches remained largely segregated and muted in their criticism. Many white Christians saw segregation as simply part of God's plan for humanity."[653] Warren Fay Carothers was an adherent of this dogma. His contribution to the Kingdom of God is like hay, wood and stubble.[654]

CHAPTER FOURTEEN

THE TEXAS SYNDICATE

"I trust, therefore, that our evangelists and workers from the North will not forget this condition of affairs [racial segregation] and embarrass the work South by well-meaning but mistaken efforts to disregard them."

-Warren Fay (W.F.) Carothers

Politics makes strange bedfellows, meaning that political alliances in a common cause may bring together those of widely differing views. In like manner, those that formed the Texas Syndicate were focused on power in a take no prisoners scheme that excluded people of color and marginalized women to create their new religious empire. Like the Galatian church, they were allegedly born in the Spirit, but sought to follow the flesh. Warren Fay Carothers was a bigoted white supremacist who deemed all nonwhites as beneath his social standing. His motive in joining with the A.F.M. is debatable. There are a few possibilities.

White Men in Dark Places

1. Carothers planned from the beginning of his connection to the Parhams to utilize the A.F.M. to advance his racially motivated agenda and create an all-white denomination just like Phineas Bresse, Alma White and other Independent Holiness ministers who were white supremacists.
2. Carothers did not realize the Parhams were not racists when he first aligned with the A.F.M.
3. Carothers realized that the Parhams, being from Kansas, were not as committed to the *Separate but Equal* vision of his Texas Syndicate, but expected the Parhams would be convinced to align with his vision.

The third point seems to be the most likely as Carothers was both very committed to his Texas Syndicate friends and wrote about his concerns that those not from the South might interfere with the way things were done in the South. Of course, the way things were done in the South was through the racial segregation of blacks by Jim Crow laws. W.F. Carothers  was in total support of the suppression of people of other races. It is clear that his friends in the Texas Syndicate supported his positions. His friends helped form the Assemblies of God and whole heartedly adopted his racial ideas.

Carothers' vision for his Texas Syndicate preceded the arrival of the Parhams in Texas. When Parham brought his A.F.M. to Texas, Carothers initially embraced the doctrines of the A.F.M. He had a number

~ CHAPTER FOURTEEN | THE TEXAS SYNDICATE ~

of meetings with Charles Parham, and they worked together on Carothers' Brunner Tabernacle. Make no mistake, Brunner Tabernacle was Carothers' project and his utopian vision of an all-white Texas style church fashioned in the manner of a Dowie or Sandford. At what point Carothers developed his extreme written concepts on people of color and women is debatable. What is certain is that Warren Fay Carothers was among the most bigoted racists of the last century.[655] More alarming, many of Carothers' concepts were included in the dogma of another former Methodist minister William Simmons, when he organized the Knights of Ku Klux Klan (KKK) reorganized in 1915.[656]

    J. G. Campbell, a fellow Texan spoke about Carothers' Texas Syndicate, "...false teachers and deceptive spirits crept in, and undermined the work and misled people all over the world where the baptism of the Holy Ghost is taught. Would-be deceivers have tried to organize the work, both here in Texas and the Pacific Coast, and other places, till there are as many divisions among the people. The Devil will seek to blind some and keep them quarreling about men."[657]

    "You slaves will go to heaven if you are good, but don't ever think that you will be close to your mistress and master. No! No! there will be a wall between you; there will be holes in it that will permit you to look out and see your mistress when she passes by. If you want to sit behind this wall, you must do the language of the text 'Obey your masters.'"[658]

    Before the KKK was reorganized by a Methodist preacher in 1915, there was Warren Fay Carothers and his Texas Syndicate. Charles Parham had for at least a decade been unalterably opposed to denominations.[659] He wrote and preached often on the subject. Yet, Warren Carothers convinced Parham to allow the appointment of officers; the A.F.M. began issuing ministerial license. Parham did not feel like he needed a title. However,

Carothers convinced him to make a title of the role he had from the inception of the A.F.M., *Projector of the Faith*. With the explosive growth of the A.F.M., Charles Parham could use some assistance. What he got was stabbed repeatedly for the rest of his natural life. Things were bad from the start of Carothers' scheme. With his shiny new badge, Carothers was the new sheriff in town. Evidently this was always Carothers' plan. Although Parham commented that Carothers became obsessed with taking over Zion, Illinois.

    Carothers certainly made haste to organize his Texas Syndicate to oppose Parham. Within months, Carothers went from one of Parham's A.F.M. leaders to being deposed. Yet, Carothers never gave up his throne. In response, Carothers brought the full force of his Texas Syndicate to bear on Parham. The first known salvo was the blackmailing of Parham by Carothers. The second round was Carothers as King and Judge; he erroneously claimed that Parham resigned from the A.F.M. Third, Carothers' hand-picked a private jury and held a kangaroo court.[660] Carothers and Goss claimed that Parham confessed something. The man Carothers picked to chair the kangaroo court said that Parham was not even in attendance and did not attempt to defend himself from the fictious charges.[661] Despite the facts, Carothers, Goss, and their Texas Syndicate friends, found Parham guilty of "conduct unbecoming a minister" (whatever that was supposed to mean). Fourth, Carothers mimicked Judas in conspiring with and bribing officials in a failed attempt to bring legal charges against Parham. Fifth, Carothers continued his quest to be the leader of the A.F.M. for years and work with the Texas Syndicate and fellow Texas Syndicate comrade to wrest as many as possible from the A.F.M. to their new organization.[662] An organization that would front on a series of names. They would be joined by the naïve, the conflicted, as well as their fellow bigots, racists and white supremacists. Together they would recreate the Kingdom of Heaven in their own image. This was a common theme in Independent Holiness groups. Jesus Christ had Judas Iscariot. Charles Parham had Warren Fay Carothers. Carothers, an Independent Holiness minister, saw potential in the Apostolic Faith Movement to advance his all-white vision. Like his comrades in the Independent Holiness Movement, he used religion to keep minorities and women in their place. Carothers bragged that he had strong ties to the Methodist church and had no immorality. Yet, he despised people of color, mistreated women, embezzled intellectual property, libeled and slandered anyone who opposed him, and his Texas Syndicate...and the list goes on.

Carothers Seeks The Preeminence

Separate but Equal was the law in the United States, but not the law of God. ***There is no Separate but Equal Jesus!*** Carothers' Texas Syndicate conveniently ignored the violations of the law of God in their pursuit of power and control. Carothers bragged he was a former Methodist, but obviously left the M.E. Church seeking something more racially intolerant. Nearly all Holiness groups were intentionally designed to give white men preeminence. Carothers' vision for the A.F.M. mirrored that of his Holiness friends. Carothers imagined that Charles Parham would give him the prominence that he desired. However, it turned out that Charles Parham was a stick-in-the-mud. Carothers was willing to allow black ministers in the ministry, but they need not have prominent roles and certainly were not the equal of a Southern man like Carothers. Carothers was in favor of a tiered approach where those he considered undesirable belonged to a subgroup or an alternative group like the Church of the Nazarene system where there was one group for the good white people and another for the rest. Carothers believed in the *separate but equal Jesus*.

The Texas Syndicate preferred the Separate but Equal approach and would continue to promote Separate but equal even after it was declared illegal. Separate but equal means always separate but rarely or never equal. In Carothers' vision, the A.F.M. would become a whites only group and another group could be created for blacks and other minorities. When Parham opposed Carothers' vision, Carothers created a separate group and chiseled as many whites as possible from the A.F.M. This left the A.F.M. still multicultural but without as many bigoted whites. It has been argued that Judas did not see his actions as betraying Jesus Christ, but rather that he was forcing His hand! Perhaps this is the thought process employed by Warren Carothers. His creation of an alternate all-white version of the Apostolic Faith was the beginning.

The primary target in the nascent days of the Texas Syndicate was Charles Fox and Sarah Eleanor Parham and their family.[663] The Texas Syndicate viewed Charles Parham as a goody two shoes. He was a pious man who had been a minister all his adult life. He had married a devout woman and lived in a sacrificial manner, helping the sick, poor, and downtrodden. The Parhams had become the foremost names in all of religion. Every minister and ministry knew of the Parhams. In the early 1900s, the Parhams had disregarded other religious denominations and leaders by claiming that the baptism of the Holy Ghost was for every believer and was evidenced by speaking in other tongues as the Spirit gave utterance.[664] Their doctrine had found a huge and growing following.

The Texas Syndicate served a need for Southern white males frustrated by societal changes that they felt threatened their rightful place. There was a great societal struggle for white men to regain the pre-eminence lost in the American Civil War and the Texas Syndicate met that need. In

~ CHAPTER FOURTEEN | THE TEXAS SYNDICATE ~

the years 1900 through 1915 there was no organization like the Ku Klux Klan to convince Christians, church leaders and others that they held the same values. The Texas Syndicate employed the rhetoric of anti-Catholicism and anti-Semitism and promoted white supremacy by degrading African-Americans, Native-Americans, Jews, Japanese, and others. Its popularity came from the combination of religion and nationalism. The Texas Syndicate promoted both religion and nationalism. This appealed to white Protestant Americans who feared that immigration and changing social mores would overthrow their social dominance. So, the Texas Syndicate filled the need until the KKK was re-established in the next decade.[665]

    The scenario was really nothing new. Warren Fay Carothers was as Apostle John wrote, one who loved to have the preeminence among the brethren.[666] "An authoritarian personality has strong feelings of inadequacy, dependency, and hostility, particularly toward those in authority, even though they may be in a position of authority. Because of these feelings of worthlessness, they tend to displace this anger and hate towards themselves onto another group. The bigot is simply transferring their own sense of low self-esteem and their own self-hatred to another racial, cultural, or religious group. The bigot will stereotype, lie, about and persecute that group no matter what the truth. They will even go so far as to accuse the persecuted of being the persecutor or fabricate instances of persecution."[667] There is really no better explanation of Mr. Carothers.

    For Charles Parham, that he would be the target of such a scheme should not have surprised him. Perhaps he was not shocked. Afterall, God had warned him those days would come. "In a letter to Howard Goss, Charles Parham warned Goss that Carothers was "trying to gain the hearts of the workers and get control of Texas." According to Parham, "Carothers had learned some rumors about him and was trying to get all the movement to follow him in revolt."⁶⁶⁸ Parham was correct, but Carothers was not alone, Goss was intimately working behind the scenes with Carothers and his Texas Syndicate. It would be a lifelong pattern of deceit and dishonor for Howard Goss."⁶⁶⁹ Although Goss was a quite willing accomplice, Carothers was the mastermind behind the Texas Syndicate. Carothers would use Howard A. Goss until Goss was no longer useful. Carothers had hoped to steer the A.F.M. away from the Parhams' multicultural vision and toward one that fulfilled his desire to restore his rightful place in the world. In Carothers' utopian view, the A.F.M. would merge with Zion City and create a predominantly white middle-class and upper-middle-class organization. This group would be led by all-white male leadership; minorities and women would also be allowed to participate. However, they were required to meet certain criteria, and "stay in their place."

In contrast to The Texas Syndicate's vision, Charles and Sarah Parham were achieving their vision which included everyone, regardless of race or gender. A decade before the serious challenges, God had warned Charles Parham that the mob would come after him. The Lord said: "Are you able to stand for the experience in the face of persecution and howling mobs?" He said: *"Yes, Lord, if you will give me the experience, for the laborer must first be partaker of the fruits."*⁶⁷⁰ In 1906, the beginning of serious leadership challenges would come to Charles Parham and Charles Mason. Both faced serious threat of schism in their movements by those who desired them to drop their resolve to expect speaking in other tongues as evidence of the baptism of the Holy Ghost. Neither Parham nor Mason would kowtow, and most of the Apostolic Faith and Pentecostal leaders agreed with them. This resulted in both facing off against detractors from within their own leadership structures and in some measure continues till this very day.

~ CHAPTER FOURTEEN | THE TEXAS SYNDICATE ~

Both Charles Fox Parham and Charles Harrison Mason were used by the Texas Syndicate. Parham was white but considered a black sympathizer, meaning he was like those abolitionists that helped slaves on the Underground Railroad. The Texas Syndicate was not interested in those like the Parhams who wanted to upset the social order. Mason was a black man from Memphis, Tennessee; that was enough for the Texas Syndicate to see him as a problem.

The Texas Syndicate was organized and led by Warren Fay Carothers who was expelled from the A.F.M. because he was a White Supremacist hellbent on turning the A.F.M. from its multicultural vision to his warped xenophobic scheme. The radical racial views of Carothers were incompatible with the vision and mission of the Apostolic Faith Movement. Carothers infiltrated the A.F.M., and then used A.F.M. connections and friendships to advance his white supremacist cause. Initially, The Texas Syndicate used their fellow Texans, who were also white supremacist, racists, etc. Next, they would attract many others who ignored or overlooked the horrible racial positions of these men. It may all sound impossible. However, consider that in the same timeframe these men implemented their mission the Ku Klux Klan was revitalized and perhaps the most racist President in American history was elected in the person of Woodrow Wilson.[671]

"A faction of the Brunner Mission, undertook to organize the movement (Apostolic Faith), after the Irvingites [the name *Catholic Apostolic Church* referred to the entire community of Christians who follow the Nicene Creed] turning against Mr. Parham saying he ought to go to hell for teaching such doctrines as speaking in tongues. These appointed a board and attempted to take control of the Apostolic Faith movement."[672] It is often said that Carothers and his friends were not bigoted *considering the times*.⁶⁷³ This is meant to mean that they were not really fanatical racists. Actually, it means whatever you want. It is an excuse for men who loathe others. In the case of the Texas Syndicate, the animosity was centered on racial intolerance. Let us consider their times. Woodrow Wilson would become President at this time. "Easily the worst part of Wilson's record as president was his overseeing of the resegregation of multiple agencies of the federal government, which had been surprisingly integrated because of Reconstruction decades earlier. At an April 11, 1913, Cabinet meeting, Postmaster General Albert Burleson argued for segregating the Railway Mail Service. He took exception to the fact that workers shared glasses, towels, and washrooms. Wilson offered no objection to Burleson's plan for segregation, saying that he "wished the matter adjusted in a way to make the least friction." In a 1913 open letter to Wilson, W.E.B. DuBois — who had supported Wilson in the 1912 election before being disenchanted by his segregation policies — wrote of *"one colored clerk who could not actually be segregated on account of the nature of his work [and who] consequently had a cage built around him to separate him from his white companions of many years." That's right: Black people who couldn't, logistically, be segregated were put in literal cages."*⁶⁷⁴

The Texas Syndicate would be a proverbial cage around all non-white persons. The Texas Syndicate was initially comprised of men who sought to remove Charles Parham from the leadership of the A.F.M. Parham's willingness to include blacks, Mexicans and others was counterproductive to the mission of the Texas Syndicate. This group was like the group who conspired to murder Julius Caesar. The similarities between the two are stunning. "The senators stabbed Caesar 23 times. The senators claimed to be acting over fears that Caesar's unprecedented concentration of power during his dictatorship was undermining the

~ CHAPTER FOURTEEN | THE TEXAS SYNDICATE ~

Roman Republic and presented the deed as an act of *tyrannicide*. At least 60 senators were party to the conspiracy, led by Marcus Junius Brutus and Gaius Cassius Longinus. Despite the death of Caesar, the conspirators were unable to restore the institutions of the Republic."[675] History regards them as double crossers.

The conspirators that formed the Texas Syndicate were similar in number and temperament. They feared Charles Parham and his A.F.M. was undermining their efforts to control their vision for the South. Together, they figuratively stabbed Charles Parham as many times as opportunity presented. To make matters harsher, many of the Texas Syndicate admitted that Parham was their spiritual father making their deeds an act of spiritual *Patricide*. Despite their horrible atrocities against Charles Parham, they failed in controlling the entire movement just as Charles Parham had prophesied. However, they did accomplish their mission. They created an all-white denomination that John G. Lake described without compliment. "... They have drifted clear away from a true scriptural Pentecostal ideal, and every day are becoming more and more a little bigoted denomination. The spirit of denominationalism in The Assemblies of God is probably narrower than even in the old churches from which Pentecostal people have been escaping for the last thirty years. So that as a power to bless mankind and put an ideal before the world such as the scriptures outline and as our soul is longing for, it does not seem to me they are worth discussing or considering."[676]

Numbered among the Texas Syndicate conspirators were **Howard A. Goss, Warren Faye Carothers, William Morwood, J. D. Sheumack, Lemuel C. Hall, Hardy Mitchell, Daniel Charles Owen (D. C. O.) Opperman, A. G. Canada, E. N. Bell, J. Roswell Flower, Cyrus B. Fockler, William Durham** and other like-minded white men. Some of these would either join or be vocal promoters of the Ku Klux Klan (KKK) when their fellow Methodist ministers resurrected the KKK in 1915. All were white, all claimed to be preachers of the Gospel of Jesus Christ.[677] By 1908 it was well-known that Carothers and Goss and their Texas Syndicate were using the A.F.M. to cloak their activities. Pressure was mounting with J. G. Campbell, Parham, Crawford, Seymour and others exposing Carothers and Goss as not being A.F.M. There were reports that Carothers had even returned to his Independent Holiness roots with his Brunner Tabernacle congregation. In December they held a meeting to discuss the way forward. W. E. Holdgate, A. L. De LaVergne, N. Cossman, R. E. Winsett, F. L. Jones, A. R. Smith, William Norwood, William Hammond Piper, are all present to discuss what Carothers called a **"new movement."**[678] However, they continued pirating the Apostolic Faith Movement name for some more years. Charles Parham said there were at least nine of them that held a secret meeting.[679] Media outlets and participants listed at least a dozen names. Over the next few years, Howard Goss would collect a list of hundreds of willing participants in whatever the scheme was he was offering. Howard Goss made a list. It may be, the Texas Syndicate was just the largest assembled bastion of butter knife bearers, but thousands of stab wounds have an impact.

The Texas Syndicate was not a public group. They were a secret group much like the KKK with which they shared mutual vision. The Texas Syndicate is the label we have applied to their covert activities. Howard A. Goss said they adopted the moniker, Pentecostal, to set them apart from the A.F.M.[680] In the end, the Texas Syndicate was accomplishing their goals. The A.F.M. would be divided between the all-white Assemblies of God on the left hand and those they deplored on the right hand. The deplorables would remain in places like the legitimate Apostolic Faith Movement, the Church

~ CHAPTER FOURTEEN | THE TEXAS SYNDICATE ~

of God in Christ, the Church of God, and more. The Texas Syndicate made it clear they were not associated with the Blacks, Mexicans, Japanese, Native-Americans or any other they deemed undesirable. While *Pentecostal* was one of the identifiers of Charles and Sarah Parham's Apostolic Faith Movement the scheme by the Texas Syndicate posed a division between all-white groups and the multicultural A.F.M. The Texas Syndicate pirated the Pentecostal moniker to separate their identity from others in the Apostolic Faith Movement. Frankly, they were happy with any name that gave them power and control. They would use several identities over a decade to advance their white supremacist agenda including for a time using the name Apostolic Faith, then Pentecostal, Apostolic Faith Church of God in Christ, Assemblies of God, General Association of Apostolic Assemblies, Pentecostal Assemblies and more.

Charles Parham labeled them *new* Pentecostals and **Holy Rollers.**[681] Neither were a compliment. In fact, the connotation of the latter label is that his detractors were horrible people. Whatever you choose to believe, there is no doubt that Charles Parham knew these men better than most and his label was more accurate than any of us want to acknowledge. It is like Frank Poretti's novel, **The Oath!**[682] The Oath was fiction. **The Texas Syndicate** was real. Parham reserved the term Holy Rollers only for the most dishonorable of religious hypocrites. In 1906, the legitimate A.F.M. continued to grow globally and nationally. By this point the A.F.M. had hundreds of thousands of adherents and was growing exponentially as Charles Parham concentrated on the evangelistic work.[683]

In short order, Parham began to realize that Carothers was working on some behind the scenes scheme so that he could accomplish his demented vision that held horrendous intentions on women and minorities. These deep concerns for Charles and Sarah Parham that Charles

Parham confided in Howard Goss. Unbeknownst to Parham, the man that he thought was his friend, Howard A. Goss, was the Brutus[684] of the conspirators. History presents Howard Goss as a man devoid of loyalty and honor. Goss stabbed the Parham's the deepest. The wound would be so intense that Goss is not as much as named when Sarah Parham wrote her book, *The Life of Charles F. Parham*.[685] It was as if Howard Goss never existed. Perhaps, Howard A. Goss' account of his importance to the A.F.M. exaggerates his role and significance.

There are few outsiders who commented on the Texas Syndicate. However, J. G. Campbell, who published The Gospel of the Kingdom from Alvin, Texas for more than a decade from 1901 through 1913, had a front row view to the activities of the Texas Syndicate. He commented, *"There are many people who have never heard of Chas F. Parham. There are others who have heard of him in connection only with slander for he was in the way of certain ones who would organize the Movement that they might control it; and because of his teachings (a restored creation, and destruction of the wicked) and because he fights sin in all alike, but probably more than any-thing else because of fighting against "demonology" and fanaticism among God's people; not withstanding God honored him as the chosen vessel on account of his teachings, to introduce to the world the baptism of the Holy Ghost… by the speaking in other tongues…"*[686]

CHAPTER FIFTEEN

THE APOSTOLIC FAITH COGIC SCHEME

"Among the white race in the Southern States there is no difference of opinion upon this subject: all are united in the opinion in reference to the political, intellectual, and social inequality between the colored people and the white races. And the people of our Commonwealth generally feel that the present condition of the colored race in this country accords both with the Word and the providence of God."

-Southern Baptist Convention

Charles Harrison Mason's Leadership Was Challenged By The Texas Syndicate.

Charles Mason had heard about the Topeka Outpouring for years. The opportunity to visit the Los Angeles Outpouring, where the A.F.M. had sent several ministers, was too good to pass. At the A.F.M. Mission in Los Angeles Mason received his own baptism of the Holy Ghost! Charles Mason's larger leadership challenge came through C. P. Jones.[687] The Texas Syndicate would concentrate on Mason after they felt they had effectively stabbed the Parham family and left them for what they hoped was dead. Starting in 1906, Both Charles Parham and Charles Mason would face serious opposition for the rest of their lives for two major positions.

1. Charles Mason and Charles Parham both believed the Gospel of the Kingdom of Jesus Christ brought equality to all mankind regardless of race, gender, or ethnicity. Charles Mason dared to adopt the vision of Charles and Sarah Parham that he saw in full display in the Apostolic Faith Gospel Mission in Los Angeles. Mason "continued the mixed-race tradition of the Los Angeles meetings when he returned to Memphis."[688] The Texas Syndicate was happy to recommend blacks and others they considered undesirable to join with Mason, but there was never a reciprocal relationship.

2. Charles Mason and Charles Parham refused to renege on the central doctrinal point.[689] The baptism of the Holy Ghost evidenced by speaking in other tongues. Mason taught that "the edificatory nature of tongues forms *solidarity with Jesus*.[690] By 1913 it had become increasingly clear that as Pentecostals moved toward denominationalism, they would follow the segregating practices of American culture rather than the multicultural model of the A.F.M. The color line that had been washed away in the blood of Jesus, reappeared. On December 20, 1913, elders E.N. Bell and H.A. Goss issued a call to convene a general council of "all Pentecostal saints and Church Of God In Christ followers," to meet the following April at Hot Springs, Arkansas. This invitation went only to the white saints.[691]

After the Texas Syndicate successfully dissected the A.F.M., they turned their attention to the Church of God in Christ (COGIC). The Texas Syndicate wanted a group for those they didn't want in their all-white society. The Texas Syndicate's master plan positioned them as the superior all-white group. Thus, they desired to have a group to be the destination

~ CHAPTER FIFTEEN | APOSTOLIC FAITH COGIC SCHEME ~

group for all those the Texas Syndicate considered deplorables. Parham had rebuffed their plan as diabolical. They had misjudged Parham's seeming indifference as weakness. Now, they found themselves defending their ill-gotten vision as opposed to Parham's still highly functioning A.F.M. In an ironic turn of events, the Texas Syndicate, although all-white, had become the "other" group with the multicultural A.F.M. holding the high ground in the minds and hearts of the people.[692]

Charles Mason was in legal peril, struggling for control of the COGIC because he had accepted Parham's doctrine of the Baptism of the Holy Ghost evidenced by speaking with other tongues. To add to his trauma, the Texas Syndicate bega to peel away those ministers who identified with organizationally minded and compatible with the racial segregationist positions preferred by the Texas Syndicate. The Texas Syndicate used the Apostolic Faith name as a front; yet, they received growing opposition from the legitimate A.F.M. In the face of this pressure, they began to move away from using Apostolic Faith, after meeting to start their *new movement* in Texas December of 1908.

At this juncture the Texas Syndicate plagiarized both the A.F.M. and the Church of God in Christ creating a Frankenstein group they labeled. God in Christ Apostolic Faith (COGICAF). They presented that Charles Mason approved their new all-white bigoted organization. This clearly was a ploy. Like their ersatz version of the A.F.M., there is nothing to suggest this was ever a legitimate alliance. Allegedly they had a roster of all-white ministers that Howard Goss provided.[693] The evidence is like gravy made from the shadow of a starving chicken! They produced a list of all-white ministers but that was so obvious.[694] While they were busy dividing up the garments of Charles Parham they always yammered about unity! Ridiculous! An all-white list was the heart of their agenda. When the Texas Syndicate helped create the A.G., they continued to see the C.O.G.I.C. as the place to direct ministers who did not fit in their all-white master race vision. The Texas Syndicate and their new Pentecostals promoted "Pentecostal Evangel articles that depicted African-Americans as ignorant and dependent on the kindness and generosity of the superior white culture. A.G. leaders supported racial segregation because they wanted to preserve the whiteness of the denomination. In addition, they feared alienation of the church's southern congregations and district officials. This was never more evident than in 1939, when the national leadership officially proclaimed its refusal to ordain African-American Ministers,"[695] just as they had in 1914.

Imagine the conversation between Howard A. Goss (bigot and racist) and Bishop Charles H. Mason. Count this author among those who do not believe there ever was such a collaborative conversation. Imagine asking Charles H. Mason (a black man) for permission to use the name of his group to create a white supremacist version? The real deal was that the Texas Syndicate did not need or ask his permission. First, they were white which made them superior in their own eyes. Why would they care about taking something from Mason? They stole from the Parhams and lied about it for decades. Additionally, the white men had Jim Crow and slick lawyers on their side. To the Texas Syndicate Charles Mason was just another *mark*. The Texas Syndicate offered an opportunity to white ministers to gather to create an all-white group. Howard Goss worked on a list of those ministers who would be in favor of an all-white organization. Mason, as a black man, was not on the list. "Many historians of Pentecostalism have observed that following the initial potential for interracial religion... after the Azusa Street Revival in 1906, most white Pentecostals progressively cut ties with their African-American coreligionists until Pentecostal denominations were almost entirely segregated by the 1930s. White evangelist James Delk joined the Church of God in Christ and became a close associate of Charles H. Mason. Like the Parhams, Delk's life shows how these rare interracial white Pentecostals maintained interracial religious ties due to a combination of their willingness to be counter cultural and go against the standards of white middle class social respectability. While going against mainstream culture was not uncommon to the Apostolic Faith Movement, the clear interracial theology Delk held was very rare among early white Pentecostals.[696]

In 1914, Texas Syndicate's Mission was accomplished; the all-white Assemblies of God was created, completing the vision. Warren Fay Carothers and Howard A. Goss were part of the new Pentecostals![697] Ironically, even though his sanction is on all their founding documents, fundamental truths and early doctrinal positions, Carothers is not even generally remembered in the Assemblies of God (A.G.). However, they retain most of his ideas, policies, and vision—especially regarding minorities and women. The A.G. is the group he helped found after he and his friends committed patricide on Charles Parham. While Carothers, and his Texas Syndicate, projected like he held the moral high ground, it is merely an optical illusion; a hollow victory at best.[698] The Assemblies of God likes to brag they are the biggest Pentecostal group in the world with some 65 million adherents.[699] This is only a small percentage of the hundreds of millions who identify with Charles Parham's message. For what will it profit a man if he gains the whole world, and loses his own soul? Or what will a man give in exchange for his soul?

Charles Fox Parham is the most renowned person in the Apostolic Faith and Pentecostal Movements. He is regarded as the Father of the modern Pentecostal Movement.[700] Every Spirit-filled believer on this planet, nearly 700 million strong,[701] have a connection to Charles and Sarah

Parham. Because of the faith and investment into the life of others by the Parham family, the restoration of genuine Spirit baptism has a global body of believers. On the other hand, Carothers is known as one of the conspirators that stabbed the Parham family without mercy. A horrible xenophobic man whose contribution to the world was hatred of all non-white persons and a chauvinistic expectation of women.[702]

When Carothers' bigoted Brunner church searched for a new pastor, they found one hand-picked by members of the Texas Syndicate. "Brother Richey was one of the most widely known ministers in the Assemblies of God. Ordained to the ministry in 1914 by Elders Arch Collins and E.N. Bell."[703] "The similarities and direct connections between religion and the Klan were anything but imagined. In the 1920s, traveling preachers like Bob Jones, Alma White, B. B. Crimm, Charlie Taylor, and Raymond T. Richey lauded the white supremacist groups in their sermons and publications." "Fittingly, in 1923 a Klan-supporting editor in Texas rhapsodized: "I find the preachers of the Protestant faith almost solid for the Klan and its ideals, with here and there an isolated minister ...who will line up with the Catholics in their fight on Protestantism, but that kind of preacher is persona non grata in most every congregation in Texas."[704]

Parham Will Not Die

The plot by the Texas Syndicate to frame Parham did not go as was planned. They had tried multiple times to get rid of Parham, but he just would not go away. The Texas Syndicate took advantage of the many religious people who felt threatened by the growing popularity of the Parhams. One of those people was Wilbur Voliva. He was a sworn enemy of Charles Parham. Parham wanted no part of Voliva or his schemes and accurately prophesied Voliva's impending demise. Carothers, his Texas

Syndicate, and Voliva were intertwined by their common goal toward the demise of Charles Parham. They fed the media half-truths that helped their hidden cause. The Waukegan Daily Sun led the charge with suggestions that Parham's sudden departure from Zion had been prompted by "mysterious men, said to be detectives, ready to arrest him on some equally mysterious charge."[705] Sounds plausible unless you ask detectives from where? Representing who? Under what authority? The only officials that could connect Zion City and San Antonio would have been Federal. There was never a federal investigation into Parham or the A.F.M. Just rumors to feed the media frenzy.

    The diabolical plan of the Texas Syndicate to present Parham in the same light as shaman Dowie, Sandford, etc., was working. People are gullible, quick to repeat rumors and very slow to admit they are backbiters, slanderers, etc. Carothers fed the same paranoia in Texas while letting Voliva take all the blame. It is evident that Voliva and Carothers contributed to the old political game of "trial by newspaper." The Waukegan paper later admitted that its report was based on rumor and that the Zion police department knew nothing of the incident. However, much damage had been done. Ironically, it seems that the Waukegan Daily may have gotten it right. The scam that was put in play in San Antonio reflects exactly this type of ridiculous scheme. The article broadcasted the method Parham's enemies were going to use to attempt their frame job on him. Obviously, someone close to the scheme tipped off the reporter.

    There was nothing nefarious on Parham's side for leaving Zion City. Despite the trials the Parhams were seeing the fruit of their labor. Tremendous historic outpourings in both Zion City and Los Angeles and smaller outpourings all over the world. For the man of God, the work was endless. With much pressure from Voliva, Sarah Parham and her children left Zion fearing for their lives. Anyone would understand that after checking on progress in Zion, meeting with Ray Davis who ran publications in Zion City and was evidently working in some way with Carothers and the Texas Syndicate, Charles Parham left for another ministry trip to the Northeast. There is absolutely no record to support the rumors that any real detectives were looking for Parham - EVER. What was happening is that Parham was fighting for his life against the leaders of the Texas Syndicate. Yes, Voliva did not like him either, but Voliva never was part of the Apostolic Faith, never on the inside and never infiltrated Parham's team.

1906 had seen incredible growth in the Apostolic Faith Movement. So much growth that nearly hundred years later the Parham's ministry would receive international recognition by Life Magazine as one of the most outstanding events of the Century. The Apostolic Faith was experiencing explosive growth everywhere. Just in Texas the **Apostolic Faith** expanded their efforts to include the following locations: Caledonian Hall (later referred to as the Apostolic Hall), 1010 ½ Texas Avenue; Mission Hall, corner of Hardy and Brooks Streets; Houston Heights under an arbor off Heights Boulevard; Houston Heights on Eighth Street; and at the corner of Seventh and Arlington Streets in Houston Heights. This would put the movement into Houston neighborhoods with an African-American population of thirty percent or more.[706] These were phase one targets in the Texas Syndicate's hostile takeover plan. Historian, **Bishop Gary W. Garrett, PhD**, notes that Parham was focusing on reaching even more black people. His close friend, Lucy Farrow, was helping him. He welcomed the addition of a new student William Joseph Seymour, who had moved to L.A. to participate in the Los Angeles Outpouring.[707]

The Apostolic Faith Newspaper announced the structure. Elders were ordained in every major town where the movement had a presence.[708] Three State Directors were appointed; **W. F. Carothers** - Texas, with State headquarters in Houston, **Rilda Cole** - Kansas, with Baxter Springs as State Headquarters (also home of the World Headquarters) and **Henry G. Tuthill** - Missouri, with State Headquarters in Carthage. **Lillian Thistlethwaite** as General Secretary. Parham retained the role he already had, "Projector of the Faith" making only he and Lilian Thistlethwaite as international officers. Parham was not enthusiastic about organizational titles. He saw them as unnecessary. All evangelists and full-time workers received credentials signed by Parham and their respective State Director. The attempt to organize met much resistance as the movement's leadership, rank and file was generally opposed to organized religion.[709] A west coast branch was soon added. The success of William Seymour and the Apostolic Faith Gospel Mission on Azusa Street brought **Florence Crawford** to serve initially as State Director for California and then for the whole Pacific Coast.[710] By the time Parham returned to Zion in December, he had dissolved all the A.F.M. positions.

The Texas Syndicate's plan to claim they were now the A.F.M. seemed to be going well. Carothers began calling himself the National Director. Kind of like a self-appointed pope. When Charles Parham dismissed Carothers from his State Director position, he just gave himself a new title. Not to worry, Parham appointed fellow conspirator Howard A. Goss. Most of the Texas Syndicate were aligned because they mutually despised people of color. They would explain that it was not that the people of color were totally hated, but the Texas Syndicate had an expectation that those of color and women should stay in their place.

The legitimate leadership role of Warren Fay Carothers was among the shortest in the history of organizations. Appointed by Charles Parham in March of 1906 as State Director, by August 1906, he was out. However, Carothers' mission was accomplished. In his short tenure he had managed to begin to assemble his Texas Syndicate into the hostile takeover of the A.F.M. Further, he would continue for years claiming that he was the National Director of the A.F.M. [711]

The Texas Syndicate initially were Carothers and Goss' fellow Texans; more would come soon. Carothers attempting to use his position to oust founder Charles Parham might have seemed premature. However, it was necessary for the Texas Syndicate. The success of A.F.M. black and women ministers in the Los Angeles Outpouring was a big red flag for the Texas Syndicate. Parham's refusal to consider withholding equal standing to women and black ministers was not acceptable.

Today, Parham's Apostolic Faith Movement still exists. Like Mark Twain, Parham could say, **rumors of my death are greatly exaggerated.**[712] Carothers busied himself trying to stop women and minorities from having ministerial standing with their white peers. He was very successful in keeping blacks, other minorities and women in their place. One of his last official acts is forwarding a letter to Charles Parham that came from William Seymour wondering why his license was being delayed.[713] The answer is that Carothers was just not interested in licensing blacks or women, and they would not have a role in his vision of the new and improved Apostolic Faith Movement which would go by the term Pentecostal. Howard Goss was appointed by Parham to replace Carothers on August 26th, 1906.[714] Carothers was out but Howard Goss would advance the Texas Syndicate's xenophobic agenda.

Much emphasis is placed on the impasse between Seymour and Parham. This is where historians take their eye off the ball. The angry and revengeful Carothers was about to even the score. If he couldn't control

Parham, he would find another way forward. Goss, whom history presents as a hideous racist without honor. He should have just resigned, but he used the appointment to help his pal in the Texas Syndicate plot against Parham. While Parham was aiding the revivals in Zion City and Los Angeles, The Texas Syndicate planned the hostile takeover of the Apostolic Faith Movement. Like Rehoboam of old, very few people noticed that Carothers, Goss, and their Texas Syndicate pals have merely traded gold for brass.[715]

Parham Follows God's Direction

Goss' appointment is important as the post was previously held by Carothers who did not agree with Parham about women ministers or blacks, Mexicans, Japanese, Native-Americans and others receiving ministerial licenses. Unknown to Parham and others was that Goss held similar views. Goss had been converted by Carothers to his way of thinking. Goss was from Kansas, but he liked the Southern way of thinking. Goss is on the record as saying he left his home state of Kansas to adopt the State of Texas. Goss' conversion was his agreement with the Jim Crow laws in the South valued by his friends in the Texas Syndicate. Parham soon realized that Goss was working with Carothers. Goss is also a conspirator. Et tu Brute?[716] With the Texas Syndicate plotting against him, Parham continues to minister leading the Apostolic Faith Encampment in Texas where 54 are baptized.[717]

In spite of the trouble brewing with the Texas Syndicate, Parham obeyed the call of God and departed for Zion City. Parham followed up *perhaps the most amazing outpouring of his ministry in Zion City* by taking a trip to Los Angeles to help his friend William J. Seymour. Seymour was having good success, but was struggling with unwanted fanaticism. In the interim,

Parham sent help to Seymour. "Anna Hall, a young student evangelist who had been greatly used in the ministry at Orchard, Texas requested leave of absence to help Seymour with the growing work in Los Angeles. He agreed and helped raise the travel costs. Parham was at the height of his popularity. Crowds of thousands would show up for his meetings. He was in great demand. The work was growing apace everywhere, not least of all in Los Angeles, to which he sent five more workers. Sensing the growing momentum of the work at the Apostolic Faith Gospel Mission in Los Angeles. Seymour wrote to Parham requesting help. He planned to hire a larger building to give full exposure to Parham's anointed ministry and believed that it would "shake the city once more" with a spiritual 'earthquake.' Seymour also needed help with handling spurious manifestations that were increasing in the meetings. He wrote 'urgent letters appealing for help, as spiritualistic manifestations, hypnotic forces and fleshly contortions... had broken loose in the meetings. He wanted Mr. Parham to come quickly and help him discern between that which was real and that which was false.' Unfortunately, Parham could simply not be everywhere, and he continued his efforts in the midwest, which was the main Centre of his 'Apostolic Faith' movement"[718]

    The Zion Outpouring is more than Parham had likely ever imagined. Those who came to find their Pentecost at Zion would number in the thousands, perhaps tens of thousands. They would forever be grateful that Parham obeyed the call of God to come to their aid. The impact that would come from the Zion Outpouring would benefit the whole world. Whole nations would be evangelized, and thousands of missionaries would be sent. There was great opposition in Zion City and while it frustrated the workers, especially Charles and Sarah Parham, there was a great spiritual harvest. The harvest at Zion would bring people into Charles and Sarah

Parham's lives that would help them through the trial of the horrible personal attacks from those in the deep South who had pretended to be their friends.[719]

While Parham was in California ministering, he received a blackmail threat via telegram from Carothers who was in Zion, Illinois. The telegram was sent by Carothers through Ray Davis who was over publications for Wilbur Voliva. Carothers was no longer a legitimate leader of the A.F.M. His alignment with friends of Wilbur Voliva was not questioned, but Parham knew that Carothers' alignment was trouble for all non-white persons. Sending the telegraph from Zion, Illinois also serves as a strawman for Carothers as Parham would later first accuse Voliva and not the Texas Syndicate. In Zion City, Carothers was on a mission to find dirt on Parham, and no one does dirt better than Wilbur Voliva. Armed by promises from his new friend, Carothers threatens to expose Parham for some crime that only Carothers was aware of. If Parham did not resign as Projector of the Faith, Carothers would expose him for the unnamed crimes. Carothers, who has an exaggerated opinion of himself, thought that he was the first person to be dismissed from their job, who suddenly has dirt on their former boss. Carothers, strutting like a banty rooster, would repeatedly parade his arrogance for the whole world to see, including a notable display of arrogance in the Houston Newspaper. In a horrible display of pride, Carothers brings shame on the entire body of Christ as he calls out Charles Parham. Carothers expected that the man of God was beholding to answer his ridiculous charade.[720] It was all religious theater of course, but religious people are so gullible. Many bought what the racially motivated Carothers was selling.

Parham, who is busy on his ministry trip, dealing with real ministry in Los Angeles telegrammed a response that he would resign as Projector.

Thinking that he has successfully completed his hostile takeover, Carothers projected he was the smartest man on the planet, Parham was not interested in what Carothers was scheming. Parham has already eliminated Carothers and nearly everyone else's position in the A.F.M. Carothers deceitfully told everyone who would listen that Parham resigned because of moral lapses. In the real world, Parham did not resign, and the Texas Syndicate would invest considerable energy the next few years and beyond trying to get him to resign and trying to convince anyone who would listen that he did resign. Of course, the all-white hate group they spawn believes their own press and sets out to promote for their racially oriented cause. There was never a letter of resignation from Charles Parham. It was all a hoax by Carothers. One of many hoaxes orchestrated by the capable Carothers.

Parham, who dismissed Carothers in September of 1906,[721] wrote that he did not need the useless title of Projector. At this point, Parham seemed unaware of the lies Carothers and Goss were propagating or has just resigned to let them run their scam. Like Jesus, he seemed to give them the "whatever you are going to do, do it quickly speech." Parham understood Carothers, Goss, and their friends despised people of color. Blackmail would not change his mind on the question. Parham was right in his assertion. He did not need the Projector title. The role was greatly misunderstood and misinterpreted. In some cases, misunderstood on purpose. In practical application, Charles Parham was the Apostolic Faith Movement. Parham was to the A.F.M. what Billy Graham was to the Billy Graham Association. While the A.F.M. did not bear Parham's name, there was no doubt he was the man of the hour. He did not need a title or the permission of the Texas Syndicate. No scam the Texas Syndicate tried ever changed that fact.

Parham continued with ministry in Los Angeles, then goes to Zion

~ CHAPTER FIFTEEN | APOSTOLIC FAITH COGIC SCHEME ~

City. In Zion City he printed an edition of his periodical, Apostolic Faith. Carothers and his Texas Syndicate told everyone that Charles Parham has resigned. The Texas Syndicate presents a series of half-truths. "The purpose and or consequence of a half-truth is to make something that is really only a belief appear to be knowledge, or a truthful statement to represent the whole truth or possibly lead to a false conclusion... A person deceived by a half-truth considers the proposition to be knowledge and acts accordingly."[722] It is purely fiction that Parham resigned from the A.F.M. Even the newspapers got this part right.[723]

"Parham returned to Zion from Los Angeles in December of 1906, where his 2000-seater tent meetings were well attended and greatly blessed." While Parham was in Zion, he published his Apostolic Faith periodical for the first time in some months; January 1907.[724] This was a very historic newsletter. Parham was putting the world on notice of several things:

He was still leading the Apostolic Faith Movement.[725]
He had not resigned from leading the Apostolic Faith, and remained available to help those who needed his input.
The Apostolic Faith publication was his. The loan to Seymour was over.

The message was received in the crumbling organizational structure of the newly independent Apostolic Faith Gospel Mission in Los Angeles. They would only print a couple more issues of their version of the publication. With Charles Parham's (and William Seymour's) permission, Florence Crawford takes the Apostolic Faith to Portland and prints the Portland version of the Apostolic Faith. This publication is still printed as of this writing.[726]

Florence Crawford was a powerful woman of God in her own right. The Apostolic Faith ministry she established in Portland remains till this day giving appropriate credit to Charles Parham as their founder.[727] Florence Crawford assumed the leadership of a mission church in Portland, Oregon and continued to lead the A.F.M. Pacific Coast. Her Portland Apostolic Faith newsletters had Charles Parham's permission. There was a long-standing relationship between Parham and the Apostolic Faith in Portland.

For Charles Parham, the A.F.M. had become much larger than anyone man or group of men can organize. He had no interest in controlling people. He wanted people to rely on the Holy Spirit for direction. Today, hundreds of millions are the beneficiaries of his far-sighted vision. "On New Year's Eve, he (Parham) preached for two hours on the baptism in the Holy Spirit. The revival created such excitement that several preachers approached Parham to become the pastor of this new church. Parham resisted the very thought, and said it was not a thought that came from God. He believed there were enough churches in the nation already. His entire ministry life had been influenced by his convictions that church organizations, denominations, and human leadership were violations of the Spirit's desire. Many before him had opted for a leadership position and popularity with the world, but rapidly lost their power. He felt that if his message was from God, then the people would support it without an organization. Parham and a handful of followers hit the road again, this time on a three-month evangelistic tour in Canada, New England and back down to Kansas and Missouri."[728] Parham completed his tasks in Zion City and returned home to Baxter Springs, Kansas to the Apostolic Faith Headquarters.

Taking his lead from the Scriptural Demas,[729] Carothers decided to pretend that his being removed from office in July of 1906 was a promotion and named himself National Director of the Apostolic Faith.[730]

~ CHAPTER FIFTEEN | APOSTOLIC FAITH COGIC SCHEME ~

It is a title he dishonestly held and promoted to anyone who was interested as long as it advanced his mission. He illegally represented himself as such in newspaper interviews, meetings with ministers, and much more. The slick lawyer from Houston was in his element. The Texas Syndicate scheme worked for a few months until Charles Parham returned to A.F.M. Headquarters. Knowing that Parham was going to return and upend the apple cart that the Texas Syndicate had hi-jacked, Carothers continued plotting. Finally, like rats with nowhere to run, Carothers and Goss both made a public show of resigning from the Apostolic Faith Movement to concentrate full time on their commitment to the Texas Syndicate. "In the summer of 1907, Goss and Carothers resigned under pressure from those who accused them of attempting to take leadership of the movement."[731] Carothers' office was dissolved more than a year before. Anyone doubting how far he would go to retain power and position should take serious notice. Goss later admitted his role had been dissolved by Parham in 1906.[732]

At the Texas Syndicate sponsored 1907 summer camp meeting, A.G. Canada was appointed field director of the split from the A.F.M. led by Carothers."[733] The Texas Syndicate was not finished. It is obvious that they ignored the legitimate leaders of the Apostolic Faith Movement. Mark Twain famously said, "A half-truth is the most cowardly of lies."[734]

About 1912, Howard Goss and fellow Texas Syndicate comrade changed the name of their deceptive *Apostolic Faith* newsletter to the Word and Witness.[735] This publication was printed during the years when Goss and his Texas Syndicate friends were supposedly involved in their new alliance with Bishop Charles Mason as the all-white Church of God in Christ Apostolic Faith. Outlandishly missing from their publication was any reference to Bishop Charles Mason. There was no mention of any of the churches associated with the C.O.G.I.C.. There was no offer to join a fellowship or organization called Church of God in Christ Apostolic Faith. There was just promotion of a meeting or two and most of those were connected to the legitimate A.F.M. in some form or fashion.[736] There was one mention of a Camp Meeting posthumously. This was billed as the Church of God in Christ of the Apostolic Faith.[737] Allegedly some 300 people made this national event held by Howard Goss, E. N. Bell, Mack Pinson, and others. No persons of color were invited. The claim that this group was a unity effort presents as damage control by Howard Goss and friendst-that his group would be so brazen to pirate the name of Mason's group to advance their cause was just too much for some. So, the ruse that they were collaborating with Mason was palatable to their audience, in what would be a constant theme for Goss and Carothers for the next couple of decades. The publication proclaimed their group was a great move of unity. Evidently, they did not understand what the word unity meant. In one edition, there was propaganda promoting what they were doing (whatever that was) as a "reform movement."[738] Evidently, "reform movement" was the Texas Syndicate code for all-white radically xenophobic hate group. Bell wrote that their reform movement was, "not a church, the church nor the churches; it is a mistake we ought to get out to call a Bible congregation of believers set in divine order by any sort of nickname. 'Apostolic church' is as sectarian in name as 'Baptist church' or 'Methodist church' or 'Presbyterian church.' None of these names are found in the Bible."[739] "Bell proposed to call them 'Churches of God' and 'Churches of God in Christ'… Why add to God's name 'Holiness church,' or Pentecostal church? All should be both."[740] In the end, they did exactly what they railed against in creating a new demonstration named the Assemblies of God, and calling their churches both Assemblies of God and Pentecostal.

CHAPTER SIXTEEN

THE RULE OF TEXAS[741]

"Nearly all men can stand adversity, but if you want to test a man's character, give him power."

-Abraham Lincoln

A case can be made that Power is the greatest pleasure on this Earth. All other drugs and addictive substances do their job by providing the user an illusion of power. So, it's easy to guess the sway it has over the human mind. It's just a feature of the human condition. We are creatures who crave power above all else. Once we get a taste of it, we are unable to give it up and lust for more and more. "A study found that power doesn't corrupt; it heightens pre-existing ethical tendencies. Which recalls a maxim, from Abraham Lincoln: "Nearly all men can stand adversity, but if you want to test a man's character, give him power."[742]

We may never satisfy those who brought spurious allegations against the Parham family. One hundred years from now, we will be right where we are today. Some will be certain that Charles Parham is a fallen hypocrite based purely on their opinion. Others will be firmly entrenched holding that Parham was a Prophet or Apostle that could do no harm based on similar stuff. The truth is somewhere in between. Even the Apostles: Peter, James, John, Paul, etc., were not perfect. They had flaws and faults. They also had enemies. The enemies of Charles Parham have written an nauseum about his alleged errors or faults. All of it speculation based on no facts. Superficial men revel in repeating unfounded rumors. Satan is the accuser of the brethren.[743] Those who ply these rumors have arrived at volumes of outrageous conclusions. It is like taking a hubcap and building a car.

Whatever the reasons or accusations, the result is fairly simple. In 1906 the A.F.M. jettisoned from their ranks, those who sought to develop an all-white organization by dissolving their positions. This was perfectly Charles Parham's right as the leader of the Movement. Those who were dismissed were free to run their own ministries based on racial hatred if that was what they chose. The trouble began when the disgruntled made personal attacks, stole intellectual property, and more from their former compatriots. While this may not be unusual, it is very un-scriptural. Jesus said, **"whoever hates his brother is a murderer, and you know that no murderer has eternal life abiding in him."**

"From a theological-ethical perspective, racism is a moral and spiritual problem. It is idolatrous worship of the self, rooted in spiritual pride. Racism is self-deification in its purest form. Unthankful arrogance and self-glorification constitute the essential notion of sin. It is self-religion. It is a decisive act of turning away from God. It is life according to the flesh (Romans 8:5). It is the worship of the creature rather than the

CHAPTER SIXTEEN | THE RULE IN TEXAS

Creator."⁷⁴⁴ The men that left the A.F.M. formed a consortium to advance their cause. Instead of leaving in peace, they sought a path of mutually assured destruction. Blinded by pride, they invested much of the rest of their lives to promoting falsehoods and disinformation agreed upon with their fellow conspirators in the Texas Syndicate. These dishonorable men caused considerable havoc for the entire A.F.M. Their obvious hatred for Charles and Sarah Parham's family was disturbing. Rather than simply walk away and continue their ministry elsewhere, they sought to exact a pound of flesh from Charles Parham. The price would be much too steep for everyone involved. Warren Carothers was disgruntled with Parham's leadership. Whether he should have been really doesn't matter. He was angry, but his response was ungodly. There was simply no excuse for such activity—and no room in the Body of Jesus Christ for this kind of malice.⁷⁴⁵

    Carothers envisioned a denomination growing out of the Apostolic Faith Movement. He dreamed of the A.F.M. merging or taking over the flailing Zion City. Carothers was not pleased with leadership appointments or developments in the A.F.M. He saw Charles Parham as a weak leader who allowed women, blacks, Mexicans and others to lead the A.F.M. Carothers expects that the A.F.M. would not retain global respect without a strong core leadership of qualified white males. He was totally against women and minorities serving in leadership roles. He wanted them in what he considered was their place. In their place means whatever Carothers wanted it to mean, but primarily it meant socially beneath Carothers.⁷⁴⁶ Carothers envied Charles Parham for allowing minorities and women liberties that were not societally accepted in the South in general, Texas in particular.⁷⁴⁷ Thus, the initial objective of the Texas Syndicate was to create their own religious empire at the expense of the Parham family. The entirety of their success was based on finding others with mutual animosity toward the Parhams, A.F.M., blacks, Mexicans, Jews, Catholics, etc.

Charles and Sarah Parham began the A.F.M. as a group for all people. They saw no need to stop that inclusion once the A.F.M. had hundreds of thousands of followers and adherents. They did not feel differently about people of color or women as ministers than they had at their inception. Of great interest, not one of their contemporaries who were women or persons of color ever brought a charge against them personally (or their ministry) regarding prejudice. When we say their enemies were white people, predominately white males, the evidence is solid.

Carothers' first response after being removed from A.F.M. leadership was to make Brunner Tabernacle an independent work.[748] Even the writer who wrote the story for the Houston Post remarked the move was "interesting."[749] Obviously, this was a direct shot at Parham's leadership. Historians often present this event as happening before Carothers was dismissed. If so, then Carothers removed Brunner Tabernacle as a preemptive strike against Charles Parham because Parham rejected Carothers' plan for an all-white male led organization. Either way, the rationale is pathological. Carothers, ever the smooth politician, proclaims that this is because of the growing maturity of the work. Brunner then becomes the center for "the main opposition to the leader (Parham)."[750] This church, by choice, was no longer part of the A.F.M. To pretend they held legitimate sway over the leadership of the A.F.M. is fraud. "It was in Brunner that the action which resulted in the publication of charges against him (Parham) originated, and all along Brunner has been regarded as the stronghold of the opposition by Parham and his adherents. Parham has roundly denounced those he claims are "hounding" him. He called them by such terms as "the rule in Texas" and the "system."[751]

The Texas Syndicate continued their charade in March of 1907.

~ CHAPTER SIXTEEN | THE RULE IN TEXAS ~

Carothers, out of the A.F.M. leadership, contributed to a newspaper article that among other things claimed that he was the "National Director (of the Apostolic Faith) and has just arrived at headquarters from Joplin, Mo."[752] Knowing that "the origin of the doctrine of initial evidence in North American Pentecostalism has almost exclusively been traced back to Charles Parham, founder of the Apostolic Faith Movement in Topeka, Kansas."[753] In 1908, Carothers began printing his own version of the Apostolic Faith, pointing A.F.M. adherents to himself at his new throne in Texas.[754] The implication in news articles and other propaganda was that Carothers had just come from headquarters in Missouri near where the public and A.F.M. ministers would expect he had met with Parham.[755] The real deal is that Carothers was not the National Director, likely never was the National Director of anything except his Texas Syndicate. It was a position that he created. No wonder Parham referred to the Texas Syndicate as "the rule in Texas."

The Texas Syndicate needed a manifesto, a Creed to explain to their white constituents what they were about. To meet the demand, Warren Fay Carothers penned the Texas Syndicate's Manifesto. It became the cornerstone of their effort. White extremists were attracted to these new Pentecostals who offered speaking in tongues to those who harbored racial hatred. Carothers' Manifesto would be their guiding principle in organizing the Assemblies of God in 1914. As of this writing, it has never been renounced. A few years later, the Ku Klux Klan (KKK) developed a similar Creed of their own.[756] These self-proclaimed Pentecostals gave this to the world. The Texas Syndicate plotted to steal as much as possible from Parham. Small wonder that Parham referred to these new Pentecostals **"as a bunch of imitating, chattering, wind-sucking, holy-roller preachers."**[757]

Like a carny or ringmaster, Howard A. Goss concocted the idea

~ 243 ~

to start referring to their scheme as "Pentecostal" to separate themselves from the A.F.M.[758] This was at least in part due to pressure from Parham, Seymour, Crawford, and others were adamant that the new Pentecostals should not refer to themselves as *Apostolic*. Previously, Pentecostal was a term used to describe the A.F.M.'s affinity toward the baptism of the Holy Ghost, but Goss wanted to separate from the Apostles doctrine and be identified merely by glossolalia.[759] At the time, many groups were using Pentecostal as an identifier.[760] As the *new* Pentecostals grew in number, most of the others using the identifier dropped the word from their titles. They wanted to be separated from the extremism that became associated with Pentecostals. For example, Carothers' fellow xenophobic Independent Holiness leader Alma White changed the name of her *Methodist Pentecostal Union Church*.[761] Most, if not all, of the groups that would be identified as Pentecostal were led by white supremacists so change was pertinent.[762] These extremists would implement many justifications as rationale to separate from people of color.[763]

In the 1890's Charles and Sarah Parham began calling their movement *Apostolic Faith* in reference to the desire to follow the teaching of the Apostles of Jesus Christ.[764] Charles Parham projected the Apostolic Faith as a Revolution.[765] **Apostolic** was a word credited to being coined by John Wycliffe who translated the Bible to English. He said, "I will do only those things that are Apostolic (meaning like the Apostles) and nothing that the Papacy dictates."[766] Apostolic was a favored word of Reformers like William Tyndale who said, "I defy the Pope and all his laws. If God spare my life, ere many years I will cause a boy that drives the plough to know more of the Scripture, than he does."[767] It was not without a price. These Reformers were branded heretics by the religious establishment and often tortured or put to death.[768] After the Topeka Outpouring, some referred to

CHAPTER SIXTEEN | THE RULE IN TEXAS

the A.F.M. as Pentecostal because of the interest in one experiencing their own personal Pentecost.[769] Pentecostal is a term referring to the similarities to the New Testament Church experience of Holy Ghost baptism that occurred on the feast day called Pentecost.[770] Parham and the A.F.M. could have simply basked in the recognition, but the experience of speaking in tongues was only part of what Charles and Sarah Parham expected when they invoked the word Apostolic.[771]

The masses were quite pleased to speak in tongues, but most were not interested in a Revolution. As William Durham began to teach his version of "Finished Work," Parham began to refer more to the Apostolic Faith as Full Gospel to give emphasis to the fact that there was more than just glossolalia.[772] Parham explained "God has thousands of perfect-love, full-gospel men and women with a non-sectarian spirit, who love every child of God, who have not bowed the knee to Baal, and who believe the full gospel wrought with signs and wonders, divers miracles and gifts of the Holy Ghost, who will never accept self-exalted man's leadership." Parham wrote this in early 1900. So, it was not a new thought; it was a well-understood part of his theology.[773] Parham emphasized the same at the Camp Meeting in Baxter Springs, Kansas in 1905 as "Of the Apostolic Faith, Holiness and Full Gospel Movement."[774]

The Texas Syndicate's adoption of the Pentecostal identifier was fitting for a white nationalist group and aligned them with other white supremacists who also used the identifier. The only difference was most of the other religious white hate groups did not adhere to speaking in other tongues. Think about it! The KKK offered nothing as amazing as speaking in tongues! With the new Pentecostals, one could promote racially oriented hate and speak in tongues. Bigotry was not required, but it was certainly encouraged.

"A thorough examination of Parham's theology of Spirit Baptism shows that Parham's understanding of the experience was adopted by later generations of Pentecostals only in word. Thus, Parham's contribution to Pentecostalism should be understood to reside at the level of hermeneutics, not doctrine."[775] The Texas Syndicate system was a good scheme; it worked amazingly, attracting vain and base people who shared a mutual vision of the superiority of the white race. People were happy to follow for a few loaves and fishes. Many did not stop to question the legitimacy of the Texas Syndicates version of Apostolic Faith. The Texas Syndicate said Parham resigned, was forced out, divorced his wife, was in prison, and was backslidden.[776] Sarah Parham was at a meeting and a lady told her that Charles Parham had left his wife and children. She did not realize she was talking to Sarah Parham.

Whatever people wanted to hear or would believe, the Texas Syndicate offered. Those who opposed the Texas Syndicate usually regretted their opposition. For Howard Goss, it seemed that he never believed many of the A.F.M. tenets anyway. Howard Goss is on the record as saying that he did not believe that speaking in tongues was essential for salvation.[777] Goss, like many others, initially followed Charles Parham but liked the Carothers way of doing things so much better. The Carothers family, like many families in the South, lost their slaves at the culmination of the American Civil War.[778] However, some things never die. The attitude of men like Warren Carothers, Howard A. Goss, Opperman, Flowers, and their friends that formed the Texas Syndicate had forever altered history. Here is the Manifesto Warren Fay Carothers wrote for the Texas Syndicate:

~ CHAPTER SIXTEEN | THE RULE IN TEXAS ~
The Texas Syndicate Manifesto

Attitude of Pentecostal Whites to the Colored Brethren in the South[779] "God that made the world, hath made of one blood all nations of men for to dwell on all the face of the earth and hath determined the times before appointed, and the bounds of their habitation. (Acts 17: -5-6)."[780] "Nor would there ever be any "race question" If men would but observe the divine arrangement and live, each nation in his own country, even as each family should live in its own separate home. There is no race question between the white people of the South and the Mexicans-or the Japanese; they are free to dine at our tables, ride in our coaches, attend our schools, churches, etc. "When the divine arrangement Is obeyed, then there may be visitors from one nation to another without any friction. In the case of the Negroes or the South, the white man. for selfish purposes, imported practically a whole nation of them into the same country with himself – broke down God's geographical barriers and in the case of the Japanese on the coast – they have done likewise.

Not only has friction arose, just as it does when families get too "thick" but the Holy Spirit also, in a final effort to preserve the integrity of the races, has intensified the racial impulse. The latter is not prejudice nor any other evil intent whatsoever, but merely the Lord's own substitute for wholesome geographical bounds of separation between the races. A proper separation of the races, looking to the integrity of each, is no more "prejudice" than is a proper separation of the sexes. Both alike are but the dictates of common decency and of a wholesome regard for the decrees of the Almighty. Praise His name. *The reality that there is real prejudice between members of both races who are not saved, and who have not the love of God in their hearts, goes without saying – but there need not be even while observing the most wholesome restraints.*

Let our Northern brethren be assured that the Pentecostal people of the South while conforming cheerfully to the general wholesale regulations made necessary in the South, have not the slightest prejudice nor is there any lack of mutual interest in the work they are doing and in the spiritual welfare. They generally get along better with the Lord than we do.

– W. F. Carothers, Houston, Texas."[781]

"What Carothers wrote was disturbing on many fronts, and a clear indication of what people of color were up against at that time... In his article he argued for racial purity and claimed that it was God's will for the races to be segregated, which was why God gave each nation its own homeland, and that each nation should be content to reside in their own country, even as each family should live in its own separate home ..."[782] In place of the men and women of God for which numerous stories have been written about their faith, their perseverance and willingness to stand for God, no matter what the cost, we have these men, hellbent on not only

accepting the repackaged racial attitudes of society, but these men doubled down and became the persecutors and would be prosecutors of their own brethren. It is beyond the comprehension of this author how men who claimed Christ could operate in such a manner. Woefully, they were not alone. More men joined their unrighteous cause.

"How then could Carothers explain, or justify, what the sons of Japheth had done to the American Indians? ... Why didn't they contentedly stay in Europe, and not come over and commit genocide on the indigenous

~ CHAPTER SIXTEEN | THE RULE IN TEXAS ~

people of the Americas?" (People that Osterholm's The Table of Nations[783] also rank as being of Hamitic descent). Carothers went on to dig himself into an even deeper pit by stating (his realization that Africans in America had not intentionally violated their bounds of habitation by leaving Africa on their own, but due to the white man's selfish motives had been forcibly imported and enslaved into the Americas ... Then to add insult to injury, Carothers went on to assert that it was actually the Holy Spirit who, in a final effort to preserve the integrity of the races, had intensified the racial impulse of segregation, calling it "the Lord's own substitute for wholesome geographical bounds of separation between the races." ... In this particular case I can only gather that Carothers was attempting to attach a "God is on our side" validation to this obvious impulse of segregation in many whites, because Civil Rights history surely denotes an otherwise sentiment of integration in the case of most black Americans - Christians included. Carothers concluded his article by assuring Northern Pentecostals that Southern white Pentecostals, while capitulating to southern racial norms, had no prejudice, or any less love for their Negro Christian siblings, and that they were yet totally interested in their spiritual welfare... Then he said something I can only attribute to be the kind of thing a person says in the clutches of a really guilty conscience, but was something of a truism none-the-less... In reference to his fellow black brothers and sisters he added, "They generally get along better with the Lord than we do."[784]

    In April of 1907, Warren Faye Carothers was no longer an officer of the Apostolic Faith Movement (although feigning he was). Relieved of his A.F.M. duties the previous September (1906) Carothers called a meeting at Brunner Tabernacle. Read that last sentence one more time. Yes, the same Carothers who Parham jettisoned from the Apostolic Faith Movement because of his horrible positions on race and women decided he would continue to make-believe he is in control of the A.F.M. The same Carothers after being relieved of his responsibilities, immediately manifests his spirit by blackmailing Parham. Carothers continued to pretend that he was the National Director, a title he created for himself.[785] His title had become his idol.[786] What is more, people followed his delusions. Brunner Tabernacle was the same that Carothers said was independent of his imprimatur and independent of the A.F.M. just four months earlier.[787] This scheme was obviously in response to Charles Parham removing Carothers from his position in the A.F.M.

This Brunner Tabernacle meeting may be the meeting that Charles Parham referred to as the *secret meeting,*[788] or there may have been more than one meeting. Most assuredly the Texas Syndicate had many secret meetings. Whatever the case, the meeting was suddenly called to discuss conduct charges against the founder of the A.F.M., Charles Fox Parham. How convenient for Mr. Carothers that he suddenly (after being dismissed from the A.F.M.) had embarrassing information about his former boss.

Wow! Imagine that! Like that had never happened before! Charles Parham either was not invited or refused to attend Carothers' meeting. Likely, he just ignored Carothers, Goss, and their racially-oriented diatribe. The answer depended on who was telling the narrative. Parham indicates that the meeting was secret. Carothers, Goss, and their camp of conspirators claimed that Parham refused to attend. Both could be correct. It would be difficult indeed for Charles Parham to attend a meeting he did not know was happening. Even more confusing, Howard Goss claims that Parham was in the meeting and confessed, but the written confessions had been lost and there are no named witnesses. One wild charge was that Parham was tried for masturbation while alone in his room at night![789] It seems Parham may have responded in writing to some inquiry where he responds about

~ CHAPTER SIXTEEN | THE RULE IN TEXAS ~

what might have happened in his sleep at night. The whole thing is a mess. Why would Parham ever agree to such a meeting? Reader, ask yourself, would you attend a meeting of men that hate you so that they can put you on some kind of mock trial? Seriously! This is like a group of former church members holding a trial of their former pastor. The outcome would be so obvious.

As to the Texas Syndicate pirating from the A.F.M.; it happens all the time. I know of ministries that have stolen the name of an organization, their trademarks, their copywrites, their logos, and more. Yet, people follow them. Howard Goss wrote in his journal that Parham was guilty (again no clue as to what) and expressed personal regret at the outcome.[790] We witness this type of thing all the time. Our former pastor was seriously messed up, so we had to find a new church! Howard Goss kept a journal but did not have a clue as to who the witnesses were or what were the charges? Really Howard? Let me say this as fairly as possible: Howard Goss was a man motivated by personal ambition. If he had true loyalty, it only showed when it benefited Howard Goss. I know that I have friends that revere him, and they can continue the adulation. No worries, but the history is accurate. Oppose Howard Goss and he would make up the story as he desired. Do we say that Howard Goss was a liar? No! Let the record show that we are accusing Howard Goss and Warren Carothers and all their Texas Syndicate of Terminological Inexactitude.

Later, Carothers publicly libeled Parham claiming that Carothers' kangaroo court had handed down a verdict of moral misconduct. This would be laughable if it were not so serious.[791] Carothers pretends that his special illegal court has come to a verdict on a topic that a duly elected District Attorney in Texas could not find enough evidence to even bring a charge. Carothers should have been disbarred in Texas. Speaking for the

Texas Syndicate, Carothers attacked not only Parham but also Parham's friends.⁷⁹² Carothers offered in his self-directed delusion that his Texas Syndicate (which he claims has the support of "every one of the men in Texas") that they were *"perfectly willing for the matter to be decided by your friends."* To be clear, Carothers did not say the support of every white man in Texas, but it was understood by his Texas Syndicate as they did not see non-whites as men. Carothers set conditions and terms that all had to meet. Among these: it had to be a trial by a group of twelve members of the Texas Syndicate.⁷⁹³ That man was simply possessed by his personal power trip. He pretended that he wielded more power than the Governor or maybe even God. The legitimate (and original) A.F.M. ignored Carothers. Like Goss, he was not even a footnote in the real story.

Carothers used his appointed post in the A.F.M. like Absalom versus King David.⁷⁹⁴ In May of 1907, as the Apostolic Faith Movement prepared for their annual encampment, the Texas Syndicate decided to have their own shadow meeting. Conspiracies can get very messy. Even though Carothers, Goss, and their friends in the Texas Syndicate were fully aware they were no longer part of the Apostolic Faith, they announced a July meeting at Brunner Tabernacle.⁷⁹⁵ In this announcement, Carothers invokes his former position as Apostolic Faith Field Director to give him credibility.

Charles Parham responded. "Let no one be disquieted by the vile rumors, persecutions and slanders heaped upon us. If any one should feel concerned enough to know the truth a personal letter will be answered gladly we cannot take valuable space in this paper devoted to the present truth, to discuss the work of our enemies."⁷⁹⁶ It seemed more than a fair response for anyone to offer.

The Texas Syndicate did not see non-whites as people; this is rooted in legal decisions, not in morality or Christian brotherhood. **"In March of 1857,** the United States Supreme Court, led by Chief Justice Roger B. Taney, declared that all blacks — slaves as well as free — were not and could never become citizens of the United States."[797] The U.S. Supreme Court ruled that **Black people "are not included, and were not intended to be included,** under the word 'citizens' in the Constitution," and so were not afforded the rights and privileges that it granted to American citizens. The Texas Syndicate totally agreed.[798] Finally, "The Fourteenth Amendment is an amendment to the United States Constitution that was adopted in 1868. It granted **citizenship and equal civil and legal rights to African-Americans and enslaved people** who had been emancipated after the American Civil War."[799] The Texas Syndicate did not agree with this decision that infringed upon Southerner's right to treat non-whites as less than citizens or as second-class citizens. As we have already seen, legitimate courts have little bearing on the Texas Syndicate or their allies. These prefer their own shadow government and fugazi trials.

The System

Carothers, Goss, and their Texas Syndicate friends set out to get a confession from Charles Parham. Confessions are generally foreign to protestants, but the Texas Syndicate didn't seem to notice. While bragging that he was a Methodist, Carothers invoked his own version of the confessional like "Pope Pius X, who was an anti-intellectual, robust restorer of Christ who demanded near military discipline and deference to superiors from priests and penitents alike."[800] Like Carothers' friend, Wilbur Voliva, Pope Pius X, "banned newspapers and radio in seminaries, restricted access to secular education for seminarians and cut out community engagement."[801] With Carothers and Goss leading the way, the Texas Syndicate and the new

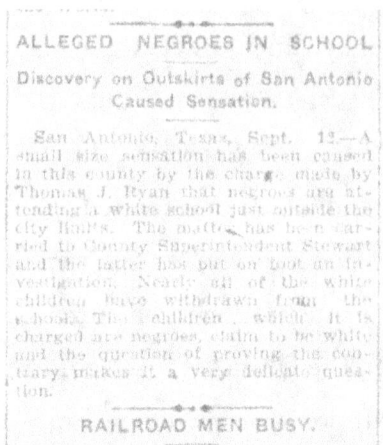

Pentecostals set up their plan for the first Pentecostal confession.

The Texas Syndicate claimed they had witnesses (in person and written) but they produced nothing. Evidently, they didn't know the qualifications for a witness.[802] Like the Golden Tablets[803] of Joseph Smith, they claimed they had them but when pressed to present the evidence, it was manifest that they had nothing. More than one hundred years later, the world is still waiting for the Mormons to produce the Golden Tablets,[804] and we are still waiting for the supposed evidence of Charles Parham's guilt and confession. The conspirators could not even agree who was in the room when they conducted their kangaroo court. The chairman of their tribunal and the leaders did not agree on who was present. The clock was ticking! Yet, zealots need no evidence. The Texas Syndicate pronounced Charles Parham guilty of conduct unbecoming a minister. The real deal is this was a meaningless charge plagued by a plethora of misdirected concepts. First, of necessity, there would need to be a legitimate measure in some bylaw or similar that outlined the procedure for censuring a minister. There was no such mechanism in the A.F.M. This was one of the things that Howard Goss explained the new Pentecostals would remedy. Yet, the long and horrid history of the new Pentecostals creations makes it painfully obvious they failed to bring remedy. Second, if a minister were to be legitimately processed on such a charge there would need to be procedures, opportunity to question witnesses, and ultimately an appeal process should the accused feel unfairly maligned. None of these things were appealing to the Texas

~ CHAPTER SIXTEEN | THE RULE IN TEXAS ~

Syndicate. They preferred the "lynch him now and try him later method!"

In May 1907, Parham sent a letter to his Apostolic Faith workers. The letter read in part:

"To the Workers and Missions,

Needville, Texas. May 18 (1907)[805] – Greetings in Jesus' name. All of the opposing forces in the "rule" in the Texas work are fast melting away and there is great need of getting the workers and all of the people who are interested together that order may again be restored. Also, that the workers again be brought into unity and in a condition where they can go forward in the work for God and the "all rule system"[806], and all of the hindering forces be broken, and that all can come into perfect harmony. We have decided to hold a convention, of a meeting where we may all come together at Katy, Texas, beginning May 23 and to continue to June 12.

The object of the convention is to prepare the workers for battle, and to free them from all bondage and send them forth to the battle so that we may move as one solid phalanx against some wicked city en masse for a grand campaign and too that we may prepare for a great State Convention for all the workers and Missions over the State, to be held in Houston at a later date.

The work in Houston is assuming shape nicely, and one by one the missions are seeing the folly of the course being taken[807] and nearly all of them have sent urgent requests that we come as soon as possible and hold meetings; later. They have united and ask that we hold the grand mass meetings in the center of the city, and with these prospects in view we believe the better plan will be to hold instead, a grand State Convention for the entire State. To this end the Katy convention is being brought out, and for the good as per above. To the Katy convention none of the workers are asked to give up important meetings nor are any of the Missions asked to send delegates, but all who can possibly arrange to be present can ill afford to miss the work to be done., and the help to be gained in this meeting. As to the entertainment at Katy, owing to the small size of the town of Katy and the Apostolic way of entertainment, we are asking that all who attend bring bedding, food, supplies, etc. etc.

All persons who can not attend and wish to aid, their children or others are at liberty to contribute anything in the way of food, bedding and supplies and can send these or means to me at Katy, Texas.

I am thanking the Lord for the wonderful work that has been done in the South, and for the victory that has been given since the first time we entered the State and trusting that He will bless the work with even greater power than ever before. Urging all of the people who can to be in the convention. I am, your humble servant, Chas F. Parham[808]

The year before, on November 25, 1906, Carothers blackmailed Parham via telegraph while Parham was ministering in Los Angeles. Carothers was a corrupt lawyer in Texas and Parham was not the first person to be railroaded by a smooth attorney. Carothers telegraphed Parham from Chicago to where he was staying in Los Angeles. In part, Carothers made reference to an accusation against Parham from a person in League City, Texas only identified by the initials, S. N. H. Carothers offered that he would expose Parham to a litany of "cases known only to me."[809] Carothers gave Parham the ultimatum to "retire to the ministry of prayer." Carothers explained that this would "wipe out the stain." This was a reference to whatever sins he was using to blackmail Parham. Carothers offers that Parham's failure to comply would end the vision of uniting the Zion Movement with the Apostolic Faith Movement.[810] Carothers was obviously in Chicago wheeling and dealing with Wilbur Voliva, associates, and former associates. It should be noted that the vision of taking over Zion City was Carothers' dream. Parham did not have interest in acquiring Zion City and comments that Carothers became obsessed with the idea of leading Zion City.

On November 27, 1906, Parham responded via Telegraph to Mr. Ray Davis, Zion City, Illinois. Where obviously Carothers is staying. "Owing to the fact that my position projector of the Apostolic Faith

~ CHAPTER SIXTEEN | THE RULE IN TEXAS ~

movement is misunderstood, many rumors afloat. I resign from such office, to devote myself to private ministry and prayer. Letter of explanation follows. Chas. F. Parham."[811] Parham said his decision to not continue as the Projector of the Faith was predicated on the fact that the A.F.M. had matured to the point where he was not needed to hold an office, leaving him as just one of the brethren. It is interesting that Carothers uses similar language in removing Brunner Tabernacle from the A.F.M.

In December, Parham concluded meetings in Los Angeles and returned to Zion City where a huge revival was still happening. Here he publishes an issue of his Apostolic Faith Newsletter. In the Apostolic Faith he says, "In resigning my position as Projector of the Apostolic Faith Movement, I simply followed a well-considered plan of mine, made years ago, never to receive honor of men, or to establish a new Church. I was called a pope, a Dowie, etc., and everywhere looked upon as a leader or a would-be leader and proselyte. These designations have always been an abomination to me and since God has given almost universal light to the world on Pentecost there is no further need of my holding the official leadership of the Apostolic Faith Movement. Now that they are generally accepted, I simply take my place among my brethren to push this gospel of the Kingdom as a witness to all nations. I shall still remain the same to my brethren in assistance, advice, and in donating to them my extra cash, as when I bore the meaningless title of 'Projector.'"[812]

Like a Mafioso family, Carothers, Goss, Hall, and their other racially motivated friends began the quest to control the A.F.M. Carothers was a man motivated by title and position. He had expected that his removal of Parham's title had ended the matter in his favor. Carothers put his hostile takeover in full swing. There was no qualified reason for Parham to leave the A.F.M.; that was the challenge. Further, short of his written resignation from anything related to the A.F.M., there was no mechanism to remove Charles or Sarah Parham from the A.F.M. They were the founders; It was not a church, but rather a movement. It would be like telling Elvis fans that he was no longer The King.

The honorable thing for Carothers and his friends to do would be to follow their independent path. However, there is no honor among thieves.[813] In March 1907, Carothers having had his position dissolved the previous year by Parham, decided he and his Texas Syndicate friend would start their own all-white group and steal the name *Apostolic Faith*. Carothers makes himself the National Director of his new group. His fugazi movement uses the Apostolic Faith name like a borrowed mule. This regime was not legitimate. Carothers understood he was more like Rex – king of Mardi Gras. Carothers continued to advertise his regime by appointing his Texas Syndicate friends to positions. He promoted W. D. Caywood of Houston as Texas State Director. Not sure why he did not make his co-conspirator Goss the State Director, but there were other appointments. A. J. Benson tooks up work among the Jews and Mrs. M. D. Fields was appointed editor of the Apostolic Faith. Carl Otto becomes Houston City Director.[814] Sounds good. Only proble was that Carothers was a King without a throne. It is interesting that they appointed someone to do the work that Charles Parham was doing with Jewish people.

Carothers decided he would make good on his threats against Parham. Allegedly, his friends have witnesses and written testimony. Wilbur Voliva brags repeatedly of having dirt on a wide range of people and produces several publications the content of which rivals the National Enquirer. In the dark of night, the plot was hatched. Carothers would expose Parham as he originally threatened, to a litany of "cases known only to me." Carothers made it clear he was taking this action in hopes of

~ CHAPTER SIXTEEN | THE RULE IN TEXAS ~

preserving the prospect of "the Zion Movement uniting with the Apostolic Faith Movement." This information was from the wire sent by Ray Davis at Zion City. Ray Davis was appointed by the receiver over Zion City to be the editor of a newspaper." Davis would be directly connected to any story that was published in Zion publications, especially those discrediting Parham.[815] Taking over Zion City was a goal that only former A.F.M. members Carothers and his Texas Syndicate hold. Charles Parham and the legitimate A.F.M. were simply not interested in what The Texas Syndicate was selling.

Carothers, a Texas lawyer with an exaggerated sense of self-importance, appoints Mr. J Charles Dowling to chair an investigative committee. J. Charles Dowling chaired a group that includes **J. M. Gates, John C. Leissier, D. A. Horn, Lars Nelson, W. C. Lyons, Alex Pecote, F Aucott, H A Goss, W A McMillon, T W Reves, and M.E. Layne.** The last one, M. D. Layne, is a benefactor of Carothers. The Layne family is wealthy and donated the land for Brunner Tabernacle.[816] Dowling, enamored with his newfound license comments *"We bear no malice toward Brother Parham. It is simply to protect this movement."*[817] Strangely, none of these men or Mr. Dowling were part of the A.F.M. Where they acquired their self-directed vision of being the protectors of the faith is apparently from Carothers. These men are all Independent Brunner Church that left the A.F.M. the previous year. Evidently, their hostile takeover was not as well planned as they presented. Carothers was going to take a no holds barred approach. Carothers decided to embark on a kangaroo court. Parham refuses to attend the circus held at Brunner Tabernacle. Some, including Howard Goss, would claim that Parham confessed. "Mr. J Charles Dowling presided as trial judge at the committee meeting which found Parham guilty of "conduct unbecoming a minister," but Parham was not even in attendance! Howard Goss said Parham was there. Yet, the Chairman, Mr. J. Charles Dowling said that Parham did not attend.[818]

Seems everyone was coached and represented by attorneys in the kangaroo court, except Parham. Dowling after being coached by Carothers claimed that "there was no hearsay evidence allowed." These men apparently thought they had some authority. Granted by whom and to do what would never be known. Mr. J. Charles Dowling admitted that Parham (recognizing these men were Carothers' pawns and held no real authority) absolutely refused to come before the committee. What that meant was that Parham did not respond to King Carothers' summons. Parham would answer none of the bogus charges, saying that he didn't propose to be tried by anybody. Dowling said, "in addition to the firsthand testimony we had letters in which the accused clearly admitted the charges."[819] Perhaps one of those letters was what they gave to Justice Ben S. Fisk in San Antonio, Texas. "There was no question in our minds, and when he absolutely refused to offer any defense or appear before the committee at all, we could not do other than what we did."[820] Parham was guilty "in their minds" before they ever held their bogus trial. Apparently, it escaped Mr. Dowling that Parham's refusal to defend his innocence placed him in very good company. The verdict was that Parham was guilty of doing something in his sleep. Thus, it was conduct unbecoming. This came from their credible witness who was allegedly a hotel maid. Parham was quoted

> **APOSTOLIC FAITH**
>
> **DIRECTOR CAROTHERS ARRIVES FROM HEADQUARTERS.**
>
> W. D. Caywood of Houston Becomes State Director—Benson Takes Up Work Among the Jews.
>
> Rev. W. F. Carothers, National director of the Apostolic Faith movement, arrived at headquarters from Joplin, Mo., yesterday after a several week's stay out of the city. Since he was here last he has conducted a Bible training school in Waco and taken part in a workers' convention in Missouri.
>
> The work of the movement, says Director Carothers, is in splendid condition, and it has never faced a brighter day. "The Texas work is fine," he continued. "The convention which we have just closed in Waco was one of the most enthusiastic I ever attended. We had about fifty student workers in attendance and they are now out in the field. The faith has taken a firm hold in Waco and I will go Monday morning to press the city campaign there."
>
> At Joplin, Mo., Mr. Carothers assisted in the ordination of twenty-one envagelist workers.
>
> Announcement is made of the following recent changes in the Texas work: W. D. Caywood of Houston becomes State director, vice A. J. Benson, who takes up the work among the Jews. Mrs. M. D. Fields becomes editor of the Apostolic Faith, the organ of the movement. Otto Carl becomes Houston city director.
>
> Plans are being formulated for the State encampment to be held in July. There will probably be some announcement relating to the encampment at a general rally to be held in the Brunner tabernacle Sunday.
>
> "There are now some half a dozen visitors in the city," said Mr. Carothers yesterday, "who have come from distant places to investigate the movement at 'headquarters.' They have been coming and investigating for some time, and all go away convinced that the movement is of God."

~ CHAPTER SIXTEEN | THE RULE IN TEXAS ~

as responding (after the fraudulent trial), "What I might have done in my sleep I cannot say but was never intended on my part...I am not guilty of an intentional crime."[821] Now, this is most interesting as this is related to the Texas Syndicate's kangaroo court in April 1907, but the newspapers report it months later verbatim. They had obviously not interviewed Charles Parham. So, this information was supplied to the reporter by someone in the Texas Syndicate. Someone who participated in the fugazi trial orchestrated by Carothers. How convenient! This information was obviously part of the alleged written testimony and witnesses from Carothers' kangaroo court.

Apostle Paul quired the Galatian Church, **Are you so foolish? Having begun in the Spirit, are you now being made perfect by the flesh?**[822] Like the Galatian Church, the church in the United States was born in the Spirit. However, like Apostle Paul suffered, **"because of false brethren secretly brought in (who came in by stealth to spy out our liberty which we have in Christ Jesus, that they might bring us into bondage). To whom we did not yield submission even for an hour, that the truth of the gospel might continue with you.**[823] *It may seem bizarre that someone would make such a personal inspection, someone was so interested in bringing accusation against Apostle Paul and Timothy that they spied out their private areas to know whether they were circumcised. ... And this occurred because of false brethren secretly brought in (who came in by stealth to spy out our liberty which we have in Christ Jesus, that they might bring us into bondage) ...*[824] *Stunning!*

When these tactics failed to stop Parham, the Texas Syndicate resorted to a more sinister approach. The San Antonio Connection via the Callahan Machine.

CHAPTER SEVENTEEN

THE SYSTEM

"But those that seek my soul, to destroy it, shall go into the lower parts of the earth. They shall fall by the sword: they shall be a portion for foxes. But the king shall rejoice in God; everyone that sweareth by him shall glory: but the mouth of them that speak lies shall be stopped."

-Psalms 63:9-11

Charles Parham made it very clear in his February 7, 1915, letter to the Apostolic Faith ministers that those who conspired against him "double crossed" him. They obviously made some pretense that they were helping Parham in the Apostolic Faith Movement, but sold him out like Judas sold out Jesus. They thought they made Parham an offer he could not refuse. Parham said they wanted him to join them when they started their group. These are indications that show those who were supposedly cooperating within the Apostolic Faith Movement actually double-crossed Parham and wanted him to join them in starting their own denomination. Parham mentioned that this group of men had pedaled their false stories about him all over the country. Their slander had finally arrived in Parhams' hometown, Cheney, Kansas. As a result of the lies, innuendo and rumors had made it all the way to Parhams' hometown appear to be the catalyst for Parham responding in writing to all the A.F.M. ministers about the deceptions.

Who were these men who Parham referred to as the new Holy Rollers? There was only one group of men who fill the bill, and they were those who conspired against him in Houston, Texas. They orchestrated an elaborate scheme to have him detained under false charges in San Antonio. They pirated what they could away from the Parhams and their Apostolic Faith Movement, later contributing to the starting of the Assemblies of God. In context, it makes sense that a group of white males who were opposed to people of color and women being treated as equals would want to start their own group diverse from Charles Parham's Apostolic Faith Movement that welcomed both people of color and women into the ministry.

As early as 1906, Parham confided in Howard Goss that Carothers was a double crosser.[825] Sadly, Parham trusts Goss, not realizing that Goss is in cahoots with Carothers. David Lee Floyd confirmed Howard Goss as one of the main prosecutors (or persecutors) of Charles Parham.[826] Carothers abused his authority as self-appointed "Field Director" and claimed that Parham resigned rather than what Parham said. Parham projected that the Apostolic Faith Movement was so well established that he did not need to have a big title. Even the media got this part correct.[827] Rather, he would just serve a role that left him promoting the A.F.M. as an equal among his brethren. Carothers was unhappy with this posture. Charles Parham would simply not play ball. He ignored growing concerns by his predominately white male leadership about the direction of the A.F.M.

~ CHAPTER SEVENTEEN | THE SYSTEM ~

Warren Faye Carothers a politically motivated lawyer who wanted the Apostolic Faith Movement to operate more like a denomination. Carothers was a very vocal and a text-book white supremacist.[828] If men like Carothers seem strange to you, please remember that the fathers of these men were a generation that was willing to go to war, and to die, if necessary, to keep blacks enslaved. Howard Goss was impressed by the slick Carothers who pastored an Independent Holiness church. Carothers was an extremely dogmatic xenophobic racist. Carothers, like many of his peers (people like Alma White and Phineas Bresse) was attracted to the independent Holiness movement as a place where racial hatred was permitted and even encouraged.

Carothers initially thought the Parhams were bigoted like him, but the more they advocated for people of color the more he became anxious. Carothers was willing to work with blacks in the Houston area in the effort for them to reach other blacks, even Jews in a similar manner. To appease Charles Parham, he was even willing to allow blacks some leeway to minister in white-oriented meetings. However, he was very opposed to blacks who did not "stay in their place." He was also opposed to Mexicans, Japanese, Jews, Catholics, and anyone else he considered inferior or second-class citizens.[829] As a member of an affluent white family in Texas, he was used to others kowtowing to him because he was white. He also was opposed to women as ministers.[830] Carothers was opposed to Parham's endorsement of William Joseph Seymour and other persons of color being sent to Los Angeles as a representative of the A.F.M.

While surrogates have postulated that the Los Angeles Outpouring, sponsored by the Apostolic Faith Gospel Mission (the Azusa Street Revival), was a black meeting. If this had been true, Carothers and his Texas Syndicate comrades would have not responded so vehemently. Carothers knew the truth. The Apostolic Faith Gospel Mission, where the Azusa Street Revival transpired, was a predominately a white meeting. The challenge for Carothers was that black ministers trained by Charles and Sarah Parham, like William Seymour, Lucy Farrow, Anna E. Hall, and others, were leading this effort. Many of the reports were not good. Parham's report was not good. This was simply not acceptable to a man like Warren F. Carothers. Parham's unwillingness to make changes did not sit well with him. As if to add insult to injury, Parham continued to promote women in the A.F.M. to the highest offices. In 1906, Parham promoted Lilian Thistlethwaite to Secretary General of the Apostolic Faith movement and Florence Crawford to Director of California. These two appointments coupled with the growing number of black ministers the Parhams were training, were the proverbial straw that broke the camel's back for Carothers.

Carothers took serious action. Parham would never attempt to create a denomination. It was the Evangelistic calling in him. He was quite happy to just be named among the brethren. His decision to merely refer to his role as a progenitor[831] of the Apostolic Faith did not sit well with men who were desirous of titles and position. What good is privilege and superiority if there is no one to lord over? It was well known that Carothers opposed people of color. Carothers opposed William Seymour, Lucy Farrow, Anna Hall and others who took a prominent role in the A.F.M. because they were not white. Carothers was happy to preach to the heathen in black churches. However, when Parham invited Lucy Farrow, the black woman whom he had sent to Los Angeles, to preach at the Houston "Apostolic Faith Movement" Camp Meeting, Carothers was less than pleased. In August 1906, as eyewitness Howard A. Goss recounts in his wife's book, The Winds of God, "Fresh from the revival in Los Angeles, Sister Lucy Farrow returned to attend this Camp Meeting. Although a

~ CHAPTER SEVENTEEN | THE SYSTEM ~

Negro, she was received as a messenger from the Lord to us, even in the deep south of Texas." Notice that Goss seemed surprised that a Negro was speaking to white people in Texas from such a lofty position. In December of 1906, Carothers continued to make his withdrawal from the A.F.M. by making his Brunner Tabernacle an Independent church. Carothers proclaimed the "sovereignty of the congregation." Carothers read from Acts 20:17-38, and spoke as though he was giving his farewell address.[832] While Carothers would attempt to throw Parham out of the A.F.M., he had no real authority. The Apostolic Faith Movement legally belonged to the founders Charles and Sarah Parham. So, while Carothers spoke great flatteries with his tongue, he held no place to overturn Charles Parham's decision to dissolve his position from the A.F.M. It didn't appear that anyone minded if he went independent. Parham did not seem affected. In fact, it seemed that Parham was pleased by the growing independence of the Apostolic Faith, but that was demonstratively not enough for Carothers who wanted the pre-eminence. Envy is horrible! Ask Joseph about the envy of his brothers.[833]

Like the secret counsel of the Biblical brothers of Joseph, Howard Goss joined Carothers as did fellow Texan Lemuel C. Hall, as well as at least six others. There were more than that on the committee but apparently only nine total made the meeting of conspirators.[834] At Waco, Texas in 1906, with Charles Parham and other key leaders away in Zion City, these men made their plan. It was a diabolical plan to oust Charles Parham and take over the Apostolic Faith Movement. Among the problems that these men hoped to resolve was the removal of blacks, Mexicans, and women from leadership, stop giving ministerial license to blacks and women, remove all that opposed them, and distance themselves from the same. In the end, they would deal a crushing blow to the Azusa Street Revival's

Apostolic Faith Gospel Mission, and seriously fracture the influence of the Apostolic Faith Movement. By 1914, they had accomplished their goals.

Howard Goss maked mention of such a *"Business Arrangement." "For some years now, we had had no organization beyond a 'gentleman's agreement,' with the understanding for the withdrawal of fellowship from the untrustworthy."*[835] Strange words, almost a confession. Goss continues, "It was becoming increasingly apparent that something would have to be done, if we were to preserve the work. New situations were arising all the time, as our work grew large and more unwieldy. New attitudes were needed. More confession, 'Men among us, in this way, became a secretary,

San Antonio Mayor Bryan Callahan 2nd from Right. Circa 1892.

a treasurer, or a leader, not by 'usurping' the place, as was sometimes suggested, nor by self-appointment, as was sometimes charged. They were chosen because they were capable, and the general public had confidence in them.'"[836]

According to Howard Goss, these men held a private kangaroo court for Charles Parham and found him guilty. Why they bothered with the scheme of holding a mock court is the work of Carothers. Of what exactly was Parham guilty? Carothers and Goss never really said. However, Goss did make a vague claim that there was a "confession, repentance... and the man is living righteous as far as I know."[837] If this was true then why were they still demanding a confession ten years later? What they did was encourage Wilbur Voliva to speak for them. Goss commented, "this growing likeness was easily traced back to the early days of the open West,

~ CHAPTER SEVENTEEN | THE SYSTEM ~

as I remember it, when groups of law-abiding citizens were forced to band together to weed out the bad men and protect the good."[838] So, Goss offered that he and his Holy Roller friends become vigilantes to set things straight as they deemed. Goss speaks of the situation after he, Carothers and their comrades hideously attempted to destroy Charles Parham, his ministry and family. "Many regrettable things began taking place at this time in our Southern work, but things so subtle and elusive as to defy remedying. As our ministers had no written credentials, they casually walked into a church for a meeting whenever they felt the impulse."[839]

Goss admits that their group was "invaded by the cleverest of confidence men, posing as our preachers."[840] This was definitely an accurate description of those who assassinated Charles Parham. Goss said that they were previously known as Apostolic Faith, but (after their coup) decided" to call ourselves Pentecostal."[841] "Pentecostal organizations have, as far as I know, been kept loosely controlled enough to protect both infant and mature saints."[842] History is not on Goss' side as to the quality control measures of groups called Pentecostal, but it is an interesting sleight of hand trick. The Apostolic Faith had been referred to as Pentecostal since the Topeka Outpouring. The real deal here is the all-white Texas Syndicate did not really want to be associated with the Apostolic Faith as they deemed them undesirable. Goss' rhetoric all sounds good until someone starts asking real questions. Anyway, this was Howard Goss' proof text for the need for him to start an organization. Apparently, based on his history, he really needed very little to start an organization as he was part of starting at least four organizations.

It is in this context that Goss told a wild story about a man and made the point of saying the man was "Apostolic." Goss said the man was a horse thief. Very clever slur, but it had nothing to do with the real A.F.M.

It may well represent the Goss and Carothers version of the Apostolic Faith as they presented like horse thieves. Howard Goss proposed that a system where pastors were called to a church by vote will be better than the way *Apostolic Faith* churches operate.[843] He obviously ignored his Texas Syndicate comrade William Durham's attempt to take over the Los Angeles Apostolic Faith Gospel Mission and the long and sordid history of organizational politics. Durham as one of Goss' fellow new Pentecostals showed only contempt for ministers of color. The bottom line is they divided up the Parham's ministry like the garments of Jesus. Goss took the evangelistic part, Carothers took the big shot title, Mack Pinson took the San Antonio Mission, D. C. O. Opperman took the college.[844]

Goss used the same Texas Syndicate tactics throughout his life to oust other quality men of God. He used closed door meetings, kangaroo courts, and other schemes to produce all-white male dominated religious organizations. If Goss opposed you, then you were guilty of something. Good men of God were flayed in these kangaroo courts. Among the victims would be Charles Parham, Sarah Parham, William Joseph Seymour, Lilian Thistlethwaite, Garfield Thomas (G.T.) Haywood, Glen Beecher (G.B.) Rowe, S.N. Norris, and many more. Goss would find his best friends among those who promoted shaman, serpent-seed doctrine and of course rabid racism. They were his favorites and the commonality in his partnering with Warren Carothers, Arch P. Collins, and other rabid haters to form the Texas Syndicate.

A historian for the Pentecostal Assemblies of the World (P.A.W.) inquired, "Was Howard Goss a racist?" My answer, "Let's describe this in terms of a bank robbery in the old West. Howard Goss was not the one in the bank, but he certainly was outside holding the horses."[845] Through a plethora of administrative efforts to create all-white male dominated religious associations, Howard Goss triumphed. His legacy of contributions to create all-white hate groups include: the Assemblies of God (A.G.), the General Association of Apostolic Assemblies (GAAA), the Pentecostal Ministerial Association (PMA) later called the Pentecostal Church Inc (PMI), and the United Pentecostal Church Incorporated. All, like Howard Goss, echo a horrible record as related to non-white people in the United States. These groups use (or used) religion like a mask in a Masquerade Ball.

In 1924, "Using the same play book that Howard Goss used in 1907, 1910 and 1913, white ministers first offer to create a white man only division within the Pentecostal Assemblies of the World (P.A.W.).[846] White ministers purposed to make separate administrative bodies for whites and blacks but stay under the same organizational structure. Of course, this was the same strawman they had offered Charles Parham, Charles Mason and others. It was a way to cloak their bigoted agenda. Backroom meetings were the nexus of discord they sowed among the brethren.[847] Even after the Supreme Court had declared that Separate but Equal was unconstitutional, Goss and his friends continued to use the scheme. The groups he was associated with still practice separate but equal dogma.[848]

Truth appears to be something foreign to the Texas Syndicate. On the one hand, Goss makes some vague reference through his wife's book to a leader having had a moral failure but confessed, repented, and as far as he knew was living righteously.[849] Yet, to appease his Texas Syndicate friends, in collaboration with Bell and Pinson makes this statement: *Notice about Parham. Chas F. Parham, who is claiming to be the head and leader of the Apostolic Faith Movement has long since been repudiated. He has refused to 'hear the church' and we are obeying the command of Christ, the Head of the church by letting him be unto us a 'heathen and a publican.' We are sorry it is so, but until he repents and confesses his sins, we cannot obey God and do otherwise. Let all Pentecostal and Apostolic Faith people of the churches of God take notice and not be misled by his claims.*"[850] Double minded men are unstable.[851] This is more of the evidence that there never was a confession by Parham as five years later these men, Goss, Bell, Pinson and S. P. Grice, are yammering about Parham. Their statement was itself contradictory as was usual when you make it up as you go. The statement said much more about the authors than it does about their intended victim. The truth is that Charles Parham was the leader and head of the Apostolic Faith Movement from 1897 till his death on January 29, 1929.

There are more questions than answers for the new Pentecostals. How? When? Where or why? Is Parham required to answer to their alleged group, the Church of God in Christ Apostolic Faith, (or whatever they call their group)? If Parham indeed had a moral failure and he was indeed a heathen, why would anyone print such in their publication? Was he the only heathen? Where is the long list of other heathens? It is evident that Parham remained extremely significant both in the U.S. and globally. Members of the Texas Syndicate continued their propaganda campaign to attempt to discredit him and everyone connected to him. These went so far as railing against using the word *Apostolic* as an explanation of doctrinal position. As usual, when these Texas Syndicate white men spoke about Parham, they assumed they were in charge. However, anyone who understands the slightest thing about an organization understands that the General Secretary would be next in line to lead the organization, Lilian Thistlethwaite. She remained in the legitimate Apostolic Faith Movement.

Veiled threats, libel, slander, and innuendo change nothing. For those who offer that they were simply trying to correct sin in the body of Christ, where is the LONG list of other offenders they sought to bring to justice?

Ironically, E. N. Bell wrote this in their Word and Witness, *"It is amazing how some otherwise good brethren who champion themselves as "defenders of the truth" make PERSONAL attacks on all who do not happen to suit their fancies. It shows a lack of good manners and proper refinement to say nothing of the weightier matters as to the true spirit of Christ, and real humble piety before God. The word teaches us that "love thinketh NO EVIL," but these dear brethren suspicion every one as a traitor to Christ who does not live up in every word and phrase to their narrow, self-made, and man-made definition of loyalty. While the word teaches us to "speak evil of no man" these call out the names of their brethren and denounce them as "compromisers" who "let down" on the truth. If you take note, the editor singles out no person or name..."*[852]
Brother Bell, we could not agree more. Thank you for making our point! Excellent job of articulating the libel and slander against Charles Parham perpetrated by your group!

Bell and his friends ignored the fact that they in fact named Parham and others in their publication, in person and in public. They did not like it when they were faced with their own methods coming back to them. Just as Scripture says, they were busy attempting to get the mote from their brother's eye while ignoring the beam in their own.[853] They would continue their charade for decades, even after Parham and Seymour were deceased. Their surrogates continue the same to this present day.

CHAPTER EIGHTEEN

HOLY ROLLERS

"The Klan symbol, displaying a white cross with a red teardrop, 'symbolizes the atonement and sacrifice of Jesus Christ, as well as others who have shed their blood for the white race."

-William Joseph Simmons

It is commonly said that Parham never responded to the horrific mess created by the Texas Syndicate; this is not the truth. Parham did respond.[854] He just did not do so on their timetable. Innocent men have the benefit of truth and time is on their side. One thing that unnerves conspirators is when the prey does not respond. For nearly a decade, the members of the Texas Syndicate drove around Charles and Sarah's Parham's new car. They showed it off to all the finest of preachers. They told them how they had

APOSTLES ARE GONE

Leaders of "Holy Rollers" Take to Flight.

ESCAPE TAR AND FEATHERS

Creffield and Brooks Accept Officers' Advice to Leave the Town---Sacrifices at Other Houses Than Hurt's.

CORVALLIS, Or., Nov. 2.—(Special.)—Creffield and Brooks, the "Holy Roller" apostles, who led the way in the recent spectacular plays of the sect in this town, have quitted Corvallis. Their going was as hasty as their work was fierce. A fear of bodily harm is supposed to have been incident to their departure.

The sheriff stayed in the house the most of Saturday night, extending the protection of the law. At noon that day a member of the sect, accompanied by his son, entered the sheriff's office, saying, "As an American citizen I demand pro-

received the new car because Charles Parham was a horrible degenerate who did not deserve such a blessing. Many people believed it must be true. What other explanation could there be? During that time the Parhams and their legitimate A.F.M. continued to do considerable ministry around the world, just like they had since the 1880's. Can you imagine how it would feel to have people steal your car and then claim it as their own? Well, we are not talking about a new car. We are discussing the Apostolic Faith Movement. As cover for their vision of Grand Theft Auto, those who comprised what we have labeled the Texas Syndicate told everyone who would listen that Charles Parham had a moral failure. They based this on two things. 1. They wanted to take over the A.F.M. 2. They had no real proof, but accusations were enough for them.

Sadly, most did not even question the premise. Those who did were told that Charles Parham's ministry ended in 1907, that he retired or whatever the ruse of the day provided. In truth, Parham was troubled by these men, but he did not stop doing ministry. 1908 found him much as previous years, with an ever-demanding schedule ministering to those that hungered for more of the Holy Ghost. For Parham, he would always be in demand to minister and would continue to have the respect of legitimate ministry the rest of his life. Another problem for the Texas Syndicate was that they did not have the title for their stolen car. So, they could drive it, but they could not sell it. Hence the reason they parted it out.

There were many people who had been impacted by the Parhams and these continued and raised up sizable ministries. Many of these continue till today. Among these were **John G. Lake, Florence Crawford, T. B. Barratt**, and others who were impacted by the Parham's Apostolic Faith and kept the same tenets as he taught.[855]

In the effort to oust Parham, the Texas Syndicate recruited the

~ CHAPTER EIGHTEEN | HOLY ROLLERS ~

most unsavory of characters. The Texas Syndicate was all white men. In addition to Carothers and Goss were E. N. Bell, J. Roswell Flowers, L. C. Hall, Mack Pinson, William Durham, and more. The way this mob behaved caused Charles Parham to refer to them and their friends with the collective term **Holy Rollers.**[856] At first blush, it would seem like a compliment or a Red Badge of Courage. However, in the timeframe the term Holy Roller was a serious charge. It was like we would say Nazis or follower of **Charles Manson**. The Holy Roller reference was to a particular group of demon possessed individuals led by one Edmund Creffield.[857]

Edmund Creffield, leader of the Holy Rollers, prison photo Courtesy Oregon State Archives

"In 1903, Edmund Creffield lured most of Corvallis's Salvation Army's soldiers to his own church. They called themselves The Church of the Bride of Christ. Everyone else called them The Holy Rollers. Most of Creffield's followers were women, and not just any women, but women who were the wives and daughters of respected men, women of high character and standing, God-fearing, decent women. Their going's on were page one news—and not just in the Pacific Northwest, but around the world. Stewart H. Holbrook, a reporter for the Oregonian and an historian, said of the Holy Roller's story: 'It seems to me, the most incredible of all the cases I have studied.' Yet few today know the story, not even many folks in Waldport, Oregon where the final chapter takes place."[858] Creffield was released from prison in 1906, he alleged that he was Christ raised from the dead—his death being his incarceration in the penitentiary. **Holy Rollers** became a pejorative term that was already widely used to refer to Pentecostal

Christians who rolled and spoke in tongues.

Parham equated these demented people to the group that was involved in attempting to oust him from his own group, the *Apostolic Faith*. This speaks to the level of animosity that was being directed to him by those claiming Christ. To Parham, and most of his peers, Edmund Creffield and his Holy Rollers, represented the most horrible beings on the planet. It well may be a fitting name for a group of men that would take it upon themselves to play God. Parham, writing about the historic event termed these men the leaders of the now **Holy Rollers**.[859] This was synonymous with his calling them the new Pentecostals. Parham used the same term Holy Rollers to describe others from the self-proclaimed Independent Holiness Movement in Los Angeles that harmed William Seymour and the Apostolic Faith Gospel Mission. Those who invaded the Los Angeles meetings Parham called, *Holy Rollers and hypnotists*.

"Apostle" Joshua Creffield

Instead of revealing his experience in a secret meeting like his detractors, Parham waited his time. For nearly another decade of ministry while his former associates parted out the pieces of his ministry including starting a series of all-white groups, bible colleges, and publications all using Parham's name—The Apostolic Faith. They wrote of their conquests to their own shame. Yet even after they were exposed, they continued on with their new all-white group. Finally, they had their own car. It was like the car in the famous Johnny Cash song, they got it one piece at a time.

Parham chose the time to set the record straight. Parham wrote the accusations in a letter to all the leaders of the Apostolic Faith Movement. The letter is dated February 7, 1915. In the letter, Charles Parham outlined the secret meeting claiming there were nine men present. It was kind of like their own version of a court as self-appointed judge and jury.[860] Apparently, there were twelve named to the inquisition. Carothers confirmed the point in challenging Charles Parham to invest in a similar quest to confront Carothers. Parham ignored the Texas Syndicate as flim-flam men.

A Prophetic Game Of Spiritual "Russian Roulette?"

The years between 1907 and 1915 were not the lost years of Charles Parham. Rather, they were the years that the Texas Syndicate thought they held the preeminence among the brethren. We are not here to be judge and jury. That would be as grave a mistake as the many the Texas Syndicate made. No, we are merely telling the historical account. For all of us, Jesus Christ will be the final judge and jury. One of the closest friends of the Texas Syndicate was William Durham. He taught a theological position that was in direct opposition of William J. Seymour. It seems that part of the reason for the difference was the newly self-crowned Pentecostals (as they billed themselves) still lusted to control The Apostolic Faith Gospel Mission on Azusa Street in Los Angeles. Afterall, one of the many misrepresentations they offered the world was that they gendered to that revival.

In a bold move, William Durham attempted to oust William J. Seymour from his Apostolic Faith church. There were at least two reasons they reviled Seymour. The first, he was black. To the Texas Syndicate that meant he was not their equal. The second was in spite of the best efforts of the Texas Syndicate to gaslight Charles and Sarah Parham and the A.F.M. as racists, Seymour was among the majority that had remained loyal and had not kowtowed. He retained the name on his church, Apostolic Faith Gospel Mission. Deep in his heart he held respect for the Parhams. Thus, when William Durham was in Los Angeles with his Texas Syndicate pals and others making his bold move, it was Charles Parham who once again rose to the occasion. That single move angered the new Pentecostals, but Parham was only sharpening his sword. In the next few years, he would make several public statements, letters, and appearances that spoke directly to the skullduggery of the Texas Syndicate and their new all-white Pentecostal movement. Of course, surrogates of the new Pentecostals ignored or maligned Parham as a mad man full of vitriol. Yet, Parham pressed on. It was said that if a man knew he was right he would argue against the whole city of New York. Parham knew he was right. In a doctrinal debate between William Howard Durham,[861] his Texas Syndicate friends, and others, "Pentecostal veteran Charles Parham (who never wavered from his strong support of Wesleyan sanctification) weighed into the fray in early January 1912. He prayed a remarkably rash—and (as it turned out) prophetic—prayer.

"If this man's doctrine is true, let my life go out to prove it; but if our teaching on a definite grace of sanctification is true, let his life pay the forfeit."[862]

Parham doubled down. In the June 1912 edition of his publication The Apostolic Faith, Parham declared: *"Durham, of Chicago, is now riding blindly to his fall. I want to say as a messenger of God, and the senior preacher of the Movement, that all men who seek leadership in this work and assume the power that alone belongs to the Messenger of the Covenant—the Holy Ghost, will fall..."*[863]
The shot across the bow at the Texas Syndicate does not go unnoticed here. Parham rails on his foes that are all men "who seek leadership" and they all "assume power" that belongs only to the Holy Ghost! Friend or foe, it must have caught everyone off guard when Durham—in the prime of his life and just shy of his fortieth birthday—died suddenly on July 7th of that same year. Says James R. Goff, Jr., one of Parham's biographers, *"Parham*

~ CHAPTER EIGHTEEN | HOLY ROLLERS ~

felt that God had properly answered his prayer." From Parham's perspective, one of the ***Holy Rollers*** was dead. Heed the warning! There would be a few more warnings, but Parham was not going to be pulled off the wall. Like Nehemiah, he worked with a sword in one hand while he continued to build with the other.

In Parham's letter recalling the events in San Antonio, Parham claimed one of them admitted the crimes against him on their death bed.[864] Could it be that the one who revealed the scheme against Parham was his nemesis, William Durham? With Parham's considerable connections in Chicago, it would be likely he would learn of such a revelation. Strangely, Durham was a convert to Charles Parham's Apostolic Faith Movement. Yet, Durham was like nearly all Parham's enemies. They were all beneficiaries of the Apostolic Faith Movement in one way or another. This person would have had to have been either in the meeting or very close to someone who was in the meeting. They would also have had to feel a great deal of allegiance to Charles Parham and his wife Sarah. They would also need to have some form of guilt associated with their proximity to the secret cabal. There was one very prominent minister that was likely part of the ***Holy Rollers:*** **William Howard Durham.**

Perhaps San Antonio was on Parham's mind when he took what was perceived as an uncharitable swipe at his deceased nemesis in the December 1912 issue of his ***The Apostolic Faith*** periodical. In an article entitled "Free-Love," Parham said, "The man who lately wrought such havoc among ***Apostolic*** people by a denial of a definite work of grace in sanctification, either fostered or was ignorant of the fact that free-love had so far permeated his work in Chicago, that some of his leading workers were sent to a certain Home in a delicate condition. This compelled the leader to make his headquarters in Los Angeles for a time..." Parham had many contacts in the Chicago area because of his ministry trips.[865] (That he would be privy to such information should not be a surprise.) Additionally, he had a number of established meetings in the Los Angeles area.

There was at least one other person that may have said something on her death bed: Millicent E. McClendon Goss. Millicent was a minister in the A.F.M. Parham called her "little David" regarding her powerful presentation on behalf of Jesus Christ. She married Howard Goss February 24, 1907.[866] Millicent died in childbirth in 1910. In Parham's letter he capitalizes the word "His" when mentioning the one who confessed on  "His" death bed. It was almost as though he was both giving a clue and yet protecting a confidence and perhaps even a dear friend. How Parham received the information is unknown. Still, no one has denied what he said. Rather, they have postulated that he never responded. The year before Millicent's death, the Goss led faction (endorsing themselves as The Apostolic Faith Movement) issued credentials to Mrs. Goss. Notice the credentials were signed by D.C.O. Opperman who was in San Antonio when they ran the scheme on Parham and quickly exited to Houston. There was also a new emphasis on "Unity" from this pseudo-Apostolic Faith Movement. There was no signature from Charles Parham. These type of credentials (from pretend groups) still plague the ministry.

Apparently, the December 1908 meeting in Texas to create a new movement resulted in the resolve of the Texas Syndicate to continue to use the Apostolic Faith name they pirated rather than creating one of their own. Opperman was posing as the State Director of the quasi-Apostolic Faith in Texas. Carothers who has moved closer to his Independent Holiness background was then signing as an advisor. Ever the lawyer, it is

~ CHAPTER EIGHTEEN | HOLY ROLLERS ~

likely that Carothers was being careful in the event they were sued for using a name they had no right to use. He could claim to just be advising them.

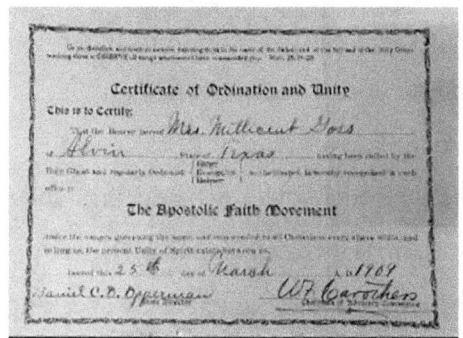

For his part, Charles Parham was not concerned with them using the Apostolic Faith name. He was concerned about all the deceit they utilize. Parham's assertion was that when they began their mission to start their all-white organization, they sought to have Parham join in with their effort. When Parham resolved not to be associated with the ones he dubbed the *Holy Rollers*, they turned on him. Parham claimed that these nine people (white males) vowed to get rid of him whatever it took, including his death. According to Parham, three of these men who were preachers, paid officials in San Antonio to frame him.[867]

The strategy was to discredit Charles Parham in any and every way possible. Those who conspired with others to make wild public accusations against Charles Parham to hide their sins, raised more questions than they gave answers. Among the questions: What crime did they accuse other Apostolic Faith officers of who were summarily dismissed from their actions? Officers of the Apostolic Faith Movement such as Secretary General, Lilian Thistlethwaite? Florence Crawford? Other than them being women of course. If Parham was guilty of something, why would they hide it? Only guilty people hide. Why did they not obey Scripture? Why would they not attempt restoration? Why did they need a confession? What witnesses did they bring? How is it that a group of preachers could find Parham guilty of something for which a seasoned Prosecutor in San Antonio could find no evidence? Why does the rhetoric in San Antonio look just like a cooked up legal version of "conduct unbecoming a minister?"

Could it be that since the frame job in Houston had failed to get Parham a formal charge his "friends" the ***Holy Rollers*** sought to make certain of their intent. "In the years 1906 to 1908 the Apostolic Faith movement fractured into several parts, mainly over issues of theological *adiaphora*[868] and along the line of personal conflict, styles of leadership and worship."[869] In 1900, Charles Parham was among the first to clarify the third work of Grace as baptism with the Holy Ghost evidenced by speaking in other tongues.[870] Even many who decided to become the enemies of Charles and Sarah Parham taught this cornerstone of their message. The Parhams' revelation was in line with the teachings of fellow Methodists like John Fletcher and Benjamin Irvin.[871] As the old saints would say, "Saved, Sanctified, and filled with the Holy Ghost!"

Reportedly, Pauline Parham, Charles Parham's daughter-in-law was shocked when she learned that Charles Parham was put through such ridicule by those pretending to be his friends. Apparently, the information was kept from the family. Those in active ministry would appreciate that this is a most difficult task to accomplish. Nevertheless, Charles and Sarah accomplished such a feat and should be commended. Evidently, the challenges of ministry, the betrayals, the heartache, and the hardship were not topics discussed in the Parham home. This would be in keeping with the character of Charles and Sarah Parham

San Antonio 1907

~ CHAPTER EIGHTEEN | HOLY ROLLERS ~

and consistent with their request not to return evil for evil.

Historians should be paying closer attention rather than being perplexed as to why Charles Parham, "increasingly attacked other branches of Pentecostalism for their "counterfeit Pentecost, with chattering, and jabbering, and windsucking," noting that "two-thirds of the Pentecostal people are being deceived by these forces."[872]

CHAPTER NINETEEN

ALL-WHITE KANGAROO COURT

"He and other Klan leaders would look to Christianity to find support for racism. Even liberal Protestant churches supported white supremacy. That seemed the natural order of things. Just as people used biblical texts to support slavery."

-Kelly Baker

In 1907, Charles Parham dissolved Howard A. Goss' position in the A.F.M.[873] Proxies claim Goss resigned under pressure once members of the A.F.M. realized that he and Carothers and others were trying to steal leadership from Charles Parham.[874] Yet, Goss said his position was dissolved.[875] Proxies favored the resigned rhetoric because it gave the appearance that Goss and his friends were actually in charge and had a choice in the matter. Neither is true.

Charles Parham was arrested during meetings that he was holding with Carothers' accomplice Lemuel C. Hall in San Antonio, Texas at a place referred to as the Majestic.[876] Let's recap.

1. Parham initially replaced Carothers with Goss. At that time, Parham was unaware that Goss was a conspirator in The Texas Syndicate with Carothers. August 26, 1906.

2. Then Parham discovered Goss and Carothers were conspiring against him. Warren Carothers whole system (Parham referenced as a scheme[877]) of organization was dissolved by Parham.[878] Carothers, Goss, and their Texas Syndicate friends discovered Parham had dissolved their positions in the A.F.M. September 1906.

3. Parham referenced this time (January - September 1906). "The saddest and most awful experience of our whole Christian life was the nine months we spent under similar control. It came as a seducing, flattering spirit, but when it gained the supremacy in our lives it used the lash."[879]

4. Carothers blackmailed (via telegram) Parham and demands his resignation as Projector. November 25, 1906. Part of Carothers' rationale may have been that since he no longer held a title then Parham did not deserve one. Parham obviously needed no title.

5. Parham responded by telegraph, "Owing to the fact that my position Projector of Apostolic Movement is misunderstood, many rumors afloat. I resign from such office to devote myself to private ministry and prayer. Letter of explanation follows" Parham sent a letter letting Carothers know that he ended Carothers' organizational scheme in September. Evidently, Parham's decision was made after Carothers expressed some scheme for the Apostolic Faith to take over Zion City while they were in that city together. Parham saw it as the last straw and expressed that Carothers had become crazed with the scheme. Sept

~ CHAPTER NINETEEN | ALL-WHITE KANGAROO COURT ~

1907.

6. Carothers told people that Parham resigned from A.F.M. for private ministry. However, A.F.M. was Parham's private ministry. Therefore, what Parham was actually communicating was that he had already dismissed Carothers. Parham said it was his plan.[880]

7. Carothers understood exactly what Parham had done. Since Carothers had only Brunner Tabernacle, he quickly moved to dissolve the affiliation with the A.F.M. November 27, 1906.

8. Parham moved forward and was more involved in ministry than ever before with an expanding A.F.M. schedule which included three months in New England. December 1906 - Feb 1907. Followed by exhaustive schedules in 1908 and for the next twenty years.

9. Carothers understood Parham did not resign and retaliateed by removing Brunner Tabernacle from the A.F.M. so that Parham would have no oversight there. He misrepresented the purpose in one of his many prevarications, December 1906.[881]

10. Led by Carothers, the Texas Syndicate (an all-white collusion group) held a phony trial allegedly in Orchard, Texas.[882] Not one alleged witness or statement was ever made public. Parham does not attend.[883] The conspirators were careful not to name Parham or even one of their bogus charges because they were instructed by Carothers that to do so would be libel.[884] April 6, 1907.

11. Howard Goss and others told the fiction that Parham attended their bogus trial.[885] The Chairman of the meeting, J. Charles Dowling, said Parham did not attend and he did not respond to anything that they said or even their order for him to attend their Kangaroo Court.[886] Goss claimed Parham confessed.[887] What did he confess? How did he confess? Howard Goss did not say because there was nothing to support their

allegations unless Goss considered the San Antonio debacle the alleged confession.[888] April 1907.

12. Charles Parham was not in attendance at the fugazi trial staged by The Texas Syndicate. So, it is evident, contrary to the Texas Syndicate's bogus claims, he did not confess anything. That was confirmed.[889] April 1907.

13. Goss claimed that there were witnesses and written statements, but they were never produced. They also claimed they had a confession, repentance and restoration,[890] but no proof was ever produced and no action by Goss or his friends ever indicates one attempt at restoration. April 1907. The only thing that seemed to be leaked from Carothers' Kangaroo court was a wild charge that a hotel maid said Parham masturbated.[891] Even if true, the Kangaroo court's actions were a criminal violation of the right to privacy? Did anyone really care about that type of accusation?[892] A testimony like that in a fake court was not proof. April 1907. Apparently, there were never either confessions or statements. It was all a clever hoax.

14. When Parham at some point learned of the accusation, responded to that masturbation claim with the simple truthful statement that what he may have done in his sleep he cannot tell.[893] Surrogates and Proxies have parlayed that response as his response to the later San Antonio disaster, but the two incidents were months apart and both without any substantiation.

15. Although he was removed from office in 1906, Carothers continued his charade for years (at least a decade), telling people he was the National Director or Field Director[894] of the Apostolic Faith[895] and that Parham resigned.[896] Supposing for the sake of argument that Parham had resigned, then Lilian Thistlethwaite, as General Secretary,

would have legally been in charge[897] – not Carothers or Goss. Certainly, smooth lawyer—Carothers knew the legalities here which explained his clandestine activity.

16. The covert operations of The Texas Syndicate come to light. Howard Goss was said to resign under pressure that he and Carothers and others were conspiring to take over the A.F.M., but Howard Goss admitted later that he knew his position had been dissolved.[898] It seemed a moot point to resign from a position that had admittedly been dissolved.[899] March 1907. Goss and Carothers conspired with their Texas Syndicate friends to continue to claim to be the Apostolic Faith. A ruse they continued for years.

17. Lemuel C. Hall, Goss, A. D. Canada,[900] W. F. Carothers, D. C. O. Opperman and other members of the Texas Syndicate with the collaboration of Wilbur Voliva plot to frame Parham. According to J. G. Campbell, the officer who brought Parham to the City Building was a Constable named Charlie Stevens. They bribed Carothers' cousin, Justice Ben S. Fisk, a corrupt San Antonio Justice of the Peace, to bring charges against Parham. They worked with the Callahan Machine in San Antonio, corrupt police, and others to pretend Parham had committed a crime. The similarities to Judas' betraying Jesus were astounding.[901] July 1907.

18. Parham was arrested under fictitious charges. Parham was physically beaten.[902] The demand at gunpoint was for Parham to sign a confession that was pre-written for him. There can be little doubt that this was a direct connection to the Carothers' previous kangaroo court.[903] Parham witnessed three of The Texas Syndicate who he labeled the Holy Rollers or new Pentecostals, pay the rest of the bribe to Justice Ben S. Fisk. Parham did not sign a confession. So, the corrupt official and

friends signed the pre-written confession for him.⁹⁰⁴ The counterfeit "confession" was forwarded to co-conspirator Wilbur Voliva and Ray Davis (Remember his friend Carothers sent the blackmail telegraph from his address) for dissemination in their news publications.⁹⁰⁵

19. The District Attorney, I. C. Baker, who had nothing to gain by pleasing the Texas Syndicate, met Charles and Sarah Parham at their scheduled hearing. District Attorney I. C. Baker told the Parhams there was simply no basis for any case. He told them to just go home. There was nothing with which to charge him. There simply was no case.⁹⁰⁶ July 1907.

20. Carothers' Texas Syndicate group held their own meeting which they called Apostolic Faith. At the same time, the legitimate Apostolic Faith was meeting. Parham and the A.F.M. meet at a hall in downtown Houston, Texas. Carothers was allegedly at independent Brunner Tabernacle.⁹⁰⁷ The Parham led meeting was standing room only with thousands in attendance.

Confession. What Exactly Is A Confession? ⁹⁰⁸

Confession, also-called **reconciliation** or **penance**, in the Judeo-Christian tradition, the acknowledgment of sinfulness in public or private, regarded as necessary to obtain divine forgiveness.' It does not present that reconciliation was the expectation of Carothers or his kangaroo court. When Parham did not attend, Carothers and his Texas Syndicate sought a quasi-legal confession⁹⁰⁹ which they also did not receive despite their crimes against Parham. On the one hand this course of events seems like a reach, but on the other it seems too contrived and easy. If Parham had realized that Hall shared the radical racial hatred of Carothers and Goss for people of color, Parham likely would not have agreed to have meetings with him. While Carothers claimed that he had all the Texas Missions on his side,

CHAPTER NINETEEN | ALL-WHITE KANGAROO COURT

there were tens of thousands or more in Texas still loyal to Charles and Sarah Parhams and the legitimate A.F.M. In truth, there was little evidence of widespread support for Carothers while Parham would have huge meetings in Texas[910] in general and even right in Houston where Carothers had set his throne.[911] Carothers made Brunner independent which left them without any leadership except Carothers, his Independent Holiness friends and the Texas Syndicate. After some of their leaders participated in the kangaroo trial of Charles Parham, many at Brunner were seen as betrayers. They were without a genuine pastor for years. In 1916, they brought another radical bigot, E. N. Richey from Illinois, to pastor Brunner. The Richey family was connected to another member of the Texas Syndicate, William Piper.[912]

Many of the Texas ministries remain connected to the A.F.M. at the time of this writing over one hundred years later. The Texas Syndicate made it clear that Parham's multicultural A.F.M. is not welcome in Texas, but the evidence is clear that all Texans do not share Carothers and his Texas Syndicates xenophobic views. The demand by the corrupt San Antonio officers for Parham to sign a confession confirming what many knew all along. There was no confession at Carothers' Kangaroo court in April 1907. This fake arrest was a last-ditch effort to get a confession out of Parham that would help the Texas Syndicate claimed Parham was a degenerate. They failed, but they presented a counterfeit version. This type of political theater is all too common.[913] For example, the elaborate fake Russian Collusion hoax orchestrated on President Donald J. Trump.[914]

Reformers like Charles Parham have been "subject to church discipline, sanctions, defamation of character and more. They have been hounded by unscrupulous leaders, anonymous letters, and threatening telephone calls. They have paid a price for the part they have played in following Apostle Paul's directive in Ephesians 4:3 to make every effort to maintain the unity of the Spirit in the bond of peace."[915] Historians, proxies, and surrogates make a variety of false claims about Charles Parham. For example, James Goff Jr., writes of Parham's "subsequent indictment of charges in Texas."[916] This is terribly a miscarriage of justice. The word "indictment" is used to give them the impression of a crime. Very typical of the type of character assassination that we are dealing with in this subject. It is like asking a man if he still beats his wife. There is no good answer. The fact remains that Charles Parham was not legally indicted – Ever! Parham was never indicted for anything of which there is any record. In an exhaustive book that researched all crimes by all preachers in the United States and Canada covering over one hundred years, Parham was not named for any legal action.[917]

In July 1907, Charles Parham was arrested but never charged. There were very few ministers of the time that commented on the subject objectively. J. G. Campbell was a Texan who spoke directly about the subject. "Those who have been condemning Mr. Parham on some-body else's say so are equally guilty of false accusation. His character was attacked by some vicious accusations. He was arrested and thrown in prison in San Antonio, Texas, but the case was thrown out of court. Following are the names of the Constables who made the arrest – Charlie Stevens – and District Attorney handling the case – Mr. Baker. Attorney for the defense – C. A. Davis and Mr. Hartman all of San Antonio, Texas. Those who have been teaching and publishing in their papers, that the Apostolic Faith Movement started on the Pacific Coast or elsewhere at a later date than 1900 A. D. ... in Topeka, Kansas are publishing and teaching falsehoods in some cases ignorantly) and the Bible tells us that the Devil is a liar, and the father of it. Therefore we can only come to the conclusion that Satan is at

~ CHAPTER NINETEEN | ALL-WHITE KANGAROO COURT ~

the bottom of it."[918]

Regardless of what we write in this chapter, some will continue to hate Charles Parham. In their minds, he will remain guilty of a crime for which:

- Parham was never charged with anything; not even j-walking.[919] There is no court record anywhere in the United States of a single charge against Charles Parham.[920] **Fact.**
- Another man (apparently a black man) was also arrested. He also was never charged. There is no real proof he was ever in San Antonio as the only arrest record is in Fort Worth, Texas that claims he was accused of taking some money from a roommate. Allegedly he traveled and was in show business.[921] **Fact.**
- Parham claimed to be innocent. He remains innocent. Fact.
- To date, over 114 plus years later, no one has produced one shred of tangible evidence. None. **Fact.**
- Charles Fox Parham was falsely arrested in San Antonio, Texas.[922] San Antonio is in the United States where the law holds that one is innocent until proven guilty. This means that Charles Parham is innocent. **Facts.**
- It is rumored, He was arrested for an "un-natural act," but where did this allegation originate as there is no charges?[923] How convenient for this rumor to have been known and spread by his enemies in The Texas Syndicate through their friends in the media; both in the Texas media and in Zion, Illinois. We know really nothing but talebearing, backbiting, and gossip. **Fact.**
- **Parham's** enemies (then and now) have created volumes of false charges and claim them as true – without any evidence. NONE.[924]
- The duly elected Prosecuting District Attorney, I. C. Baker could find

no reason to charge or detain Charles Parham.[925] Fact.
- The goal of all of this was to discredit Charles Parham and his leadership in the Apostolic Faith Movement.[926] Fact. Who benefited?
- Someone made all of this up. The person used legal terms. There was one lawyer who hated Parham. His name was **Warren Carothers.** Fact. If Parham really resigned, then why did Carothers need to do all this charade.
- If it were true that **Unnatural act** is why Parham was arrested. This is a legal term. A legal term comes from a legal person. The only lawyer connected to Charles Parham (as far as is known) was also his self-avowed enemy Warren Carothers![927]
- Fact: "These laws are unconstitutional to enforce for sexual conduct between consenting adults in light of Lawrence v. Texas (2003)."[928]
- Fact: Charles Parham denied any guilt.[929]
- Fact: There is no known reason to not accept Charles Parham at his word. He was not perfect but certainly was not known as a fabricator of the truth.
- What the false arrest did do was stop successful meetings that Charles Parham was having at the Majestic in San Antonio. Fact.

Charges Against Members Of The Texas Syndicate

Ironically, a seldom known point of fact is that at least two of the Texas Syndicate that became leaders in future all-white hate groups had serious legal charges against the that are never mentioned by surrogates. Lemuel C. Hall had previously been arrested under almost the same conditions as Charles Parham. The events around the accusations against Charles Parham were as though they used Hall's experience as the script. According to Hall's first wife, Mary, while ministering in Saint Louis

~ CHAPTER NINETEEN | ALL-WHITE KANGAROO COURT ~

Lemuel C. Hall was arrested and charged with **"very obscene charges."** His wife had to come to his aid. In August 1902, the daily papers contained stories of dissension in the church Hall pastored. This caused grave charges against Pastor Hall to be nailed on the church door. On a Saturday night while Hall was preaching on a corner, two plain closed policemen hidden in the crowd arrested him. One of them told Sister Hall that he would be taken where she would not see him for forty years! Sister Hall began singing and the officer pushed her and struck her with his club. In a little while they filed charges against Lemuel C. Hall. Sister Hall claimed that they were the most outrageous lies about Pastor Hall. He was treated brutally and placed in a cell. In a couple of days, they went before the judge who dismissed the whole case claiming the prosecutor had failed to make any case at all.[930]

His relationship to Warren Carothers is uncertain but in 1902, one of Warren Carothers' fellow moral Methodists found himself in serious legal challenge. "Carothers, Rev. Mr., Hackensack, N. J. Methodist. Conspiracy; intimacy with a sister of the church."[931] Unlike the trumped-up case against Parham, Carothers case went to conviction. The Texas Syndicate focused much attention on the wild false accusations against Charles Parham because it was part of their agenda. Yet, they explained away similar wild accusations aimed at their own Texas Syndicate colleagues, **Cyrus Barnette Fockler** and Lemuel C. Hall. The Texas Syndicate promoted both to key leadership positions through proxies of their all-white clique. In fairness, "Wilbur Voliva had a history of accusing those he opposed of sexual misconduct including, "'Bingley, a self-confessed dirty old kisser;' 'Fockler, a self-confessed adulterer;' and 'Brudder Tom, ... an immoral man ... caught ... hugging and kissing **Sister Hall**' ... 'the accusation of sodomy against one of Dowie's overseers.'"[932] Although

Fockler came into the A.F.M. through the influence of John G. Lake and F. F. Bosworth, he conspired with and accepted a position from the leaders of The Texas Syndicate.

In M.E. Billings exhaustive work, *Crimes of Preachers*, Mr. Billings covers crimes by ministers covering one hundred years or more. Charles Parham is not in the book. This separated those religiously and politically motivated situations from real crimes.[933] So, what really happened in San Antonio. Obviously, the same thing that happened with Hall in Saint Louis. Naught of a criminal nature! Just an excuse for accusers to bring accusation. The only one willing to go on the record was the victim, Charles Parham. Parham's enemies took opportunities and license with the accusations. Parham claims that his abuse came at the hands of a corrupt mayor of San Antonio. Someone politically connected had to influence some of that attention toward Parham. Parham ID's the Mayor as being Mexican, white, and Catholic. Turns out that Bryan Callahan, nine-time mayor of San Antonio was all of that and more. "The Callaghan machine has been accused, with justification, of a variety of sins, including the unethical distribution of patronage, opposition to civil-service reform, lenience toward gambling and vice operations, favoritism in awarding municipal contracts, and widespread vote manipulation."[934] The Callahan machine was nothing to be trifled with in those days. Parham was known in some circles as a Prohibitionist. This is likely the ruse that the Texas Syndicate used to get the Callahan Machine involved. Callahan had his own police force in that time as he had fired all the legitimate police in 1905 and implemented his own police force. The Callahan Machine opposed several ministers, especially those who were Prohibitionists.[935]

Parham wrote that an officer, Constable Charlie Stevens approached him about needing to answer some questions. Whether this was one of

~ CHAPTER NINETEEN | ALL-WHITE KANGAROO COURT ~

Callahan's men or a legitimate officer we do not know. It does explain Parham's charge of Callahan's involvement. Also, Parham said that Callahan fought with him "terribly" to stop his meetings at the Majestic.[936]

> "Parham not answering makes him no more guilty than Jesus when He did not answer Pontius Pilate."

Parham claims that three ministers came to the San Antonio City Building and offered Callahan "*evidence of Parham's filthiness.*" They even paid an official to take Parham up and get a confession from him. What was so important that one would pay bribes to corrupt city officials? Parham responded

    This author has been told that Charles Parham never addressed his false arrest. The implication is: because he would not answer, he is guilty. Parham not answering makes him no more guilty than Jesus when He did not answer Pontius Pilate.[937] When I learned that Oral Roberts University Archives had a letter about the subject written by Charles Parham, I was frankly amazed. I had been convinced by denominational surrogates posing as historians, that Parham never had responded to the unfounded charges against him in San Antonio. Obviously, this was part of the Texas Syndicate's and their proxies well-organized disinformation campaign. When I acquired a copy of the letter, I realized what they were hiding. Until I read Parham's letter to the Apostolic Faith Ministers, I wondered why his enemies needed a confession. Afterall, they claimed they had the confessions from their kangaroo court during their fugazi trial of Charles Parham in Orchard, Texas. Then the lights came on! There were no confessions! That was a clever ruse to get Parham to admit something – just anything. This was where the passing of fluids in the night came to light and the honest admission was turned into sexual deviancy through propaganda. Carothers, ever the lawyer, knew they had nothing! The

Texas Syndicate needed a confession of some kind. A confession they were determined to get - no matter what!

Parham explained that the officer (Constable Stevens) came to him and said that Parham was wanted at the City Building to answer some questions. Parham expected it was about the revival meetings they were holding. Parham was ushered into a room and told he needed to explain certain things. They produced a paper for him to sign that was supposedly a declaration of guilt. Who knew what to write on a predetermined confession? Apparently, many of the officials being Catholic, they did not understand that Protestants were not that keen on confessions. The officials in the room told Parham to sign and that would be the end of the matter. How could a confession end the matter? What was the matter? The only parallel to this is the blackmail telegram from Carothers through Ray Davis to Parham.[938]

Fortunately, Parham refused to sign their statement. Three men that Parham described as "rough necks" came in from the adjoining room and proceeded to beat Parham unmercifully while demanding he sign said confession. Parham expected he would die. Yet, he did not relent. In fact, Parham claimed he said, "you can Kill me, but I'll not sign."[939] Next, Parham recounted, they threw him in a chair. One man pulled a gun on him, the other used his fists and they yelled, "Sign! Sign!" while they beat him nearly to death. One of these placed a pen in Parham's hand and with his hand "traced my name (Parham) on the paper." Then, "the official wrote something more."[940]

This is how the evidence presented. No wonder District Attorney I. C. Baker wanted no part of this circus. Like Pontius Pilate, District Attorney Baker knew the best path forward was to wash his hands of the mess. It appeared that the original letter was prepared by someone before

~ CHAPTER NINETEEN | ALL-WHITE KANGAROO COURT ~

Parham arrived. Likely, in keeping with the spirit of the conspirators of the Texas Syndicate, Carothers dictated the letter and someone else wrote it, so that Carothers could present it to his cousin Justice Ben Fisk, and it would not be in his handwriting. This would give Carothers the position of claiming it was for a client and he could enlist his cousin to help. Fisk was also promised some other incriminating evidence on Parham apparently by his cousin a fellow attorney, Warren Fay Carothers. The promised evidence never materialized! Imagine that! Carothers knew what the confession needed to say and what the legal mind of the corrupt Justice of the Peace, Ben S. Fisk, [who was his relative] would accept as having the air of legitimacy. Allegedly, this is the content of the Texas Syndicate letter that was given covertly to Justice Ben S. Fisk masqueraded by the Texas Syndicate as a confession:

> *"One man pulled a gun on him the other used his fists and they yelled, 'Sign! Sign!' while they beat him nearly to death. One of these placed a pen in Parham's hand and with his hand 'traced my name (Parham) on the paper.' Then, the 'official wrote something more.'"*

"I hereby confess my guilt in the commission of the crime of sodomy with one J. J. Jourdan in San Antonio, Texas on the 18th of July 1907." (In a different handwriting)
"I am a helpless degenerate."

Chas F. Parham

The wording of the supposed "confession" was from signs printed by Wilbur Voliva (several years later). Likely, the letter was destroyed as Fisk would not have risked his career on such a scheme. In 2021 and 2022, we asked for this alleged confession and supposed case to be reviewed by a couple of attorneys and other legal minds. Here are some of the observations about the supposed confession.

18 U.S. Code § 3501 - Admissibility Of Confessions

(a) In any criminal prosecution brought by the United States or by the District of Columbia, a confession, as defined in subsection (e) hereof, shall be admissible in evidence if it is voluntarily given. Before such confession is received in evidence, the trial judge shall, out of the presence of the jury, determine any issue as to voluntariness. If the trial judge determines that the confession was voluntarily made it shall be admitted in evidence and the trial judge shall permit the jury to hear relevant evidence on the issue of voluntariness and shall instruct the jury to give such weight to the confession as the jury feels it deserves under all the circumstances.

(b) The trial judge in determining the issue of voluntariness shall take into consideration all the circumstances surrounding the giving of the confession, including (1) the time elapsing between arrest and arraignment of the defendant making the confession, if it was made after arrest and before arraignment, (2) whether such defendant knew the nature of the offense with which he was charged or of which he was suspected at the time of making the confession, (3) whether or not such defendant was advised or knew that he was not required to make any statement and that any such statement could be used against him, (4) whether or not such defendant had been advised prior to questioning of his right to the assistance of counsel; and (5) whether or not such defendant was without the assistance of counsel when questioned and when giving such confession.

The presence or absence of any of the above-mentioned factors to be taken into consideration by the judge need not be conclusive on the issue of voluntariness of the confession.

~ CHAPTER NINETEEN | ALL-WHITE KANGAROO COURT ~
More Challenges To The Texas Syndicate's Confession Scheme

- This presented as evidence of coercion.[941] [It may be that the promised "evidence" of the Texas Syndicate was supposed to give justification to the means. However, no collaborating evidence was ever presented to the District Attorney or to anyone else].The alleged confession was so weak that the defendant's claim the confession was coerced, was by itself obviously enough for the case to be dismissed.
- "Black's Law Dictionary defines duress as "any unlawful threat or coercion used... to induce another to act [or to refrain from acting] in a manner [they] otherwise would not [or would]."[942]
- Mr. Parham's previously established blackmailers (see the telegraph from Chicago from one W. F. Carothers published in Texas Newspapers[943]) would establish sufficient cause for claiming duress.
- Mr. Parham's explanation of the situation brings in several actionable legal remedies against the agents responsible.
- Sodomy under the cited Texas Statute is a crime. Since the alleged confession names the victim, why was the victim arrested and held as a criminal? What was his crime?
- This presents that J. J. Jourdan was not considered the victim by the arresting officer. Thus, who was the supposed victim? Where was the information about the interview with the victim or complaint from the victim?
- "I am a helpless degenerate," the words allegedly added by Justice Fisk, presents as a topic for the confessional booth of a priest, not evidence for a court. There is no admission of any crime in this statement. In fairness, "I am a helpless degenerate." the statement might well be made by any honest person. We are all helpless degenerates without Christ.
- Since this presents that J. J. Jourdan was not the victim, why is there no mention in the alleged confession about the alleged victim?

- What exactly is he supposedly confessing?
- IF there was a relationship with J. J. Jourdan as surrogates imply, how does this meet the statute for a crime? IF it was a crime, why did J. J. Jourdan not file the complaint?
- "Recent DNA exonerations have shed light on the problem that people sometimes confess to crimes they did not commit. Drawing on police practices, laws concerning the admissibility of confession evidence, core principles of psychology, and forensic studies involving multiple methodologies."[944]
- First reaction from one of our legal team, "It is a silly confession that lacks substance."
- Where in San Antonio? Under what circumstances? Why was there only one accusation?
- This presents more like a shakedown in hopes of some evidence coming to light that would aid in a crime being investigated. If so, what was the crime and who was investigating?
- There is the alleged confession date, but What date did the crime take place?
- "This is why our criminal justice system needs to have procedural safeguards in place to keep the innocent from being falsely charged."
- "No self-respecting attorney would use this supposed confession to bring a legal charge." [Exactly how District Attorney I. C. Baker saw the situation. No case].
- Granted in 1907, it was a much different time, but apparently this was not even a good confession at that time.

Here are some other challenges with the supposed confession.
- As presented, this was not a confession.

~ CHAPTER NINETEEN | ALL-WHITE KANGAROO COURT ~

- There appeared to be a group of people involved in this confession.
- Someone wrote the confession.
- Someone gave the confession to the Justice of the Peace before the accused was present.
- Why were there two or even three different types of handwriting in the alleged confession?
- Where was the information from? In other words, what is the source of this information alleged?
- Why was there no handwriting analysis? What evidence was there of a signature?
- There does not appear to be a legitimate signature:
  - First the name was from a published name of a well-known person who was a publisher. It was his published name.
  - The signature presents as being based on his published signature. Not a legal signature one would use in a legal matter. Lending one to conclude the alleged confession was a forgery.
  - The defendant denied signing this document. Claims the signature was a form of forgery. Forgery is a crime.
  - There were no collaborating witnesses to the signing of the confession. Why?
  - Where did these witnesses go?
  - Where was the confession written and by whom?
  - Under what circumstances was the confession written and exactly where?
  - Why was such a confession, if legitimate, not signed in the presence of an official willing to collaborate the signature? Why did no official collaborate the signature?
  - A huge question that would have been brought up in the case of

a trial was who wrote this and why did they give it to the Justice of the Peace. Why were there no witnesses, collaborations, or even anonymous statements?

Returning to Parham's 1915 letter. Next, the Justice of the Peace called into the room three of Parham's enemies. Three preachers of those Parham called the *Holy Rollers* and later by the name they chose, new "Pentecostals." No wonder even the racists in the Church of the Nazarene and Alma White's KKK wanted no part of these men that were the new Pentecostals. Strangely, no one has ever figured out the identity of the three preachers. Surely, Parham knew but it does not appear he revealed their names to anyone. Perhaps this is because it was obvious at the time. We know **Lemuel C. Hall** was part of the Texas Syndicate and is with Parham when the trouble starts, but is conspicuously absent from any of the reports. He also does not present as accompanying Parham to the City Building or bail him out of jail. Interesting! A. C. Canada is also in San Antonio according to Howard Goss.[945] Another preacher, one **Daniel C. O. Opperman** was not only in San Antonio, but shortly after these events relocated to Houston where Carothers was putting together his fugazi[946] headquarters. Oh, and Opperman's payment? He took over the Houston Bible School that Parham had started. This the new Pentecostals would claim as their own. How convenient. Follow the money. Parham charges that these three preachers paid the official some money which they said was, *"the rest of what we agreed to give you for this confession."*[947]

We also establish that Carothers and Justice Fisk were related. The official is unnamed in Parham's letter, but news outlets identify him as **Justice Ben S. Fisk**. Fisk was Justice of the Peace, Precinct No. 1, Place 2.[948] The evidence presents that Fisk took the bribe mentioned by the Holy

~ CHAPTER NINETEEN | ALL-WHITE KANGAROO COURT ~

Roller preachers in Parham's letter. Parham said the official was expecting evidence to be presented to him from these three members of the **Holy Rollers,** but they produced none. The Texas Syndicate had claimed since the kangaroo trial a few months before that they had signed confessions and witnesses. They failed to produce either. Sarah Parham wrote, *"One day I received word that he (Charles) had been arrested while preaching. The city attorney told him that he would not have to appear, because he (the attorney) would not even call the case for trial for he "was satisfied it was all spite work. I was with him in Texas, at the date set in the indictment, but the case was never called, the prosecuting attorney declaring that there was absolutely no evidence which merited any legal recognition."*[949]

Parham claimed, the official realized that he had also been double crossed and Parham had been framed, but as the official's hands were also dirty, he merely released Parham and likely destroyed the fraudulent statement associated with Parham's detainment.[950] This was not only an interesting account, but it also has a biblical ring. When David plotted to kill Uriah, he released him to go home. When Amnon raped his sister Tamara he sent her home after the dirty deeds.[951] After the fragments of what was supposedly a case are passed to District Attorney, I. C. Baker, Charles and Sarah have their appointed day in court. Despite all the illegal acts against Charles Parham, he was never charged with anything. When the mess was turned over to District Attorney I. C. Baker,[952] Baker said there was simply no case. Charles and Sarah Parham had returned to the court to face whatever charge would be brought. However, District

Warren Fay Carothers (Center) with his son in his lap and father and grandfather behind him. Four generations of white Southern men.

Attorney Baker told them to just go home.[953]

To be certain, District Attorney Baker was no saint. Ironically, both he and Mr. Fisk found themselves in a quagmire of their own the very next year when the Governor of Texas withheld their Commissions as Officers, as well as several others pending investigation.[954] Baker was elected as a Democrat District Attorney for San Antonio. As such, he was certainly in favor of the Jim Crow system. Even with that he found no reason to charge Parham. No charge! Everyone should have rejoiced!

Most did rejoice, but not the Texas Syndicate! The Texas Syndicate and their proxies used this as the basis for outrageous bogus allegations till this day! On the other hand, Parham's instruction to his A.F.M. ministers was not to fight his enemies for him.[955] Perhaps that was the reason he left their names out of his account. This demonstrated more honor than all the Texas Syndicate. The honorable thing would have been way back in 1905 when they realized that Parham was not a fellow racist or white supremacist to just walk away. However, they just were not honorable men. History is NOT on their side.

The Justice who held Charles Parham on the trumped-up charge was an elected Justice of the Peace.[956] His name: Ben S. Fisk.[957] If you believe in coincidence, you can ignore that the honorable (or less than honorable) Ben Fisk was a cousin of one of Charles Parham's enemies. Fisk was raised in one of the San Antonio area's wealthy and well-connected Texas families. He came from a long line of politicians and lawyers. Coincidentally, one of his ancestors was Mary Rachel Euphemia Carothers Fisk.[958] Yes, exactly, Justice Ben Fisk and Warren Fay Carothers were cousins. Imagine that!

If Parham was really compromised, then why didn't the Texas Syndicate have a legitimate public meeting where real people would present real evidence of wrongdoing to the legitimate leaders of the Apostolic Faith

~ CHAPTER NINETEEN | ALL-WHITE KANGAROO COURT ~

Movement? You know, do what the Bible says and take it to the Church.⁹⁵⁹ Or since they were so carnal, why did they not publish real evidence in one of their newspapers' hit pieces on Charles Parham? Reader, you miss the point. This was NEVER about anything except control. Carothers wanted control for him and his racist friends in the Texas Syndicate. Without any real evidence, they would use something better: lies, deceit, innuendo, slander, libel and more.

Next tactic: use the little spat between Parham and the Apostolic Faith Gospel Mission leaders in Los Angeles to create propaganda to drive a wedge between the white A.F.M. and the blacks by whatever means necessary. Gaslight the Parhams as racist. How does that explain the disconnect of all the California and West Coast ministers? They used the opportunity of the Apostolic Faith Gospel Mission impasse to flush as many blacks as possible from the group they now set out to create. They also did not want women in leadership. So, Florence Crawford's disagreements with Seymour and ultimate departure were wonderful in their eyes. No blacks and no women. They were already publishing their own pirated version of the Apostolic Faith newsletter from Houston, Texas! After being released from the leadership in the Apostolic Faith, Carothers seized on his opportunity and stole the Apostolic Faith newsletter and started printing it in Houston. It fit well with the stolen Bible College that they turned over to D. C. O. Opperman.

Parham rallied his forces and continued publishing his Apostolic Faith newsletter.⁹⁶⁰ Parham's first responsive newsletter came from Zion in 1907.⁹⁶¹ Like most seasoned men of God, it seems Parham was sure footed. However, Carothers, a man who would have given Cain his due as a rival, apparently had no morals. He despised men of color, disparaged women, was jealous of William Seymour, and made haste to press his advantage. He started printing the Apostolic Faith in Houston, Texas. Carothers claimed he would make certain that Parham was "disciplined" for his willingness to violate Jim Crow laws and be seen with men of color in public. It seems they tried to make J. J. Jourdan (a man of mixed race) Parham's downfall. Mr. Jourdan was a jazz musician from New Orleans. As far as was known, was never convicted of a crime. Unless like Carothers and his Texas Syndicate friends, you count being born black as a crime.

Sarah Parham said the *"main secret of the fight against him, was that he did not believe in organizations."* [962] While the Texas Syndicate plotted their next scheme, Charles Parham continued with the work of the Lord. He returned to Los Angeles and ministered in the winter of 1907 into 1908. On January 12, 1908, he began meetings at the W.C. T. U. Temple in Los Angeles. At Easter, Sunday April 19, of 1908 he ministered in Orchard, Texas. In Houston, May 9, 1908, he wrote of the Orchard meeting in a letter to followers in Kansas and Missouri:

"... the multitudes who attended the meeting were fed free. There were people there from Missouri, Kansas, Virginia, California and from all over the State of Texas, who came specially to attend this meeting. At the close of ten days session (the time advertised for the meeting), it was impossible to close, so it was continued a week longer, closing with power, light, life and truth to all. Thus ended the third annual Easter meeting at Orchard, Texas. After the conclusion of the battle here in Houston, I am going to Alabama, Mississippi, for a little season... I am your father in the gospel, Chas. F. Parham."[963] "Parham held a convention in Houston and left May 17, 1908."[964]

For all of Warren Carothers and Howard Goss' presentation of the demise of Charles Parham, Parham was right in Houston having powerful meetings. They surely knew he was there. The crowds could not be missed.

CHAPTER TWENTY

NEW PENTECOSTALS AND THE KKK

"I'd grown up fearing the lynch mobs of the Ku Klux Klan; as an adult I was starting to wonder if I'd been afraid of the wrong white people all along - where I was being pursued not by bigots in white robes, but by left-wing zealots draped in flowing sanctimony."

-Clarence Thomas

Charles Parham pledged to clear his name and refused suggestions to leave town to avoid prosecution in San Antonio. Subsequently, on July 24th the case was dismissed, "the prosecuting attorney declaring that there was absolutely no evidence which merited legal recognition." Parham's name disappeared from the headlines of secular newspapers as quickly as it appeared. There is now overwhelming evidence that no formal indictment was ever filed. There is no record of the incident at the Bexar County Courthouse, as the San Antonio Police Department routinely disposed of such forms in instances of case dismissal.[965] It may even be that the whole thing was fabricated in hopes of a real confession by Parham. Yet, he gave them nothing. Of course, innocent men have little confession to give.

Even the alleged bail amount of $1000.00 is suspect. Cases for Murder and other capital crimes in 1907 held maximum bail amounts of $750.00[966] Additionally, the amount seems consistent with cases in other states.[967] One has to ask why was his bail so high? Ironically, allegedly, San Antonio has a long history of jailing innocent people before they are found guilty.[968] In contrast, in the same court of Justice Ben Fisk, in a case where the suspect was charged with assault, the suspect was fined $5 and released.[969]

Parham immediately fought back with rage. He secured a lawyer, C. A. Davis, and announced that he had been "elaborately framed" by his old nemesis, Wilbur Voliva. Parham was certain that Voliva was furious over a Zion city church that Parham had preached in. It had once belonged to Zion but left the Zion association. It had joined the Apostolic Faith Movement. It does seem that Voliva worked in collusion with the Texas Syndicate, and he certainly was afraid of Parham's influence, but he may not have had anything directly to do with this event in Texas. No one would ever know in this life.

The other man arrested was a young man named J. J. Jourdan. Apparently, Mr. Jourdan was a jazz musician from New Orleans. While surrogates claim he was previously arrested in San Antonio, there is no evidence for their assumptions. It is true that Mr. Jourdan was arrested the 21st of May 1907 in Fort Worth, Texas on charges he took $60 from a roommate in Fort Worth.[970] It is likely that his crime in both San Antonio and Fort Worth had more to do with the fact that he was a non-white than anything else. Fortunately for Mr. Jourdan, both charges were simply dismissed. Jourdan was known to work in a Jazz Club known as the Ramblers.[971] In 1907, he served on the governing board of their 23rd Annual

~ CHAPTER TWENTY | NEW PENTECOSTALS AND THE KKK ~

Ball.[972] No record exists of any formal charge being brought against Mr. Jordan in either of the noted arrests. It seems that Mr. Jourdan was a man of color and a fan of New Orleans style jazz music. In Fort Worth and San Antonio there were jazz clubs patronized by blacks. Those who frequented there were often "victims of systematic racial discrimination begun against Negroes throughout the South, and this discrimination eventually emerged in the form of segregation. Stringent laws were passed relating to apprenticeship, labor contracts, vagrancy, voting restrictions, and the incompetency of Negroes to testify in court, each a deliberate attempt to nullify the Thirteenth Amendment."[973] Jourdan seems to have been a victim of these hateful laws.

There is no record of the incident at the Bexar County Courthouse.[974] Possibly there never was a legitimate incident. Perhaps the whole event was staged. One account says that J. J. Jourdan was a creole man (a man of color). An accuser in Zion City casts aspersions saying that the man was a Jew. The Texas Syndicate despised both Jews and persons of color so it really did not matter to them. Two newspapers that took liberty with the story were the Burning Bush, and the Zion Herald (the official newspaper of Wilbur Voliva's church in Zion). These newspapers were said to have quoted the San Antonio Light, along with an eyewitness account of Parham's alleged improprieties, including a written confession. When researched, it was found the articles "quoted" in the Herald and Bush never appeared in the San Antonio paper. It was also learned that the scandal was only publicized in certain areas—every source of which could be traced to the Zion Herald. If the rumor went nationwide, it traveled by the grapevine.[975] These facts indicate that persons in Texas fabricated the story and spread the rumors in an elaborate disinformation campaign. There never was a document that qualified as anything close to a legal confession, a point made clear by District Attorney I. C. Baker. The proposed document was obviously another fabrication of the same group aiding the Texas Syndicate disparaging the Parham family.

Without a doubt, it seemed that Voliva was making the best of the scandal, "leaving no stone unturned." Though no one could pinpoint Voliva as the instigator of the accusations, he had been known to spread rumors frequently about immorality against his chief rivals including some who joined the Texas Syndicate. In addition to Parham, Voliva had launched many verbal attacks on his associates in Zion, including Cyrus Fockler and Lemuel C. Hall, calling them "adulterers," and "immoral." The Zion Herald, Voliva's megaphone of righteous indignation disguised as a newspaper, railed against Parham taking delight in his plight in San Antonio. In a cavalcade of smear Voliva called out Cyrus Fockler, John G. Lake, John Spiecher, A. F. Lee, William H. Piper, and Tom Hezmalhalch branding them thieves, drunks, adulterers, and lovers of indecency.[976]

Never mentioned by the new Pentecostals was the actual arrest and real trial of Cyrus Fockler for fraud.[977] Unlike Parham's case where there was no charge ever filed, Texas Syndicate member Cyrus Fockler and other defendants faced three days of testimony in a full-blown real trial in Massachusetts. Judge W. A. Kingsbury dismissed their case, but not without serious doubts saying, "it required some self-denial on his part not to refer the case to the grand jury."[978] He charged the defendants which included Earl Clark and Maria Woodworth-Etter that the tactics they used to raise money were "repugnant to the general public."[979] The new Pentecostals presented to the public as grifters rather than people of God.

Parham's legal team and associates attempted legal action with the U. S. postal authorities for "unlawful defamation," but they refused to act on the matter.[980] Evidently, they had the evidence that Carothers and

CHAPTER TWENTY | NEW PENTECOSTALS AND THE KKK

his Texas Syndicate comrades had. The arrest of Parham was referenced by his enemies as evidence that Parham was a sodomite. The reference to Parham as a Sodomite stemed on the surface from a false arrest of Parham. However, it was much deeper. Parham's opponents were all white supremacists, segregationists, and deeply hated people of color in the deep South. They were not bashful about telling people exactly what I just wrote. Most of them were actively involved in activity that would today be deemed hate crimes.[981] Many of them would either join the Ku Klux Klan or be counted among their supporters. Many of the written documents of the KKK contain statements that reflect as quotes from Independent Holiness groups.

Marjorie Haire who traveled extensively with the Parhams responded to the accusation against Charles Parham with simplicity, *"That was a lie."* [982] Rev. Algernon Benoni Stanberry Jr., who traveled with Charles Parham did not even know of the allegation until after his friend's death in 1931. He responded, "I slept with him (meaning in the same room with Parham), eat with him and... I could swear on a stack of bibles that there was never one immoral approach in our ministry together."[983] Stanberry's response pointed to the secret nature of the high cabal held by Goss, Carothers, Hall, Bell, Opperman and comrades in the Texas Syndicate.

In one retelling, Mr. Jourdan became an "angel-faced boy," a "young man hymn singer." In another, he was a "Jew boy," apparently based on nothing, but adding a layer of antisemitism to the homophobia.[984] What a mess we weave when first we seek to deceive. The Texas Syndicate wiped their mouths and claimed they did no wrong. Apparently, someone wrote a confession for Parham[985] to sign; it is quite apparent that the Texas Syndicate played a part. All these white supremacists had commonality.

Many white supremacist Holiness preachers became actively involved in activities that led to the resurrection of the Ku Klux Klan in 1915.

Serpent Seed

Prominent among these groups was the doctrine of two seeds. It is a doctrine that is still believed among many white Pentecostal ministers. "The doctrine of the serpent seed, also known as the dual-seed or the two-seedline doctrine, is a controversial and fringe Christian religious belief which explains the biblical account of the fall of man by stating that the Serpent mated with Eve in the Garden of Eden, and the offspring of their union was Cain." "Genesis 9 talks about Noah and his three sons Shem, Ham and Japheth, from whom 'the whole earth overspread,' to follow the biblical narrative. After Ham told his two brothers that he had seen their father drunk and naked, Noah finds out and curses Canaan, Ham's son, to be 'a servant of servants unto his brethren.' Out of this biblical story, a racial exegesis derives proclaiming that Ham is the originator of the black race, Shem of the Semitic race, and Japheth of the Aryan race.

This racial reading of the ninth chapter of Genesis was part of legitimizing slavery in the United States since it was argued that God had predestined blacks to slavery or at least to be subordinated those of the white race."[986] All of KKK apologist Alma White's credibility was self-appointed. Methodism would not even grant her a license to preach.[987] Apparently, everything was evil and "revolting" to Alma White, including the way the people in the Apostolic Faith Movement held Godly love one to another.[988] Alma White offered solutions for getting rid of those who spoke in other tongues as the Spirit gave utterance. She suggested the Old Testament solution, "stoned to death that the land might be rid of witches, and it is necessary to wage as vigorous warfare against this evil today as it was in olden times."⁹⁸⁹ Thus, Alma White, her friends, denominational proxies, offered that those who spoke in other tongues should be stoned to death. To put an end to her enemies was Alma White's life goal and the reason she changed the name of her cult to **Pillar of Fire**.⁹⁹⁰ Only those who quote her as a legitimate contributor to the conversation would justify such vivitrol. Alma White was happy to play the role of white master as long as her subjects understood she was superior to them. "Despite the positive spin with which the women's Klan present their views on race, white supremacy inherently signifies the inferiority of all other races. In their official materials, the women's Klan frowns upon the consociation of white and black Americans, and Bishop Alma White bolsters the inherent inequalities of the races with Scriptural evidence.⁹⁹¹ However, in the midst of her argumentation, Alma conceded the underlying reasons for her racism, which may be applicable to the Women of the Ku Klux Klan of Colorado. It would seem that the political enfranchisement of black men prior to that of white women was an open wound, even after the ratification of the Nineteenth Amendment.'⁹⁹²

The A.F.M. and the Parhams held no regard for Jim Crow or his racist laws. If a black man was with Charles Parham in public that would be a violation of the Jim Crow laws of San Antonio. Among the norms that Jim Crow demanded that were violated by Charles and Sarah Parham and their less than desirable friends:

- A black male could not offer his hand (to shake hands) with a white male because it implied being socially equal.
- A black male could not offer his hand or any other part of his body to a white woman, because he risked being accused of rape.

J. J. Jourdan

- Blacks and whites were not supposed to eat together. If they did eat together, whites were to be served first, and some sort of partition was to be placed between them.
- Blacks were not allowed to show affection toward one another in public, especially kissing, because it offended whites.
- Jim Crow etiquette prescribed that blacks were introduced to whites, never whites to blacks. For example: "Mr. Peters (the white person), this is Charlie (the black person), that I spoke to you about."
- Whites did not use courtesy titles of respect when referring to blacks, for example, Mr., Mrs., Miss, Sir, or Ma'am. Instead, blacks were called by their first names.
- Blacks had to use courtesy titles when referring to whites and were not allowed to call them by their first names.
- If a black person rode in a car driven by a white person, the black person sat in the back seat, or the back of a truck.
- White motorists had the right-of-way at all intersections.
- Education. The schools for white children and the schools for Negro children shall be conducted separately.
- Teaching. Any instructor who shall teach in any school, college, or institution where members of the white and colored race are received and enrolled as pupils for instruction shall be deemed guilty of a misdemeanor, and upon conviction thereof, shall be fined....[993]

"Sodomite was used as a slur toward Parham because of his close association with people of color. The Texas Syndicate knew Parham was fond of his black friends and it provoked them! Traces of this racial exegesis is found in the official 'k-reed' of the Klan, which states, '*We avow the distinction between the races of mankind as same has been decreed by the Creator, and we shall ever be true in the faithful maintenance of white supremacy and will strenuously*

~ CHAPTER TWENTY | NEW PENTECOSTALS AND THE KKK ~

oppose any compromise thereof in any and all things."[994] Warren Fay Carothers' work was in cohesion with the positions of the Ku Klux Klan. These all-white detractors taught that persons of color were the seed of Satan.

A rare photo of a bearded Charles Fox Parham. Courtesy of Apostolic Archives.

"Through the analytical concept of 'racial exegesis'—meaning a biblically based view on the supposed origin of human races—the main argument is that the Klan did not invent anything in the racial and theological domains. The Klan's self-proclaimed mission to uphold white Protestant hegemony in America resulted in the identification of imagined racial and cultural threats. As important were mythical interpretations of history, according to which the white race was believed to be destined by God to thrive on American soil. The synthesis of racial ideology and Protestant theology in the Klan resulted in a self-identified vanguard of white, native-born, Protestant Americans seeking to follow Christ as 'Criterion of Character' by which Klansmen hoped to enhance the resurgence of American nation in accordance with the Founding Fathers' alleged religious and racial ideals."[995] Much of what is being argued in America at the present day—the addition of whiteness and Christian faith as basis for national identity as well as notions of America as god-ordained territory—was also proclaimed by the Klan.[996]

A white woman was arrested in San Antonio within days of Parham. She was arrested for the crime of being with a black man.[997] This was serious. Justice Ben S. Fisk, the same justice that was involved with Parham's

WHITE WOMAN WAS WITH NEGRO

Residents Near 100 Block on Eda Street Indignant and Appeal to Separate Mismated Couple.

Citizens living on and near Eda street in the neighborhood of the 100 block were thrown into excitement and indignation this morning by the discovery that a white woman was living with a negro man in one of the houses.

Agent Mathews of the humane society was notified and made an investigation, with the result that he found the woman in the house. An effort will be made to prosecute the parties and break up the relation.

The discovery was first made last night by Gabe Headen, who lives in the neighborhood. He saw a white woman approach the house and hesitate in a peculiar manner when she saw him. He retired and watched her from concealment, and saw her enter the house. Late last night he says he saw the couple in the back yard.

When the other neighbors heard of it this morning they became very much wrought up. Mr. Headen notified the humane society and Agent Mathews went to the house. The woman would not admit him at first, but he insisted, and when he got inside he found her in bed. The girl admitted she was white, gave her name and said she had recently come to San Antonio from Houston. The man was not in the house at the time.

Mr. Headen went with agent Mathews to Justice Fisk's office to make an affidavit against the woman, but the justice referred them to county attorney Newton.

case, referred her case to the District Attorney. Nearly all Christian Denominations were all-white or led by whites. "In 1915, white Protestant nativists organized a revival of the Ku Klux Klan near Atlanta, Georgia, inspired by their romantic view of the Old South as well as Thomas Dixon's 1905 book "The Clansman" and D.W. Griffith's 1915 film "Birth of a Nation." This second generation of the Klan was not only anti-black but also took a stand against Roman Catholics, Jews, foreigners, and organized labor."[998]

Rather than look inward for racism, the historians from various denominations gaslight Charles Parham. This has left the general impression that the Parham's and their A.F.M. were like these various hate groups. It was a horrible injustice to the Parham family and the Apostolic Faith Movement, that such historians would malign the Parhams. At the same time, they gave people like Warren Fay Carothers and Alma White a pass; this is disturbing to say the least. "One of many publications on racial theology that most likely influenced becoming Klansmen on such matters was *Anthropology of the People*, published pseudonymously in 1891 under the name Caucasian. In the book, Caucasian compares three theories about the origins of mankind and argues for which is believed to be most in accordance with Scripture. The theories are monogenesis (every race derives from Adam and Eve), polygenesis (only the white race derives from Adam and Eve), and evolutionary biology.[999]

Caucasian also rejects the monogenetic theory on the basis that it, if true, would have degenerated mankind due to miscegenation and thus turned Creation into failure. The theory is portrayed as humiliating God and incompatible with mankind's 'natural instincts' to hold on to one's own race. Caucasian considers it 'so absurd and preposterous, that it never could have been entertained by intelligent minds.'[1000] Based on these amplifications, Caucasian argues for the polygenetic theory as most compatible with the Bible. This implicates that non-white are not descendants of Adam, but inferior beings created by God before Adam and Eve."[1001] Thus, to these adherents and their all-white denominations people like Parham who would dare promote, encourage, or create an atmosphere conducive to miscegenation are like the people of Sodom — thus Parham was a Sodomite. Mission accomplished. No number of facts will likely ever get it the way of people's opinions.

Those who joined the Invisible Empire were focused on their mission. It would be a decade before they formally organized. However, the rhetoric used against Charles and Sarah Parham and their Apostolic Faith Movement would be the script that they would use repeatedly. No one said it better than when Edwin

Edwards joked with reporters: *"The only way I can lose this election is if I'm caught in bed with either a dead girl or a live boy."*[1002] The enemies of Parham and the Apostolic Faith Movement were not particularly focused on sodomy, but it was a very effective tool in getting the attention

of the Right and they needed the attention of the Right to advance their malevolent cause. Conservative Christian groups would carry their water much more and much farther than they realized. "[1003]

Claiming someone was a sodomite was a very effective political stunt. It seems it would have been much easier to arrest him in Illinois or Kansas where he lived, but Texas better fit the agenda. The law was much more favorable. At least one of Parham's enemies was well versed in the law, specifically Texas law. History proves that there was no place in the United States where the laws could be more influenced than Texas and more people were charged with such than any other state. The exact meaning of an act of unnatural offense came into question in the majority of these cases.[1004]

How convenient for Parham's enemies. The fact that there was never a formal charge, trial, conviction, etc. does not matter. This trial, like many others, was in the court of public opinion and the deck was already stacked. Historian Jacqueline N. Moore determined that, of all the cases in Texas where sodomy was charged, only eight were appeals to actual sodomy convictions.[1005] In the scheme against Parham conviction was not necessary, only an arrest was needed. In fact, formal charges and a trial would have been counterproductive to those who sought to bring accusation against Charles Parham and the Apostolic Faith Movement.

Consider Alma White's personal testimony, "In the spring of 1906, a colored man, introducing himself as Seymour, called at our Bible School at Denver. He was on his way to Los Angeles, California, and took the opportunity of visiting our School while passing through the city. We did not know he was in the building until He walked into the dining room. Someone had shown him through the building and brought him into the dining room. He had a strange appearance which somewhat aroused our curiosity, and as he claimed to be a preacher of the Gospel, we called on

~ CHAPTER TWENTY | NEW PENTECOSTALS AND THE KKK ~

him to pray. He responded with a good deal of fervor, but oh the feeling that came over us. We thought of demons, and other slimy creatures before he had finished praying. After he had left the room, a number of the students told that they felt that he was possessed with evil spirits. He was very untidy in his appearance; he wore no collar..." Alma White was an officer in the KKK. What else needs to be said?

When Parham arrived in Los Angeles, the leadership at the **Apostolic Faith Movement** had become a global force. The Apostolic Faith Gospel Mission on Azusa Street was enjoying the limelight of global attention and the lure of the money that was flowing to the Mission. It was William J Seymour's proverbial 15 minutes of fame. Most of the Apostolic

Faith Gospel Mission leaders were white and had a plethora of religious backgrounds. None of them had much experience as a leader of a local body of believers. Some would become much more renowned than Seymour.

Certainly, Florence Crawford, Glen Cook, and perhaps others. Seymour's race played a factor. The only place he was readily welcomed had been the Apostolic Faith Movement. His team had bitten the hand that fed them. Florence Crawford quickly moved on and Seymour made an enemy of her. Tragic. The new Pentecostals as they called themselves did not want black ministers and no doubt when they organized in 1914 as an all-white hate group, Seymour was shocked. Those that claimed to be interested in his branch of the Apostolic Faith Movement left him out of their all-white denomination.

Howard Goss and his friends in the Texas Syndicate did not want Seymour. They worked diligently from the time that Seymour's team barred Parham from their Mission church to alienate all black ministers and to discourage women ministers. Goss became their lead evangelist and he partnered with William Durham and E. N. Bell in Chicago. Bell then joined Goss in Malvern, Arkansas where Goss was printing a publication in the name of Charles Parham's ministry, Apostolic Faith. Realizing that they were living the lie and facing the uncertainty of potential legal challenges from the legitimate A.F.M., they changed the name to Word and Witness in 1910.[1006] Fortunately for all of us, the Parhams never responded by returning evil for evil.

Whether the white men who opposed them did so because of lust for preeminence[1007] or because of deep seeded racial hatred can be debated. Likely both persuasions are represented. Some acted so that, like Demetrius, they could be in charge. Bishop G. B. Rowe[1008] concluded that to be the primary motivation by such men as did Apostle John in his writing in 3 John. However, others clearly held deep seeded racial hatred. Whatever the rationale, it is certainly not pleasing to God. Following Parham's multicultural lead, Ambrose Jessup (A. J.) Tomlinson adopted a similar approach. Like the Parhams, he was a Midwesterner and did not agree with the cultural proclivities held by many in the Southern United States and apparently held by most denominational leaders of the era. Under the leadership of A. J. Tomlinson, the Church of God (Cleveland, TN.) adopted a centralized form of Church government with an inclusive International General Assembly (1906), launched a world evangelization effort beginning in the Bahamas (1909), inaugurated the *Church of God Evangel* (1910), and established educational opportunities for ministers and members (1918). Today Church of God ministries include more than 7 million members in 178 nations and territories. Some 36,000 congregations serve around the world.¹⁰⁰⁹

Carothers argued against allowing women to preach.¹⁰¹⁰ His defenders claim he was a staunch segregationist. History shows Carothers was extremely racist. Quakers, like Sarah Parham and Lillian Thistlethwaite, were part of the earliest denomination opposing the slavery system since 1776. Methodist banned slavery in 1784 while Presbyterians in 1818. Church started not only to ban the slavery, but also welcome the participation of the black in church activities and services. With the profound influence of the Great Awakening, by the end of the eighteenth century, there were about one quarter of blacks in the Methodists and Baptists in the South.¹⁰¹¹ Apparently, Carothers was not a member of these groups for reasons beyond his identification as a Pentecostal. He preferred separate groups for his black associates.

Parham and Carothers

"Nevertheless, because of the racist and exclusivist practices in the white Baptist and Methodist churches, separate black Baptist and Methodist religious bodies came into existence in the beginning of the eighteenth century. The black slaves not only took part in church with a sense of a personal and egalitarian God who gave them an identity and dignity not found in American society, but also enjoyed the right to control over their own ecclesiastical institutions."¹⁰¹² This arrangement let the political establishment retain its systems of power and control.

Let me translate some of Warren Fay Carothers' manifesto. "I am a racist. I expect that God must have intended that people should be divided by nations. Blacks should stay in their country which is Africa. Whites in their country which is the United States." (That an educated man would think that Africa is a country is quite alarming.) Anyone claiming the United States is a white nation by some sort of Divine decree, as though the natives were not God's creation, is simply ludicrous. Carothers was also advocating for the Mexicans and the Japanese to "stay in their place," which apparently in Reverend Carothers and the leaders of the Assemblies of God's view IS NOT IN THE UNITED STATES. Does anyone really wonder why this racist agenda could not co-exist with the Parham family? This type of writing played well at Carothers' country club and to his other racist friends and apparently to his growing group of friends in the all-white Assemblies of God, but this is not compatible with the blood shed by Jesus Christ for whosoever will...[1013]

> *"Anyone claiming the United States is a white nation by some sort of Divine decree, as though the natives were not God's creation, is simply ludicrous."*

Carothers advocated for a policy that strictly prohibited any kind of contact between whites and blacks. His writing served as proof text for the new KKK when they organized in 1915. "The Ku Klux Klan undoubtedly reflected such mythical historical accounts. Hiram Wesley Evans asserted that 'the hand of God was in the creation of the American stock and nation.'"[1014] This was based in fear of miscegenation and seen as justified by a belief that racial animosity was a corrective gift from God which helped ensure the separation of the races. W.F. Carothers justified southern segregation by arguing that although all humanity shared one blood (Acts 17:24-26), God had created a multiplicity of nations which God divided along color lines. From his perspective the U. S. was white, and Africa was black. Because of slavery "a whole nation" of blacks had been "imported" into the South thereby breaking down the natural "geographical barriers" which God had instituted. Racial friction was the inevitable result

CHAPTER TWENTY | NEW PENTECOSTALS AND THE KKK

of this intense intermingling of persons because God had intended to maintain "racial purity and integrity of the different nations." This racial friction was only intensifying because the Holy Spirit was now "at work" in what Carothers called "a final effort to preserve the integrity of the races." Carothers went on to argue that while prejudice existed within much of southern society, it did not exist among Pentecostals. Segregation within the churches as it was practiced by southern Pentecostals could not be used as a sign that they were racially prejudiced, but rather that they were in cheerful conformity to what he called "wholesome regulations" which were necessary in the South. "...The Pentecostal people of the South," he contended, "have not the slightest prejudice or lack of divine love for the colored people, nor is there any lack of mutual interest in the work they are doing and in their spiritual welfare." Indeed, "A proper separation of the races looking to the integrity of each," Carothers reasoned, "is no more 'prejudice' than is a proper separation of the sexes. Both alike are but the dictates of common decency and of a wholesome regard for the decrees of the Almighty."[1015] "It also became a divine mission to counteract miscegenation. The purpose was to preserve what the Ku Klux Klan considered to be divine order. For instance, the Deluge was seen as biblical evidence for miscegenation as opposing the Words of God and as such contradicting God's plan for mankind."[1016] Regardless the form of racial exegesis, the general goal for the Ku Klux Klan was to maintain the Founding Fathers' religious and racial ideals as imagined in order to counteract the alleged defilement of American society. To do so, the Klan formulated six premises. First, the Republic was established by white men; second, it was established for white men; third, it should never fall into the hands of an 'inferior' race; fourth, blacks must be kept outside of politics; fifth, blacks ought to comprehend that whites are the ones who rule in America; sixth, purity of the white blood must be maintained.[1017] The sixth premise appeared to be especially important to the Klan's racial exegesis, both under the Simmons and Evans eras. Two important Klan documents from each of these eras—Constitution and Laws of the Knights of the Ku Klux Klan (1922) and Klansman's Manual (1924)—establish that one of the fundaments of the Klan was 'to maintain forever the God-given supremacy of the white race.'"[1018] I hope the reader finds this self-justification as sickening as the author concludes. Yet, the A.G. continues to defend these men and their anti-Christ behavior.

While Carothers laid the groundwork for latter inclusion of the KKK, some of his Texas Syndicate friends were happy to outright join the KKK. **A. B. Cox,**[1019] Charter member of the General Council joined the KKK and was a member for at least seventeen years. He served as A.G. District Official in the old Central District and has been called by Assemblies of God historian William Menzies a "giant in the faith." "Cox claimed that no one could be a true American and not be a part of the KKK. "I have more respect for a man true to his country than [sic] with NO Religious profession at all, than for a weak kneed [sic] religious man." Though he mentioned nothing of the KKK's racial bigotry, he lauded its anti-Romanism." In response to one of Cox's parishioners who had written complaining of his promoting the clan, A.G. General Superintendent Welch suggested it was better to "stay free of entanglements in these last days no matter how good they look on the surface. He did not suggest that his friend, Cox, was wrong in being a member of the KKK."[1020] His (Carothers) opposition to women ministers would be transferred to the Assemblies of Ged where Carothers found a home in their organizational meeting in 1914.[1021]

Howard Goss generally sided with or agreed with Carothers' position on blacks since he partnered with Carothers. Goss would continue to have a long history of leading racial strife. There is some doubt that the two did not agree on women in ministry as both of Howard Goss's wives (Millicent and Ethel) were licensed ministers. These ladies were powerful evangelists in their own right.[1022] The reasons for Howard Goss' repeated alliances and lifelong connection to white supremacism is extremely troubling. The organizations he helped create and lead continue to ignore or attempt to explain away his racism; this is even more troubling.

CHAPTER TWENTY-ONE

THE BIG LIE

"[T]he anointing of the Holy Spirit is given to illuminate His Word, to open the Scriptures, and to place the spiritual man in direct communication with the mind of God."

-Charles Fox Parham

Early on in "Narrative of the Life of Frederick Douglass," the first of three autobiographies Douglass wrote over his lifetime, he recounts what happened—or, perhaps more accurately, what didn't happen—after his master, Thomas Auld, became a Christian believer at a Methodist camp meeting. Douglass had harbored the hope that Auld's conversion, in August 1832, might lead him to emancipate his slaves, or at least "make him more kind and humane." Instead, Douglass writes, "If it had any effect on his character, it made him more cruel and hateful in all his ways." Auld was ostentatious about his piety—praying "morning, noon, and night," participating in revivals, and opening his home to travelling preachers—but he used his faith as license to inflict pain and suffering upon his slaves. "I have seen him tie up a lame young woman, and whip her with a heavy cowskin upon her naked shoulders, causing the warm red blood to drip; in justification of the bloody deed, he would quote this passage of Scripture—'He that knoweth his master's will, and doeth it not, shall be beaten with many stripes,'" Douglass writes. Douglass was so scornful about Christianity in his memoir that he felt a need to append an explanation clarifying that he was not an opponent of all religion. In fact, he argued that what he had written about was not "Christianity proper," and labeling it as such would be "the boldest of all frauds." Douglass believed that "the widest possible difference" existed between the "slaveholding religion of this land" and "the pure, peaceable, and impartial Christianity of Christ."[1023] Those who formed the Assemblies of God and other related white supremacist groups perpetrated "the boldest of all frauds."

"The more racist attitudes a person holds, the more likely he or she is to identify as a white Christian. The correlation is just as pronounced among white evangelical Protestants as it is among white mainline Protestants and white Catholics—and stands in stark contrast to the attitudes of religiously unaffiliated whites."[1024] "If you were recruiting for a white supremacist cause on a Sunday morning, you'd likely have more success hanging out in the parking lot of an average white Christian church—evangelical Protestant, mainline Protestant, or Catholic—than approaching whites sitting out services at the local coffee shop,"[1025] "The theologian Jonathan Edwards pressed for the evangelization of the enslaved but owned several slaves; he believed the practice could be countenanced as long as they were treated humanely. "Within this evangelical framework, one could adopt an evangelical expression of Christianity yet remain

~ CHAPTER TWENTY-ONE | THE BIG LIE ~

uncompelled to confront institutional injustice."[1026]

If you tell a lie big enough and keep repeating it, people will eventually come to believe it. The lie can be maintained only for such time as the State can shield the people from the political, economic and/or military consequences of the lie.[1027]

Missionary Jeffrey Nelson wrote, "'As a young man growing up in the Assemblies of God, I was told that while other churches had a human founder such as Luther or Wesley, the Pentecostal Movement had no human origin, but it was simply a move of the Spirit. It was explained as a latter rain[1028] that God spontaneously poured out beginning at the turn of the 20th century. While in some ways this is true, the fact that God used one man, **Charles Parham**, to discover the doctrine of Bible evidence and then work indefatigably until his death to spread it was never taught—at least to me. I heard his name and read the stories of Stone's Folly and Topeka. I heard about the great outpouring of Azusa Street. It was often noted that no man began the movement.'[1029] Thank you, Jeff Nelson. When I read these words, I wept! I feel that for most of my life, I have been separated from my compatriots in Christ by an invisible wall where reality has imprinted this brutal division on the Army of God, standing before every Gate of so-called 'Truth' is a man separated from his fellow compatriot in the Gospel! Every man today in honesty ought to look upon a scar bespeaking of the brutality of unnecessary separation and division! There needs to be repentance before God!"[1030]

As a young man, this author's father pastored a church in another all-white male-controlled hate group. They are a sister organization to the all-white male-controlled hate group called the Assemblies of God. Both sides make the claim that they are different. Still, if the two organizations were living beings the DNA match would be nearly one hundred percent. The areas where the two groups differ is so minuscule it is hardly discernible: like a blemish in an unseen part of the body. One of the similarities is that both are all-white religious organizations. Ironically, both claim their genesis from what they have named the *Azusa Street Revival* which they both pretend was a black or African-American revival. This they claim, gives them a multicultural genesis. Since they know black people, they cannot be racist. Sound familiar?

One of the miniscule differences is that the Assemblies of God used the ruse of minor doctrinal differences to rid their organization of black ministers and women ministers.[1031] The group my father held membership, now United Pentecostal Church International (U.P.C.I.), took more than twenty years to also purge themselves of black ministers and most women ministers. Certainly, a minor difference but the same result. For the record, I am not offering that these two groups may not have some token[1032] representation from a minority group or women, but the fact remains that these groups were by design all-white and by edict male controlled. These always claim the bigotry of their group was someone else's fault or simply the way things were at the time. However, there are groups like the Church of God, Cleveland, Tennessee and C.O.G.I.C. that were part of the same times and did not have the same conclusions.

Inside their corporate walls some might jest that the U.P.C.I. leaders were slow learners in getting rid of their perceived deplorables, but this was not some jest. It was real and lives were destroyed, and people will likely miss eternal life as part of the consequences of the actions of the Texas Syndicate and their posterity in all-white hate groups that hide behind the cross. I am not in any way visiting the sins of the fathers upon

~ CHAPTER TWENTY-ONE | THE BIG LIE ~

the children. Yet, as I once commented to one of the self-righteous, the jury is still out! Fortunately, in the end, this will not be decided by a jury, it will be decided by our great God and Righteous King, Jesus Christ. He is ruler over everything. I am certain He is not amused in the slightest by our contrived reasons to be divided one from another. What is this I am writing? A rebuke? Yes, a rebuke long overdue! Who am I to write such a rebuke? NOBODY. In the words of Winston Churchill, *"I was not the lion, but it fell to me to give the lion's roar."* Thus, I am not the lion, but it is past time for excuses. I pray to God, some hear me. What is the big lie? ***The big lie is a riddle, wrapped in a mystery, inside an enigma. A conspiracy to defraud a man of his reputation so that ambitious men could rule in his stead.***

All-white Pentecostal groups claim a revival as their beginning. The same revival they created a name for and carefully developed the propaganda surrounding. They

The all-white Assemblies of God. First executive presbytery in 1914. Seated (L-R): T.K. Leonard, E.N. Bell, Cyrus Fockler; Standing (L-R): John W. Welch, J. Roswell Flower, D.C.O. Opperman, Howard A. Goss, M.M. Pinson.

claimed all were united at this revival they renamed Mission from the reference. Thus, distancing themselves from their real genesis and at the same time creating the basis of some of their self-serving propaganda. They claimed Charles Parham divided us all from our brothers and sisters because he was a racist! They claim they were all gender from this revival in Los Angeles. Yet, most of those making the claim, were never there. The division between the A.F.M. and the Neo Pentecostals is clear as a line drawn in the sand.

The truth is that all of these groups can make some claim to gendering to the Apostolic Faith Movement, but they do not mention that because the truth is way too uncomfortable. The Pentecostals were neither born at or united in the Apostolic Faith Gospel Mission (they call it Azusa Street). *Azusa Street* as these all-white hate groups have presented it, is a myth. There was no revival called the Azusa Street Revival. Wait, bear with me. There was a revival at the Apostolic Faith Gospel Mission in Los Angeles. This was a Mission of the Apostolic Faith Movement. The Mission was on a street called Azusa. William Joseph Seymour was one of several Apostolic Faith Movement ministers that participated in the Revival, and he emerged as the Past or of the Mission, a position he would hold till his death in 1922. The real deal is that there is a propagandized effort to make Azusa Street look like a black revival. They use this for a variety of reasons. Among the reasons is so they could have yet another outrageous charge to put at the feet of Charles and Sarah Parham. They also used this position to feed white guilt while giving reasons for the horrible treatment of the A.F.M., the Parhams, the Bishop Seymour and his wife Jeannie.

The organizers of both aforementioned hate groups (and other similar factions) were predominately white supremacists organizations using religion as a front. They claimed to be about unity,[1033] "but the Klan's unity, they are narrowly limited to those people they thought qualified as truly American—only white Protestants."[1034] In every one of these efforts there will be much emphasis on unity. They always claim "unity." In Truth, these practice their own brand of religious bigotry. These involve character assassination and harassment of members of religious minorities and the people that associate with them. Often members of religious minorities or those who are their benefactors are excluded from social functions or community gatherings. They may be falsely accused of crimes or framed for crimes they did not commit. Sometimes, religious bigotry will be cloaked with false accusations that members of minority religions are lazy or insane or an undesirable element. The most common form of persecution is to accuse the minority religious group of being a cult or Satanic. Early Christians were accused of sacrificing babies, cannibalism, and one piece of ancient Roman graffiti shows Christ with a donkey head. No one would accuse Christianity of such things now."[1035] Those who do participate in groups with such agendas are guilty by association.[1036] It is not a criminal allegation (although it may be). Rather as Merriam Webster defined, it is "moral guilt or unfitness presumed to exist on the basis of one's known associations. *Like Cain, we should inquire, "Am I my brother's keeper?"*[1037]

In a rare departure from the "THE BIG LIE" of the Assemblies of God, one of their top historians, Cecil Robeck, Jr., offered a rare glimpse into the truth. In fairness to Mr. Robeck, he at least vocalized what has been a historical fact that no one in the leadership of the Assembly of God has had the moral fortitude to address. I must give a *tip of the hat* to Mr. Robeck. I do not know him, but I trust he was a sincere man of God. I pray my response is not perceived as mean spirited as I have friends in the Assemblies of God. Robeck writes, "In the Fall of 1970, I moved to Pasadena, California, to begin my Master of Divinity studies at Fuller Theological Seminary. Our orientation to seminary life took place at a hotel in the San Bernardino Mountains. I drew a young United Methodist from Alabama as a roommate. As we introduced ourselves to one another, he asked me what my denominational affiliation was. I replied that I had been a member of the Assemblies of God all of my life. I didn't know quite how he would respond, because at that time, Pentecostals were still a rare novelty at Fuller. I can tell you that I was not at all prepared for his response."

"Oh," he said with a straight face, "then you are a racist!"[1038]

"A racist," I protested, "you don't even know me. I've never been a racist. I've been reared in a home in which my father has always preached the equality of persons regardless of color, where he has always argued for equal opportunity for everyone, and where the "N" word has never been tolerated. I'm no racist. In fact, some of my best friends in high school and college have been black."[1039]

Mr. Robeck, I understand. Like many of us, you have been given the mushroom treatment. What these all-white denominations fail to acknowledge is that after the Civil War, when *Separate but Equal* became a shiny new package for slavery, their leaders failed to denounce the horrors of the agenda. The church had opportunities to lead the way but kowtowed to their own lusts, and even persecuted those who dared to stand for the right. Thankfully, where religious people like the Assemblies of God and others make excuses, the United States Supreme Court ultimately made a way. On May 17, 1954 (more than fifty years after Charles and Sarah Parhams' Apostolic Faith Movement broke down the color barriers), the Supreme Court of the United States unanimously ruled that segregation in public schools is unconstitutional. The Court said, "separate is not equal," and segregation violated the Equal Protection Clause of the Fourteenth Amendment.[1040] Hallelujah! Great God Almighty We are NOT Free at Last, but it is getting Better!

Secluded in his all-white denomination Mr. Robeck was apparently unaware that he was "channeling a tried-and-true myth: the belief that proximity to blackness immunizes white people from having attitudes that are rooted in racism or doing racist things. In other words, offering the "some of my best friends are black" defense, which has so often been relied

~ CHAPTER TWENTY-ONE | THE BIG LIE ~

on by those facing accusations of racism that it has become shorthand for weak denials of bigotry a punch line about the absence of thoughtfulness and rigor in our conversations about racism.[1041] Nearly all racists resort to it at some point when challenged.

Mr. Robeck continues, "How is it that you can call me a racist?" "Well," he said in a Southern drawl, "that's not been my experience of the Assemblies of God. I've found them to be narrow and bigoted where I come from. Their churches are all white. Their record on civil rights has been terrible, and some of them even belong to the Klan."[1042]
All of the United Methodist preachers' statements have the same challenge. They are all facts. To say that the new Pentecostals that lusted for control and wrested the same away from Charles Parham were narrow and bigoted is an understatement. Ironically, John G. Lake made the same conclusion in 1927, calling the A.G. *more bigoted than the denominations from which they came*.[1043] We have outlined only the surface of these accusations in this book. There is far more to this than just the tip of the iceberg. In the United States at the time of this writing less than half of churches preach equality. Believing in equality is another discussion altogether.

Racists often think that one must know them to recognize racially oriented hatred. They think because they claim they preach "racial equality" that this has fixed the challenge. If it were only that easy preaching would have solved all humanities challenges. These always offer that they have friends of color. Classic racism. I notice in Mr. Robeck's response he does not try to prove that members of the Assemblies of God are not connected to the Ku Klux Klan (KKK). Warren Fay Carothers' manifesto was completely compatible with the KKK. The founders of the Assemblies of God were among the most bigoted of white supremacists. All supported KKK ideology and some openly joined the KKK. Dare we name them? Get ready, most of the Assemblies of God 'heroes' are on the list! **Howard A. Goss, Warren Fay Carothers, E.N. Bell, J. R. Flower, F. F. Bosworth, A. P. Collins, Andrew L. Fraser, D. W. Kerr, T. K. Leonard, D. H. McDowell, M. M. Pinson, H. G. Rodgers, J. W. Welch, D. C. O. Opperman, and B. P. Lawrence.** These are but the tip of the iceberg. We cited these because their names are affixed to the official racial position of the Assemblies of God as it stood at their inception and to make sure all were aware, was published in the Weekly Evangel for all the world to Witness. At the time it was published the all-white Assemblies of God was preparing yet another assault on people of color.[1044]

"If our God had Intended for men to have only one color, as he did that, they should have only One blood. doubtless be would have attended to that in the making of the nations. And his purpose to preserve the racial purity and Integrity of the different nations he had made Is plainly indicated by his appointment of the bounds of their habitation. Nor would there ever be any "race question" if men would but observe the divine arrangement and live, each nation in his own country, even as each family should live in its own separate home. There is no race question between the white people of the South and the Mexicans—or the Japanese; they are free to dine at our tables, ride in our coaches, attend our schools, churches, etc. "When the divine arrangement Is obeyed, then there may be visitors from one nation to another without any friction."

There is much more of this written, but I am pausing to give us all time to vomit. These men in the above name list believed and strictly adhered to this dogma. It was their Creed while they moved on to their next project, drafting their list of Fundamental Truths! This is the Creed of the Assemblies of God. Even as horrible as it manifests, there is more.

~ CHAPTER TWENTY-ONE | THE BIG LIE ~

Dear Reader, despite what they wrote, blacks were NOT welcomed at the table of many of these men. In fact, they lived in places where it was against the law to have blacks or Mexicans, or others sit at their tables, and they would not dare stand up for a black or Mexican brother in Christ in opposition to the Jim Crow laws. In fact, rather than take such a stand they organized against all-white ministers who would stand up for minorities. Do I hate the Assemblies of God? No, of course not. **I have friends who are in the Assemblies of God.**[1045] Are any of them black you might ask? No, of course not. None of them are black as far as I know. However, all of them are happy to support black missionaries and causes in other countries where black people live. Just like Assemblies of God founder Warren Fay Carothers proposed, *"Negroes should be in their country – Africa."*

Assemblies of God surrogates posing as historians have tried to gaslight Charles Parham with the most ridiculous of overtures in this arena. Robeck continues, "I went away from that conversation a bit off balance, insisting that I was not a racist. Still, this incident caused me to think, and I began to wonder why, even in 'progressive' California, I saw so few African-Americans in our congregations. In most churches, black faces weren't even present, and when they were, they were so few in number they could easily be overlooked. I wondered why I had never heard a sermon on racism, or for that matter on civil rights. I wondered, too, if I really was a racist but I didn't know it. For the next two years I was troubled deeply by these questions."[1046]

Let me help you Mr. Robeck. First, you do an excellent job of communicating with your writing. We have briefly outlined why the Assemblies of God and other all-white organizations have few or only token membership among black people in America. Sadly, Mr. Robeck, even after your confession (which we applaud the admission) on the horrible racially-oriented history of the Assemblies of God. You decided to pivot and give a lecture on what racism really entails, and then try to make the feeble case of blaming Charles and Sarah Parham. Seriously?! It is like a child caught with his hand in the cookie jar attempting to blame the cat. It is the same old strawman that A.G. apologists have used from even before their inception. Instead of accepting the challenge, they gaslight their opposition.

The article written by Mr. Robeck is a prime example of how racist people respond to real racial challenges:

A. make excuses,
B. blame other people,
C. attempt to show that they are "not as racist as others,"
D. etc.

What they never do is just own the charge and make changes (you know – REPENT).

Charles and Sarah Parham's openness to black, Hispanic, and other minority ministers was decades ahead of their time. It is not cute or excusable that men like **Carothers, Collins, Flower, Leonard, Kerr, and Goss** used people of color as stepping stones for their political agendas. Stop! You may want to read that again, more slowly. It is even more inexcusable that their proxies continue to make excuses. Sorry, Mr. Robeck. I have taken the gloves off here. I apologize in advance. You and the group you champion have not been anywhere near as fair. People like Charles and Sarah Parham, Lilian Thistlethwaite and others, had been attacked by this group of all-white men, like rabid dogs on fresh meat. I am certain there are more tombstones in this graveyard of good men and women than just our departed leaders. How they sleep at night blaming men they do not know without evidence is ridiculous! Just stop it!

Charles Parham understood that his message of Apostolic Restoration was for more than his predominately white audiences in the central part of the United States. There were very many more than just Charles Parham attacked by those with anti-Christ agendas. For starters there was Sarah Parham and her Sister Lillian Thistlethwaite. Their contribution to a multicultural ministry is substantial, well-documented and un-equaled. No one in the entire history of the all-white Assemblies of God has a comparable resume to either of these amazing women of God. Any surrogate from the A.G. attempting to smear their good names to prop up their horrible racial bigotry continues to manifest the true spirit of the Assemblies of God. The A.G. leadership presents that **Women and people of color are inferior.**

There is no long list of persons of color associated with the Assemblies of God, because there are no black ministers connected to their ministry. Please don't bring up some token or the political posturing for a black minister or two in the late 1960's. White men with political agendas have re-rewritten the history of the Apostolic Faith Gospel Mission and named it after a street (Azusa Street). They have successfully passed it off as though their organization was born in that Revival. It was not called that in the beginning. This was the Apostolic Faith Gospel Mission in Los Angeles. This was a Mission Church of the Apostolic Faith Movement. To believe that the Assemblies of God was born at the Apostolic Faith Gospel Mission would be like believing that large white Southern Baptist Churches in the deep South were readily welcoming black people to take the Lord's Supper from a common cup with the high affluent white folks. If only!

The so-called Azusa Street Revival of the Apostolic Faith Gospel Mission in Los Angeles was NOT connected to the Assemblies of God –

EVER! The Assembly of God did not exist in the heyday of either the Los Angeles Outpouring or the Revival at the Apostolic Faith Gospel Mission in Los Angeles. This was an **Apostolic Faith Movement** revival. I hear the voice of Joe Friday - JUST THE FACTS MAAM.[1047]

Here is a fact. When the Assemblies of God organized in 1914, William J. Seymour saw them for what they were. An all-white group that opposed him, his ministry and even his friends in the Apostolic Faith Movement.[1048] In response to the organizing of the Assemblies of God Seymour led his congregation to amend the Articles of Incorporation and the Constitution of the Apostolic Faith Gospel Mission. The changes outlined that all elected leaders would be limited to people of color.[1049] This would keep the all-white Assemblies of God from controlling the ministry. Instead, the Assemblies of God claimed the Apostolic Faith Gospel Mission (which they renamed Azusa Street) as their beginning![1050] Some say that Seymour's move was a tribute to his old friend Charles Parham who even though they had some disagreements, had been the only white preacher to come to the defense of the black preacher, Seymour, when he was faced with another leader of the all-white Texas Syndicate trying to take over his little church. Another man who had no regard for black ministers and a close associate of the Texas Syndicate, William Durham.[1051]

For Seymour, whatever mandate he set for his local mission, he attempted to back up with a biblical precedent. For example, in describing the "prejudices and discrimination" of several of their "white brethren," he uses a biblical passage from Galatians.[1052] In this passage, Paul writes of a time when he felt it necessary to rebuke a fellow apostle, Peter, for discriminating, as a Jew, against Gentile believers. Thus, this provides the scriptural precedent for his own forthcoming rebuke. Furthermore, in describing the way African-Americans in the congregation should respond to this discrimination, Seymour cited two passages, Matthew 17:8, and the entire 23rd chapter of Matthew. Interestingly, the first verse comes from a context unrelated to church unity, or even anything to do with race; rather, it comes from the account of the transfiguration of Jesus (when Jesus brought a few disciples up onto a mountainside, where Jesus temporarily traded his human form for a radiant one, while the ancient prophets Moses and Elijah appeared and talked with Jesus). The verse itself says, "When [the disciples] looked up, they saw no one except Jesus." Thus, it that Seymour's exhortation was for his congregation to focus on spiritual things—specifically, on Jesus—and to ignore acts of discrimination against them. In 1915, looking back at the development of the Apostolic Faith Gospel Mission and the Pentecostal movement, Seymour recalled, "Very soon division arose through some of our brethren, and the Holy Spirit was grieved." The message of unity was one that Seymour believed truly was important to God.[1053] While Seymour and Parham had some disagreement, they both held that the Holy Spirit was Supreme and more important than their individual concerns. Both championed the A.F.M. till their death.

The Assemblies of God and their proxies have systematically and purposefully misrepresented the history of Charles and Sarah Parham and the A.F.M. because the actual history was so damning to their propaganda. They prevaricate and rewrite the history to make it seem they were connected. The facts remain, they were just as Mr. Robeck's Methodist friend and others at Fuller Theological charged - RACISTS. If the dress fits, just wear it!

Charles Parham did not just embrace black and other minority ministers. More to the point, he sought them out, embraced and promoted them.[1054] This was especially true in reaching black audiences. Key in this pursuit was Lucy Farrow.[1055] Farrow began to impact a hungry audience in black churches in Houston. This led to a request for someone to come to a black church in Los Angeles.[1056] Parham's willingness not just to promote women, but to treat them as ministerial equals was one hundred years or more ahead of his time. Parham's contribution to giving women opportunities generally reserved for women gave rise to a plethora of women ministers. Not just those with the imprimatur of his own Apostolic Faith movement, but in a larger arena with women like Aimee Semple McPherson, Maria Woodworth-Etter, and others.[1057]

Howard Goss and **W. F. Carothers** attempted to persuade **Charles F. Parham** about the subject early on, but Parham was not to be coaxed to take a stance against ministers of God based on color or gender.[1058] So, the next step: these men failed in a coup to run Charles Parham out of the group he started, **The Apostolic Faith**. Despite a considerable campaign against Parham, Goss and Carothers failed in their mutiny. So, they began to form their own group. The first scheme was a counterfeit group for which they pirated the name Apostolic Faith Movement. Parham, for his part, wanted no schism. Thankfully Parham stood up when they thought he would kowtow. The Apostolic Faith Movement survived with independent Missions all over the world and an overabundance of renowned ministers promoting the core doctrine of the Apostolic Faith in the United States and around the World. Several major A.F.M. leaders led considerable ministries in their own right, Florence Crawford, William J. Seymour, Garfield Thomas Haywood, Thoro Harris, B. M. David, G. B. Rowe, and others.

Much drama had been associated with the departure of **Florence Crawford** from Los Angeles. If she were a man, her departure would likely never be mentioned. Rumors of racial rift here are also misplaced. Crawford felt compelled by God to assume the A.F.M. in Portland. Portland strongly identified as Apostolic Faith even before Crawford's arrival.[1059] As the A.F.M. Director of the Pacific Coast, this was part of her area of responsibility. The ensuing challenge with the Apostolic Faith publication was also overplayed. The publication continued to be printed with the permission of the Parhams. Just from a different location. Claims that the mailing list was stolen are way overplayed. Nothing stopped the A.F.M. in Los Angeles from creating their own independent publication or mailing list. Many of the names on the mailing list were not originally from Los Angeles A.F.M. These accounts never acknowledge that the A.F.M. in Los Angeles had decided to become independent of the Parhams. Crawford edited a version of the Apostolic Faith while she was in Los Angeles. The Los Angeles leadership never took into account that their decision to separate from the Parhams might have extenuating circumstances. This was one of the consequences. Florence Crawford's publishing of the Apostolic Faith in Portland was approved by the Parhams. The A.F.M. in Portland continues to be connected to the Parhams' legacy. Additionally, there is solid evidence that Seymour agreed to continue working with Crawford with the Apostolic Faith publication moving to Portland.[1060] Jeannie Seymour even helped with the organizational documents showing the general spirit of collaboration within the A.F.M. and gave explicit permission for publishing the "Apostolic Faith."[1061]

    Florence Crawford and her multicultural Apostolic Faith Mission in Portland, OR was a target of hostile takeover by the new or *Neo-Pentecostals*.[1062] They were at war with the A.F.M. and Crawford was connected to the A.F.M. and the Parhams. Effectively, Portland was an independent A.F.M., but that did not matter to the Texas Syndicate. As in Los Angeles, the Texas Syndicate sent their comrade William Durham to split Crawford's work with his new racially divisive dogma.[1063] He opened a competing church three blocks away.[1064] Strange that Goss claimed their new Pentecostal group was about stopping such activity.[1065] Durham threatened to take all of Crawford's people. Crawford responded, "You are welcome to every member you can get."[1066] Durham succeeded in taking about half the Portland congregation and dealing crushing blows to both the Apostolic Faith Gospel Mission in Los Angeles and Elmer Fisher's congregation. Defectors from the Apostolic Faith Gospel Mission in Los Angeles included Glen Cook.[1067]

Crawford responded by establishing an Apostolic Faith Mission on East 1st Street in Los Angeles.[1068] It was at this point that Seymour decided he was the head of these Independent Apostolic Faith Missions. Crawford merely followed the pattern established by the Los Angeles leaders and separated from Seymour as an Independent Apostolic Faith Mission. Still, there was solidarity against William Durham, Frank Ewart and all the Texas Syndicate as "Charles Parham, William Seymour, and Florence Crawford denounced them as no longer being Apostolic. Some people addressed them as *Neo-Pentecostals* or 'new Pentecostals.'"[1069]

The attempt by Goss and Carothers and their Texas Syndicate was wrought with challenges. Howard Goss admitted, "Many people seemed to think of this movement as some new competitive doctrine which a bunch of young irresponsible had recently hatched and certainly not as the good news of the gospel..."[1070] With their hostile takeover of the A.F.M. flailing they created more schemes. **First,** they created a group they called the ***Apostolic Faith Church of God in Christ***. This was an attempt to proselytize the names of the two most recognized groups of the time and persuade white ministers to join with their group. You can see the endorsement of the slick lawyer from Houston, Warren Fay Carothers in making the name just different enough to avoid being litigated. Not that either Parham or Mason was inclined to such, but even those good men of

~ CHAPTER TWENTY-ONE | THE BIG LIE ~

God could tolerate only so much larceny. The tactics of the Texas Syndicate apparently ate away at Howard Goss' soul as he became like a press secretary attempting to explain away the anti-Christ nature of the counterfeit movement. Like a crime family, the Texas Syndicate sought to legitimize their movement. The focus was only on white ministers. Historians refer to this effort as the Church of God in Christ (white) in reference to their propensity toward a list of all-white, like-minded ministers.[1071]

Historians have imagined some alignment between this group and Charles H. Mason's Church of God in Christ. Goss allegedly approached Bishop Charles Mason and offered to create an all-white version of the Church of God in Christ. It is an oft told tale among the Assemblies of God, United Pentecostal, and other all-white racially oriented groups. However, it presents like more of the Big Lie. Why would Mason, who was in court from 1907 to 1914 fighting for control of the Church of God in Christ be interested in such a racist arrangement? Why would Mason agree to license white ministers separately when his group already licensed white ministers?

There is a list of all-white ministers that Howard Goss claimed authorship and ownership, but no record exists of any of the ministers on the list being licensed with or ordained by the Church of God in Christ of Charles H. Mason. There were no documents, licenses, ordination papers, train tickets, conference schedules, etc. Simply nothing but a list that could mean many things. All sides agree – it is a list of all-white ministers. When this scheme failed, the Texas Syndicate moved on to the next plot.

Second, these men formed the Assemblies of God. "When the all-white Assemblies of God was formed in 1914,[1072] the largest contingent of incoming ministers came from a loosely-organized group identified by historians as "Apostolic Faith Church of God in Christ (white)." This was

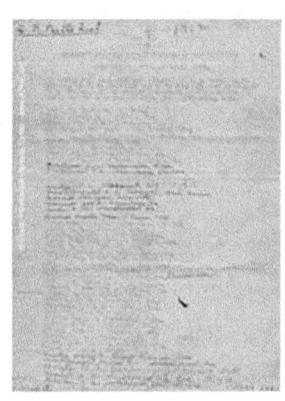
Howard Goss's list of white ministers that became the basis of organizing the Assemblies of God.

an all-white group led by Warren Carothers and loyal to Howard Goss and his Texas Syndicate. Goss organized several groups over the next forty years. The groups that Howard Goss organized were always all-white. In 1915, E. N. Bell continued the Texas Syndicate charade with the **Weekly Evangel** claiming that W. F. Carothers was connected to a multicultural outpouring in Houston. Simutaneously, he pretended that Parham was disposed. After naming Parham, he claimed they never name anyone.[1073] The reality is that Carothers brief stint at A.F.M. ministry in Texas ended in 1906. He turned his attention to a variety of business interests including a law practice, writing policy for the Assemblies of God, selling abstracts and inventions related to weather. In the secular world, Carothers appears to have had some successes. Meanwhile the legitimate A.F.M. had a strong base of more than 100,000 actively involved in their ministry.[1074]

White Pentecostal organizations are racially oriented in the selection of their members. Most notable of these organizations are the Pentecostal Ministers Inc. (P.M.I.),[1075] the Assemblies of God[1076] and their sister organization, The United Pentecostal Church.[1077] These were organized with the idea that only white people would be members and/or hold important positions in their group. Howard Goss was in the forefront of this effort. His best skill was salesman. He was opposed to black and minority ministers being his equal and his friend W. F. Carothers was like-minded. Carothers also was opposed to women ministers as equals. Their warrant in the founding of the Assemblies of God is substantial. The only problem for Goss was they did not put him in charge of the A.G. As a result, Goss

~ CHAPTER TWENTY-ONE | THE BIG LIE ~

Howard Goss

joined with a faction of all-white ministers who left the nascent group and started another scheme. This group they called the General Association of Apostolic Assemblies - G.A.A.A. Howard Goss admitted that he was not necessarily in agreement with their side of what was couched as a doctrinal debate, but since the A.G. had not put him in charge, he threw his lot in with the all-white G.A.A.A. It is not certain what Goss believed. The commonality of both groups reviled Charles Parham and the A.F.M.[1078] The enemy of my enemy is my friend.

In 1924, Goss, Texas Syndicate comrade Hall, and their fellow collaborators revolted against Garfield Thomas Haywood (black secretary of the P.A.W.) because of his race and formed yet another all-white group they labeled the Pentecostal Ministerial Alliance.[1079] Later they changed the name to the Pentecostal Ministers Inc. These groups were totally designed and organized for white men by white men. These white men openly endorsed racial segregation and other forms of animosity that seemed acceptable to the general society. Race was more important than doctrine to these men. This was a schism of white ministers from the multicultural Pentecostal Assemblies of the World (P. A. of W.). The P. A. of W. began as a predominately white group but by 1924 had a strong and growing presence of minority ministers. As before with the A.F.M. white men resurrected their racial bigotry as more valuable than the Gospel of Jesus Christ. As in their opposition to the A.F.M., they withstood black ministers having leadership positions. They were okay in the same group as minorities but they didn't see them as their equals. Their primary target in the 1924 scheme was Garfield Thomas (G. T.) Haywood.[1080]

In 1931, after the death of Bishop Haywood, Goss led a failed effort to gain control of the P.A. of W. However, it was only a matter of time and manipulation. There was a merger of the P. A. of W. with the A. C. of J. C. that resulted in the creation of the Pentecostal Assemblies of Jesus Christ (P.A. of J. C.). Initially the P.A. of J. C. boasted an equal composite of white and black ministers. Until the white members in clandestine activity with Howard Goss created a path to oust or urge black leaders to leave the group. This exodus of black leaders throughout the mid to late 1930's created a path to a merger of the two all-white hate groups. The P.M.I. merged with the P.A. of J. C. to become the **United Pentecostal Church Inc.** Nearly forty years after they started, the Texas Syndicate had accomplished the lofty goal of two all-white racially bigoted Pentecostal organizations. After forty years of racial oriented animosity against non-whites, the U.P.C.I. leaders boldly announced itself as a UNITY effort and named their group "UNITED"![1081]

CHAPTER TWENTY-TWO

BAPTIZED IN JESUS' NAME

"For my enemies I have only an abiding sympathy; no words of condemnation, but only sorrow for the souls, who, through their fight on me, have been wrecked and ruined. I think the greatest sorrow of my life is the thought that my enemies, in seeking my destruction, have ruined and destroyed so many precious souls."

-Charles F. Parham

There were no women leaders permitted in the Texas Syndicate. As an executive in the Assemblies of God, Warren Fay Carothers used his position to keep women in their place. Carothers was not just focused on keeping blacks and other minority men in their place; he was an equal opportunity controller. His misuse of Scripture to prop up his ideas was at the center of the "way things are done" in the Assemblies of God. Charles Parham called it "the rule in Texas." Racism and sexism were two favorite dogmas of the A.G. and Carothers liked to pontificate about both. Carothers' book on Church Government published in 1909 became a manual for the nascent Assemblies of God.[1082] Carothers, ever the lawyer, used nine New Testament Scriptures to outline his view of the place of women in the Church. Carothers offered that Man was created in the image of God and therefore destined to rule all things – including women. Of course, when Carothers spoke about men, he was talking about white men, as he did not see nonwhites as equals. "In theory, ordination gives women and men equal access to all levels of leadership, but no woman has ever seriously contended for elective or appointive offices within the Assemblies of God structure.[1083] This was the core element of the creation of the Texas Syndicate. Nonwhites and women could not be permitted to hold any role of equality with white males. Like a group of judges, nine white men were placed in charge of the A.G.

If you doubt the strength of the Texas Syndicate in the A.G., this will stun you. In 1916, in what presents as a bad joke, the A.G. appointed Warren Fay Carothers to lead the "General Field Department." Sound familiar? This was a regurgitation of Carothers' "scheme" from 1906. Parham had rejected Carothers' scheme but his Texas Syndicate friends embraced the theory like a new cart to move the Ark of the Covenant. Just as Carothers had previously orchestrated, the General Field Department was created "as a medium for keeping our Executive Presbytery and General Council in daily, co-operative touch with the General Bodies of Pentecostal peoples the world over, this General Field Department would be able to promote good fellowship, actual unity, co-operation, and gradually eliminate friction, misunderstanding, and disorder in general in all fields home and abroad."[1084] Carothers said, "ALL FRICTION and TRESPASSING will be avoided.[1085] Wow! Really! This is like appointing Adolf Hitler to unite all Europeans in love! Carothers, ever the power broker, was the architect of the 1916 **Fundamental Statement of Faith** and was helped by others in the all-white Syndicate.[1086] Carothers used his

~ CHAPTER TWENTY-TWO | BAPTISED IN JESUS NAME ~

contribution to parlay his new role as National Director which effectively put him in charge of all the people in the world. Finally, Carothers was legitimately a National Director. This was his utopian dream – an all-white group. Carothers served the A.G. as kind of a black Pope,[1087] a role that Carothers knew so well. Who would have guessed that Carothers, white supremacist, would be given the role of General Field Director in an all-white group?

"The Assemblies of God congregations exclude women from church boards, even as women pursue ordination. These issues have agitated the constituency since the Assemblies of God was formed in 1914. For a short time, it seemed that women might overcome Carothers and his friend's sanction to keep them *in their place*.[1088] Like Charles and Sarah Parham, these women of God seriously underestimated the warrant of Warren Carothers and The Texas Syndicate in their new Pentecostal experiment. They not only dominated the first decade, but they put policies and disciples in place that would continue to secure their policies. In 1931, a strongly worded resolution discouraging women pastors passed."[1089] Women placed a pivotal role in planting churches early on but since the nineteen thirties no women evangelists have[1090] had national appeal in the denomination, and most of the handful of prominent female pastors who once exerted influence have died. The A.F.M. had welcomed and encouraged women, the neo-Pentecostal embraced no such unanimity.

Unlike the new Pentecostals and the A.G., the first assemblies in Australia bore the likeness of the Apostolic Faith Movement. Established New Year's Eve 1909, and led by fifty-year-old grandmother, **Sarah Jane Lancaster.** (It is noteworthy that, prior to 1930, not only was Lancaster the informal leader of pentecostalism in this country, but over half of the assemblies established prior to 1930 were planted and led by women.)

Early Australian Pentecostalism in the model of the A.F.M. had little in the way of structure or doctrine that could identify it as a "church." What formed and sustained communities was a shared experience and theology of baptism in the Spirit. Baptism in the Spirit was symbolically representative of the pentecostal identity and worldview and, in this way, functioned at the level of cultural values by enriching self-understanding. The notion of Spirit-baptism as universally available, and universally empowering for people of all genders, all races, all classes, and all intelligences, was a vital symbol of unity. At the same time, since the Spirit was understood as a sign of the end-times, as facilitating personal holiness, and as empowering for mission, it also acted as a force for cultural and social change."[1091]

"It can thus be said that baptism in the Spirit facilitated pentecostal ecclesiology, despite the fact that early assemblies were structured informally, and there were no ordained ministers. There was no formal connection between assemblies, and no agreed statement of doctrine, a fact that was to become a major issue when some pentecostal assemblies discovered that Lancaster did not believe in the doctrine of the Trinity.[1092] She was an annihilationist, rejecting traditional views of hell which is another of the positions that were acceptable in the A.F.M.[1093] Lancaster was open to fellowship with people of diverse opinions on these matters. Like many voluntarists, she believed that a shared experience of the Spirit was enough to constitute "the church," that the church was an "organism not an organization,"[1094] and that unity was possible without so-called divisive doctrine and restrictive structure. She was in very good standing. The Parhams and their A.F.M. concurred.

The Texas Syndicate vision for women and minorities had been accomplished. Women, like blacks, had been regulated to their place. In a no holds barred letter, title Leadership,[1095] Charles Parham let the cat out of the bag on the Texas Syndicate giving a laundry list of those connected with the desire for power and control. Parham wrote, "My reason for writing this article is to make my position clear and warn honest men to fight the spirit of leadership that has seized and destroyed so many able men in this movement. The first man who sought leadership was a Mr. Carothers, of Texas, pastor of a small holiness church in Houston, who had a hobby of church government or polity which he thought superior to any tried or used by old line churches. He sought position in the work by urging me to blaze the way and he would follow with his organizing scheme, tithing system, etc. After a visit to Zion City, he became crazed with the desire for leadership and sought the destruction of everyone and everything that stood in the way of the realization of his dream. I refused to be a party to his plans and methods; in seeking my destruction, he backslid hundreds of true hearts and he himself went to the wall."[1096] Result – he has no following and has long been engaged in secular work."[1097] Leaving ministry behind as he had no genuine ministry.[1098]

Other Candidates that Parham mentioned for pre-eminence in Carothers' Texas Syndicate included a Brother Fink from Denver, Colorado who wanted to have a bunch of Bishops that would answer to Parham. Parham had no interest. [*Lupton of Alliance, Ohio and Mr. Piper of Stone Church in Chicago.*] Piper wrote Parham a bitter letter barring him from attending his church. Parham "warned him that if he did not repent, two years would be the limit of his life. Six months before the two years were up, he took sick and died. Fisher of Spring Street in Los Angeles, who stole his congregation from Azusa and sought leadership. Durham of Chicago and many others.

BAPTIZED IN JESUS' NAME

One would expect that since Christ followers are instructed to do everything in the name of Jesus Christ, baptizing in His name would be natural – not controversial.[1099] However, since 1914 baptizing while invoking the name of Jesus Christ has become synonymous with controversy. Among the lesser publicized doctrines promoted by Charles Parham was baptism invoking the singular name of Jesus Christ (circa 1900).[1100]

In 1915, nearly everyone was being baptized or even re-baptize invoking baptism in the single name of Jesus Christ. This was nothing new for the A.F.M. as Charles and Sarah Parham had baptized in Jesus' name since about 1901.[1101] Charles Parham wrote as much in his book in 1902 and later said that neither he nor Sarah Parham had ever been baptized with the Triune formula.[1102] Despite the fact that Charles Parham and the A.F.M. had championed Jesus' name baptism as opposed to the Roman triune formula.[1103] Some of the new Pentecostals expected baptism in Jesus' name was a revelation. Good for them! As the new wave of Jesus' name baptism seized the country many of the new Pentecostals were swept up in the wave. Howard Goss, who had already been baptized in Jesus' name by Charles Parham got baptized again in Jesus' name.[1104] For Goss, this latter baptism was presented as a publicity stunt to impress his Texas Syndicate friends and their new A.G. and Goss dare not mention that this was how Parham baptized.[1105] Yet, to his credit, Goss would stay the course in holding to Jesus' name baptism.

Goss's close associate, Texas Syndicate adherent and Chairman, E. N. Bell, of the newly formed Assemblies of God was baptized in Jesus' name and wrote a marvelous tract about the experience. Bell's publication was called, "Who is Jesus Christ" and one of the issues featured pictures

~ CHAPTER TWENTY-TWO | BAPTISED IN JESUS NAME ~

of E. N. Bell and his friend Howard A. Goss. This issue is preserved at Apostolic Archives.[1106] The Jesus name baptism resurgence was going quite well until Warren Fay Carothers, leader of the Texas Syndicate and powerful member of the A.G. Executive Board had a meeting with the A.G. leadership. Most notably with J. Roswell Flower. Carothers pointed out that most black and other minority ministers were already baptizing in Jesus' name. These had learned this mode of baptism from Carothers' enemy, Charles F. Parham. Carothers was very concerned that this would bring a new wave of interest and inquiry to the all-white A.G. from those they had already dismissed as undesirables. The last things the A.G. wanted was a 14th Amendment challenge to their all-white alliance[1107].

Carothers understood that Jesus' name baptism was a foundation stone of Charles Parham's A.F.M. Carothers and Flower were among the nine men appointed to the first Executive Presbytery of the A.G.[1108] The Texas Syndicate influence could not be denied. The embracement and endorsement of the same by A.G. leaders would lend credence to those that considered the A.G. a counterfeit movement. While the A.G. loved to pretend and even published that Parham was irrelevant, everyone understood that Parham was still the senior leader. **E.N. Bell** General Superintendent of the **Assemblies of God** said that God spoke to him about being baptized in the Name of Jesus.[1109] The conviction was so irresistible that he called for **Evangelist L.V. Roberts** to baptize him.[1110] He then published an article strongly supporting Jesus' name baptism and his Christocentric position. This was of course before the Texas Syndicate had time to respond. The letter by E. N. Bell would be so strong that Flower (Assistant Editor) severely edited the content before printing the letter. Bell was forced to resign as Superintendent of the Assemblies of God and **Arch P. Collins** (as xenophobic as Carothers) was temporarily appointed.[1111] Bell made it clear that he supports Baptism in Jesus' name. He also encouraged the ministers not to make this a point of contention. However, history proves that neither side of the argument was willing to listen. Bell quickly found himself *persona non grata* with his Assemblies of God "friends."[1112] The truth is that E.N. Bell's article would have made even Charles Parham pleased. The doctrinal positions he expounds are superior to anything that the so-called "oneness" organizations have produced. One of Bell's many points was that he denounces the study of the Trinity as never causing anyone to be saved and presents that exalting Jesus Christ as the mighty God would bring thousands and thousands to Christ![1113] Afterall, the railing against Charles Parham and the A.F.M., it is evident that he was right all along.

Carothers brought his Texas Syndicate to bear, forcing E. N. Bell out of leadership. Bell then writes in his Word and Witness that baptism in Jesus' name is just a fad and would fade away.[1114] The A.G. began to call baptism in Jesus' name, "the New Issue." Of course, this was falsehood. There was nothing new about baptism in Jesus' name. First, it was in the Bible and second, Charles Parham and the A.F.M. had baptized in Jesus' name for more than a decade. E. N. Bell began to give due penitence to his all-white brotherhood. Four years later after the successful organizing of the Pentecostals Assemblies of the World, Bell attempted to do damage control over his repudiation of his baptism in the name of Jesus Christ.[1115]

For cover, the A.G. began publicizing their "New Issue" and created

~ CHAPTER TWENTY-TWO | BAPTISED IN JESUS NAME ~

a back story that the whole thing started at a camp meeting in Arroyo Seco, California in 1913. Sounds good, if you don't ask questions. However, *the Apostolic Faith World-Wide Camp-Meeting* was the event and those there were not in opposition of baptizing in Jesus' name. No one there thought much of the subject at the time as the A.F.M. had baptized in Jesus' name for more than a decade. The only thing "NEW" was the A.G. claiming it was new. The Apostolic Faith Worldwide Camp Meeting was organized by R. J. Scott and George Studd. They spoke directly to the subject of who was to be given credit for the meeting. **"This camp meeting belongs to the Apostolic Faith people."**[1116] One thing that was new, was that the new Pentecostals attempted to take the credit for the success of the meeting.[1117] George Studd organized, promoted, and attended the A.F.M. Camp Meeting. He was a strong proponent of baptism in Jesus' name and later served on the board of the Original Pentecostal Assemblies of the World (P.A. of W.) when it organized in 1919.

The organizers, R. J. Scott and Studd said, "God is gathering His saints together in this city of Los Angeles, where he first set down his power in such a mighty way in 1906. We stand squarely for the whole Word of God, and the full Gospel - Jesus Christ crucified, risen and ascended, and the baptism with the Holy Ghost with the seal of speaking in tongues as the Spirit gives utterance. (Acts2:4)." [1118] This statement speaks volumes. The doctrinal position outlined is clearly Apostolic Faith Movement. The point about full Gospel is in direct opposition to William Durham and his finished work. Directly in support of Charles Parham's Full Gospel position. Mrs. Woodworth Etter was the Camp Evangelist. Other than using their influence to draw attention to their nascent organization, the new Pentecostals only gave lip service to women ministers, barring them from licensure and offices. Those in attendance at the Apostolic Faith

Camp Meeting did not promote any of the dogmas that the A.G. surrogates have accused. No one at this meeting claimed to be "Oneness." This was a slur offered by A.G. apologists and antagonists. Later, some who were maligned by the A.G. began to use the term "oneness" like a Red Badge of courage.

The Texas Syndicate's goal was the same as when they initially attacked Parham. Also, the same as when they sent their friend William Durham to attempt to wrest the Apostolic Faith Gospel Missions away from William Seymour, Florence Crawford, and Elmer Fisher. Now there was even more at stake. Another Apostolic Faith minister was making serious waves and he pastored one of the largest and growing churches in the country. What was even more reprehensible to the Texas Syndicate was that this man was BLACK. This was not a Parham or a Seymour, Garfield Thomas Haywood was a powerful, gifted preacher in his own right. This was a real challenge to the all-white Assemblies of God. Their response had to be firm; they had to appear to be responsive.

The new Pentecostals or *Holy Rollers* if you prefer, rejected Jesus' name baptism not because it was "new." Rather, they were just continuing their campaign of attacking and distancing themselves from the A.F.M. and Charles Parham (Father of the Modern Pentecostal Movement)[1119] and those associated with Parham. Among the many strategies was claiming Parham was not part of the Los Angeles Outpouring at the Apostolic Faith Gospel Mission. They intended to rename the wonderful outpouring of the Holy Ghost at Bishop William J. Seymour's Apostolic Faith Gospel Church after a street (the Azusa Street revival). These claim to trace their roots to the outpouring in Los Angeles but named it after a street! This has resulted in a horrible mischaracterization of the Los Angeles Outpouring as though it all took place at one location rather than a city-wide outpouring.

~ CHAPTER TWENTY-TWO | BAPTISED IN JESUS NAME ~

Then, they claimed it was a Pentecostal revival steering the credit to their new Pentecostal group that was not even in existence in 1906. Ironically, this theory is the work of obliviousness. What they term The Azusa Street Revival was an Apostolic Faith Movement revival. These postulate that Azusa Street became independent. There is half-truth to the latter point. When the Apostolic Faith Gospel Mission became independent, they did not change their church name, doctrine or expectation. The Outpouring was already waning.

Those who adopted the opposition to Parham because of his racially and gender inclusive doctrine have systematically rewritten or distorted historical accounts to their liking. Ironically, while they renamed ***How Pentecost came to Los Angeles***, the *Azusa Street Revival*. The catalyst of what they term the Azusa Street Revival[1120] was a minister of Parham's Apostolic Faith Movement. One of Charles Parham's spiritual sons, William Joseph Seymour.[1121] The *new* Pentecostals brought to the fore a display of smoke and mirrors never seen in religious circles. Since their inception, they have paraded channelers like William Branham,[1122] shaman like Jim Jones,[1123] a long list of racially oriented haters (like Finis Dake, A.G. minister, and author of "30 Reasons for Segregation of Races"[1124]) masquerading as ministers, and prominent members of the KKK to impress and possess members of their congregations. All of this with the full endorsement of the A.G. leadership and of course their Texas Syndicate founders.

When the Assemblies of God was formed as an all-white group in 1914, the white men who led the effort to start the Assemblies of God ignored the key leaders of the legitimate Apostolic Faith Movement to set up their new all-white enterprise. The legitimate leaders at the time, Charles Fox & Sarah Eleanor Parham, Charles H. Mason, Florence Crawford, Lilian Thistlethwaite, William J. Seymour, and many more Black, Hispanic,

Native-American men and women of God. These were not welcome among the new Pentecostals in the all-white Assemblies of God.

In short order, even some of the white men found themselves *persona non grata* to the new Pentecostals because they dared have an unsanctioned opinion. The new Pentecostals claim the difference was doctrinal. Yet, many of the white men on both sides had in some measure or fashion embraced what they called the "New Issue." Some of these remained with the A.G. even after the Great Pentecostal Schism of 1915. So, it is fair to ask who created the "New Issue?" The so-called "New Issue" was born in the shadow of The Texas Syndicate. Charles Parham rightfully called them the new Pentecostals. In this light everything could be labeled "new" to the A.G. Their decade long experiment to seize control of the Apostolic Faith Movement was only partially working. Parham warned them that no man or group of men could control this movement, but they would try anyway. A.G. leaders in the persons of J. Roswell Flower, E. N. Bell, Howard Goss, Warren Carothers, and others used nearly every politically motivated ruse they could to pry people away from the legitimate leaders of the A.F.M. As these politically motivated men moved their agenda forward, they chose to resurrect not a new issue but an old one. These claimed that at the Apostolic Faith Camp Meeting in 1913 the supposed "New Issue" began. Yet, key leaders that were at the meeting did not know there was a "New Issue." From the beginning the Apostolic Faith Movement baptized in Jesus' name. There was no change in their camp. From the perspective of the Apostolic Faith Movement, "There was nothing unusual about this gathering."[1125] "Even a message about various methods applied historically was clearly presented as not an attempt at suggesting innovation on current baptism methods."[1126]

Apologists for this "new issue" controversy make the Apostolic

Faith camp the watershed moment for controversy. Nonetheless, there were serious gaps in the evidence.[1127] Two key leaders that were present gave some insight, but not in support of such a controversy. First, the Camp evangelist and main speaker, Maria Wood-worth Etter made no mention of a water baptism controversy although she wrote extensively.[1128] Second, Andrew Bar-David Urshan, a participant in the camp meeting, also wrote extensively. Yet, he did not reference a baptism controversy connected with the Apostolic Faith Camp meeting.[1129] The explanation is rather simple. This was not a new issue in the A.F.M. Andrew Urshan certainly had a position on the subject. However, he was less energized about what the A.G. thought about the subject and more interested in the practical application. Urshan wrote: "The foolishness of the practice of baptizing or pouring water on a person in three names, and calling it baptism, is too obvious to need comment. A person ignorant of the gospel is no subject for baptism. Those who practice sprinkling or pouring can certainly have no proper knowledge of the gospel. Their irregular use of water is in keeping with their irregular faith, and the whole accompaniment of a swarm of errors. The man who comprehends the glorious gospel, needs not be told that he must be buried in water..."[1130] Urshan was apparently baptized in the name of Jesus Christ by a Senior Elder in the Ukraine.[1131]

For more than a decade Charles Parham and other Apostolic Faith ministers were baptizing simply using the name of Jesus Christ rather than the tri-theist formula developed by the Roman Church[1132] and continued in use by most Protestants.[1133] "In the early stages of his ministry, Charles Parham struggled with the absoluteness of water baptism as it related to regeneration. Soon he had a clearer understanding, that not only did Jesus expect it from a believer, but that water baptism would be the imminent response of a believer's faith in Christ, and one of the identifying marks of the Apostolic faith. In his theology, Parham realized that as believers, we are buried with Christ by baptism into His death. In his book entitled, *A Voice Crying in The Wilderness,* which he first published in 1902, Parham deals with the subject of water baptism as it pertained to the doctrines of his Apostolic Faith Movement."[1134]

Parham writes, *'For years after entering the ministry, we taught no special baptism of water, believing the Baptism of the Holy Spirit to be the only essential one; having been marvelously anointed from time to time, and received the anointing that abideth, we put the question of water baptism aside. One day, while meditating alone in the woods, the Spirit said, 'Have you obeyed every command you believe to be in the Word.' I answered, yes; the question repeated, and the same answer was given. The third time the question was asked, I answered, no! for like a flood, the convincing evidence of the necessity of obedience rushed in upon me, how Peter said, 'Repent and be baptized every one of you in the name of Jesus Christ.' Was not this one baptism?"*[1135]

"Then came the second; and ye shall receive the gift of the Holy Ghost. Again, Peter preceded at once to baptize Cornelius, and all his house, who had received the Baptism of the Holy Spirit, with the Bible evidence of speaking with other tongues. Thrusting aside all arguments, Peter replied, 'Can any man forbid water, that these should be baptized, which have received the Holy Ghost as well as we.' Paul did not recognize the baptism of John to repentance as sufficient, but rebaptized them in the name of the Lord Jesus Christ before he would lay hands upon them that they might receive the baptism of the Holy Spirit. These and other Scriptures were so convincing that the next day we were baptized by single immersion."

Parham continues by saying, **"I can well remember when we sought God in this cleansing, how some of the teachings we had believed to be so Scriptural, and some we had loved so dearly were**

~ CHAPTER TWENTY-TWO | BAPTISED IN JESUS NAME ~

wiped from our minds. Among them was triune immersion; we could not afterward find a single argument in its favor. One day at the Bible School we were waiting upon God that we might know the Scriptural teaching on water baptism. Finally, the Spirit of God said: 'We are buried by baptism into His death.' Although we had known that for years, again the Spirit said: 'God the Father and the Holy Ghost never died." Then how quickly we recognized the fact that we could not be buried by baptism in the name of the Father, and in the name of the Holy Ghost, because it stood for nothing, as they never died or were resurrected. So, if you desire to witness a public confession of a clean conscience toward God, and man, faith in the divinity of Jesus Christ, you will be baptized by single immersion, signifying the death, burial, and resurrection: being baptized in the name of Jesus Christ." Parham's position on baptism in the name of Jesus Christ is without debate. Sarah Parham confirmed as much in her book, The Life of Charles Parham.[1136]

A.G. leaders saw this as another opportunity to pilfer followers away from Parham and the A.F.M. The so-called "New Issue" was actually the same old issue – *discredit Parham and anyone connected to him or his doctrinal positions so that we can be in charge.* "In the end, it didn't matter, nor did the words of John McAlister who merely taught an historically accurate Bible class on baptism. Key leaders like Charles Parham and William Seymour were not present or even invited to the lynching of black ministers by the A.G. leadership who would later offer the lame excuse that they had disfellowshipped Parham. The same Parham who was never part of their all-white boys club. The rhetoric of the Assemblies of God apparently played well to many in their all-white constituency.

Neither Parham (nor Seymour) was never part of the Assemblies of God. This was by the design and imprimatur of The Texas Syndicate.

Seymour was not a member because he was black and considered "less than" by the leadership of the Assemblies of God. The new Pentecostals demonstrated no respect for Seymour. They conspired to control him and the revival that happened at his church. Even sending one of The Texas Syndicate to try to steal his church. Charles Parham was not a member because he saw their effort as illegitimate. Parham was considered by the A.G. as too invested in the promotion of people of color and women as ministers. There is a slur for this, I opted not to use it in this writing. The new Pentecostals wanted control. "Charles (Parham) said God had told him to Baptize in Jesus' name, that's why he started doing so in the first place."[1137] The A.G. leaders rejected all those whom they could not control with their new all-white club.[1138] Parham was not the only one they despised. In 1913, they "DISOWNED H. H. HALL." The terminology is interesting. It shows they held some premonition that they owned the man. They stated that "The Church of God in Christ of the Apostolic Faith at Ottumwa, Ia., had withdrawn from one H. Howard Hall. He had been given scriptural opportunity to amen and walk in the ways of the Lord, but refused to do so. "Hence, we warn all the saints against him." — Joseph A. Darner, Pastor. Strange business, but this was how the Texas Syndicate operated.[1139]

CHAPTER TWENTY-THREE

LYNCH MOB JUSTICE

"I'm from Georgia," a reference to their propensity to kill and lynch Blacks. To which Peter J. F. Bridges from the Eastern States and an Apostolic pioneer rose to his feet on the other side of the room and said, "I am Peter Jan Bridges from New York, and I want you to know that I wouldn't care even if you came from hell."[1140]

-Gerloff Saunders

There is a famous scene in the first Star Wars movie where Luke Skywalker and Obi-wan Kenobi walk into a bar. They are accompanied by two robots. The bartender stops Luke and says, "Hey, we don't serve their kind here." C-3PO decided that he and R2-D2 will stay outside to avoid trouble. The moment was perplexing. As the camera circled the room, we saw every manner of wondrous creature; they were not just from different races but different planets. The clientele was as diverse as they come. For some reason, we do not understand, androids are not welcome. For reasons beyond the understanding of this author, insecure white supremacists posing as ministers of Jesus Christ created a secret high cabal to control the free flow of the Holy Ghost. These planned and orchestrated a series of hostile takeovers, orchestrated propaganda, and separated men and women of like precious faith from each other based on the color of their skin and/or their gender. They hold signs for everyone who is not a white male to see: YOU ARE NOT WELCOME!

"White lynch mobs in America murdered at least 4,467 people between 1883 and 1941, hanging, burning, dismembering, garroting and blowtorching their victims."[1141] Their violence was widespread but not indiscriminate: About 3,300 of the lynched were black, according to the most recent count by sociologists Charles Seguin and David Rigby. The remaining dead were white, Mexican, of Mexican descent, Native-American, Chinese or Japanese. The full human toll of racial lynching may remain ever beyond reach. Religion was no barrier for these white murderers. White preachers incited racial violence, joined the Ku Klux Klan and lynched black people."[1142] The reader might pause here at the mention of the KKK, but this history does not speak well for the protégé of the Texas Syndicate. These are most notably the *Assemblies of God* (A.G.), *The Pentecostal Ministerial Association* (PMA) the *United Pentecostal Church International* (U.P.C.I.) and others who barred nonwhite ministers until at least 1969. Yet, in the 1940's, and 50's and beyond these same men celebrated and promoted debauchers like the shaman William Branham despite his close ties to the KKK.[1143] It might have appeared that they chose Branham, but the reality is Branham chose them because the anti-black, all-white group appealed to him and his racially oriented, two-seeds doctrine backers and friends. All the groups that were targeted by lynch mob justice are named by Warren Fay Carothers in his manifesto that was adopted by the Assemblies of God founders and leaders.

White religious institutions in the post-bellum South were intimately involved in maintaining the existing racial hierarchy. Indeed, the predominant Christian organizations disseminated a theology rooted in white superiority and providing ideological justification for separation of the races[1144] became a primary function of white religious groups.[1145] None of these more prevalent than the Southern Baptist Convention that organized in 1845 manifesting that retaining black slaves held more importance to them than the Scriptures they claim to represent.[1146] Like their fathers, the organizers of most Pentecostal organizations would have an all-white constituency.

In this vein, On October 1-10, 1915, J. Roswell Flower, acting as the interim overseer of the Assemblies of God convened a Third General Council for the nascent A.G. to be held from October 1 through the 10th at Turner Hall in St. Louis, Missouri. The advertised challenge was specifically to address, discuss, and debate the issue of baptism. The council passed a resolution stating that the use of a baptismal formula would not be a test of fellowship for white ministers. Of course, the A.G. had no nonwhite ministers. All ministers were advised against preaching on the issue in a way that would divide "the brethren"[1147] until a final decision could be rendered at the next General Council. Few knew that the Texas Syndicate had already made the decision. Warren Fay Carothers was working behind the scenes with A.G. leaders and would soon re-emerge as the National Field Director. Carothers was not about to let the Jesus name faction bring Charles Parham's A.F.M. back into the forefront. Too much was at stake. He had made a career of spreading exaggerations about Apostle Charles Parham and although he was not active in pulpit ministry.[1148] He reasserted himself in this new war with Parham and the A.F.M. The South was rising again.[1149] His comrade, J. Roswell Flower was an all too willing pawn in Carothers' scheme.

Flower was determined to make good on his vow to stamp out the Jesus name baptizers. He reaffirmed his commitment to his friend, Carothers. The meeting in Saint Louis was a witch hunt from the beginning. Newly elected Chairman **John W. Welch** replaced fellow Parham hater, E. N. Bell. Carothers privately encouraged Bell to step down because of his allegiance to Jesus' name baptism. While Bell explained his revelation away later, his Jesus' Name baptism article of 1915 put him on the Texas Syndicate's blacklist. Therefore, Bell is not present at the 1915 meeting. **Daniel Opperman** who was originally elected Assistant Chairman joined Bell in being pressured out of office because of disagreement over baptismal formula. These failed to see the obvious connection of Jesus name baptism to Charles Parham and the A.F.M. ***The Great Pentecostal Schism*** brought division to the Texas Syndicate's most senior members. In the end, Opperman would leave but Bell would repudiate his new baptism and kowtow to the Texas Syndicate. Bell would be repaid for his obedience and once again regain his former standing with the A.G. Both Bell and Opperman were at the time proponents of the Apostle's baptismal method which was simply in baptism in Jesus' name. They were not people that Flower wanted in the debate.

Like Carothers, Flowers was bigoted and would have a storied history with the all-white xenophobic A.G. From his lofty office, Flower actively participated in this lynch mob. He was heavily invested in his fellow haters. Flower "never made any official effort to end the racist practices in the Assemblies of God that were designed to exclude African-American from full participation in the denomination. He repeatedly supported the idea that the Church of God in Christ was more appropriate

~ CHAPTER TWENTY-THREE | LYNCH MOB JUSTICE ~

for African-Americans than the Assemblies of God. Flowers' letters to the denomination's ministers and statements to the general presbytery support this assertion."¹¹⁵⁰ Carothers' vision for a superior all-white group with lesser groups for those he considered inferior was accomplished.

Garfield Thomas (G. T.) Haywood, who was black and thus not welcome as a member of the xenophobic all-white A.G. was brought into a new kangaroo Court. This one would be held far from Texas, in St. Louis, Missouri. Haywood is presented by A.G. surrogates as being 'privileged' to speak.¹¹⁵¹ Historians write that it was esteem! This was like David Duke inviting Jesse Jackson to speak at a KKK rally! The A.G. saw this as a privilege because since Haywood was black they deem him inferior due to his race. Thus, the A.G. considered him privileged to speak to his betters. It is a set-up by the racially bigoted A.G. leaders, but Haywood and others attempt to dialogue in hopes of not seeing division over baptismal formula, mode or method. They did not yet know that the debate was really about

control, and more control was in process. Even today, proxies present that this was a genuine effort at compromise. These same men reportedly have ocean front property for sale in Kansas! Haywood's race was the perfect excuse. Haywood, who pastored an Apostolic Faith Mission¹¹⁵² in Indianapolis represented the view of many non-whites and others considered undesirable by the all-white leaders of the A.G. Many of the Jesus name persuasion had strongly been influenced by Charles Parham and the A.F.M. From the Texas Syndicate perspective this would be a purge to separate the Apostolic Faith from the new Pentecostals. The debate outcome had very little to do with doctrine. The war against the multicultural A.F.M. was another battle. In the end, the A.G. leaders pretended that there would be more discussion, but they were already working to create a Creed for the nascent group.[1153] It is common for white supremacists groups to have a creed.[1154] This is in sharp contrast to the A.F.M. which was often referenced as having no creed to adhere to or church to join.[1155]

Haywood who was not part of the A.G. because he was a black man,[1156] was there to debate for those who sought to continue the Protestant tradition of protesting or ignoring the Papacy, Papal edicts, man-made Creeds and Counsels of the Roman Church. The Texas Syndicate instructed Flowers to give the impression that because of the influence that Haywood carried he was allowed to make his points and A.G. surrogates sold this version to all who listen or read. Haywood solidified the point that he was the spokesperson for non-white ministers who were not in the A.G. Additionally, and perhaps surprisingly, there were more than 150 white ministers that agreed with him. The A.G. wanted to give the appearance that Haywood's point of view would be considered even though they would not allow black membership. In reality, they were already drafting a position piece that would leave any white men who disagreed on the outside of their all-white group. **They called their Creed: Statement of Fundamental Truths.**

Historian Walter J. Hollenweger said, **"If the issue was theological or dogmatic it certainly came at a most convenient time. The Assemblies of God bowed to pressures of their American middle-of-the-road Protestantism to distance themselves from fellowship with blacks."**[1157] This was not a "new issue," this was the same old issue. This was just another chapter in the war with Charles Parham and the inclusive multicultural A.F.M. If Jesus Christ had bodily manifested in the room while Haywood was speaking and said, "Haywood is right - Hear him!," the outcome would not have been different. This was not about the work of God; this was all about the control of men. Couching this as a "doctrinal debate" gave the A.G. great leniency in areas of race. The KKK was much more straightforward in simply stating that minorities were the enemy.

Haywood's problem, from the perspective of white leaders like Flowers, Kerr, Carothers and friends, was that he was black. The Texas Syndicate had been in an open war with Parham for nearly a decade. A black preacher from Indianapolis was a challenge they were well prepared to handle. They had already dispatched many others, including the notable William J. Seymour. The A.G. leaders were quite happy for him to lead black people, but he was not (in their estimation) qualified to lead white people. Even the historic baptismal service at Haywood's church where many were re-baptized in Jesus' name, had two baptisms. One baptismal service for white people and one for black people. So, couching their racial hatred in the guise of a doctrinal dispute was quite convenient for the nascent Assemblies of God.

To hide their shame these same men claimed that they had disfellowshipped Parham. Strangest thing since Parham was never part of the Assemblies of God. How do you disfellowship someone with whom you were never in fellowship? Why was there not a long list of others they disfellowshipped? Parham was not having any of what they were offering. Charles F. Parham denounced those men as *"a bunch of imitating, chattering, wind-sucking, holy-roller preachers"* before they even organized their 1914 group.[1158] Parham had also accurately prophesied the physical death of one of their mentors.[1159] William J. Seymour and Florence Crawford joined Parham in calling these the neo-Pentecostals.[1160]

W. F. Carothers, a close associate of Flowers and Kerr, wrote the manifesto for these like-minded men. **Warren Faye Carothers,** was a self-taught attorney.[1161] His responsibilities would include training evangelists and pastors.[1162] Carothers argued against allowing women to preach and was busy working behind the scenes directing the A.G. to continue their bigoted racially segregated vision.[1163] Bishop Saunders also recalled a man on the Flowers side shouting, *"I'm from Georgia,"* a reference to their propensity to kill and lynch Blacks. To which **Peter J. F. Bridges** from the Eastern States and a Pentecostal pioneer rose to his feet on the other side of the room and said, *"I am Peter Jan Bridges from New York, and I want you to know that I wouldn't care even if you came from hell."*[1164] This is what A.G. historian Carl Brumbeck called *"a spirited and sometimes humorous debate."*[1165] Here we have yet another A.G. proxy attempting to explain away racial bigotry. There is absolutely nothing humorous about anyone threatening to lynch another. Yet, the Texas Syndicate was quite comfortable pushing their agenda forward. "Brutality and savagery mark all lynching. Young and old, male and female, have been tortured by fire; a pregnant colored woman was hanged by the ankles and her unborn child ripped from her abdomen.   This ruling class savagery has a purpose: to strike terror into the hearts of the oppressed Negro people so that they dare not strike out for liberation."[1166] The A.G. message was clear to the black ministers. Obey the will of the superior white people or you might find yourself at the end of a rope.

During this meeting **G. T. Haywood** was publicly insulted as the target of racial slurs and innuendo. This supposedly for his and others baptizing in Jesus' name and not the fact that he was black. However, the slurs were racially oriented not doctrinal debate. The A.G. ministers jeered that Haywood's teachings were "hay, wood and stubble" and "they are all in the wilderness and they have a voice in the wilderness" (the latter

~ CHAPTER TWENTY-THREE | LYNCH MOB JUSTICE ~

interpreted by historians as a reference to Haywood's publication), "A Voice in the Wilderness."[1167] However, Haywood's publication was in deference to a more well-known publication by the same name, Charles Fox Parham's book. In the book, Chapter II is about Water Baptism. This whole fight is a continuation of the war with Parham. There is nothing to be won in this debate. If God had bodily manifested in the room and said, "Haywood is right! Hear him!" The result would not have been different, and G. T. Haywood would not have been magically allowed to join the all-white hate group called the Assemblies of God.

This rebuke was led by two prominent Assemblies of God ministers: Kerr[1168] and Flower. These would claim that doctrine was the issue and not race. It could be argued that neither was relevant. The facts tell us that this was simply a corporate takeover. The real dividing issue was the Fundamental Statement. To a room full of ministers who generally opposed denominations, Warren Fay Carothers' newest innovation was just too much. Ever the counter of noses and nickels, Howard Goss claims some 153 ministers left the A.G. In any case *The Great Pentecostal Schism* was in full swing. Pentecostals would formally divide from the Apostolic Faith Movement and over time form so many organizations [both Jesus name and Trinitarian persuasions] that it is very hard to count them. The New Issue as the A.G. called it was brought to the fore. Factions among the attendees championed either the Apostolic Faith position of Jesus' name baptism like the Apostles baptized, or the traditional Roman Catholic position. The Jesus' name group was slurred as "Oneness" by Flowers who led the charge. It was really well placed as it gaslighted his opponents and took the emphasis off his racial hatred. Offended by the slurs, the Jesus' name adherents wore the designation "Oneness" like a red badge of courage. The Jesus' name group countered by calling Flowers and Flowers' group "Trinitarians." One hundred years later, many are still divided because of these near-sighted men. It is sad to think that the A.G. leaders hypothesized baptism in Jesus' name inferior to the Roman version and a Roman Catholic inspired man-made created creed superior to the Apostles of Jesus Christ.[1169]

The easy solution would have been to allow either or both as men like **Andrew Urshan** proposed. However, that position is presuming that there was a desire for unity. The leaders of the A.G. were mostly focused on holding control, keeping blacks and women in their place and not giving Parham's A.F.M. any satisfaction. "There would be no 'come and let us reason together.' Bishop Garfield T. Haywood pastored one the largest assemblies in the whole Pentecostal movement. From that vantagepoint of he represented the problem." Bishop Monroe R. Saunders, Sr., recalled it this way, "Haywood and a few others were called on to defend the doctrine of baptism in Jesus' name. Flowers and a few others were called upon to defend the Trinity. Well, after about two days of that, Haywood and his group had the Bible on their side. The Assemblies of God had Church history on their side. Needless to say, [1170] Church history won over Bible revelation."[1171]

All references to black ministers were removed from the new "Ministerial List of the General Council of the Assemblies of God."[1172] A.G. surrogates claim G. T. Haywood was an A.G. member, but it was merely a history revision.[1173] The Texas Syndicate would set the wheels of the A.G. machine in motion so that they were all dead before the A.G. would allow black or other people of color membership in their white supremacist denomination. "Quite a number of Black Pentecostal churches adopt the baptism in Jesus' name formula without formally joining organizations in the movement. Some of these were in the all-black Church of God in

Christ. Others were in the **Original Glorious Church of God in Christ Apostolic Faith, Glorious Church of God in Christ, Apostolic, New Bethel Church of God in Christ** (Richmond, CA)**, Church of God in Christ Apostolic,** and more.[1174]

Andrew D. Urshan

Fourth General Conference of the fledgling Assemblies of God. They adopt their new creed which they call the *Statement of Fundamental Truths*. Pledging to be a branch of the "one, holy, universal, and apostolic" church an obvious reference to the Roman Catholic Church.[1175] All ministers were told they had to accept the document or not join or remain a member of the nascent organization. In the end, 156 ministers chose not to remain. How the vote went down is debated with neither side agreeing on what happened.

G. T. Haywood wrote about it this way, "There were quite a number who withdrew from the Council at the close of the session, because there was a spirit of drifting into another denomination manifested, when they began to draw up a "creed," which they termed "fundamentals." It is no doubt the same thing under a different name. I have no complaints to make, but by the grace of God, I shall endeavor to press on with the Lord, "without the camp, bearing His reproach, for here we have no continuing city, but we seek one to come."[1176] The early Apostolic Faith movement unalterably opposed denominationally minded men; this is without question. It continued to be evident in the actions of Haywood.

The division was clearly racially motivated. The idea of doctrinal division was a straw man. Those who followed the "Haywood faction" see their theology as a life language, not done outside a particular racial, cultural, or socio-political, and therefore a means for racial redemption. In contrast, those who followed the "Flowers faction" hold to an impoverished theology, a language of argument outside and above the harsh realities of a segregated society, and therefore a possible vehicle for self-promotion and oppression. In a nutshell, for Blacks the "new issue" took on the stance of a liberating force in Jesus' name, because for them the dogmatic and racial issues were closely intertwined, as God is life-giving power in this world. For many Whites, if not all, the new issue became social upward mobility, a speculative argument of past and present orthodoxy which could render them almost completely ignorant of the racial and political implications and help them to dissociate themselves from the Blacks. In this way, the doctrinal controversy developed into an expedient means of fighting the "enemies" and of expelling "heretic" leaders.[1177] The Texas Syndicate was clearly running the A.G. **J. W. Welch** was elected Chairman, **J. R. Flower** Secretary, John Goben Treasurer, and Stanley H. Frodsham elected General Secretary of the Assemblies of God.[1178] Executive Presbyters were E. N. Bell, R. A. Brown, Arch P. Collins, Andrew L. Fraser, A. G. Garr, S.A. Jamieson, D. W. Kerr, B. F. Lawrence, D. H. McDowell and Will C. Trotter. The departure of Howard Goss is rarely mentioned.[1179]

Meanwhile, **Charles Parham** began another series of powerful meetings in Zion, IL.[1180] Songwriter Thoro Harris[1181] was among the notable participants at the **Lake Street Mission.** About this time **Thoro Harris** shocked the A.G. Council by being baptized in Jesus' name and would follow up with writing his song, "Baptized in Jesus' name." His baptismal hymn opens defiantly, "Today I gladly bear the bitter cross of scorn, reproach and shame; I count the worthless praise of men but loss, baptized in Jesus' name.[1182] Harris followed up in 1917 with his most well-known hymn, **"All That Thrills My Soul is Jesus."** The alliance between Parham

~ CHAPTER TWENTY-THREE | LYNCH MOB JUSTICE ~

and Harris at this meeting showed that Parham is still very much the leader of the Apostolic Faith movement. His working with Harris made it obvious that he has some affinity with ministers that were baptizing in Jesus' name as opposed to the titles.

"What is clear is that there was a departure from the multicultural and non-denomination focus of the Apostolic Faith movement. These new "Pentecostals" only admitted whites and men as ministers. The imprimatur of Howard Goss and W. F. Carothers on these points is certain. Goss opposed black ministers and Carothers opposed all non-whites and women ministers. The A.G. opposed both blacks and women. However, in the end, even Goss was not happy with what they had created and found himself on the outside of the A.G. For the Texas Syndicate, Goss had served his purpose. He would continue for the rest of his life to be a preacher killer, a despiser of good men and ten years later would return to give G. T. Haywood a bitter blow. Those who cross Howard Goss were always attacked in a vicious manner."

Reader, if you have been drinking the purple Kool-Aid offered by white supremacists and really thought that Charles Parham was irrelevant like the Texas Syndicate and their creation the Assemblies of God had been selling. This next point will show more proof of the Big Lie. The *Weekly Evangel*, written and published by *Flowers,* claims that **Charles Fox Parham** has been "disfellowshipped"[1183] and W. F. Carothers was now in charge.[1184] The fact is that Carothers, as Flowers well knew, joined the Assemblies of God at its inception in 1914. He held no capacity in the Apostolic Faith Movement in 1916. This is the worst kind of slime by men who present as willing to do anything to advance their agenda. Flowers was working hard to discredit Parham as part of his (Flowers) campaign to lead the all-white Assemblies of God against Blacks, women and their supporters, like the Parhams.[1185] Otherwise, why would he print this in his publication? There is NO RECORD of Parham ever being in fellowship with either Flowers or the Assemblies of God. In fact, Parham denounced them as pretenders. The fact is that the September 2nd Issue of the Weekly Evangel contains a report from W. F. Carothers who was working as the New Director of the "General Field Department" of the Assemblies of God and operating from his base in Houston, Texas.[1186]

Why would there be a need to disfellowship a man who was never in your fellowship? The Texas Syndicate leader Warren Faye Carothers was wielding its control over the A.G. **Weekly Evangel,** edited by **Flowers,** confirms the position of the Assemblies of God on Women Pastors. *"We do not find in the New Testament examples where any woman acted as pastor or is authorized especially by Scripture to do so."*[1187]

> *"There is NO RECORD of Parham ever being in fellowship with either Flowers or the Assemblies of God. In fact, Parham denounced them as pretenders."*

The Assemblies of God was serious about keeping blacks out of their white supremacist hate group. The Assemblies of God continued to use questionable methods to distance their organization from all those they deem undesirable by refusing to ordain a Chicago man named Alexander Howard as a missionary to Liberia — on account of his race.[1188]

Charles Parham's openness to black ministers was more than fifty years ahead of his time. Parham understood that his message of Apostolic Restoration was for more than his predominately white audiences in the central part of the United States. He did not just embrace black ministers. More to the point, he sought them out, embraced them and promoted them. This was especially true in reaching black audiences. In 1917, Charles Parham was ministering at Lake Street Mission. Thoro Harris who is known as a black songwriter said that when Parham preached the people loved the message and the messenger and look[ed] forward to his (Parham's) return. Harris described the meetings as a "feast of good things."[1189] Despite volumes of excuses written by Assembly of God and United Pentecostal Church historians and their surrogates explaining the challenges as part of the culture of the times, other groups such as the Church of God, Cleveland, Tennessee and the legitimate Church of God in Christ (C.O.G.I.C.) made no such excuses and welcomed people of all colors.

At a camp meeting at Arroyo Seco, California, many people noticed the miracles that came in response to prayers, "in the name of Jesus." Amid this focus, a man named John Scheppe claimed to have had a revelation of the power of the name of Jesus. Another minister remarked that the apostles did not mention baptizing in the "name of the Father, Son, and Holy Ghost" but rather "in the name of Jesus." After the camp meeting, many began to rebaptize in "the name of Jesus" only. Gradually, some began to consider what baptizing in "Jesus Only" implied. Some preachers began to preach that when Scripture speaks of "the name of the Father, the Son, and the Holy Ghost" that it meant that the Father, the Son, and the Holy Ghost had a name: Jesus. Eventually, this led to the understanding that there was only one person in the godhead – Jesus Christ. The teaching spread that Jesus IS the Father, and the Son, and the Holy Spirit. This was a teaching that Charles Parham and the A.F.M. had been implementing for more than a decade.

Rev. Alexander and Margaret Howard

E. N. Bell, the first general chairman (later called general superintendent), in the Sept. 6, 1919, *Pentecostal Evangel* addressed this issue in an article entitled, "The Great Controversy and Confusion." Some of the brothers advocating the "Jesus Only" position had reported that the newly formed Assemblies of God was opposed to baptism in the manner in which the apostles baptized in the book of Acts and that church leadership was preventing "teaching that exalts Him (Jesus) as God." Bell explained that the General Council of the Assemblies of God did not raise any issue over people baptizing in the name of Jesus until "there came to be attached to it certain fundamental errors" that "made only the entering wedge for other teaching not found in Acts" or "a single line in the whole New Testament." Apparently, Bell believed that men held the power of salvation through what they said while baptizing someone. Of course, this is just damage control. Bell ended his 1919 article with these words, "If the other brethren had never introduced other matters dishonoring to the Father and to the Son, and contrary to the Scriptures, and had held only for the matchless and glorious TRUE DEITY of the blessed Son of God, then we would be all pulling together today ... if they will drop all these unscriptural issues and hold only for His true Deity, we can do it yet." This was simply more damage control and of course the A.G. favorite: half-truths. In contrast, "Haywood received a message from God telling him to walk in the light, after reading a letter sent by independent A.F.M. Apostle Glen Cook telling him to baptize in Jesus' name. The letter from the Assemblies of God telling him to uphold their doctrine came too late."[1190] Today's Christians who rejected Jesus' name, most have NO baptism at all, and no Holy Spirit speaking in tongues either. The Bible tells us men will give heed to doctrines of devils. They now proclaim Romans 10:9 to be their doctrine. Most either neglect it or do not know about Charles Parham and the A.F.M. There was a lot of persecution of the A.F.M., and any who agreed

CHAPTER TWENTY-THREE | LYNCH MOB JUSTICE

with their Jesus' name baptismal position. They were attacked by the Ku Klux Klan and staunch trinitarians. Jesus' name people were criticized, ostracized and called heretics for using the name of Jesus."[1191]

Most local and national religious organizations were racially segregated, and to the extent that blacks were incorporated into white-controlled denominations, they were typically relegated to separate congregations, or separate areas of the church in mixed-race congregations.[1192] Once most of the black ministers were dispatched from the Assemblies of God sphere of influence to follow Haywood and others that the Assemblies of God leadership made all manner of names and slurs to malign, the A.G. became even bolder towards persons of color. "In 1917, a black minister from Chicago approached the newly formed Assemblies of God (A.G.) with a request. Alexander Howard wanted the denomination to send him as a missionary to Liberia. A.G. leaders refused to let him go because of his race."[1193] 100 years later the A.G. made a token apology on the subject. Sadly, everyone who joined with Haywood's side of the baptismal debate was not in agreement on racial equality. Soon after being dismissed by the all-white Assemblies of God because he failed to meet their cookie cutter, he was faced with more ministers who saw his skin color as a major detractor. These would follow Howard Goss for the next thirty plus years until they had also firmly established another all-white ministerial group. The differences between the Assemblies of God and the United Pentecostal Church are so minute they can generally be summarized in one sentence. "The UPC baptizes adherents using the singular invocation of 'In the name of Jesus Christ.'" The debate over Charles F. Parham's early 1900 revelation on water baptism has firmly entrenched itself in two all-white camps. The Assemblies of God and the United Pentecostal Church.

Beyond the all-white camps that still follow the Jesus' name baptismal method invoked by the Apostolic Faith movement are a number of sizable groups including several that are multicultural much like the vision of Charles and Sarah Parham. The multicultural groups include the Apostolic World Christian Fellowship (A.W.C.F.),[1194] the International Circle of Faith (I.C.O.F.)[1195] and others. Some groups have migrated to all black (or predominately) such as Bible Way, C.O.O.L.J.C., Pentecostal Assemblies of the World (P.A.W.) and others. There is a street named in Haywood's honor in his hometown Indianapolis, Indiana and a plethora of churches and ministries (hundreds) have come from his spiritual sons and daughters.

The lynching of **Horace Duncan, Fred Coker,** and **Fred Allen** led to the exodus of hundreds of blacks from Springfield to less hostile areas. The ethnic makeup of Springfield, to this day, reflects that horrific event. Not surprisingly, just a few years later, the all-white Assemblies of God chose this city for their headquarters.[1196] In contrast, some of those who participated in the lynching found their way to Charles Parham's Apostolic Faith meetings in Joplin. Notably, a Brother Geisler, who participated in the Springfield lynching. At the time, Geisler was an unsaved alcoholic. Afterward, in about 1907, he visited Joplin, where he encountered a Pentecostal street preacher confronting people and asking if they had participated in the lynching. The preacher said, "Everybody that gave their consent for killing these Negroes was a murderer and has committed murder."[1197]

CHAPTER TWENTY-FOUR

DETRACTORS

"If I were to try to read, much less answer, all the attacks made on me, this shop might as well be closed for any other business. I do the very best I know how - the very best I can; and I mean to keep doing so until the end. If the end brings me out all right, what's said against me won't amount to anything. If the end brings me out wrong, ten angels swearing I was right would make no difference."

-Abraham Lincoln

The greatest attacks in Parham's life and ministry were hatched in 296 days between October 1, 1906, to July 24, 1907"[1198] After nearly a decade of growth and advancement of the nascent Apostolic Faith Movement (now numbering 100,000 or more adherents),[1199] "suddenly all hell broke loose. Three distinct events arose, which would be thorns in his flesh the rest of his days. These three events are related to Zion City, IL and Wilbur Glenn Voliva; Los Angeles Outpouring (aka Azusa Street Revival)[1200] and William J. Seymour; and San Antonio, TX, with an allegation Parham declared to be connected to Voliva as well. Any of these events might have stopped lesser men from continuing to carry on public ministry, but the indefatigable Charles Parham was more determined to carry on the call God had placed on his life.[1201]

Through all the years, the trials and the triumphs, the travel, the personal assaults on their family, Charles and Sarah Parham became parents to six children and shared their family home with many others. "His wife and children were loving and loyal family members who believed in him and the message he taught. The preacher in the pulpit was the man they knew at home."[1202] The Parham family lived by faith. They trusted God to supply their every need. Few people in history have accomplished much without people becoming envious. The first reference that men hear of Charles and Sarah Parham is probably some negative story. Forgotten are the orphans for whom they found homes, the widows who were aided, the people who were physically healed, those who were spiritually changed, lives renewed and more. Although Charles Parham took the brunt of the acrimony, one can only imagine what his wife Sarah unfairly endured. There had to be times when they must have thought, "this is not worth it!" Surely, when they laid their precious child in his grave, they must have had doubts about the cost of their sacrifice. Yet, they journeyed on, the Celestial City and Eternal Life is their reward.

No person of color: Black, Hispanic, Chinese, Native-American, or any other ever accused the Parhams of being less than authentic. What Warren Carothers, Howard Goss, and their many bigoted friends gave the world is a sordid tale of a good man and his family. A tale that simply has no evidence. A tale that even a District Attorney in the Jim Crow era in Texas found so lacking in authenticity that he would not even file a charge. A tale sold in the media and through the works of the flesh. The only ones that benefit from the tale were those who were members of the Texas Syndicate and the bigoted religious organizations they founded starting with the A.G. These men hold a repugnant place in history. They took control of the only known inter-racial movement of their day (A.F.M.) and replaced it with one in their bigoted, white supremacist image (the Assemblies of God).[1203] Every one of them should have hung their head in shame. Yet, like the whorish woman that Solomon wrote about, they wiped their collective mouths and pretended they did no wrong.[1204]

Lilian Thistlethwaite who lived with the Parhams offered some keen insight into their world. "Many wear scars, deep soul scars, made by friends who rudely, crudely thrust their clumsy fingers among their heart-strings. We say cruel words. They may even be ill-timed words of truth, and we do not stop to consider how brutally they pierce and sting. I have often thought that there would have been very few that would have been willing to stand the persecutions and hardships that he and his faithful wife endured as they were being tried as gold in the fire. Bro. Parham was often wounded in the house of his friends, and mistreated by those who he did the most for, which we know sometimes he felt very keenly, even though he did not retaliate or resent it."[1205]

Some years ago, I visited a preacher friend who had recently become the new pastor of a church. I was unfamiliar with the church before my friend's arrival there. The church facility was beautiful. As we sat in the very nice pastor's office and chatted. He sat at the beautiful desk, and I was sitting in a chair across from the desk. I asked him where the previous pastor went? My friend stared at me in silence for a few moments. I could tell that he was measuring his words.

Then the pastor spoke, "Do you see the stain there on the carpet?" I looked down and there was a large very visible stain on the carpet round my chair, but much larger. It ran up under the desk as well. I nodded that I did see the stain. It seemed like the only blemish in an otherwise immaculate office.

The pastor took a deep breath and then said, "That stain is from the blood of my predecessor. We had the carpet professionally cleaned but the stain would not come out. New carpet is on order. The former pastor came into this study and took his own life with a gun."

I was stunned. I didn't know if I should move my chair or just sit there. The pastor pressed on. "You see, there were rumors that the pastor had been unfaithful to his wife. After I arrived, there were some men that came to me and admitted that they wanted the pastor out. They had not intended for the false rumors that they spread to end so tragically. They had just decided that they wanted a different pastor. They expected he would resign and move on. Some of them sobbed right here in this same office as they told the horrible tale."

The pastor paused and then continued. "Those men went down to the parsonage and told the pastor's widow and his young daughter the truth that their husband and father was not unfaithful. Then they sold their homes and left this town."

It is a heart wrenching and tragic story. Like the story of Charles Parham, there are many rumors and lies, but none of them have ever been substantiated with even one witness. Horribly, no one has ever repented for starting the lies, telling the lies, retelling the lies, and much more. We leave justice to our Great God and Righteous King, Ruler over Everything. Nearly every fallen spiritual leader was connected to financial irregularities. Except Parham. Seriously. Historian Jeff Nelson notes, "Charles Parham did not even receive offerings in his meetings."[1206] Certainly not a good financial plan. Nelson also chronicles, "He lived by faith throughout his entire ministry.

Indefatigable Ministry

"Many times, he would preach two or three times a day for weeks at a time in a town, a village, or a city. When he was in Zion City and had to meet in homes rather than a hall, he would travel to five homes in a night, preaching typically from 7:00 pm until Midnight.[1207] Many years Charles Parham traveled between 5,000 and 8,000 miles by horse and buggy, then train, and then automobile holding campaigns across the U.S. He likely traveled between 100,000 and 200,000 miles in his thirty-five years of ministry. Additionally, he started Bible schools,[1208] healing homes,[1209] orphan and widow ministries,[1210] and took teams of workers to the streets and missions.[1211] He kept up this evangelistic ministry for about 35 years, and he never seemed to tire of reaching people for Jesus.

When he was only about thirty-two years old, The Houston Chronicle reported in 1906, "He remarked on the doctrine of healing held by the adherents of his faith. 'Over 100,000 people in the United States today are trusting God for healing.'"[1212] Near the end of his life in 1928, Connelly wrote in A Standard History of Kansas and Kansans, "A New York statistician has given Mr. Parham credit for the conversion of fully 2,000,000 persons." If these numbers are indicative of the growth of the Pentecostal movement during his lifetime, it is not surprising that today, there are over 650 million Pentecostal/Charismatic believers around the world. Jesus said, "But the seed falling on good soil refers to someone who hears the Word and understands it. This is the one who produces a crop, yielding a 100, 60, or 30 times what was sown" (John 13:23 NIV).

In the writings of both Charles and Sarah there are some references to the hurt of the betrayals. Much like when Apostle Paul wrote, "Demas has forsaken me, having loved this present world."[1213] It almost seems that people lined up just to take a pot shot at this couple. In fairness, their doctrinal positions angered a lot of important very religious people. Their ideas on racial equality angered most of those same people and some more.

Their insistence that women were co-equals in ministry irritated not only religious people, but many in society at large. Like the mob waiting to stone the Apostle Stephen[1214] these people and groups would all line up to hurl a proverbial stone in the direction of Charles and Sarah Parham. The likely reason some only hurled proverbial stones was not born from some sense of doing the right thing, but rather only that literally hurling a stone is illegal.[1215]

I want to thank my new friend, Jeffrey Nelson,[1216] for his permission to quote from his excellent work on Charles Parham. **Charles F. Parham, Indefatigable Toil and Launching the World-wide Pentecostal Movement: A New Look at a Forgotten Leader**, I would encourage readers to read his entire work. I want to thank my friend John Collins[1217] for his help in research. John was a tremendous researcher, writer, and presenter. He is without doubt the foremost expert in the world on the shaman known as **William Branham.** If you as the reader are among those who think *William Branham was a man sent from God*. John Collins' work is a must read material.[1218] When I was first introduced to John, I challenged some of his premises. I have since learned that he does his homework! Branham convinced many people that he too was a man of God even though he dabbled in the occult, practiced channeling, and used stage props to deceive the masses. These facts are the subject of much of John Collins' research.

A year or so before I began writing this book, I asked John Collins to help me find the "dirt" so to speak on Charles Parham. Not the regurgitated fabrications of people trying to sell themselves as experts. Legitimate proof like eyewitnesses, legal charges, sworn testimony, etc. Particularly we sought proof beyond a reasonable doubt the credibility of allegations against Charles Parham in 1907 at San Antonio, Texas. Parham told his followers that he had been framed by his Zion City opponent, Wilbur Voliva. Was there any proof? There is no doubt that Voliva was among the conspirators that worked with Warren Fay Carothers, Howard A. Goss, and their intolerant Texas Syndicate. Despite the horrible atrocities of the Texas Syndicate, because of the vitriol of Voliva. Parham still held a higher opinion of them than Voliva. Parham changed his mind as time passed and more information presented. These men continued to conspire against him. The dust up with Voliva seemed to have settled after Voliva got the control he sought in Zion City. The dust up with Seymour was much like the rift between Paul and Barnabas. Like Barnabas, Seymour continued on with commendable ministry. Like Paul, Parham was much more in the forefront of a global ministry and wrote epistles that still encourage the church. When needed, Parham came to the defense of his fellow compatriot in the gospel, his former student and friend, William J. Seymour.

The claim that Parham became more hostile toward some Pentecostals is true. Yet not all who claimed their Pentecost. Instead, it was those who we have linked to the Texas Syndicate, that Parham referred to as the new Pentecostals and Holy Rollers. These were those who began to self-identify as Pentecostals in direct opposition to the A.F.M. Whatever may be said about these men, it is certain that there was very little that resembles Christ in their actions. Mrs. Parham felt their enemies must have had great faith in Parham's beliefs because, if this kind of onslaught had befallen a secular person, court action would have surely followed. Surely, she is correct. Certainly, if it had been anyone else the crimes committed against him would have been litigated in courts in Texas, Illinois, Kansas, California, and other places. Charles Parham left the matter to the discretion of his followers, believing that those who were faithful would never believe the unsubstantiated charges.[1219] On his fortieth birthday

Parham wrote:

"I think the greatest sorrow of my life is the thought that my enemies, in seeking my destruction, have ruined and destroyed so many precious souls."

Sorrow and destruction make no difference to those who oppose the ministry of God. When Parham returned to preach in Zion nine years later, Voliva followers fabricated posters and fliers that showed the fabricated signed confession of guilt. These are the source of the statement written by the Texas Syndicate and given to a corrupt official. If these are really words, they wrote on the paper they wanted Parham to sign may never be known. In 1913, Parham was met by a mob in Wichita who were armed with clubs and pitchforks. A friend rescued Parham by secreting him away by a different route, and the meeting continued as scheduled. Hundreds were said to have repented in Wichita, and many were healed. Wounded by those he thought were his friends, Parham never backed away from the cities to which God had led him. He led the most dominant ministry of the teens and twenties, preaching meetings in so many Texas cities it is hard to track. He even returned to Los Angeles and held a tremendous meeting, in which thousands were converted, baptized in the Holy Spirit, healed and delivered. In the winter of 1924, Parham held meetings in Oregon and Washington. It was at one of these that Gordon Lindsay found salvation. Lindsay went on to do a great work for God, establishing the international Bible college, Christ for The Nations, located in Dallas, Texas.

The Parhams' youngest son, Robert, quit his job with a department store to come home to fast and pray in the house where his father lay. After several days, he came to Parham's bedside to tell him he had also "surrendered his life to the call of ministry." Thrilled in the knowledge that two of his sons would carry on the work of the Gospel, Parham gained enough strength to say:

Though several men sought to destroy him, they couldn't touch the pillar of strength that was built within his spirit. "I can't boast of any good works I have done when I meet my Master face to face, but I can say, I have been faithful to the message He gave me, and lived a pure, clean life." Sarah said she would never forget her beloved's face, knowing "with a joy and a look of peaceful satisfaction that his prayer for many years was answered." His last day on earth, Charles Fox Parham was heard quoting, "Peace, peace, like a river; that is what I have been thinking all day." During the night, he sang part of the song, "Power in the Blood," then asked his family to finish the song for him. When they had finished, he asked them to, "sing it again." Here are a few pages of small matters concerning Parham.

Lodge

In the early 1900's, while living in Baldwin, Kansas, Charles Parham obtained an insurance policy from a fraternal order of some kind. Such insurance is referred to as Fraternal Insurance.[1220] This connection to a lodge was not a conflict from the standpoint of Charles' M.E. church but for his new bride, the birthright Quaker, Sarah Parham, who's church had taught her not to have part with secret organizations it was a concern.[1221] Charles made the decision to agree with his new bride and let the fraternal insurance policy lapse and refrain from being connected to such organizations in any manner.[1222] A plethora of pretenders have postulated that Parham was a member of the Ku Klux Klan. Such assertions are authored by writers who pose as Historians but are proxies for denominations. These statements are made to sell books by the creation of sensations. "Usually, the purpose of historical negation is to achieve a national, political aim, by transferring war-guilt, demonizing an enemy, providing an illusion of victory, or preserving a friendship."[1223] The actions of those persons employ a plethora of methods which may even be criminal.[1224] Parham made one known statement about the KKK. The KKK was working hard to buy the loyalty of ministers. Parham was certainly a target. His response was to say they presented well.

Haters say that Parham praises "these splendid men" and the "organization that has won ten million to its standards in ten years" and their "high ideals for mankind." Like most of the stories about Parham, it is out of context. In context, Parham was saying that all their ideas for mankind's betterment would not "be of any lasting use to the human race unless it shall begin with an old-fashioned conversion and a real change of

heart...if they all could be really converted and could spend their time and strength and money...to bring the world to really know Christ and have his character wrought out in them. Only by this method will the Ku Klux Klan ever be able to better mankind."[1225]

Parham did not leave his position to question. He spoke directly about all these type groups a decade or more before there was a formally organized group called the KKK. He spoke against all lodges and named a few such as the Knights of Pythias, the Mason, the Odd Fellows, and thousands more. Like Moses pleading before God, Parham presented that if these are the Church then, "I Quit!"[1226] He did not specifically mention the KKK because it did not exist at the time (the KKK was reorganized in 1915).

Unlike Alma White, Phineas Bresse, Warren Carothers, many

~ CHAPTER TWENTY-FOUR | DETRACTORS ~

members of the all-white Assemblies of God, he did not promote the Klan or its message and was certainly not a member. Parham was not in any way aligned with the KKK or any secret order. It was a lifelong position to which he was true. At a ministry meeting in Kingman, Kansas a designer employed some coy marketing in creating the flyer announcing the event. Because of the two Ks in Kingman, Kansas, they thought it would be a clever marketing ploy to change the three Cs at the bottom of the flyer to three K's. Good marketing? Obviously, it was very good marketing. More than one hundred years later we are still talking about the flyer. From this simple creative outreach to announce a meeting for Charles Parham surrogates for the new Pentecostals have claimed this as proof Parham was in the KKK. These same proxies conveniently ignore William Branham's direct involvement with the organizers of the Klan in 1915 and his lifelong commitment to the same. They ignore a plethora of others in their all-white hate groups they organized as ministerial fellowships who marched in goose-step with Branham and other leaders of the KKK. For the record, the Apostolic Faith continued to have multicultural meetings in Kingman, Kansas for decades.[1227]

Annihilation Of The Wicked

It is accurate to say that Charles Fox Parham unalterably believed that one must be born of the water and of the Spirit to gain eternal Life. Obviously, one would ascertain that those who do not have such an experience will not live forever. The challenge is that Protestants generally believe that you will live forever somewhere. Protestants even sing songs to that end. Early in Parham's ministry he came into contact with Baptist adherents that proposed predestination and concluded mankind was eternal and would live forever somewhere. These claim it was predestined for all mankind. They believed that some people are predestined for eternal life (primarily the white ones) and some predestined for eternal punishment (primarily the non-white ones).

Parham responded that the eternal punishment of sinners was simply death. Theologians have argued the finer points of the subject for generations and regardless of our doctrinal position we realize Scripture gives us limited information on the topic. "In annihilationism he believed that God would welcome repentant sinners into Heaven to be with him but lovingly destroy the souls that rejected him so that they would not suffer eternal punishment."

Pacifism

Strongly influenced by his pacifist friends and family in the Quaker (or Friends) tradition, Parham was preaching pacifism decades before the 1st World War. While other groups sought their footing on the subject, Parham had been preaching pacifism. It does seem that in the emotional state of losing one his closest friends, who was killed in action during the 1st World War that Parham sought unsuccessfully to enlist.

Language

Historians have made much ado about Parham's quotes. We make no excuse and agree he quoted words and used phrases we find unacceptable. The N word should never be used. Regrettably, a version of the same is found acceptable in modern music. For Parham, there are at least a couple of times that the word was used in an article in the Apostolic Faith.[1228] This article was not written by Parham, but it is in his publication and as such he is responsible. It seems that Parham was quoting one of his many detractors, **Alma White.** However, he should have been clear.

~ CHAPTER TWENTY-FOUR | DETRACTORS ~

Perhaps he was, but it was lost. In any case, this is certainly not a pattern of how he conducted his life. Further no one has ever substantiated the various claims by his enemies of his blatant racism.

Chemical Gold

It appears Parham may have been the victim as an investor of a scheme. There were never charges against him, but there were charges against the founder of the scheme. Stockholders of Chemical Gold Company Become Clamorous. 1902, Nov 6. the Wilkes Barre Record. "George A. Francis, president of the Francis Chemical Gold Company, is in the county jail in default of $300 bonds to await a hearing before Justice Ben Spitz tomorrow, charged with obtaining money under false pretenses. The Rev. Charles F. Parham, projector of the Apostolic Faith Movement, editor of the Apostolic Faith, and founder of the College of Bethel, at Topeka, not an official of the company but erst-while confidant and advisor of its president, cannot be found. Five stockholders and directors are clamoring for the return of their investments, or other satisfaction."

British Israel

Parham was an adherent of the idea that the Anglo people were ten lost tribes of Israel. As such they held responsibility to the whole world to lead them to Christ. "It is important that one does not judge historical figures by present theological understanding. Presentism is the "uncritical adherence to present-day attitudes, especially the tendency to interpret past events in terms of modern values and concepts."[1229] This concept evolved into the Christian Identity movement. Parham was not a participant.

New Pentecostals

Many writers had postulated that Charles Parham became

increasingly hostile toward the Pentecostal people. They wrote this as though it was some strange malady. First and foremost, the Apostolic Faith Movement is Charles and Sarah Parham's ministry. Anyone who used the name, the associated publications, etc. without permission is simply a thief and a robber. However, the Parhams present as being very generous with their friends and compatriots in the Gospel of Jesus Christ.

That either of the Parhams, or the actual representatives would stand up against petty larceny, was their legal right. No one has ever taken that from them. Those who wanted to have their own ministry should have merely created their own. Yet, that was not enough. Over the intervening years the Texas Syndicate ran a plethora of schemes and a surfeit of lies to support their schemes. Parham labeled these the "New Pentecostals" and opposed them. It was more than his right; it was his responsibility.

Schemes of The Texas Syndicate (Howard A. Goss, Warren Fay Carothers, their A.G.).

- 1906 - Blackmail Charles Parham in an attempt to gain control of the A.F.M.
- 1907 - Hold kangaroo Court and find Parham guilty of something that can be called "Conduct unbecoming a Minister." This charge is rich. Perhaps the Parhams should have said, "you first." In other words when "Carothers and his friends were tried for their "Conduct unbecoming a Minister," then we can have a conversation.
- 1907 - Conspire to have Parham arrested on bogus claims.
- 1907- Pretend they are the leaders of the A.F.M. after Parham dissolved their positions. Carothers left active ministry and began a number of business interests. Goss had credibility only because he married 2 A.F.M. ministers. On his own there is very little positive to say.
- 1908 - Continue to Pretend they lead the A.F.M. while Parham was

~ CHAPTER TWENTY-FOUR | DETRACTORS ~

evangelizing in a 2000 seat tent, Carothers was busy scheming, and Millicent Goss was ministering with Howard tagging along.

- 1910 – Pretended they have an agreement with Charles Mason to start a Frankenstein group they title, *Apostolic Faith Church of God in Christ*.
- 1911 – Began to put together a list of white ministers who might have interest in an all-white group in direct opposition to the A.F.M., C.O.G.I.C., and the Church of God Cleveland Tennessee which are all multicultural.
- 1913 – Put out a call for white ministers to come to Hot Springs, Arkansas.
- 1914 – The Texas Syndicate helped organize the Assemblies of God.
- 1915 – Texas Syndicate and their prodigy, the A.G., opposed blacks on bogus doctrinal claims.

W. F. CAROTHERS,
Attorney.
Room 622 First National Bank Bld. tf

In 1908, Carothers had a large article printed in the Houston Newspapers (and perhaps others) proclaiming his personal righteousness. In the letter he challenges Charles Parham to pick twelve men to judge him. It is presented like some kind of one-up-man-ship. As though he and Parham were in a duel. Perhaps Carothers thought he was in a duel, but Parham was not participating. Carothers lived by the old code of the South where white men were like kings, blacks were slaves, other minorities were servants and women kept their mouths shut.

Mr. Carothers new law practice[1230] and real estate businesses[1231] in Houston were getting the best of his spirit man. He had long confused carnal things with spiritual things and continued to manifest the same. Please note: none of his shortcomings, lies, hatred, racism, or white supremacy mattered to his friends in The Texas Syndicate. Nor did those things matter to his new friends as they formed alliances with William Durham and later created the Assemblies of God. When I first learned of the story of Charles Parham's legal challenges in San Antonio, I wondered why his Texas lawyer "friend," Warren Faye Carothers, did not go to his rescue. That was before I understood that Carothers was the Parhams' and the A.F.M.'s archrival, conspirator, and chief persecutor.

> "Why, would Bishop Mason want to start a white group when his group was receptive to all peoples (including whites)? Bishop Mason's Church of God in Christ already had white ministers."

While Carothers was busy with directing kangaroo courts and false arrest schemes, his fellow conspirator Howard Goss was developing a new scheme. The Texas Syndicate was losing face. Parham had completed a very extensive ministry schedule in 1908, shattering the lie that his ministry was over. Goss realized they needed a new plan. The word had gotten out that they are interlopers who are not really in charge of the A.F.M. So, they propose a new scheme. They would use the name Church of God in Christ (in a similar manner to how they used the name Apostolic Faith). They would combine the two and call it *Apostolic Faith Church of God in Christ*. They told people that they approached Bishop Charles Mason and he agreed to let them use the name for a white version of his movement. Sounds plausible until you ask questions. Why would Bishop Mason want to help start a racist group?

APOSTOLIC FAITH

DIRECTOR CAROTHERS ARRIVES FROM HEADQUARTERS.

W. D. Caywood of Houston Becomes State Director—Benson Takes Up Work Among the Jews.

Rev. W. F. Carothers, National director of the Apostolic Faith movement, arrived at headquarters from Joplin, Mo., yesterday after a several week's stay out of the city. Since he was here last he has conducted a Bible training school in Waco and taken part in a workers' convention in Missouri.

The work of the movement, says Director Carothers, is in splendid condition, and it has never faced a brighter day. "The Texas work is fine," he continued. "The convention which we have just closed in Waco was one of the most enthusiastic I ever attended. We had about fifty student workers in attendance and they are now out in the field. The faith has taken a firm hold in Waco and I will go Monday morning to press the city campaign there."

At Joplin, Mo., Mr. Carothers assisted in the ordination of twenty-one evangelist workers.

Announcement is made of the following recent changes in the Texas work: W. D. Caywood of Houston becomes State director, vice A. J. Benson, who takes up the work among the Jews. Mrs. M. D. Fields becomes editor of the Apostolic Faith, the organ of the movement. Otto Carl becomes Houston city director.

Plans are being formulated for the State encampment to be held in July. There will probably be some announcement relating to this encampment at a general rally to be held in the Brunner tabernacle Sunday.

"There are now some half a dozen visitors in the city," said Mr. Carothers yesterday, "who have come from distant places to investigate the movement at headquarters. They have been coming and investigating for some time, and all go away convinced that the movement is of God."

~ CHAPTER TWENTY-FOUR | DETRACTORS ~

Why would Bishop Mason want to start a white group when his group was receptive to all peoples (including whites)? Bishop Mason's Church of God in Christ already had white ministers.

Lies, fabrications, and more
- Charles Parham's Ministry ended at Azusa Street in 1906.
- Charles Parham divorced His Wife
- Charles Parham resigned from the Apostolic Faith Movement
- The Parhams are racists
- Charles Parham turned the Apostolic Faith Movement over to Warren Fay Carothers and his friends.
- Charles Parham joined the KKK

The Frankenstein created by the neo-Pentecostals was alive. After the interracial period 1906 to 1929, white Pentecostals with few exceptions torn asunder the interracial worshiping community of equals in their struggle for dominance and conformity to particular fundamentalistic interpretations of the Bible.[1232] The new Pentecostals replaced Parham's A.F.M. works with their grandiose vision of global unity.

Sarah Parham reflected, Parham's approach was *"letting each minister go forward doing his work, and, leaving local assemblies under local elders; and as often as God permits revisit to strengthen the missions."*[1233] "The Pentecostal work has been organized not only into one church, but many different organizations. Many small churches have been built, and many beautiful and expensive churches and temples, which have equaled or excelled those which have been built by the old-line organizations."[1234] "But the sad fact faced the Pentecostal work today, is the strife and bitterness that exist between the different churches of faith, in many places. How do you imagine it appears to the eyes of our God of love as He sees two or three churches in the same town, practically of the same belief at variance with each other? Each church magnifying the others faults and failures, that they may keep their own bunch in their own particular church."[1235]

Parham said, "Unity by organization never can be realized; for all churches, movements, and leaders want the supervision of that unity."[1236] The Texas Syndicate had killed the proverbial golden goose. For the last two decades of his life Charles Parham never faced a moral charge or accusation. The fake rumors, lies and innuendo had accomplished the mission of the Texas Syndicate. Apparently, all his enemies were united in the Texas Syndicate and their new creation which they named the Assemblies of God. Firmly entrenched in their various xenophobic endeavors the Texas Syndicate has spawned.

Parham remained in contact with his core A.F.M. following. He was widely appreciated by ministers around the world who gave proper credit to his priceless contribution to the Kingdom of Jesus Christ. Parham ministered for two more decades and held considerable revival campaigns in California, Idaho, Oregon, Michigan, New York, Kansas, Missouri, Oklahoma, and more.[1237] He preached in a number of venues including using his 40' x 80' tent that would seat 2000 people.[1238] Parham was first in many things related to his role as Father of the Pentecostal Movement including first developing the idea that speaking in tongues is the evidence of Holy Spirit baptism. "Parham was clearly the first nationally known Pentecostal prophet. His work covered every section of the continental United States except for the Southeast. "[1239] He was developing the foundation of what is referred to as the Pentecostal movement a decade before he met William Seymour. "Undoubtedly, he was a great speaker and everywhere he went crowds came to hear his message.[1240] The response was legendary. "With few conventions of organization, he succeeded in establishing a lasting affiliation of churches. Often called, "Daddy Parham" in his later years, he himself remained the center of the group's identity.[1241] Parham repeatedly denied any desire for recognition.[1242]

In closing, I give honor to those who pioneered a more excellent way for all of us. If Charles and Sarah Parham and the faithful Lilian Thistlethwaite had not dared to expect more from the Holy Ghost, we may not know that speaking with tongues as the Spirit of God gives utterance is available to all, I wonder if those speaking in tongues would still be regulated to remote places, woodsheds, and the outdoors as places where the Spirit of God would have liberty. I bow my head in thanks and humble appreciation for the example the Parhams led. To all those the Lord deems Righteous, whom I mention in this book, I give you the highest respect, honor, and appreciation.

Charles Parham said, "Twenty-eight years ago, baptized in the Holy Ghost and scarcely a day since that, I have not spoken in tongues. My dear friends of many years will know that I have served faithfully through days of indefatigable toil and nights of blackness and storm. No days were so cold and terrible or nights so frightful but what it was joy to run His errand, ever on the wing on errands of mercy and missions of love. The mighty deserts or rugged mountains, or distances long, but what it was joy to me to rush to help, feed, or comfort my loved ones in the Lord. Brethren, let us rise to the emergency of the hour, to the privilege that God has given us, and to spread the Gospel of Full salvation and preparation for our coming redemption to the end of the earth. Remembering that selfish motive in our work for God is un-Christ-like and that He left an example, that without considering ourselves, our own comforts or convenience or our own pleasure in the matter that we should pour our lives out in unselfish sacrificial service to our fellow men. Anything less than this would be unworthy of the high and holy calling to which God has ordained us."[1243]

On January 29, 1929, Charles Fox Parham went to be with the Lord, aged fifty-six years and he received his "Well done, good and faithful servant" from the Lord he loved.[1244] Over twenty-five hundred people attended his funeral at the Baxter Theatre. It took over an hour for the great crowd to pass the open casket for their last view of this gift of God to His church. A choir of fifty occupied the stage, along with a number of ministers from different parts of the nation. Over his casket people who had been healed and blessed under his ministry wept with appreciation. Offerings were sent from all over the United States to help purchase a monument. The family chose a granite pulpit with an open Bible on the top, on which was carved "John 15:13," which was his last sermon text, "Greater love hath no man than this, that a man lay down his life for his friends."[1245] Lilian Thistlethwaite said, "If there could be one thing more than another that proved to me the wonderful Christian life Bro. Parham lived, it is his family of four sons and a daughter, who, with their families, are every one of them honest, honorable, upright Christians, proving that through his faithful Christian life they too have accepted their father's God."[1246]

As I started, Charles and Sarah Parham, I came not to praise you. I came to bury you. May you rest in the Peace of our Lord and Savior Jesus Christ, in whose name you pledged your lives, your fortunes, and sacred honor. Till we all get to heaven!

Endnotes

1. https://www.apostolicarchives.com/page/page/5834251.htm
2. https://william-branham.org/site/john_collins
3. https://www.willistower.com/history-and-facts
4. https://theopolisinstitute.com/leithart_post/spirit-of-segregation/
5. https://william-branham.org/site/books/pbtwh
6. https://www.cambriapress.com/pub.cfm?bid=96
7. Ethics in the Age of the Spirit. Race, Women, War and the Assemblies of God. Howard N. Kenyon. 2019.
8. https://theoldblackchurch.blogspot.com/2018/10/is-there-racism-in-united-pentecostal.html
9. Charisma. Why the Azusa Street Revival Ended. J. D. King. 2016. J.D. King is the director of the World Revival Network and associate pastor of World Revival Church.
10. Sixth Amendment. In all criminal prosecutions, the accused shall enjoy the right to a speedy and public trial, by an impartial jury of the State and district wherein the crime shall have been committed, which district shall have been previously ascertained by law, and to be informed of the nature and cause of the accusation; to be confronted with the witnesses against him; to have compulsory process for obtaining witnesses in his favor, and to have the Assistance of Counsel for his defense. https://constitution.congress.gov/constitution/amendment-6/
11. See Zachariah 7:9-10.
12. The cleansing power of the blood of Jesus. The blood of Jesus has two-fold cleansing power! Read how in this enlightening article. Elias Aslaksen. See 1 John 1:7-9.
13. See Job 33:9.
14. https://www.loc.gov/exhibits/magna-carta-muse-and-mentor/trial-by-jury.html
15. See II Corinthians 7:11
16. See Matthew 17:24
17. https://drjimmann.com/2018/10/04/bible-even-points-to-idea-of-innocent-until-proven-guilty/
18. 1 John 4:20
19. https://www.fairtrials.org/the-right-to-a-fair-trial/the-presumption-of-innocence/
20. https://www.law.cornell.edu/wex/right_to_counsel
21. The First Circuit has repeatedly stated that "reasonable doubt is a fundamental concept that does not easily lend itself to refinement or definition." United States v. Vavlitis, 9 F.3d 206, 212 (1st Cir. 1993); see also United States v. Campbell, 874 F.2d 838, 843 (1st Cir. 1989). For that reason, the First Circuit has joined other circuits in advising that the meaning of "reasonable doubt" be left to the jury to discern. United States v. Cassiere, 4 F.3d 1006, 1024 (1st Cir. 1993) ("[A]n instruction which uses the words

reasonable doubt without further definition adequately apprises the jury of the proper burden of proof." (Quoting United States v. Olmstead, 832 F.2d 642, 646 (1st Cir. 1987)); accord United States v. Taylor, 997 F.2d 1551, 1558 (D.C. Cir. 1993) ("[T]he greatest wisdom may lie with the Fourth Circuit's and Seventh Circuit's instruction to leave to juries the task of deliberating the meaning of reasonable doubt."). The constitutionality of this practice was reaffirmed by the Supreme Court in Victor v. Nebraska, 511 U.S. 1, 5-6 (1994). It is not reversible error to refuse further explanation, even when requested by the jury, so long as the reasonable doubt standard was "not 'buried as an aside' in the judge's charge." United States v. Littlefield, 840 F.2d 143, 146 (1st Cir. 1988) (quoting Olmstead, 832 F.2d at 646).

22   False Witness: A Lawyer's History of the Law of Perjury. Richard H. Underwood University of Kentucky College of Law, runderwo@uky.edu Fall 1993.

23   False Witness: A Lawyer's History of the Law of the Law of Perjury. Richard H. Underwood. University of Kentucky College of Law. 1993.

24   Brooks Ayers Isn't Alone: 8 Famous Lies and the Liars Who Told Them. History has proven, the truth always comes out. NATALIE FINN. NOV 12, 2015.

25   4 Famous People Convicted of Perjury. ETHAN TREX. AUGUST 26, 2010

26   June 25, 1948, ch. 645, 62 Stat. 773; Pub. L. 88-619, § 1, Oct. 3, 1964, 78 Stat. 995; Pub. L. 94-550, § 2, Oct. 18, 1976, 90 Stat. 2534; Pub. L. 103-322, title XXXIII, § 330016(1)(I), Sept. 13, 1994, 108 Stat. 2147.

27   https://www.gotquestions.org/false-witness.html

28   This instruction does not use a "'guilt or innocence' comparison" warned against by the First Circuit. United States v. DeLuca, 137 F.3d 24, 37 (1st Cir. 1998); United States v. Andujar, 49 F.3d 16, 24 (1st Cir. 1995). A "guilt and non-guilt" comparison is "less troublesome," but still "could risk undercutting the government's burden by suggesting that the defendant is guilty if they do not think he is not guilty." United States v. Ranney, Nos. 01-1912, 01-2531, 01-1913, 2002 WL 1751379, at *5 (1st Cir. Aug. 1, 2002).

29   For the rationale of Self-defense, see: Boaz Sangero, Self-Defense in Criminal Law 11 - 106 (Hart Publishing, 2006).

30   https://deathpenaltyinfo.org/policy-issues/innocence/executed-but-possibly-innocent

31   https://www.mad.uscourts.gov/resources/pattern2003/html/patt4cfo.htm

32   https://sddefenseattorneys.com/blog/famous-wrongful-conviction-cases/

33   Accomplices, Accessories, Aiders, and Abettors
How criminals are defined–from accomplices to aiders and abettors to conspirators–depends on their participation in the crime. Micah Schwartzbach, Attorney

34   A defendant is never to be convicted on suspicion or conjecture. https://www.

mad.uscourts.gov/resources/pattern2003/html/patt4cfo.htm
35   https://www.lynchingintexas.org/
36   https://www.law.cornell.edu/rules/frcrmp/rule_16
37   Reasonable Doubt. WILL KENTON. September 28, 2021. Reviewed by ROBERT C. KELLY. Fact checked by ARIEL COURA.G.E
38   Arrests That Don't Result in Criminal Charges. Janet Portman, Attorney
39   Matthew 5:7.
40   https://www.opensocietyfoundations.org/publications/justice-denied-americas-continuing-neglect-our-constitutional-right-counsel
41   What Do States Owe People Who Are Wrongfully Convicted? STATELINE ARTICLE March 14, 2017. Scott Rodd
42   Galatians 5:19-21.
43   I Corinthians 6:9.
44   Understanding a charge of aiding and abetting On Behalf of Juan L Guerra Jr & Associates | Nov 19, 2019
45   Exodus 23:1.
46   Jude 1:12.
47   Konstantin Stanislavski.
48   https://www.apostolicarchives.com/newsletters/newsletter/9117400/100620.htm
49   Acts Chapter 2.
50   The Theology of Charles Fox Parham. James R. Goff. Pg. 59.
51   "A Short History of Methodism," WJW, 9: 348.
52   The Real Meaning of Sola Scriptura. MARTY FOORD. 25/08/2017
53
54   Ibid. Goss. Goss spoke honestly of Parham in the early days, even though Goss later conspired with W. F. Carothers and others in a coup to overthrow Parham's leadership in his own Apostolic Faith Movement.
55   The Life of Charles Parham. Sarah E. Parham. Dedication page. 1930. Joplin, Mo.
56   https://www.asbury.edu/about/spiritual-vitality/faith/wesleyan-holiness-theology/#footnotes
57   "Principles of a Methodist," BE, 9: 50 ff.
58   Apostolic Faith Bible College. 335 West 10th Street Baxter Springs, Kansas. 66713. www.Afbiblecollege.com
59   Frank D Macchia. Baptized in the Spirit: A Global Pentecostal Theology. Grand Rapids, MI. Zondervan, 2006. 20.
60   https://seedbed.com/happy-birthday-henry-clay-morrison/
61   Seven Ways John Wesley Preached about the Holy Spirit. Chris Ritter. May 30, 2017.
62   The Los Angeles Times. Los Angeles, California. 18 Apr 1906, Wed. Page 17

63	Ibid. Ritter.
64	https://place.asburyseminary.edu/cgi/viewcontent.cgi?article=1000&context=firstfruitsheritagematerial
65	https://www.britannica.com/topic/Pentecostalism#ref187934
66	Later, some Pentecostals would pick up the name of the magazine as though they invented the concept, however the original belongs to Henry Clay Morrison.
67	https://www.gospeltruth.net/tongue_fire.htm
68	https://www.gospeltruth.net/tongue_fire.htm
69	The greatest missionary you've never heard of. [Christian History originally published this article in Christian History Issue #136 in 2020]. Robert G. Tuttle Jr. is emeritus professor of world Christianity at Asbury Theological Seminary and the author of In Our Time: The Life and Ministry of E. Stanley Jones.
70	See the Book of the Acts of the Apostles.
71	Asbury Theological Seminary 90th Anniversary Publications. Henry Clay Morrison "Crusader Saint". Percival A. Wesche a Short History of Asbury Theological Seminary. Howard Fenimore Shipps. The Distinctive Emphases of Asbury Theological Seminary. Harold B. Kuhn
72	Lilian Thistlethwaite wrote this in The Life of Charles Fox Parham. The Wonderful History of the Latter Rain. Sarah E. Parham. Pg. 59.
73	Acts Chapter 2.
74	https://www.biblegateway.com/resources/encyclopedia-of-the-bible/Apostolic-Age
75	Southland Church. The Case against Cessationism. Page 8. www.mysouthland.com
76	https://romans1015.com/1901-topeka-outpouring/
77	William W. Menzies, Robert P. Menzies, "Spirit and Power: Foundations of Pentecostal Experience", Zondervan, USA, 2011, page 16
78	Apostolic Faith. Los Angeles California. September 1906.
79	Ibid. Apostolic Faith.
80	6 Ibid., Loc. 738.
81	The Apostolic Faith. Official Organ of the Original Apostolic Faith. Charles F. Parham. Founder. Bethel Bible School. Topeka Kansas. 1900. Volume XXVII-XXVIII. December 1950. January 1951. No. 12-1. Pg.1.
82	Ibid. Apostolic Faith. Pg. 1
83	Apostolic Faith. August 1925. Cove
84	https://www.apostolicfaith.org/the-apostolic-faith/january-2017-viewpoint
85	https://www.catalystresources.org/methodist-bands-past-and-present-salvation-happens-in-community/
86	The Personal Pentecost and the Glorious Hope. Charles Haddon Spurgeon June 13, 1886. Scripture: Romans 5:5. Metropolitan Tabernacle Pulpit Volume 32
87	https://www.britannica.com/topic/Pentecostalism

88   https://biography.yourdictionary.com/charles-fox-parham

89   Jeff Nelson, Pentecostal Missions: Past 100 and Beyond, International Journal of Pentecostal Missiology (Dec. 2019) 6:1, 25.

90   CYBERJOURNAL FOR PENTECOSTAL-CHARISMATIC RESEARCH Table of Contents #5 February 1999 Hispanic Pentecostals: Azusa Street and Beyond Carmelo Alvarez. Pg. 1.

91   Ecclesiastes 9:11.

92   https://plato.stanford.edu/entries/dubois/

93   http://www.prca.org/resources/publications/articles/item/5373-the-parting-of-his-garments

94   Howard Goss, who conspired with eight other men in a coup against Charles Parham wrote of Parham's humility. See: The Winds of God. Ethel Goss.

95   Revelation 13:7

96   Apostolic Faith. September 1906. Volume 1. No. 1 from Los Angeles. Page 1.

97   Ibid. Apostolic Faith.

98   UNDERSTANDING CONFLICT AND WAR: VOL. 3: CONFLICT IN PERSPECTIVE. Chapter 4. Misperception, Cognitive Dissonance, Righteousness, And Conflict. R.J. Rummel.

99   https://christianhistoryinstitute.org/magazine/article/pentecostalism-seymour

100   https://rafu.com/2014/02/walk-of-remembrance-commemorates-beginning-of-pentecostal-movement-in-little-tokyo/

101   https://www.revival-library.org/revival_heroes/20th_century/seymour_william.shtml

102   https://www.revival-library.org/revival_heroes/20th_century/seymour_william.shtml

103   Azusa Street, the Roots of Modern-day Pentecost, an Eyewitness Account Paperback – January 1, 1980. Frank Bartleman.

104   HOW PENTECOST CAME TO LOS ANGELES. As It Was in the Beginning. FRANK BARTLEMAN. 2nd Edition F. BARTLEMAN 5606 Bushnell Way, Los Angeles, Calif. This issue does not contain any of the information added later by Pentecostals.

105   https://www.apostolicarchives.com/articles/article/8801925/173591.htm

106   Ibid. Apostolic Faith. Pg. 1.

107   Apostolic Faith. September 1906. Volume 1. No. 1 from Los Angeles. Page 1.

108   Ibid. Goss.

109   Across the Lines: Charles Parham's Contribution to the Inter-Racial Character of Early Pentecostalism. Eddie Hyatt. December 20, 2004.

110   https://www.encyclopedia.com/environment/encyclopedias-almanacs-transcripts-and-maps/seymour-william

111   Lucy was very much a part of the Parham family. The Parham children called her "Auntie." Lucy Farrow has been called "the central prophet igniting the Holy Ghost fires in Southern

California."4 She was known for her

success in praying with people to receive the gift of the Holy Spirit. Even before the first outpouring on Bonnie Brae Street,

Seymour sent for Farrow to come to Los Angeles and help him pray with seekers. Once in the city she was responsible for leading

many at the Azusa Street Mission into the baptism in the Holy Spirit.

112   Apostolic Faith. September 1906. Volume 1. No. 1 from Los Angeles. Page 1.
113   The Life of Charles Parham. Sarah E. Parham.
114   https://www.apostolicarchives.com/articles/article/8801925/173189.htm
115   https://www.apostolicarchives.com/articles/article/8801925/173189.htm
116   The Life of Charles Fox Parham. Sarah E. Parham. Page 137. Also See Apostolic Archives. Bishop William J. Seymour. www.apostolicarchives.com
117   The Life of Charles F. Parham. Sarah E. Parham. Page 142.
118   Ibid. Gary W. Garrett. Apostolic Archives.
119   Winds of God. Ethel Goss. Page 73.
120   See Apostolic Faith Report. May 1921. Page 5.
121   Ibid. Apostolic Archives.
122   Charles W. Shumway, □A Critical Study of the Gift of Tongues '. (A. B. diss., University of Southern California, 1914), 173.
123   Shumway. Gift of Tongues. Page 158-9.
124   Proverbs 16:28.
125   https://www.merriam-webster.com/dictionary/a%20needle%20in%20a%20haystack
126   Revelation 12:10 & John 19:6.
127   See: Job 1:6-12.
128   See: Exodus 23:1.
129   Pneuma Review. Fall 2004. Across the Lines: Charles Parham's Contribution to the Inter-Racial Character of Early Pentecostalism. Eddie Hyatt. December 20, 2004
130   Ibid. Hyatt.
131   James 1:26.
132   Ibid. Parham.
133   Julia W. Hutchins became acquainted with the Apostolic Faith through William F. Manley and his 1905 Los Angeles Tent Meetings.
134   This presents as an escalation of Carothers agenda against negros, Mexicans, women and others. Los Angeles would further inflame Carothers. The Los Angeles Apostolic Faith Gospel Mission was located in Little Tokyo prompting Carothers to add Japanese to his long list of undesirable people for his manifesto.
135   Carothers was a very bigoted man. He did participate in a service to send Seymour to Los Angeles but was not interested in the promotion of blacks to speak to white audiences.

136   Parham promised Seymour ministerial license. Seymour got the license, but they took longer than expected as Carothers took his time getting the man his credentials. See the letter from Seymour to Parham asking about the delay in his credentials.

137   William J. Seymour letter to the Apostolic Faith Movement. Carothers is supposed to be fielding such correspondence but the letter from Seymour appears that Carothers has been ignoring Seymour's requests. Parham is notified on the bottom of the correspondence that the documents have finally been processed. This indicates that Carothers was conspiring behind the scenes against Parham and Seymour as part of his growing scheme. Later, Carothers would steal the Apostolic Faith newsletter from Seymour. https://digitalshowcase.oru.edu/cgi/viewcontent.cgi?article=1002&context=correspondence

138   https://christianhistoryinstitute.org/magazine/article/american-pentecost

139   Criticisms of Azusa Street. Duke Press. July 2014

140   The Lower Light. No. 7, 4, 6.

141   Faith-Based Racism and the Rise of the White-Supremacist Nation. Reviewed Work: Reforging the White Republic: Race, Religion, and American Nationalism, 1865-1898. Edward J. Blum

142   Ibid. French. Pg. 31.

143   Robeck, "Pentecostal Origins" 170; Goff, "Problems of History." 188.

144   The Life of Charles Parham. Sarah E. Parham, Pages 148-150.

145   Ibid. Parham. Page 153-155.

146   Ibid. Parham. Page 155.

147   Ibid. Parham. Page 148.

148   The Life of Charles Parham. Sarah E. Parham. Page 162.

149   Ibid. Parham. Page 163. Sarah Parham quoted this from the Gospel to the Kingdom. J. G. Campbell. Texas.

150   https://issuu.com/charismata/docs/apostolic_faith_and_pentecostal_time-table_of_key_

151   https://azusastreet.org/ParticipantHallAnna.htm

152   https://312azusa.com/blog/page/26/

153   Seymour's 1906 letter is archived at Apostolic Archives. Www.apostolicarchives.com

154   Ibid. Hyatt. Pg. 4.

155   Ibid. Hyatt. Pg. 4.

156   "The Apostolic Faith Movement," Apostolic Faith (Los Angeles), 1:1. September 1906, 2.1.

157   The Apostolic Faith Movement," Apostolic Faith (Los Angeles), 1:1. September 1906, 2.1.

158   https://www.notablebiographies.com/supp/Supplement-Mi-So/Seymour-William-Joseph.html

159   Ibid. J. D. King.

160   Ibid. J. D. King.

161   See. HISTORICAL ESSAY: IN THE NAME OF GOD; AN AMERICAN STORY OF

FEMINISM, RACISM, AND RELIGIOUS INTOLERANCE: THE STORY OF ALMA BRIDWELL WHITE. KRISTIN E. KANDT.

162

163   Sarah Parham and others have her name as Lucy F. Farrar. See, the Life of Charles Parham by Sarah E. Parham. 1930. Lucy was part of the Parham family and lived in their home. The only known document with her name spelled on it, is her death certificate. Although unlikely, it is possible that one was her maiden name. If not, we do not know her maiden name. The photo of her was submitted as Mrs. Lucy F. Farrar.

164   Lucy Farrow - The Woman Who ignited the Flame at Azusa Street. Tamera Lynn Kraft. Friday December 29. 2017.

165   D. J. Nelson, in "For Such a Time as This: The Story of Bishop William J. Seymour and the Azusa Street Revival" (Ph.D. diss., University of Birmingham 1981), 35, suggests that Seymour settled in Houston about 1903.

166   Ibid. Nelson.

167   https://aaregistry.org/story/lucy-farrow-pastor-born/

168   3. (Christian Churches, other) Christianity someone who performs Christian service without pay but earns a living by another means. https://www.thefreedictionary.com/tentmaker

169   https://wordsharpeners.wordpress.com/2018/05/21/lucy-farrow-the-woman-who-ignited-the-flame-at-azuza-st-revival/

170   CYBERJOURNAL FOR PENTECOSTAL-CHARISMATIC RESEARCH. THE PAST: Historical Roots of Racial Unity and Division. in American Pentecostalism. Cecil M. Robeck, Jr., Ph.D.

171   https://www.revival-library.org/revival_heroes/20th_century/farrow_lucy.shtml

172   https://www.revival-library.org/revival_heroes/20th_century/farrow_lucy.shtml

173   Across the Lines: Charles Parham's Contribution to the Inter-Racial Character of Early Pentecostalism. Eddie Hyatt. December 20, 2004

174   https://lamp-stand.com/2012/09/08/i-historical-reconstruction-of-the-apostolic-doctrine-subpart-g-pentecostal-movement-article-2-azusa-street-revival/

175   Apostolic Faith. Charles F. Parham. Melbourne Kansas. 1905.

176   Apostolic Faith and Pentecostal Timetable of Key Events. Bernie L. Wade. Published on Nov 30, 2015. Pg. 45.

177   Ibid. Hyatt.

178   See B. F. Lawrence, The Apostolic Faith Restored (St. Louis: Gospel Publishing, 1916), 64.

179   See B. F. Lawrence. The Apostolic Faith Restored. 66.

180   Jude. Chapter 1.

181   a person who kills their father. plural noun: patricides

182   Speech: "Friends, Romans, countrymen, lend me your ears." WILLIAM SHAKESPEARE (from Julius Caesar, spoken by Marc Antony).

183   Psalms 23:23 NKJV.

184   The Third Great Awakening, according to historians, occurred from approximately the late 1850s to the early 1920s. Much like the First and Second Great Awakenings, this time period experienced a resurgence in religious interest and vigor. The "Great Prayer Meeting Revival of 1857-58" was the catalyst and carried into the 1870s, as Dwight Moody's urban campaigns spread across the United States.

185   https://www.thearda.com/timeline/movements/movement_51.asp

186   Acts 14:17 NKJV.

187   https://www.apostolicarchives.com/newsletters/newsletter/9117400/100620.htm

188   Apostolic Faith & Pentecostal Timetable of Key Events 1880-1910 6th Edition ©2012, 2013, 2014, 2015, 2016, 2020, 2021 Bernie L. Wade, PhD. Coker Creek. Pg. 19.

189   Ibid. Wade. Pg. 20.

190   https://www.loc.gov/rr/scitech/battle.html

191   There is no reference to the name Fox as Charles Parham's middle name. As the name is quite unusual it seems likely that the reference was an attempt by the pious mother to make him the namesake of the founder of the Quakers.

192   See Acts Chapter 17.

193   The Life of Charles Fox Parham. Sarah E. Parham. The Latter Reign. Pg. 55-57.

194   Ibid. Apostolic Archives. Topeka Outpouring.

195   Confidence. April 1908. No. 1.

196   https://www.bcwales.org/1904-welsh-revival

197   https://en.wikipedia.org/wiki/W._T._Stead

198   https://www.bcwales.org/1904-welsh-revival

199   https://romans1015.com/welsh-revival-1904-05/

200   https://www.bcwales.org/1904-welsh-revival

201   Acts Chapter 2:6

202   Apostolic Faith Report. August 1905. Volume 1. No. 3. Melrose Kansas.

203   https://www.desiringgod.org/articles/the-american-revival-of-1905

204   God Found His Moses" A biographical and theological analysis of the life of Joseph Smale (1867-1926) Welch, Timothy Bernard (2009). "God Found His Moses" A biographical and theological analysis of the life of Joseph Smale (1867-1926). University of Birmingham. Ph.D.

205   Apostolic Faith & Pentecostal Timetable of Key Events 1880-1910 6th Edition ©2012, 2013, 2014, 2015, 2016, 2020, 2021 Bernie L. Wade, PhD. Pg. 57-58.

206   How Pentecost Came to Los Angeles. Frank Bartleman. Pg. 11.

207   Published and blessed. A Case study in Early Pentecostal Publishing 1906-1926. Malcolm John Taylor. University of Birmingham. January 1994.

208   John Piper (@JohnPiper) is founder and teacher of desiringGod.org and chancellor of Bethlehem College & Seminary. For 33 years, he served as pastor of Bethlehem Baptist Church,

Minneapolis, Minnesota. He is author of more than 50 books, including Desiring God: Meditations of a Christian Hedonist and most recently Providence.

209   https://www.asbury.edu/academics/resources/library/archives/biographies/henry-clay-morrison/

210   https://churchleaders.com/outreach-missions/outreach-missions-articles/257668-brief-history-spiritual-revival-awakening-america.html

211   http://media.sabda.org/alkitab-6/wh2-hdm/hdm0529.pdf

212   https://place.asburyseminary.edu/firstfruitsheritagematerial/1/

213   http://media.sabda.org/alkitab-6/wh2-hdm/hdm0529.pdf

214   HENRY CLAY MORRISON Prophet, Warrior, Orator. George Whitefield Ridout. Chapter 2. THE PROPHET. Pentecostal Publishing Company. Louisville, KY. 1944.

215   Jonathan Edwards, "A Narrative of Surprising Conversions," Jonathan Edwards on Revival, Carlisle: The Banner of Truth Trust, first published in 1736, p. 2.

216   https://www.desiringgod.org/articles/the-american-revival-of-1905

217   http://plainshumanities.unl.edu/encyclopedia/doc/egp.rel.038

218   See: The Life of Charles F. Parham. Sarah E. Parham.

219   https://quaker.org/legacy/northbranch/equality.html

220   SIR JOHN HARRIS (1874-1940), Secretary for many years of the Anti-Slavery Society. QUAKER TESTIMONY A.G.AINST SLAVERY AND RACIAL DISCRIMINATION An Anthology compiled by STELLA ALEXANDER. Published for the Race_ Relations Committee by FRIENDS HOME SERVICE COMMITTEE. FRIENDS HOUSE, EUSTON ROAD, LONDON, N.W.1

221   Fields White unto Harvest. Charles F. Parham and the Missionary Origins of Pentecostalism. James R. Goff, JR. 1988. Introduction.

222   Charles F. Parham. "Baptism of the Holy Ghost," A Voice Crying in The Wilderness. 36.

223   John Wesley, "Christian Perfection." Sermon 40. 150.

224   Henry Clay Morrison. The Baptism of the Holy Ghost (Wilmore, KY" First Fruits Press, 2021. Originally 1900), 4, 22.

225   JW Journal 11/8/74; cf. JWJ 2/10/67 and 12/25/85 for similar examples.

226   JW Christian Perfection II.11.

227   JW Journal 10/28/62. The reader should take note of Charles' qualification of Pentecost "fully come." This possibly implies a concept of degrees in the Wesley brothers understanding of Pentecost.

228   https://www.loc.gov/resource/dcmsiabooks.tongueoffireortr00arth_0/?sp=7

229   Tongue of Fire or the True Power of Christianity. William Arthur. A.M. New York. 1857. Pg. 35.

230   Baptism of the Holy Ghost. Henry Clay Morrison. Page 12. 1900. Pentecostal Publishing Company. Louisville, KY.

231   Baptism of the Holy Ghost. Henry Clay Morrison. Page 12. Pentecostal Publishing Company. Louisville, KY. 1900.

232   Ibid. Morrison. Acts Chapter 2:38-40

233   The history of Kentucky Methodism has no more loyal name among her sons and daughters than that of Durham. The Durham home was known as a haven for the circuit-rider.

234   https://en.wikipedia.org/wiki/Henry_Bidleman_Bascom

235   A Biographical Sketch of Henry Clay Morrison, D.D. Editor of The Pentecostal Herald. The Man and His Ministry. C. F. WIMBERLY. Page 30.

236   https://en.wikipedia.org/wiki/Manumission

237   https://en.wikipedia.org/wiki/Henry_Bidleman_Bascom

238   https://en.wikipedia.org/wiki/Henry_Clay_Morrison

239   Acts 2:1-40.

240   The Baldwin Ledger (Baldwin, Kansas). August 02, 1895. Pg. 3.

241   Ibid. Baldwin Ledger.

242   https://www.britannica.com/topic/DePauw-University

243   Ibid. Baldwin Ledger

244   Baldwin City (Douglas County). Kansas Messenger. A Methodist paper "devoted to news, education, and religion." Jan. 1, 1859 - Jan. 8, 1859. https://www.kshs.org/p/kansas-territorial-newspapers/13875

245   https://www.goodreads.com/quotes/675958-we-hold-these-truths-to-be-self-evident-that-all-men#:~:text=Quotes%20%3E%20Quotable%20Quote-,%E2%80%9CWe%20hold%20these%20truths%20to%20be%20self%2Devident%2C%20that,and%20the%20pursuit%20of%20Happiness.

246   https://politicalstrangenames.blogspot.com/2018/04/werter-renick-davis-1815-1893.html

247   https://politicalstrangenames.blogspot.com/2018/04/werter-renick-davis-1815-1893.html

248   https://politicalstrangenames.blogspot.com/2018/04/werter-renick-davis-1815-1893.html

249   https://www.bakeru.edu/

250   The publication dealt with news from the perspective of the M.E. Church and had a strong abolitionist flavor.

251   Appletons' cyclopedia of American biography, Vol. II, New York, D. Appleton and Company, 1887.

252   Minute of the Annual Conferences of the Methodist Episcopal Church. Spring Conferences of 1879. Kansas Conference, Held in Leavenworth, Kansas. March 12-17, 1879. Bishop Wiley, Presiding. William Smith, Secretary. Pg. 37. From the Library of The Ohio State University. Cincinnati. 1879.

253   https://www.google.com/books/edition/Minutes_Taken_at_the_Several_Annual_Conf/J?hl=en&gbpv=1&dq=Reverend+J+C+Telford+methodist+pastor+Kansas&pg=PA38&printsec=frontcover

254   https://www.history.com/this-day-in-history/john-browns-raid-on-harpers-ferry

255   The Baldwin Ledger. Baldwin Kansas. August 02, 1895. Page 3. Reprinted from the

Methodist Review. New York City. August 1895. Dr. W. A. Quayle. Page 618.

256   Ibid. Baldwin Ledger. https://www.google.com/books/edition/The_Methodist_Review/QAAMAAJ?hl=en&gbpv-1&dq=werter+renick+davis&pg=PA618&printsec=frontcover

257   http://www.ksgenweb.org/civilwar/Werter_R_Davis.htm

258   Ibid Baldwin Ledger.

259   Wesley, the Almost Charismatic. Peter J. Bellini. June 1, 2020.

260   Acts Chapter 2:39. NKJV

261   https://en.wikipedia.org/wiki/John_William_Fletcher

262   Timothy Smith, The Promise of the Spirit, 25.

263   Gresham, John Jr. Charles G. Finney's Doctrine of the Baptism of the Holy Spirit, 65.

264   https://en.wikipedia.org/wiki/High_church#:~:text=High%20Church%20clergy%20and%20laity,an%20orderly%20and%20dignified%20churchmanship

265   Apostolic Faith & Pentecostal Timetable of Key Events 1880-1910 6th Edition ©2012, 2013, 2014, 2015, 2016, 2020, 2021 Bernie L. Wade, PhD. Pg. 21.

266   Joel 2:28 NKJV

267   https://www.biblegateway.com/passage/?search=Joel%202%3A28-32&version=NKJV

268   https://robcanobbio.files.wordpress.com/2020/01/104.pdf

269   The Life Millennium: The 100 Most Important Events and People of the Past 1,000 Years Hardcover – November 1, 1998. Robert Friedman. Time.

270   Romans 13:7. NKJV.

271   The Progressive Mystery. Tracing the Elusive Spirit in Scripture & Tradition. Myk Habets.2019. Page 161.

272   Boddy, B.J. & Lioy, D., 2016, 'The intercession of the Holy Spirit: Revisiting Romans 8:26-27', Conspectus: The Journal of the South African Theological Seminary 21(03), 2-37.

273   https://fullerstudio.fuller.edu/women-in-the-pentecostal-movement/

274   https://www.christianitytoday.com/history/issues/issue-58/silent-pentecostals.html

275   https://christianhistoryinstitute.org/magazine/article/pentecostalism-did-you-know

276   Four times the church got weird... and was better for it. Michael Frost. April 18, 2018. Anabaptists, Celtic Christianity, Cistercians, Pentecostals

277   https://www.britannica.com/topic/Oberlin-College

278   https://www.berea.edu/about/history/

279   https://place.asburyseminary.edu/cgi/viewcontent.cgi?article=1000&context=apostolicfaith

280   https://www.amazon.com/LILIAN-THISTLETHWAITE-Evangelist-Pentecost-Christian/dp/1888435305/ref=sr_1_1?keywords=Lilian%20Thistlethwaite%20by%20Linda%20Miller&qid=1580605448&s=books&sr=1-1&fbclid=IwAR1L7OA.G.Av21JL-_i9oKHfJ819e0jyCZVV6vtUpCb3JLiQt-Fi4fNsA10Mk

281   https://fullerstudio.fuller.edu/women-in-the-pentecostal-movement/

282   https://www.britannica.com/topic/Pentecostalism

283   https://ghanachurch.com/charles-f-parham-the-father-of-pentecost/
284   https://www.wikitree.com/wiki/Thistlethwaite-43
285   https://www.umc.org/en/content/timeline-of-women-in-methodism
286   https://www.umc.org/en/content/timeline-of-women-in-methodism
287   Alma Bridwell White, The Ku Klux Klan in Prophecy, 135.
288   "We Want No Hatchet-Wielding Amazons:" The Feminism, Racism, and Nativism of the Women of the Ku Klux Klan
Honors Thesis Submitted to The Department of History of The University of Colorado Boulder. Nora Hickins Boulder, Colorado April 2018. Pg. 24.
289   See: Race and the Assemblies of God Church: The Journey from Azusa Street to the "Miracle of Memphis"
290   https://www.law.cornell.edu/wex/separate_but_equal
291   Britannica. Jim Crow laws. United States [1877-1954]. Melvin I. Urofsky |
292   Linda Gordon, The Second Coming of the KKK, 121.
293   Race and the Assemblies of God Church: The Journey from Azusa Street to the "Miracle of Memphis"
294   https://www.learnreligions.com/history-of-the-nazarene-churches-700057
295   Church of the Nazarene.
296   Ibid. Sarah E. Parham. Pg. 24.
297   Pentecostals Renounce Racism. Memphis gathering begins mending historic rift. J. LEE GRADY. DECEMBER 12, 1994
298   https://en.wikipedia.org/wiki/Charles_Fox_Parham
299   https://www.kshs.org/kansapedia/settlement-in-kansas/14546
300   https://www.kshs.org/kansapedia/education-in-kansas/14231
301   http://www.tonganoxiemirror.com/news/2001/feb/28/delaware_footprints/?print
302   https://tonganoxielibrary.org/tonganoxie-history/
303   Origins of Southern Radicalism. Lacy K. Ford. 1988. Pg. 345.
304   http://www.tonganoxiemirror.com/news/2016/jun/09/chief-tonganoxie-man-who-shaped-us/
305   https://tonganoxielibrary.org/tonganoxie-history/
306   http://www.tonganoxiemirror.com/news/2016/jun/09/chief-tonganoxie-man-who-shaped-us/
307   Captain David L. Payne," Archived May 19, 2017, at the Wayback Machine Chronicles of Oklahoma, Vol. 14 No. 3: December 1935. Accessed March 1, 2015.
308   https://abandonedks.com/pleasant-valley-school/
309   https://www.tonganoxiehistoricalsociety.org/newsletters/TCHS-newsletter-mar-2008.pdf
310   ART. XXXVI.–The Tonganoxie Meteorite; [Contributions from the Chemical Laboratory of the University of Kansas, No. II.]

Bailey, E H American Journal of Science (1880-1910); New Haven Vol. 42, Iss. 251, (Nov 1891): 385. https://www.google.com/books/edition/Report_of_the_Commissioner_of_Education/J?hl=en&gbpv=1&dq=Tonganoxie+Friends+Academy&pg=PA2040&printsec=frontcover

311   https://tonganoxielibrary.org/tonganoxie-history/

A New Kansas Meteorite. F. H. SNOW SCIENCE. 2 Jan 1891. Vol ns-17, Issue 413, p. 3. DOI: 10.1126/science. ns-17.413.3. b

https://www.science.org/doi/epdf/10.1126/science.ns-17.413.3.b

312   https://ghanachurch.com/charles-f-parham-the-father-of-pentecost/

313   The Life of Charles Parham. Search the Scriptures. Chapter 2. Sarah E. Parham. Pg. 11.

314   https://www.umc.org/en/content/methodist-history-the-mourners-bench

315   https://www.revival-library.org/revival_heroes/20th_century/parham_charles_fox.shtml

316   https://www.wikitree.com/wiki/Thistlethwaite-44

317   https://www.wikitree.com/wiki/Baker-27983

318   Thistlethwaite, Bernard. The Thistlethwaite Family. A study in genealogy. Vol. I. Headly Brothers, Bishopgate, London, E.C. 1910. page 203.

319   The Life of Charles Parham. Search the Scriptures. Chapter 2. Sarah E. Parham. Pg. 11.

320   https://www.ebooksread.com/authors-eng/jesse-a-hall/history-of-leavenworth-county-kansas-lla/page-46-history-of-leavenworth-county-kansas-lla.shtml

321   Miss Lucy Baker, a co-partner with her sister, Mrs. Mary Ellen Dawes, in the ownership and managing of 110 acres of land in Stranger Township, is a native of England. She was born near Durham, England, on Broad-wood farm, a daughter of David and Anna Marie (Thompson) Baker. David Baker was born near York, England, and was engaged in the wholesale tea business in London, England, before coming to the United States, in 1869. He came to New-York state and remained there until 1870, coming to Stranger Township, Leavenworth County, Kansas, in that year. Upon his arrival he purchased 160 acres of land, the present home
of the daughters. Anna Maria (Thompson) Baker was born in Reeth, Yorkshire, England, and died in 1888 on the farm in Stranger Township. David Baker died in 1898. Mr. and Mrs. David Baker were married in England and they were the parents of eight children, as follows: Lucy, Ann Maria, Mrs. Anthony Thistlethwaite, with Miss Lucy; Mary Ellen, widow of Edward K. Dawes, who died in 1893; Mary Ellen Dawes now lives with the subject of this sketch; Emily, deceased, was the wife of Alfred Thistlethwaite now living in Kansas City, Missouri; Margaret Evangeline, died in 1901; Thomas Hedley, married Mary Thistlethwaite; David, Kansas City, Missouri, married Hattie Driesbach; and Herbert Henry, of Stranger Township, married Kezia Nickson. Lucy Baker taught school for two years in Stranger Township and Mrs. Dawes taught in the Indian schools for twenty-three years and taught in the district schools of Stranger Township six years. Miss Baker and her sister, Mrs. Dawes, are capable and successful farmers and are highly respected in the community in which they live. They are members of the Friends Church, an organization of which their parents were also members.

322   http://www.tonganoxiemirror.com/news/2019/oct/02/remember-when-community-review-oct-2-2019/?print
323   The Life of Charles Parham. Search the Scriptures. Chapter 2. Sarah E. Parham. Pg. 14.
324   The Life of Charles Parham. Search the Scriptures. Chapter 2. Sarah E. Parham. Pg. 11.
325   The Life of Charles Parham. Search the Scriptures. Chapter 2. Sarah E. Parham. Pg. 14.
326   https://ghanachurch.com/charles-f-parham-the-father-of-pentecost/
327   The Life of Charles Parham. Search the Scriptures. Chapter 2. Sarah E. Parham. Pg. 19-20.
328   https://christianhistoryinstitute.org/magazine/article/peaceniks
329   https://christianhistoryinstitute.org/magazine/article/peaceniks
330   http://sonnenhof.com.br/commitment-in-etg/07ed2b-how-long-do-methodist-pastors-stay-at-a-church
331   The United Methodist Church Should Give Up Its Game of Musical Chairs. John A. Murdock. July 9, 2015
332   Ibid. Murdock.
333   https://www.revival-library.org/revival_heroes/20th_century/parham_charles_fox.shtml
334   Ibid. Sarah Parham. Pg. 24.
335   The Life of Charles Parham. Search the Scriptures. Chapter 2. Sarah E. Parham. Pg. 20-22.
336   Kansas Trails. Leavenworth County, Kansas. Louis Dolton.
337   Parham. Life. Page 25. Parham. Everlasting Gospel. Page 7.
338   https://en.wikipedia.org/wiki/Eudora,_Kansas
339   Indian-White Relations in the United States: A Bibliography of Works Published 1975-1980. Lincoln: University of Nebraska Press, 1982. Supplement to 1977 edition, published by University of Chicago Press.
340   The Century of the Holy Spirit: 100 Years of Pentecostal and Charismatic Renewal. 1901-2001. Vinson Synan · 2012
341   Ibid. Sarah E Parham. Chapter 5. The Great Physician. Pg. 29.
342   John Wesley, 1703-1791. Thoughts upon Slavery in "A Collection of Religious Tracts." Philadelphia: Re-printed in Philadelphia, with notes, and sold by Joseph Crukshank, 1784. Summary
343   Slavery and the founders of Methodism. Rev. William B. Lawrence. Aug. 13, 2020 | CHAPEL HILL, N.C. (UM News)
344   United Methodist History Doctrine and Polity Online Courses System Requirements. Course Structure.
345   Ibid. Lawrence.
346   http://gcah.org/history/harry-hosier
347   https://www.francisasburytriptych.com/book-series/characters/harry-hosier/
348   https://www.francisasburytriptych.com/book-series/characters/harry-hosier/

349   Slavery and the founders of Methodism. Rev. William B. Lawrence. Aug. 13, 2020, | CHAPEL HILL, N.C. (UM News)

350   The Journal of the Gilded Age and Progressive Era, Volume 18, Issue 2, April 2019, pp. 155 - 173.

351   Church and Culture. Indianapolis, IN: Wesleyan Publishing House, 2011. p. 11

352   LILIAN THISTLETHWAITE: Ardent Follower of Jesus, Bible Teacher, Evangelist, Pioneer of 20th C. Pentecost (The Int'l Christian Women's Hall of Fame Series). February 1, 2019, Linda A. Miller

353   https://www.thaddeusstevenssociety.com/quotes

354   https://www.cliffsnotes.com/cliffsnotes/subjects/american-government/what-did-abraham-lincoln-mean-by-a-house-divided-against-itself-cannot-stand

355   https://www.britannica.com/topic/racial-segregation

356   http://commonplace.online/article/kingdom-of-satan/

357   June 13, 1866, on the alteration of his original proposal for the 14th Amendment.

358   http://encyclopediaofalabama.org/article/h-1182

359   American Christianity's White-Supremacy Problem. History, theology, and culture all contribute to the racist attitudes embedded in the white church. Michael Luo. September 2, 2020

360   "Regret' Over Maryland Role in Slavery. Ovetta Wiggins. Washington Post Staff Writer. Saturday, March 17, 2007

361   https://www.britannica.com/event/Holiness-movement

362   https://www.britannica.com/biography/Alma-Bridwell-White

363   https://classroom.synonym.com/how-to-become-an-ordained-united-methodist-minister-12085015.html

364   "A Quaker Education | Discover Education in UK Quaker Schools." A Quaker Education. Retrieved 13 June 2019.

365   https://www.quaker.org.uk/about-quakers/our-history

366   Kyle Haselden, The Racial Problem in Christian Perspective, New York: Harper Torch Book. 1964.

367   Present: The Problem of Racism in The Contemporary Pentecostal Movement. Leonard Lovettt, Ph.D. Page 2.

368   Thaddeus Stevens.

369   William Branham among the most favored preachers of the all-white Assemblies of God and the United Pentecostal Church International. Before certain audiences, William Branham sided with the Ku Klux Klan's stance against Civil Rights? Why did he do so? And why are dark-skinned cult followers not told that he made such statements? https://william-branham.org/site/blog/20161006_william_branham_using_ku_klux_klan_slogan_for_segregation

370   Labor Unions and the Negro: The Record of Discrimination. THE removal of the sanction of law from racial segregation has sharply posed the issue of the Negro's status in...

by Herbert Hill

371   https://www.britannica.com/topic/Ku-Klux-Klan

372   Charles William Sloan, Jr., "Kansas Battles the Invisible Empire: The Legal Ouster of the KKK From Kansas, 1922–1927," Kansas Historical Quarterly Fall, 1974 (Vol. 40, No. 3), pp. 393–409 (ed. explains in detail how the KKK worked in Kansas.)

373   Baptist History Homepage. Kentucky Baptist History, 1770 - 1922. William Dudley Nowlin. The Anti-Missionary Controversy of Baptists in Kentucky from 1832 to 1842

374   https://en.wikipedia.org/wiki/Manichaeism

375   https://digital.library.sbts.edu/bitstream/handle/10392/5954/Lee-ThM-Daniel%20Parkers%20Doctrine%20of%20the%20Two%20Seeds-ocr.pdf?sequence=1&isAllowed=y

376   Britannica, The Editors of Encyclopedia. "predestination." Encyclopedia Britannica, 30 Jan. 2022, https://www.britannica.com/topic/predestination. Accessed 12 February 2022.

377   https://christianity.stackexchange.com/questions/64079/how-is-the-election-of-adam-and-eve-according-to-the-calvinist

378   DANIEL PARKER: PIONEER PREACHER AND POLITICAL LEADER by DAN B. WIMBERLY, B.A., M.A.

379   https://www.tshaonline.org/handbook/entries/parker-daniel

380   Henry c. Vedder, A Short History of the Baptists (Philadelphia: American Baptist Publication Society, 1907), p. 389. See Peck, "Historical Sketches," pp. 198-99, A. H. Dunlevy, History of the Miami Baptist Association. Cincinnati: George S. Blanchard and Co., 1869), p. 79; Spencer, History of Kentucky Baptists, I, 577-78; H. K. Carroll, The Religious Forces of the United States, Vol. I: American Church History (New York: The Christian Literature Co., 1893), pp. 49-50; States East of the Mississippi-Philadelphia: American Baptist Publication Society, 1896), p. 124; B. F. Riley, History of the Baptists in the Southern States East of the Mississippi (Philadelphia: American Baptist Publication Society, 1898 , pp. 356-57; Sweet, The Baptists, p. 75; Frank S. Mead, Hand- ~ of Denominations in the United States (New York: Abingdon Press, 1951), p. 44; Jesse L. Boyd, A History of Baptists in
America Prior to~ {New York: The American Press, 1957), p. 131; Lynn E. May, Jr., "Two-Seed-in-the-Spirit Predestinarian Baptists," Encyclopedia of Southern Baptists, ed. Norman Wade Cox, II (1958, 1433; Clifton E. Olmstead, History of Religion in the United States (Englewood Cliffs, N. J.: Prentice-Hall; Inc., 1960), p. 273.

381   https://www.merriam-webster.com/dictionary/classism

382   https://www.dw.com/en/east-africas-forgotten-slave-trade/a-50126759

383   https://alajamwalarab.com/the-jet-black-descendants-of-adam-are-going-to-hell/

384   The Life of Charles Parham. Search the Scriptures. Chapter 2. Sarah E. Parham. Pg. 20-22.

385   Ibid. Sarah Parham. Evangelistic Work. Pg. 24.

386   Glenn Miller, "'The Doors of Opportunity': Methodist Theological Education and the

University, 1866-1929," paper presented at the "United Methodism in American Culture" conference, St. Simon's Island, Georgia, August 1995.

387   II Chronicles 12:22

388   Ibid. Hyatt.

389   Ibid. Hyatt.

390   Ibid. Hyatt.

391   Leslie R. Marston, From Age to Age A Living Witness: A Historical Interpretation of Free Methodism's First Century (Winona Lake, IN: Light and Life Press, 1960)

392   Ibid. Marston.

393   See Kenneth E. Rowe, "Redesigning Methodist Churches: Auditorium Style Sanctuaries and Akron-Plan Sunday Schools in Romanesque Costume, 1875-1925," paper presented to the "United Methodism and American Culture" conference, St. Simon's Island, GA, August 1995.

394   https://worldmethodistcouncil.org/member-churches/

395   Britannica, The Editors of Encyclopedia. "Southern Baptist Convention." Encyclopedia Britannica, 5 Apr. 2021, https://www.britannica.com/topic/Southern-Baptist-Convention. Accessed 20 December 2021.

396   http://baptisthistoryhomepage.com/missions.controversy.html

397   https://www.nytimes.com/2011/11/27/books/review/the-not-so-invisible-empire.html

398   https://wordhistories.net/2019/08/12/more-equal-than-others/

399   Ibid. Britannica.

400   This reference is from the book of Job but has serious hidden meaning to those who distort the accounts of Genesis 6 promoting several Luciferian concepts. See: War on Earth. Bernie L. Wade. 2021. Your Life Press. 2021.

401   Ibid. Britannica.

402   The title page of the Second Dose lists 1826 as the publication date. However, Parker did not conclude the writing until February 1827. (Daniel Parker, The Second Dose of Doctrine on the Two Seeds, Dealt Out in Broken Doses Designed to Purge the Armenian Stuff & Dross Out of the Church of Christ and Hearts and Heads of Saints [Vincennes, Indiana: Elihu Stout, 1826], p. 83.).

403   First minutes of the General Association of Baptists in Kentucky, organized at Louisville, Friday, October 20th, 1837. Page 11.

404   https://www.merriam-webster.com/dictionary/antinomian

405   John Mason Peck, "Historical Sketches of the Baptist Denomination in Indiana, Illinois, and Missouri," The Baptist Memorial and Monthly Chronicle, I (July 1842), 19. See also "Parkerism in Indiana?" The Baptist Encyclopedia, ed. William Cathcart, II (1880J 883; William T. Stott, Indiana Baptist History, 1798-1908 {Franklin, Indiana: William T. Stott, 1908), p. ~Walter Brownlow Posey, The Baptist Church in the Lower Mississippi Valley, 1776-1845 (Lexington, Ky.: University of Kentucky Press, 1

406   J. H. Spencer, History of Kentucky Baptists from 11Q2 to 1885 (Cincinnati: J. R. Baumes,

1885, I, 576; William Warren Sweet, The Baptists 1783-1830, Volo I: Religion the American Frontier (Chicago: The University of Chicago Press, 1931), p. 75.

407   Ibid. Spencer. P. 577.

408   Private conversations. The names and places have been recorded but are not being made public to protect the identities of those providing information This author stakes his honor on the authenticity of the testimonies.

409   www.treeoflifeks.org

410   The Apostolic Faith 1. no. 3 (April 1925). Cover. digitalshowcase.oru.edu

411   Winds Of God Chapter III Pg. 15

412   The Apostolic Faith. Topeka Kansas. Vol. 2. No. 3. Page 1. Page 7.

413   https://en.wikipedia.org/wiki/In_His_Steps

414   Sheldon, "The Statesmanship of Christ," box 1, folder 3, Sheldon/ Central Congregational Collection, chap. 7, p. 8.

415   Parham, A Voice Crying in the Wilderness, 57.

416   Sanders, Seymour, 13. Martin. Seymour. Pg. 326.

417   Vinson Synan, "Classical Pentecostalism," p.220.

418   https://william-branham.org/site/people/charles_fox_parham

419   https://william-branham.org/site/people/charles_fox_parham

420   https://www.christianitytoday.com/history/people/martyrs/polycarp.html

421   Fair Clear and Terrible by Shirley Nelson, unpublished page notes, refer to text p. 157.

422   Shumway, "Glossolalia," 111, depicted Parham as conceiving of his theological scheme at Shiloh. See: Shumway, "Tongues," 165; Goff, Fields, 73ff; Sarah E. Parham, The Life of Charles F. Parham (Birmingham: Commercial Printing, [1930] 1977) 48.

423   Tongues of Fire July 1 & 15, 1900 p 111 & 115

424   Tongues of Fire. August 1, 1897.Volume 3. Number 15. Sanford. Lisbon Falls, Maine.

425   "Cleveland Bible College." Ohio History Central. Retrieved October 2, 2010.

426   https://www.malone.edu/

427   Songe, Alice H. (1978). American universities and colleges: a dictionary of name changes by Alice H. Songe. Rowman & Littlefield (1978), p. 79. ISBN 9780810811379. Retrieved 2012-09-14.

428   https://www.gordon.edu/

429   Songe, Alice H. (1978). American universities and colleges: a dictionary of name changes by Alice H. Songe. Rowman & Littlefield (1978), p. 79. ISBN 9780810811379. Retrieved 2012-09-14.

430   https://www.apostolicarchives.com/articles/article/8801925/173155.htm

431   https://www.apostolicarchives.com/articles/article/8801925/173155.htm

432   http://www.fwselijah.com/dowie.htm

433   The Salt Lake Tribune. Salt Lake City, Utah 30 Jan 1904, Sat. Page 1

434   https://www.williambranham.com/elijah-55-0301/

435   1906, Sep 29. the Tennessean.

436   Chattanooga Daily Times. Chattanooga, Tennessee. 06 May 1906, Sun. Page 13

437   https://www.google.com/books/edition/Encyclopaedia_of_Religion_and_Ethics/IC?hl=en&gbpv=1&dq=sanford+claimed+to+be+elijah&pg=PA320&printsec=frontcover

438   Ibid. Chattanooga Times.

439   Nashville Banner. NASHVILLE, TENNESSEE. Saturday, April 7, 1906

440   https://www.hmdb.org/m.asp?m=38186

441   https://www.mrbreakfast.com/cereal_detail.asp?id=779

442   https://en.wikipedia.org/wiki/National_Enquirer

443   Zion City Religious Situation," "Moved to Shiloh Tabernacle," ZCN, June 14, 1907; "News Items," ZH, June 29, 1907; Council Minutes, June 3, 1907; "City Council Proceedings," June 28, 1907; "Casket of Jewels," ZCN, June 19, 1907; "Gospel Dynamite Bombs," ZH, July 19, 1907. Pg. 148-164.

444   Gardiner. Out of Zion. 2: Brumback, Suddenly... from Heaven, 72. Waldron was baptized in Zion City on May 1, 1904.

445   Ibid. Gardiner.

446   The Century of the Holy Spirit: 100 Years of Pentecostal and Charismatic Renewal. 1901-2001. Vinson Synan · 2012.

447   LILIAN THISTLETHWAITE: Ardent Follower of Jesus, Bible Teacher, Evangelist, Pioneer of 20th C. Pentecost (The Int'l Christian Women's Hall of Fame Series) Paperback – February 1, 2019. Linda A. Miller. Pg. 53.

448   The Apostolic Faith. Volume XXVII-XXVIII. December 1950 – January 1951. No. 12-1.

449   A. B. Simpson, "Words of Cheer for Christian Workers," CAMW, April 28, 1893, 295

450   Charles Nienkirchen, A. B. Simpson and the Pentecostal Movement (Peabody, MA: Hendrickson, 1993), 139-140.

451   Grant Wacker, Heaven Below: Early Pentecostals and American Culture (Cambridge, MA; London, Eng.: Harvard University Press, 2001), 317, note 27.

452   https://www.wikiwand.com/en/Historical_negationism

453   Ibid. Shumway.

454   https://moodycenter.org/articles/tag/second-great-awakening/

455   Charles W. Nienkirchen A.B. Simpson and the Pentecostal Movement p.30.

456   John G. Lake Letter of Endorsement of Charles Parham November 1, 1924, John G. Lake

457   Nellie is from Sarah's middle name, Eleanor.

458   The Century of the Holy Spirit: 100 Years of Pentecostal and Charismatic Renewal. 1901-2001. Vinson Synan · 2012

459   Ibid. Sarah Parham. Chapter VIII. The Wonderful History of the Latter Rain. Pg. 57.

460   https://www.kansasmemory.org/item/216406

461   https://stonesfolly.com/main/index.php/history

462   Apostolic Faith. Houston Texas. December 1905. Vol. 1. No. 7. Page. 6.

463   https://stonesfolly.com/main/index.php/books

464   https://www.apostolicarchives.com/articles/article/8801925/173171.htm

465   https://www.britannica.com/topic/Watch-Night

466   Christianity Without the Cross. Thomas Fudge. Currents and Confluence in Pre-Oneness Theology. Page 17.

467   According to Agnes Osman it was the night of January 1. "History of the Pentecostal Movement from January 1, 1901. 2. Agnes N. O. LaBerge, Letter to E. N. Bell, 28 February 1922. 1. Archives of the Assemblies of God, Springfield, Missouri. Record Group 17, Personal Papers – LaBerge.

468   Personal Testimony of being the first person to Receive the Holy Ghost at "Stones Folly" in Topeka, Kansas. (January 1, 1901)

Printed in the Apostolic Faith April - 1951

469   https://www.apostolicarchives.com/articles/article/8801925/173163.htm

470   https://journeyonline.org/devotionals/journey-to-pentecost-part-2/day-19-pentecost-in-topeka/

471   There is a problem regarding the actual time this occurred. Mrs. Parham, Charles Fox Parham (Baxter Spring, 1969) gives two differing accounts. Mrs. Parham's sister may have remembered the day as being December 31, 1900, (p.59) but Agnes is quoted (p. 66) as singling out January 1, 1901. Agnes repeats this date in her own book, Agnes N.O. LaBerge, What God Hath Wrought (Chicago: Herald n.d.) 29. See: Ethel E. Goss, The Winds of God (Hazelwood: World Aflame Press, 1977); Synan, Old-Time Power, 104. Whatever the case all agree that it was within the same 24-hour period.

472   A Rhetorical History of Race Relations in the Early Pentecostal Movement, 1906-1916 Erik J. Hjalmeby, M.A. Advisor: Martin J. Medhurst, Ph.D. Chapter 2. Pg. 15.

473   www.apostolicarchives.com/articles/article/8801925/173673.htm

474   The Inter Ocean, Chicago, Illinois 27 Jan 1901, Sun. Page 37

475   Goss. Pg. 108.

476   https://christianheritagefellowship.com/the-wright-brotherssons-of-bishop-milton-wright/

477   One Wright was wrong, but two Wrights were right. The Glendale Star. Pastor Ed Delph Nov 8, 2019.

478   https://jddeklerk.wordpress.com/2018/02/20/calvin-the-cessationist/

479   Ibid. Morrison. Pentecost.

480   Acts 2:38.

481   A Biographical Sketch of Henry Clay Morrison. C. F. Wimberly. 1922. Published on Apr 13, 2012

482   Apostolic Faith Report. August 1905. Pg. 14.

483   W. E. Warner, "Lawrence, Bennett Freeman," in The New International Dictionary of

Pentecostal and Charismatic Movements, ed. Stanley M. Burgess (Grand Rapids, MI: Zondervan, 2002), 834.

484   B. F. Lawrence, The Apostolic Faith Restored, in Three Early Pentecostal Tracts, ed. Donald W. Dayton (New York: Garland, 1985), 11-13.

485   Pentecostal and Apostolic Faith are both terms that became synonymous with Charles and Sarah Parhams' group of ministers.

486   The Pneuma Review. Journal of Ministry Resources and Theology for Pentecostal and Charismatic Ministries & Leaders. Across the Lines: Charles Parham's Contribution to the Inter-Racial Character of Early Pentecostalism. Eddie Hyatt. December 20, 2004

487   W. F. Carothers, "The Race Question in the South," Apostolic Faith vol. 1, no. 8 (Dec. 1905).

488   See: Confidence printed from 1908-1913. https://pentecostalarchives.org/search/index.cfm?fuseaction=search.FullTextResults

489   Confidence. December 15, 1908. No. 9. Page 19.

490   Ibid. Confidence.

491   Confidence January 1909. Vol. II. No. 1. Page 22.

492   Confidence. March 1912. Vol. 5. No. 8. Page 68.

493   Apostolic Faith Report. Melrose Kansas. September 1905. Page 7.

494   Apostolic Faith Report. September 1905. Melrose Kansas. Page 9.

495   The Apostolic Faith. Houston, Texas. Charles F. Parham. Vol. 1. No. 7. Page. 7.

496   Pneuma Review. Hyatt. Across the Lines: Charles Parham's Contribution to the Inter-Racial Character of Early Pentecostalism. Eddie Hyatt. December 20, 2004.

497   https://www.ferris.edu/jimcrow/what.htm

498   Pneuma Review. Hyatt. Across the Lines: Charles Parham's Contribution to the Inter-Racial Character of Early Pentecostalism. Eddie Hyatt. December 20, 2004.

499   Randall Herbert Balmer, "Encyclopedia of Evangelicalism," Baylor University Press, USA, 2004, page 619

500   Apostolic Faith. Houston, Texas. December 1905. Page 14.

501   Ibid. Hyatt.

502   Gary B. McGee, "Lake, John Graham," in Biographical Dictionary of Christian Missions, ed. Gerald H. Anderson (New York: Macmillan Reference USA, 1998), 380.

503   Martin and Seymour, The Words that Changed the World 110.

504   Ibid. Fudge. Pg. 27.

505   Parham, Sarah, Loc. 2642.

506   Joe Creech, "Visions of Glory: The Place of the Azusa Street Revival in Pentecostal History,"
Church History. 65:3. Sept 1996, 405-24: 406.

507   Jeff Nelson, Pentecostal Missions: Past 100 and Beyond, International Journal of Pentecostal Missiology (Dec. 2019) 6:1, 25.

508   A Voice Crying in the Wilderness. 2nd Edition. Charles F. Parham. Pg. 6. 1910.

509   The Azusa Street Mission and Latin American Pentecostalism Douglas Petersen.

510   Lawrence, The Apostolic Faith, 32-52.

511   Ibid. Lawrence.

512   Ibid. Fudge. Page 39.

513   "SPIRIT-BAPTISM AND THE 1896 REVIVAL IN CHEROKEE COUNTY, NORTH CAROLINA." Harold D. Hunter. as published in Pneuma 5:2 (Fall 1983)

514   Parham, Sarah, Loc. 2259-2267.

515   Apostolic Faith & Pentecostal Timetable of Key Events. 1880-1910. 6th Edition ©2012, 2013, 2014, 2015, 2016, 2020, 2021 Bernie L. Wade, PhD. Pg. 53.

516   The Los Angeles Times. Los Angeles, California. 23 September 19-2. Page 13.

517   http://daibach-welldigger.blogspot.com/2015/09/azuza-street-and-welsh-revival.html

518   The Los Angeles Times. Los Angeles California. 11 September 1905. Page 5.

519   http://daibach-welldigger.blogspot.com/2015/09/azuza-street-and-welsh-revival.html

520   Los Angeles Herald, Volume 33, Number 57, 27 November 1905

521   THIS WEEK IN A.G. HISTORY – OCT. 7, 1962. DARRIN J. RODGERS on October 10, 2019

522   The Los Angeles Times. Los Angeles, California. 18 September 1905. Page. 4.

523   The Los Angeles Times. Los Angeles, California. 18 September 1905. Page 4.

524   The Long Beach Tribune. Long Beach, California. 19 September 1905. Page 6.

525   Robeck, Azusa Street, 60.

526   "FOR CHINA AND TIBET, AND FOR WORLD-WIDE REVIVAL" CECIL HENRY POLHILL (1860-1938) AND HIS SIGNIFICANCE FOR EARLY PENTECOSTALISM. John Martin Usher. A thesis submitted to the University of Birmingham for the degree of DOCTOR OF PHILOSOPHY. School of Philosophy, Theology and Religion. College of Arts and Law. University of Birmingham. August 2015

527   https://digitalcommons.fuller.edu/cgi/viewcontent.cgi?article=1020&context=findingaids

528   Voice Crying in the Wilderness. Charles F. Parham. Pg. 40. 2nd Edition. 1910.

529

530   https://www.merriam-webster.com/dictionary/Black%20Pope

531   Los Angeles Daily Times. Wednesday Morning. April 18, 1906. Front Page.

532   The Journal of the WESLEYAN THEOLOGICAL SOCIETY/ A Fellowship of Wesleyan-Holiness Scholars Editor and Chair of the Editorial Committee: Barry L. Callen. 2008. IS YOUR ALL ON THE ALTAR? THE QUEST FOR WESLEYAN PERFECTION IN CAMPUS REVIVALS AT OBERLIN

AND WHEATON COLLEGES. Louis B. Gallien, Jr. Pg. 171,

533 https://www.ferris.edu/HTMLS/news/jimcrow/what.htm

534 https://en.wikipedia.org/wiki/Cessationism_versus_continuationism

535 See Daniel Chapter 6.

536 https://www.nationalgeographic.com/history/article/remembering-red-summer-white-mobs-massacred-blacks-tulsa-dc

537 http://www.zionchristianministry.com/azusa/the-life-and-ministry-of-lucy-farrow/

538 The Los Angeles Evening Express. Los Angeles California. 20 September 1906. Page 7.

539 HOW PENTECOST CAME TO LOS ANGELES As It Was in the Beginning. FRANK BARTLEMAN 2nd Edition. F. BARTLEMAN 5606 Bushnell Way, Los Angeles, Calif.

540 E.A. Girvin, Phineas F. Bresee: A Prince in Israel (Kansas City, MO: Pentecostal Nazarene Publishing House, 1916; New York: Garland Publishing, Inc., 1984), 82-83. 31

541 Ibid.

542 https://www.apostolicarchives.com/articles/article/8801925/173157.htm

543 Apostolic Faith. Los Angeles, September 1906.

544 W. F. Carothers, The Baptism of the Holy Ghost and Speaking in Tongues (Zion City, IL); W. F. Carothers, 1906/7; W. F. Carothers, Church Government, Houston, TX.; W. F. Carothers, 1909.

545 Ibid. Carothers.

546 50 Pentecostal Theology. March 7, 2022.

547 See: Telegraph from Warren Fay Carothers in Zion Ill, via Ray Davis to Charles Parham in Los Angeles.

548 https://www.newspapers.com/image/95169712/?terms=W.%20F.%20Carothers&match=1

549 The Los Angeles Times. Los Angeles, California 18 Apr 1906, Wed. Page 17

550 https://www.goodreads.com/work/quotes/1137159-the-souls-of-black-folk

551 American Pentecost. The story behind the Azusa Street revival, the most phenomenal event of twentieth-century Christianity. TED OLSEN

552 https://www.revival-library.org/revival_heroes/20th_century/parham_charles_fox.shtml

553 The Earth is flat. Idaho State Journal. Mike O'Donnell Mar 4, 2017

554 Ibid. O'Donnell.

555 THE PLANE TRUTH. A HISTORY OF THE FLAT-EARTH MOVEMENT. Robert J. Schadewald. Copyright © 2015. Wendy S. Schadewald. Chapter 8. Voliva and Zion.

556 LILIAN THISTLETHWAITE: Ardent Follower of Jesus, Bible Teacher, Evangelist, Pioneer of 20th C. Pentecost (The Int'l Christian Women's Hall of Fame Series) Paperback – February 1, 2019. Linda A. Miller

557 LILIAN THISTLETHWAITE: Ardent Follower of Jesus, Bible Teacher, Evangelist, Pioneer of 20th C. Pentecost (The Int'l Christian Women's Hall of Fame Series) Paperback – February 1, 2019. Linda A. Miller.

558   Ibid. Miller.
559   Voliva would end in bankruptcy.
560   The Topeka Daily Herald: September 26, 1906.
561   Independence Daily Reporter Independence, Kansas 06 Nov 1906, Tue • Page 1
562   The Kansas City Star. Kansas City, Missouri. 20 September 1907. Page 4.
563   See The War of the Worlds (1938 radio drama).
564   https://disney.fandom.com/wiki/Chicken_Little_(1943_short)
565   The Houston Post. Houston, Texas. 22 May 1907, Wed. Page 5
566   Wilbur Glenn Voliva, who believes the world is flat, was declared "flat broke" today. Federal Judge Charles G. Briggle confirmed a bankruptcy composition taking all the property of the former business dictator and religious leader of Zion City. New York Times. August 38, 1937. Page 4.
567   https://ncse.ngo/taking-voliva-challenge
568   Los Angeles Evening Express. Los Angeles, California. 20 September 1906. Pg. 7. https://www.newspapers.com/browse/us/california/los-angeles/los-angeles-evening-express_21928
569   Ibid. Evening Express.
570   Ibid. Evening Express.
571   https://www.christian-oneness.org/tongues-gifts-and-related-issues/holy.html
572   Bartleman. Pentecost. Page 6.
573   Ibid. Parham. Pg. 163.
574   The Silent Pentecostals. Until recently, Latinos have been the most overlooked members of the Pentecostal family.
GASTON ESPINOSA
575   Ibid. Espinosa.
576   Ibid. Espinosa.
577   The Silent Pentecostals. Until recently, Latinos have been the most overlooked members of the Pentecostal family. GASTON ESPINOSA
578   Lucinda Davis in Works Progress Administration: Oklahoma Writers Project, Slave Narratives (Washington: U.S. Government Printing Office, 1932) 58. Preston Kyles in Works Progress Administration: Arkansas Writers Project, Slave Narratives (Washington: U.S. Government Printing Office, 1932) 220. J. Leitch Wright, Creeks and Seminoles, 95. bell hooks, "Revolutionary Renegades: Native-Americans, African-Americans, and Black Indians" Black Looks: Race and Representation (Boston: South End Press, 1992), 183.
579   With Walt Whitman in Camden. WITH WALT WHITMAN IN CAMDEN. March 28-July 14, 1888. Horace Traubel. BOSTON
SMALL, MAYNARD & COMPANY. 1906 Page 109.
580   Frank Bartleman, Azusa Street. Whitaker House. Kindle Edition. Loc. 517-523. Also, Dylan Tate, MA Paper.
581   Acts Chapter 2.

582   Ibid. Hyatt. Page 4.
583   Charles F. Parham, The Apostolic Faith, no. 3 (April 1925): 10.
584   What caused Paul and Barnabas to disagree? A mention in the letter to the Colossians (Col 4, 10) informs us that Mark was a cousin of Barnabas....3 This became a reason for the conflict between Paul and Barnabas, because Paul would no longer accept Mark as a helper (Ac 15, 36☐40). Consequently, while Barnabas and Mark went to Cyprus, Paul was alone.
585   William J. Seymour, letter to W. F. Carothers. 12 July 1906.
586   D. J. Nelson. For Such a Time as This; The Story of Bishop William J. Seymour and the Azusa Street Revival. Unpublished PhD dissertation, University of Birmingham. 1981.
587   William J. Seymour: Father of Modern Pentecostalism. Journal of the Interdenominational Theological Center. 4. No. 1. 1976. 34-44.
588   Ibid. Fudge. Page 32.
589   The Apostolic Faith. Unity. Charles F. Parham. July 1925. Page 9.
590   Los Angeles Herald Los Angeles, California 07 Nov 1906, Wed • Page 7
591   Parham, Sarah, Loc. 2110.
592   Los Angeles Herald. Los Angeles, California 11 Jan 1908, Sat. Page 5
593   Sarah Parham, The Life of Charles F. Parham, 246.
594   Robert Mapes Anderson, Vision of the Disinherited (New York: Oxford, 1979), 123.
595   Apostolic Faith Newsletter. Charles F. Parham. Zion Illinois. December 1907.
596   The Life of Charles Parham. Sarah E. Parham. Page 168.
597   http://agts.edu/wp-content/uploads/2020/09/IJPM-7-1-2-Nelson-Parham.pdf
598   Goff. Pg. 128.
599   This committee was also tasked with overseeing finances and publications for the nascent Apostolic Faith Mission. "For Such a Time as This: The Story of Bishop William J. Seymour and the Azusa Street Revival" (Ph.D. Dissertation, University of Birmingham, 1981).
600   The Twentieth-Century Pentecostal Revival. David Bernard.
601   Iain MacRobert, "The Black Roots of Pentecostalism," in African-American Religion: Interpretive Essays in History and Culture, ed. Timothy E. Fulop and Albert J. Raboteau, eds, (New York: Routledge, 1997), 295.
602   MacRoberts, 295.
603   Ibid. Pneuma Review. Hyatt. Pg. 4.
604   Dr. Gary W. Garrett is the founder of Apostolic Archives and perhaps the foremost expert on Charlee Parham in the world. www.apostolicarchives.com
605   Jennie Evans Moore Seymour - Vanguard of Pentecost. Charisma Magazine. Glenn Clark. 2004.
606   https://atwistedcrownofthorns.com/2011/04/20/charles-f-parham-learning-from-errors-in-church-history/
607   The Spirit in Black and White: Early Twentieth-Century Pentecostals and Race Relations.

1905-1945. Blaine Charles Hamilton. Houston, Texas. 2013.

608   https://christianhistoryinstitute.org/magazine/article/sanctification-scuffles

609   The Azusa Street Revival: No Racism; Only Persecution of Jesus Name...Amen. "Charles Parham, the Father of the Oneness Apostolic Pentecostal Movement. A Brief Life of Charles Fox Parham from Apostolic Archives. Hannah Faith. Pg. 80.

610   https://www.christianitytoday.com/history/issues/issue-45/rejecting-negro-pew.html

611   https://www.christianitytoday.com/history/issues/issue-45/rejecting-negro-pew.html

612   https://www.christianitytoday.com/history/issues/issue-45/rejecting-negro-pew.html

613   Ibid. Lovett.

614   https://www.christian-oneness.org/tongues-gifts-and-related-issues/holy.html

615   Apostolic Faith. Volume 1. No. 9. Baxter Springs, Kansas. Page 2.

616   Ibid. Dart.

617   Los Angeles Times. Flourishing Church Began Modestly. JOHN DART. FEB. 25,1995 12 AM PT

618   https://www.graceandpeacemagazine.org/articles/19-issue-summer-2013/354-the-worship-style-of-phineas-bresee

619   Los Angeles Times. Flourishing Church Began Modestly. JOHN DART. FEB. 25,1995 12 AM PT

620   Ibid. Dart

621   Bishop Alma White, Preacher, Author. Founder Of Pillar of Fire Dies At 84. Established Several Schools and Colleges." New York Times. Associated Press. June 27, 1946. Retrieved August 21, 2007. Bishop Alma White, founder of the Pillar of Fire Church and author of thirty-five religious tracts and some 200 hymns, died here today at the headquarters of the religious group at near-by Zarephath. Her age was 84.

622   Alma White (1925). The Ku Klux Klan in Prophecy. Pillar of Fire. ISBN 978-1-4286-1075-0.

623   Alma White (1925). The Ku Klux Klan in Prophecy. Pillar of Fire. ISBN 978-1-4286-1075-0.

624   The Ku Klux Klan in Prophecy. Alma White. Pg. 30.

625   Hiram Evans on the "The Klan's Fight for Americanism" (1926).

626   https://www.britannica.com/biography/Alma-Bridwell-White

627   http://lavistachurchofchrist.org/LVanswers/2004/2004-08-24a.htm

628   https://www.britannica.com/biography/Alma-Bridwell-White

629   Hiram Evans on the "The Klan's Fight for Americanism" (1926)

630   https://www.lavistachurchofchrist.org/cms/what-do-you-think-about-the-azusa-street-revival/

631   https://www.revival-library.org/revival_heroes/20th_century/farrow_lucy.shtml

632   Britannica, The Editors of Encyclopedia. "Christian Identity." Encyclopedia Britannica,

21 Oct. 2009, https://www.britannica.com/topic/Christian-Identity. Accessed 18 February 2022.

633   A number of surrogates add slurs to what R. A. Torrey said about Charles Parham. However, we could not authenticate such hyperbole. Like many of those who write on these subjects, write to accomplish sensationalism rather than factual \\ account. In fairness to R. A. Torrey, his account of the matter details some very strange meetings in the Los Angeles area. None of these were associated with Charles Parham but rather were meeting led by the splinter Pentecostals and others.

634   Torrey, The Baptism, 5

635   https://www.lavistachurchofchrist.org/cms/what-do-you-think-about-the-azusa-street-revival/

636   https://www.jbhe.com/news_views/62_bobjones.html

637   The Story of Bob Jones University v. United States: Race, Religion, and Congress' Extraordinary Acquiescence
Olatunde C.A. Johnson. Columbia Law School, olati.johnson@law.columbia.edu

638   https://www.jbhe.com/news_views/62_bobjones.html

639   https://www.lavistachurchofchrist.org/cms/what-do-you-think-about-the-azusa-street-revival/

640   Alma White. The Story of My Life. 62. (1919). Volume II.

641   Ibid. White.

642   Volume 1. Supra note 3. At 174.

643   White. Volume II, supra note 53, at 176.

644   Galatians 3:28.

645   White. Volume III. Supra note 72, at 105.

646   Journal of Gender, Social Policy & the Law. Vol. 8:3. Pages 768-782.

647   In the Name of God; An American Story of Feminism, Racism, and Religious Intolerance: The Story of Alma Bridwell White Historical Essay. Kandt, Kristin E. Page 753.

648   White. Volume IV, supra note 7, at 125.

649   See Edwin S. Gaustad. A Documentary History of Religion in America. The Knights of Columbus was "the major Roman Catholic fraternal order, which started out as a heavily Irish mutual aid society in New Haven, Connecticut in 1882.

650   Volume V, supra note 7, at 166. Kent left Alma White's organization permanently in 1909 and visited Alma White infrequently. Volume VI, supra note 110, at 53.

651   https://www.amazon.com/Word-God-Coming-Again/dp/B00T9IX6FK

652   Demons and Tongues. Mrs. Alma White. Published by The Pentecostal Union, Bound Brook, N. J. 1910.

653   American Christianity's White-Supremacy Problem History, theology, and culture all contribute to the racist attitudes embedded in the white church. Michael Luo. September 2, 2020

654   I Corinthians 3:12.

655   See: THE GOSPEL ACCORDING TO THE KLAN: THE KU KLUX KLAN'S VISION OF WHITE PROTESTANT AMERICA, 1915-1930. KELLY J. BAKER.

656   Chester L. Quarles, The Ku Klux Klan and Related American Racialist and Antisemitic Organizations: A History and Analysis, (Jefferson, NC: McFarland & Company, 1999), 55.

657   The Gospel of the Kingdom. J. G. Campbell. Alvin Texas. Vol. 3. No. 1.

658   Frank Roberson, a paraphrase of the type of sermon which he and other slaves were subjected to

659   https://www.revival-library.org/revival_heroes/20th_century/parham_charles_fox.shtml

660   The Houston Post. Houston, Texas. 22 May 1907, Wed. Page 5

661   Ibid. Houston Post.

662   Ibid. Houston Post.

663   Matthew 26:31.

664   https://www.apostolicarchives.com/newsletters/newsletter/9117400/100620.htm

665   Religion and the Rise of the Second Ku Klux Klan, 1915-1922. Kelly J. Baker. Instructor, University of New Mexico

666   3 John 1:9.

667   THE NATURE OF RELIGIOUS BIGOTRY. An essay by Swain and Eric Wodening. Used by permission.

668   Charles F. Parham, Toronto, Canada to Howard A. Goss, 31 January 1907. Flower Pentecostal Heritage Center, Springfield, MO.

669   Apostolic Faith & Pentecostal Timetable of Key Events. 1880-1910. 6th Edition ©2012, 2013, 2014, 2015, 2016, 2020, 2021. Bernie L. Wade, PhD. Page 127.

670   The Apostolic Faith Volume 1 Issue 2, October 1906 http://www.azusabooks.com

671   How Woodrow Wilson Tried to Reverse Black American Progress By promoting the Ku Klux Klan and overseeing segregation of the federal workforce, the 28th president helped erase gains African-Americans had made since Reconstruction. BECKY LITTLE. JUL 14, 2020.

672   The Gospel of the Kingdom. Pg. 14. December 18, 1910. Parham's reference to the Irvingites represents his strong resolve toward Apostolic reformation. Like most of his contemporaries he is opposed to Creeds and other dogmas and doctrines of men.

673   Woodrow Wilson was extremely racist – even by the standards of his time. Matthew Dylan Matthewsdylan@vox.com Nov 20, 2015

674   Woodrow Wilson was extremely racist – even by the standards of his time. Dylan Matthewsdylan@vox.com. Nov 20, 2015

675   https://en.wikipedia.org/wiki/Assassination_of_Julius_Caesar

676   John G. Lake. Letter to Charles F. Parham. Written by Florence Lake. March 24, 1927. ORU Archives.

677   The Houston Post. Houston, Texas. 26 Oct 1907, Sat. Page 14

678   The Houston Post. Houston, Texas. 25 Dec 1908, Fri. Page 7

679   Oral Roberts Archives.
680   See: The Winds of God. Ethel Goss.
681   Charles F. Parham. Letter to Apostolic Faith ministers. Baxter Springs, Kansas. February 7, 1915.
682   The Oath By Frank E. Peretti. June 22, 2016. Donna Feyen
683   Charles. Parham. Progenitor. of. Pentecostalism. Leslie d. Callahan. Parham, The Life of Charles F. Parham, Founder of the Apostolic Faith Movement, The Higher Christian life (New York: garland, 1985) 1. 2. S. e. Parham, Life, 2. 3. Chapter 18. Page 210.
684   https://en.wikipedia.org/wiki/Marcus_Junius_Brutus
685   https://www.amazon.com/Life-Charles-Parham-Apostolic-Pentecostal-ebook/dp/B00SI6IPPU
686   The Gospel of the Kingdom. J. G. Campbell. Alvin Texas. Vol. 3. No. 1.
687   https://en.wikipedia.org/wiki/Charles_Price_Jones
688   Ibid. Jones. Page 171.
689   White, Calvin, Jr. "In the Beginning, There Stood Two: Arkansas Roots of the Black Holiness Movement." Arkansas Historical Quarterly 68 (Spring 2009): 1–22.
690   The Continuing Relevance of Wesleyan Theology. Essays in Honor of Laurence W. Wood.
691   https://eastsidecommcogic.tripod.com/id1.html
692   http://www.originalapostolicfaith.org/reports-1920-1929.html
693   JUNE 25, 2008. Church of God in Christ and in unity with the Apostolic Faith. https://ifphc.wordpress.com/2008/06/25/church-of-god-in-christ-and-in-unity-with-the-apostolic-faith/
694   Howard Goss compiled a list of all-white ministers to invite to his all-white ministerial groups. The list was printed in the Word and Witness. December 1913. Goss invested his whole life in creating an all-white hate group.
695   Ibid. Jones. 173.
696   "Loving all People Regardless of Race, Creed, or Color": James L. Delk and the Lost History of Pentecostal Interracialism." Abstract.
Brown, Kenan Aaron
697   Britannica, The Editors of Encyclopedia. "Assemblies of God." Encyclopedia Britannica, 1 Aug. 2018, https://www.britannica.com/topic/Assemblies-of-God. Accessed 4 February 2022.
698   Mark 8:36-37.
699   Britannica, The Editors of Encyclopedia. "Assemblies of God." Encyclopedia Britannica, 1 Aug. 2018, https://www.britannica.com/topic/Assemblies-of-God. Accessed 4 February 2022.
700   http://plainshumanities.unl.edu/encyclopedia/doc/egp.rel.038
701   Pew Research Center. https://www.pewforum.org/2011/12/19/global-christianity-movements-and-denominations/
702   https://nosweatshakespeare.com/quotes/famous/et-tu-brute/
703   https://www.findagrave.com/memorial/53698031/raymond-theodore-richey

704 Colonel Mayfield's Weekly, December 8, 1923, quoted in Charles C. Alexander, The Ku Klux Klan in the Southwest (Lexington, KY: University of Kentucky Press), 90.

705 https://www.revival-library.org/revival_heroes/20th_century/parham_charles_fox.shtml

706 See □The City in Brief, □ HC, 7 January 1906; □Church Notices, □ HC, 13 January 1906, p. 6; □Sunday Church Services, HP, 7 April 1906, p. 5; □Sunday Church Services, HP, 9 June 1906, p. 14; □Church Notices, HC, 7 July 1906, p. 5; □Church Notices, HC, 28 July 1906, p. 6.

707 Despite horrible historical accounts claiming Parham as a racist, the historical facts show Parham was very open to people of other cultures. Lucy Farrow (who was black) was a friend and part of the Parham family. Lucy Farrow was a frequent speaker at Parham's Apostolic Faith events. Parham welcomed Seymour in like fashion and enrolled him in his bible school along with everyone else. Contrary to more horrible historical accounts, there is no real evidence that Seymour was treated different from other students. When the request comes for someone to come to Los Angeles, Parham pays the train fare and sends Seymour. Neither of them could foresee the amazing results the trip would bring. Also see www.apostolicarchives.com

708 This concept of Elders exists even today in some groups with roots to the Apostolic Faith movement.

709 Goff. Pg. 118. March Apostolic Faith. 1906.

710 Pentecostalism in America, R. G. Robins. Pg. 37.

711 The Houston Post. Houston, Texas, 25 Dec 1908, Fri. Page 7

712 https://www.dictionary.com/browse/the-reports-of-my-death-are-greatly-exaggerated

713 William J. Seymour writes to Warren Fay Carothers requesting the license Charles Parham had promised. Carothers is behind in completing his duties as National Director of the Apostolic Faith Movement. Within days he is removed from his position and replaced by Howard A. Goss.

714 Parham. Chapter XVI. A Call to Zion City. Page 151.

715 I Kings 14:27. 2 Chronicles 12:10.

716 https://en.wikipedia.org/wiki/Et_tu,_Brute%3F

717 Parham. Chapter XVI. A Call to Zion City. Page 151.

718 Apostolic Archives. Dr. Gary W. Garrett. Charles Fox Parham (1873-1929). Charles Fox Parham. https://www.apostolicarchives.com/articles/article/8801925/173673.htm

719 https://www.biblestudytools.com/proverbs/17-17.html

720 The Houston Post. Houston, Texas 19 May 1908, Tue. Page 9.

721 Blumhofer, Restoring the Faith, 117.

722 https://en.wikipedia.org/wiki/Half-truth#:~:text=The%20purpose%20and%20or%20consequence,lead%20to%20a%20false%20conclusion.&text=A%20person%20deceived%20by%20a,be%20knowledge%20and%20acts%20accordingly.

723 Parham Still in Apostolic Faith Cult. The Waukegan Daily Sun. December 3, 1906. Pg. 3.

724 Apostolic Archives. Charles Fox Parham (1873-1929). Dr. Gary W. Garrett. https://www.

apostolicarchives.com/articles/article/8801925/173673.htm

725   Ibid. Waukegan Sun.

726   "Florence Louise Crawford," The New International Dictionary of Pentecostal and Charismatic Movements, Ed. Stanley M. Burgess, 2002; Cecil M. Robeck, Florence Crawford: Apostolic Faith Pioneer, in Portraits of a Generation: Early Pentecostal Leaders. Ed. James R. Goff Jr. and Grant Wacker University of Arkansas, Fayetteville, 2002, pp218-235.

727   https://www.apostolicfaith.org/ministers-manual/our-name

728   Ibid. Garrett. Parham.

729   2 Timothy 4:10.

730   The Houston Pos. Houston, Texas. 04 Oct 1906, Thu. Page 16

731   https://www.apostolicarchives.com/articles/article/8795590/187464.htm

732   Ibid. Winds of God. Goss.

733   Apostolic Archives. Warren Faye Carothers (1872 - 1953). Dr. Gary W. Garrett. https://www.apostolicarchives.com/articles/article/8795590/187464.htm

734   https://www.goodreads.com/quotes/119070-a-half-truth-is-the-most-cowardly-of-lies

735   Glory and Unity at the Eureka Springs Camp. Word and Witness. August 20, 1912. Volume 8. No. 6. Page 1. Bell published this publication for a couple of years.

736   Glory and Unity at the Eureka Springs Camp. Word and Witness. August 20, 1912. Volume 8. No. 6.

737   Glory and Unity at the Eureka Springs Camp. Word and Witness. August 20, 1912. Volume 8. No. 6. Page 1.

738   Glory and Unity at the Eureka Springs Camp. Word and Witness. August 20, 1912. Volume 8. No. 6. Page 2.

739   Glory and Unity at the Eureka Springs Camp. Word and Witness. August 20, 1912. Volume 8. No. 6. Page 2.

740   Glory and Unity at the Eureka Springs Camp. Word and Witness. August 20, 1912. Volume 8. No. 6. Page 2.

741   Charles Parham referred to the activities of Carothers and Goss as "The Rule in Texas" and the "System". These were references to the xenophobic agenda of the Texas Syndicate.

742   Why Power Corrupts. New research digs deeper into the social science behind why power brings out the best in some people and the worst in others. Christopher Shea. October 2012

743   Revelation 12:10.

744   Ibid. Lovett. Page 3. See George Kelsey, Racism and the Christian Understanding of Man, New York: Charles Scribner and Sons, 1965, p. 146; also, Waldo Beach, "A Theological Analysis of Race Relations, "Faith and Ethics, Paul Ramsey (ed), New York: 1957, p. 211.7.

745   The Houston Post. Houston, Texas. 19 May 1908, Tue. Page 9

746   https://www.merriam-webster.com/dictionary/keep%20%28someone%29%20in%20

his%2Fher%20place

747 Apostolic Faith. Oct. 1912. Supplement.

748 The Houston Post. Houston, Texas. 31 Dec 1906, Mon. Page 6

749 Ibid. Houston Post.

750 The Houston Post. Houston Texas. 22 MAY 1907. Page 5.

751 Ibid. Houston Post.

752 The Houston Post. Houston, Texas 22 Mar 1907, Fri. Page 16

753 The Called Out of the Called Out: Charles Parham's Doctrine of Spirit Baptism. Aaron Friesen Ph.D. candidate in Pentecostal and Charismatic Studies at Bangor University in Bangor, Wales. July 23, 2015.

754 Ibid. Houston Post.

755 Ibid. Houston Post.

756 https://www.thehenryford.org/collections-and-research/digital-collections/artifact/326607/

757 Christianity without the Cross. Thomas A. Fudge. Page 44.

758 See: The Winds of God. Ethel Goss.

759 https://www.apostolicarchives.com/articles/article/8801925/173157.htm

760 https://www.christianity.com/church/denominations/the-apostolic-church-origin-history-and-beliefs-of-apostolic-faith.html

761 Britannica, The Editors of Encyclopedia. "Alma Bridwell White." Encyclopedia Britannica, 22 Jun. 2021, https://www.britannica.com/biography/Alma-Bridwell-White. Accessed 3 February 2022.

762 https://askanydifference.com/difference-between-pentecostal-and-apostolic/

763 https://www.oikoumene.org/church-families/pentecostal-churches

764 https://www.etymonline.com/word/apostolic

765 Charles F. Parham, "Forsaking All and All Things in Common," A Voice Crying in The Wilderness (Joplin, MO: Joplin Printing Corporation, 1902, 1910), 56.

766 https://www.historytoday.com/archive/john-wycliffe-condemned-heretic

767 https://quote.org/quote/i-defy-the-pope-and-all-his-585878

768 See Foxes Book of Martyrs.

769 The Apostolic Faith 1 no. 6 (July 1925)

770 https://www.merriam-webster.com/dictionary/Pentecostal

771 Ibid. Parham. Apostolic Faith. July 1925.

772 Although Parham used the term full gospel earlier, it seems he reverted to the term more in opposition to what he called the new Pentecostals. This is a definite reference to those who had conspired to steal his family's life work away from him.

773	Charles F. Parham, "Forsaking All and All Things in Common," A Voice Crying in The Wilderness (Joplin, MO: Joplin Printing Corporation, 1902, 1910), 56.

774	Charles F. Parham, "Grand Encampment," The Apostolic Faith (Melrose, KS), Vol. 1, No. 3 (August 1905): 14.

775	The Called Out of the Called Out: Charles Parham's Doctrine of Spirit Baptism. April 2009. Journal of the European Pentecostal Theological Association 29(1):43-55

776	See: The Life of Charles F. Parham by Sarah E. Parham.

777	Personal interview of Howard A. Goss by Bishop William Garrett at Garrett's parsonage. Source: Apostolic Archives.

778	See Carothers v. Thor 21 TX 358. Wheeler.

779	There are no coincidences in this manifesto. The writers saw blacks, Mexicans, Jews, Japanese and any other non-whites as inferior. They also were not interest in women being fellow ministers as noted in their address to "Brethren."

780	Weekly Evangel. August 14, 1915. Note on Page 2 they certain all are aware that this is "A Pentecostal Newspaper. The are making certain that their all-white supremacy is known.

781	Ibid. Weekly Evangel. This Manifesto of the Texas Syndicate, written by Attorney Warren Fay Carothers became a cornerstone document of the Assemblies of God. In 1915, the Assemblies of God printed this front page on their official organ, the Weekly Evangel and affixed their names to the same. It included all of their leaders.

782	A Call for A/G and COGIC Reunification in the Racial Harmony that was the Original Intent of Holy Spirit's 1906 Pentecostal Movement. Rahman Reuben DD. Page 13. "A Call for A/G and COGIC Reunification ~ in the Racial Harmony that was the Original Intent of Holy Spirit's 1906 Pentecostal Movement" https://www.academia.edu/34861518/_A_Call_for_A_G_and_COGIC_Reunification_in_the_Racial_Harmony_that_was_the_Original_Intent_of_Holy_Spirit_s_1906_Pentecostal_Movement_

783	https://pc-freak.net/files/the-table-of-nations-and-the-origin-of-races-history-of-man.html

784	Ibid. Reuben. Page 14.

785	The Houston Post. Houston, Texas. 22 Mar 1907, Fri. Page 16

786	When Ministry Becomes an Idol. Chiree Patterson. https://www.reviveourhearts.com/articles/when-ministry-becomes-idol/

787	This is more parlor games by Carothers as Brunner Tabernacle would advertise for years after the fact as an Apostolic Faith church. He further uses Brunner for a plethora of other pseudo-Apostolic Faith meetings. The Houston Post. Houston, Texas. 31 Jul 1906, Tue. Page 9. The real deal is that like Satan, Carothers sets his seat in the North (or in this case, the South) and defies Parham as he claims the new headquarters of the Apostolic Faith Movement is in Houston, Texas. See: Isaiah 14:12-15

788	Parham's February 7, 1915, letter to the Apostolic Faith ministers.

789 Sensation at San Antonio. The Houston Chronicle. 21 July 1907.

790 The Diaries of Howard A. Goss, entries for 30 January and 6 April 1907.

791 The Houston Post. Houston, Texas. 19 May 1908. Page 9.

792 Ibid. Houston Post.

793 Ibid. Houston Post.

794 See the Book of Second Samuel.

795 The Houston Post. Houston, Texas. 28 July 1907. Page 11.

796 Ibid. Sarah E. Parham. Pg. 185.

797 https://www.pbs.org/wgbh/aia/part4/4h2933.html#:~:text=Find%20Your%20Local%20Station%3A&text=In%20March%20of%201857%2C%20the,citizens%20of%20the%20United%20States.

798 https://www.archives.gov/research/african-americans/vote/laws-and-courts

799 https://www.britannica.com/topic/Fourteenth-Amendment

800 https://www.irishtimes.com/culture/books/a-little-box-and-a-dark-history-the-collapse-of-confession-1.1730886

801 https://www.irishtimes.com/culture/books/a-little-box-and-a-dark-history-the-collapse-of-confession-1.1730886

802 https://www.merriam-webster.com/dictionary/witness

803 Kirk B. Henrichsen, comp., "How Witnesses Described the 'Gold Plates,'" Journal of Book of Mormon Studies, vol. 10, no. 1 (2001), 16-21, 78-79. John W. Welch, "The Miraculous Translation of the Book of Mormon," in John W. Welch, ed., Opening the Heavens: Accounts of Divine Manifestations, 1820-1844 (Provo, Utah: Brigham Young University Press, 2005), 76-213.

804 Joseph Smith claimed in 1823 he had found the Golden Tablets.

805 Christianity Without the Cross. Thomas Fudge. Page 362.

806 This is a direct reference to Warren Carothers and his leadership methods.

807 This is a direct reference again to Warren Carothers and more pointedly to his obsession with merging with the fallen Zion City movement and creating an international denomination.

808 The Houston Post. Houston Texas. 22 May 1907. Page 5.

809 Ibid. Houston Post.

810 Ibid. Houston Post.

811 Ibid. Houston Post.

812 Apostolic Faith. Zion City, Illinois. December 1907.

813 https://heartofashepherd.com/2014/06/21/proverbs-2110-11-there-is-no-honor-among-thieves/

814 Carothers The Houston Post Houston, Texas 22 Mar 1907, Fri • Page 16

815 Progressivism in Zion City, Illinois, a Conservative Protestant. https://epublications.marquette.edu, GA Kiszely · 2018

816 https://www.apostolicarchives.com/articles/article/8795590/187464.htm

817   The Houston Post. Houston Texas. 22 May 1907. Page 5.
818   Houston Post. Houston Texas. 22 May 1907. Page 5.
819   Ibid. Houston Post.
820   Ibid. Houston Post. Houston, Texas. 22 May 1907. Page 5.
821   Sensation at San Antonio. The Houston Chronicle. July 21. 1907.
822   Galatians 3:3. NKJV.
823   Galatians 2:4-5.
824   Galatian 2:4.
825   Apostolic Faith and Pentecostal Timetable of Key Events. Published on Nov 30, 2015. Pg. 89.
826   David Lee Floyd interview with Wayne Warner. Tape #3. Assemblies of God Archives. Springfield Missouri.
827   Parham Still in Apostolic Faith Cult," The Waukegan Daily Sun. December 3, 1906. 6.
828   Supporting the belief that white people constitute a superior race and should therefore dominate society, typically to the exclusion or detriment of other racial and ethnic groups, in particular black or Jewish people.
829   https://www.dictionary.com/browse/second-class-citizen
830   https://ancestors.familysearch.org/en/L7F4-VST/warren-fay-carothers-1872-1953
831   From Aldersgate to Azusa Street: Wesleyan, Holiness, and Pentecostal visions of the new creation. Henry H Knight. Eugene, Or. Pickwick Publications, ©2010.
832   The Houston Post. Houston, Texas. 31 December 1906. Page 6.
833   Genesis Chapter 37.
834   Ibid. Parham letter 1915. ORU Archive.
835   The winds of God: the story of the early Pentecostal days (1901-1914) ...Ethel Goss. Chapter XXVII. Page 183.
836   Ibid. Goss. Pg. 185.
837   Ibid. Goss. Pg. 166
838   Ibid Goss. Page 167.
839   Ibid Goss. Page 168.
840   Ibid. Goss. Page 168.
841   Ibid Goss. Page 168.
842   Ibid. Goss. Page 172.
843   Ibid. Goss. Page 170.
844   Word and Witness. Malvern Arkansas. Vol. 9. No. 3. March 20, 1913. Page 2.
845   Phone conversation with Brother Moore, Historian for the Pentecostal Assemblies of the Word (PAW) and Bishop Bernie L. Wade. July 2005.
846   Apostolic Faith & Pentecostal Timetable of Key Events. 1920-1930. 7th Edition ©2012, 2013, 2014, 2015, 2016, 2020, 2022. Bernie L. Wade, PhD

847   Tyson. The Body is Rent Asunder. Pg. 248.
848   https://www.history.com/topics/black-history/brown-v-board-of-education-of-topeka
849   Ibid. Goss.
850   Word and Witness. October 10, 1912.
851   James 1:8.
852   Word and Witness. Malvern Arkansas. June 20, 1913. Vol. 9. No. 6. Page 4.
853   Matthew 7:5.
854   See Parham's Letter to the Apostolic Faith Ministers. February 7, 1915. ORU Archives. There were other previous written responses in private correspondence and in person to people like John G. Lake, Florence Crawford, etc.
855   A Historical Account of the Apostolic Faith (Portland: 1965) 45, 59; Nichols, Pentecostals, 41f; Bloch-Hoell, Pentecostal Movement, 87.
856   https://www.oregonencyclopedia.org/articles/creffield_edmund_and_the_brides_of_christ_church/#.YdN8V2jMKUk
857   Edmund Creffield and the Brides of Christ Church. Theresa McCracken
858   https://mchumor.com/edmundcreffield.com/

859   Charles Parham to Apostolic Faith Ministers, 1915. Letter to Pauline Param. Oral Roberts Archives.
860   Charles Parham to Apostolic Faith Ministers, 1915. Letter to Pauline Param. Oral Roberts Archives.
861   https://www.revival-library.org/revival_heroes/20th_century/durham_william.shtml
862   Edith Waldvogel Blumhofer; The Assemblies of God: A Popular History; (Springfield, MO: Radiant Books/Gospel Publishing House, 1985), p. 43. This type of prophet vs. prophet showdown isn't completely unprecedented in Scripture. In fact, two Old Testament scripture passages come to mind. The more well-known of the two is Elijah on Mt. Carmel (1 Kings 18:17-40) when the Tishbite challenged, "How long halt ye between two opinions? ...the God that answereth by fire, let Him be God." (vv. 21,24). By day's end, 450 false prophets had met their doom. Then there is the story in Jeremiah 28 about the opposition the false prophet Hananiah made against Jeremiah's word from God. God spoke through Jeremiah, telling him that He would kill Hananiah "this year" (v.16), and Hananiah died later that same year (v.17). As sobering and unpopular as the thought may be, God is not averse to taking the life of one who opposes Him (even in the New Testament, as witnessed by the sad story of Peter's prophetic pronouncements against Ananias and Sapphira in Acts 5:1-11).
863   Charles F. Parham, The Apostolic Faith (Baxter Springs, Kansas), Vol. 1, No. 4, June 1912, pp. 8-9. Whether by popular demand or (one is tempted to think of this as more likely) as a "See, I told you so!" Parham reprinted this article in its entirety in Vol. 2, No. 7 (September 1913) on pp. 9-10.

864   Charles Parham to Apostolic Faith Ministers, 1915. Letter to Pauline Param. Oral Roberts Archives.
865   Apostolic Faith. Free Love. Baxter Springs, Kansas. December 1912.
866   https://www.apostolicarchives.com/articles/article/8795590/187474.htm
867   "Apostles are Gone: Leaders of Holy Rollers Take to Flight," Morning Oregonian, Nov. 3, 1903.
868   https://www.britannica.com/topic/adiaphorism
869   Christianity Without the Cross. Currents and Confluence in Pre-Oneness Pentecostal Theology. Thomas Fudge. Page 13.
870   Parham. A Critical Analysis of the Tongues Question. Apostolic Faith. June 1925. Page 2-6.
871   Ibid. Fudge. Page 15.
872   Charles F. Parham and His Role in the Development of the Pentecostal Movement. A Reevaluation. James R. Goff, Jr. Page. 233.
873   Ibid. Goss.
874   Johnston, Robin M. (March 2010). "Howard A Goss: A Pentecostal Life." ProQuest.
875   See: The Winds of God. Ethel Goss.
876   "Meetings Halt at the Majestic," San Antonio Light. July 20, 1907, 8. Parham Free Again; Preaches," San Antonio Gazette. July 23, 1907, 7.
877   Apostolic Faith. Charles F. Parham. Baxter Springs. Kansas. Page 7.
878   The Winds of God. Ethel Goss. Page 79.
879   The Apostolic Faith. Volume 3. No. 1. Baxter Springs Kansas.
880   Apostolic Faith. Baxter Springs. Vol. 3. No. 1.
881   Ibid. Houston Post.
882   The Houston Post. Houston, Texas. 22 May 1907, Wed. Page 5
883   Ibid. Houston Post. J Charles Dowling who was chairman of the phony trial admits that Parham was not in attendance.
884   Ibid. Houston Post.
885   Ibid. Goss. Page 79
886   Ibid. Houston Post.
887   Ibid. Goss. Page 79.
888   Ibid. Goss. Page. 79.
889   Ibid. Houston Post.
890   Ibid. Goss. Page 79.
891   https://brill.com/view/journals/pneu/41/1/article-p31_4.xml
892   https://en.wikipedia.org/wiki/Lawrence_v._Texas
893   https://lamp-stand.com/tag/charles-parham/
894   The Houston Post. May 19, 1908. Front Page.

895   The Houston Post. 22 March 1907.

896   Weekly Evangel. Saint Louis, MO. March 11, 1916. No. 130.

897   The Everlasting Gospel: The Significance of Eschatology in ...https://books.google.com › books
D William Faupel · 2019. Pg. 179.

898   Ibid. Goss.

899   Ibid. Goss. Pg. 79.

900   A. G. Canada works closely with Carothers and Goss who appoint him Texas Director of their replica A.F.M. Ironically, they sent him to San Antonio in early 1907 where Parham is arrested.

901   Mathew 27:3-5.

902   See Parham's letter to the Apostolic Faith Ministry. February 7, 1915.

903   Strangely, there is no dissenters that claim the supposed confession was not prewritten. This single point begs the question, Who wrote the confession and why? Who knew in advance that Parham would be arrested on fictious charges? Also, why did the Justice add the supposed line to the confession?

904   Ibid. Parham. Feb. 7, 1915.

905   Ibid. Houston Post.

906   See. The Life of Charles Fox Parham. Sarah E. Parham.

907   City in Brief, HC, 24 August 1907, p. 5 and Church Notices, HC, 24 August 1907, p. 7

908   Britannica, The Editors of Encyclopedia. "confession." Encyclopedia Britannica, 25 Jan. 2021, https://www.britannica.com/topic/confession-religion. Accessed 14 February 2022.

909   Haas, Kenneth C.. "confession." Encyclopedia Britannica, 7 Apr. 2014, https://www.britannica.com/topic/confession-law. Accessed 14 February 2022.

910   City in Brief, HC, 24 August 1907, p. 5 and Church Notices, HC, 24 August 1907, p. 7

911   Isaiah 13:14.

912   Assemblies of God. Volume 22. No. 4. Winter 2002-3. Page 4.

913   The Washington Post. Notes on Political Theater. Nelson Pressley. November 18, 2016.

914   Hillary Clinton was the mastermind behind the Trump-Russia collusion hoax and may never face justice. Make no mistake –it was Clinton who invented the elaborate collusion hoax, financed it, and directed the process. Greg Jarrett. February 15, 2022.

915   Harold Hunter, "Two Movements of the Holy Spirit in the 20th Century? A Closer Look at Global Pentecostalism and Ecumenism," One in Christ. 38, No. 1 (January 2003), 31-39. Reprinted in Wolfgang Vondey, ed. Pentecostalism and Christian Unity: Ecumenical Documents and Critical Assessment (Eugene, OR: Pickwick Publications, 2010), 20-33.

916   Charles F. Parham and His Role in the Development of the Pentecostal Movement. A Reevaluation. James R. Goff, Jr. Page. 233.

917   Crimes of Preachers in the United States and Canada. M.E. Billings. August 24, 2018,

918   The Gospel of the Kingdom. J. G. Campbell. Alvin Texas. Vol. 3. No. 1.

919   Vinson Synan. The Holiness-Pentecostal Tradition: Charismatic Movements in the Twentieth Century. Grand Rapids, Michigan: William B. Eerdmans Publishing Company, 1997, p. 106 n.

920   Crimes of Preachers in the United States and Canada. M.E. Billings. August 24, 2018,

921   J J Jourdan. San Antonio Gazette 21 May 1907, Tue • Page 10

922   https://brill.com/view/journals/pneu/41/1/article-p31_4.xml

923   "Evangelist is Arrested." San Antonio Light. July 19, 1907. Page. 1.

924   Tony Cauchi, Charles Fox Parham Archived 2015-12-13 at the Wayback Machine, Revival-library.org, United Kingdom, 2004.

925   San Antonio Gazette (July 19, 1907), 1.

926   https://en.wikipedia.org/wiki/Unnatural_Acts

927   https://definitions.uslegal.com/u/unnatural-act/

928   https://en.wikipedia.org/wiki/Crime_against_nature

929   "Evangelist Denies Charges But Pleads On Knees for Mercy." San Antonio Gazette. July 19, 1907, 1.

930   Leaves of Healing. August 27, 1902. Evangelist Mary McGee Hall. Pg. 705.

931   Crimes of Preachers. In the United States and Canada. M.E. Billings. Release Date: August 24, 2018 [EBook #57764]

932   Goff, Loc. 4351. Cyrus B Fockler, later to be a founding executive presbyter of the Assemblies of God (1914),
fell under similar false accusation and persecution from Voliva.

933   Ibid. Billings.

934   Handbook of Texas. Callaghan, Bryan V., Jr. (1852-1912). J. Kaaz Doyle

935   San Antonio Light. San Antonio Texas. 27 Oct. 1908. Tuesday. Page 7.

936   Parham 1915 Letter to the Apostolic Faith Ministers.

937   https://www.britannica.com/biography/Pontius-Pilate

938   Ibid. Houston Post.

939   Ibid. Parham Letter February 7, 1915.

940   Ibid. Parham. Feb. 7, 1915.

941   https://www.findlaw.com/criminal/criminal-charges/what-is-coercion-law.html

942   https://www.findlaw.com/criminal/criminal-charges/what-is-coercion-law.html

943   Ibid. Houston Post.

944   Police-Induced Confessions: Risk Factors and Recommendations. Saul M. Kassin Æ Steven A. Drizin Æ Thomas Grisso Æ
Gisli H. Gudjonsson Æ Richard A. Leo Æ. Allison D. Redlich. Published online: 15 July 2009

945   Ibid. Goss. Pg.79.

946   https://www.urbandictionary.com/define.php?term=fugazi

947   Oral Robert University Archives. Charles F. Parham letter to Apostolic Faith. February 7,

1915.

948   San Antonio Gazette. San Antonio, Texas. July 25, 1908. Page 10.

949   The Life of Charles F. Parham Founder of the Apostolic Faith Movement. Sarah E. Parham. Page 198.

950   Ibid. ORU Archives. Parham Letter.

951   II Samuel Chapter 13.

952   I. C. Baker was an elected District Attorney representing San Antonio. Even though he was a Democrat and as such would have held certain views on the treatment of those who violated Jim Crow laws, he found no evidence of anything to bring to a trial and dismissed the whole mess. See the Houston Post. Houston, Texas. November 7, 1906. Page 7.

953   Ibid. Sarah Parham. Pg. 198.

954   San Antonio Gazette. San Antonio, Texas. December 12, 1908. Page 1.

955   Ibid. Parham. Feb 7, 1915, letter.

956   San Antonio Gazette. San Antonio Texas. December 12, 1908. Page 1.

957   "Justice Ben Fisk's Court," The San Antonio Daily Express. July 20, 1907, 12.

958   https://www.findagrave.com/memorial/32344612/mary-rachel_euphemia-fisk

959   Matthew 5:23-24.

960   Parham is Rallying Forces. The Houston Post. May 22, 1907. 5.

961   1/18/22. Correspondence between Apostolic Faith Bible College Resident Historian and Bishop Bernie L. Wade, PhD. "There is no evidence that Parham loaned the use of the report to Seymour in any of our records. We know that Seymour began printing a report from LA in the early 1900's, but to our knowledge that was something he started from scratch in the image of what Parham had already established; and not the actual existing report itself."

962   Ibid. Parham. Page 201.

963   Ibid. Parham. Pages 203-206.

964   Ibid. Parham. Page 206.

965   https://www.scribd.com/doc/201031459/charles-parham-arrest

966   Ibid., Loc. 744, 755, 765, and 1001.

967   https://newspapers.library.in.gov/?a=d&d=PT19070418.1.1&e=——en-20–1–txt-txIN——

968   https://bailproject.org/san-antonio/

969   San Antonio Gazette. San Antonio Texas. 23 November 1907. Page. 12.

970   J J Jourdan. San Antonio Gazette 21 May 1907, Tue • Page 10

971   The Times-Democrat. New Orleans, Louisiana. 01 Feb 1907, Fri. Page 5

972   Ibid. Times-Democrat.

973   TOLSON, Arthur Lincoln, 1924—THE NEGRO IN OKLAHOMA TERRITORY, 1889-1907; A STUDY IN RACIAL DISCRIMINATION. The University of Oklahoma, PhD., 1966 History, modern. University Microfilms, Inc., Ann Arbor,

Michigan

974 Ibid., Loc. 5240.

975 Jacobs, Joseph (1901). "Anglo-Israelism." In Singer, Isidore (ed.). Jewish Encyclopedia: Anglo-Israelism. New York: Funk and Wagnalls. p. 600. ISBN 978-1117918952.

976 Living in Bible Times: F. F. Bosworth and the Pentecostal. Christopher J. Richmann · 2020. 5.

977 The Boston Globe. PA.G.E 1. Boston, Massachusetts. Friday, August 29, 1913

978 The Evening Herald. Fall River, Massachusetts. 03 Sep 1913, Wed. Page 5

979 Ibid. Herald.

980 Parham, Sarah, Loc. 682.

981 A crime, typically one involving violence, which is motivated by prejudice on the basis of race, religion, sexual orientation, or other grounds.

982 Interview with Marjorie Haire. Rogers, Arkansas. July 12, 1985.

983 Interview with A. B. Stanberry, Jr. Alvin, Texas. 16, August 1985.

984 The 1st Pentecostal scandal July 28, 2016. Daniel Silliman

985 Ibid. Silliman.

986 Harvey, op. cit., pp. 13-27; Gerbner, op. cit.

987 Ibid. Kandt. Page 777.

988 White. Demons and Tongues. Pg. 9.

989 Ibid. White. Demons and Tongues. Pg. 13.

990 Ibid. White. Page 13.

991 "We Want No Hatchet-Wielding Amazons:" The Feminism, Racism, and Nativism of the Women of the Ku Klux Klan Honors Thesis Submitted to The Department of History of The University of Colorado Boulder. Nora Hickins Boulder, Colorado April 2018

992 Susie Cunningham Stanley, Feminist Pillar of Fire, 38.

993 This list was derived from a larger list composed by the Martin Luther King, Jr., National Historic Site Interpretive Staff. Last Updated January 5, 1998. The web address is: http//www.nps.gov/malu/documents/jim crowlaws.htm.

994 Ku Klux Klan, Kloran, op. cit., p. 2.

995 Blood, Cross and Flag: The Influence of Race on Ku Klux Klan Theology in the 1920s. Gustaf Forsell.

Gustaf Forsel

996 Linda Gordon, The Second Coming of the KKK: The Ku Klux Klan of the 1920s and the American Political Tradition (New York: Liveright, 2017).

997 San Antonio Gazette. San Antonio, Texas. 12 April 1907. Page 6.

998 https://www.history.com/topics/reconstruction/ku-klux-klan

999 W.H. Caucasian, Anthropology for the People: A Refutation of the Theory of the Adamic Origin of All Races (Richmond: Everett Waddey, 1891), p. 39.

1000   Ibid., pp. 17-26.

1001   W.H. Caucasian, Anthropology for the People: A Refutation of the Theory of the Adamic Origin of All Races (Richmond: Everett Waddey, 1891), p. 39.

1002   Eric Benson (July 12, 2014). "Return of the Guv." National Journal. Retrieved September 4, 2014.

1003   https://www.christianpost.com/news/this-week-in-christian-history-great-schism-pentecostal-leader.html?page=2

1004   Katz, Love Stories: Sex Between Men Before Homosexuality (Chicago: University of Chicago Press, 2001), 61

1005   Jacqueline N. Moore, Cowboys and Cattlemen: Class and Masculinities on the Texas Frontier, 1865-1900 (New York: New York University Press, 2010), 241n

1006   The Twentieth-Century Pentecostal Revival. David K. Bernard.

1007   3 John 1:9.

1008   Interview with Faith Barnaby by this Author. She said that her father, Bishop G. B. Rowe thought the schisms were more about "who wanted to be in charge."

1009   https://churchofgod.org/about/a-brief-history-of-the-church-of-god/

1010   Encyclopedia of Evangelism by Randall Herbert Balmer.

1011   Ibid. Balmer. Pg. 7. William E. Montgomery, Under Their Own Vine and Fig Tree: The African-American Church in the South 1865-1900 (London: Louisiana State, 1993), p. 18.

1012   Cheryl J. Sanders, Saints in Exile: The Holiness-Pentecostal Experience in African-American Religion and Culture (New York & Oxford: Oxford, 1996), p.18. The first separate black Baptist church was organized between 1773 and 1775 in Silver Bluff, South Carolina, and the black Methodist church was in 1787.

1013   Mark 8:34-38.

1014   Evans, 'Americanism', op. cit., p. 51.

1015   Carothers, "Attitude of Pentecostal Whites to the Colored Brethren in the South,"

1016   Wright, Religious and Patriotic Ideals, op. cit., pp. 43-44.

1017   Ku Klux Klan, Ideals, op. cit., p. 5.

1018   Ku Klux Klan, Constitution and Laws, op. cit., p. 5; Ku Klux Klan, Klansman's Manual, op. cit., pp. 17-18.

1019   https://www.apostolicarchives.com/articles/article/8795236/172423.htm

1020   Ibid. Kenyon.

1021   The Baptism with the Holy Spirit (1906). Warren Faye Carothers. Idem. Church Government. (1909).

1022   Blumhofer, Pentecost in My Soul, 121-122. Ruth Goss Nortje, "Ethel Elizabeth Goss" in Pioneer Pentecostal Women, Volume 3, Mary Wallace, ed. (Hazelwood, MO: Word Aflame Press, 2003), 63.

1023   American Christianity's White-Supremacy Problem History, theology, and culture all contribute to the racist attitudes embedded in the white church. Michael Luo. September 2, 2020. Pg. 1.

1024 Ibid. Michael Luo.

1025 White Too Long: The Legacy of White Supremacy in American Christianity Hardcover – Illustrated, July 28, 2020. Robert P. Jones

1026 The Color of Compromise: The Truth about the American Church's Complicity in Racism. January 7, 2020. Jemar Tisby

1027 https://www.jewishvirtuallibrary.org/joseph-goebbels-on-the-quot-big-lie-quot

1028 Joel 2:23 and Hosea 6:3.

1029 Charles F. Parham, Indefatigable Toil and Launching the World-wide Pentecostal Movement: A New Look at a Forgotten Leader. Jeffery Nelson. Pg. 44.

1030 The Believers Magna Carta. John R. Crist. 2004.

1031 https://ifphc.wordpress.com/2013/10/22/1916-general-council/

1032 https://www.merriam-webster.com/dictionary/tokenism

1033 https://www.apostolicarchives.com/articles/article/8795236/172433.htm

1034 The Klan, White Christianity, and the Past and Present | a response to Kelly J. Baker by Randall J. Stephens, Joel A Brown. Jun 26, 2017.

1035 https://www.religioustolerance.org/relbigot.htm

1036 https://www.merriam-webster.com/dictionary/guilt%20by%20association

1037 See Genesis 4:1-13.

1038 David Edwin Harrell, Jr., White Sects and Black Men in the Recent South, Nashville: Vanderbilt University Press, 1971; Vinson Synan, The Holiness Pentecostal Movement in the United States, Grand Rapids: William B. Eerdmans Publishing Company, 1971, especially 165-184; Iain MacRobert, The Black Roots and White Racism of Early Pentecostalism in the USA, New York: St. Martin's Press, 1988; Douglas J. Nelson, "For Such A Time As This: The Story of Bishop William J. Seymour and the Azusa Street Revival," unpublished Ph.D. Dissertation, University of Birmingham, Birmingham, England, 1981; Howard N. Kenyon, "An Analysis of Ethical Issues in the History of the Assemblies of God," unpublished Ph.D. Dissertation, Baylor University, Waco, Texas, 1988, pp. 42-176; Howard N. Kenyon "Black Ministers in the Assemblies of God," Assemblies of God Heritage 7:1 (Spring, 1987), 10-13, 20; Walter J. Hollenweger, Pentecost Between Black and White: Five Case Studies on Pentecost and Politics, Belfast, Ireland: Christian Journals Limited, 1974, 13-32; Hans A. Baer, "The Socio-Religious Development of the Church of God in Christ," in Hans A. Baer and Yvonne Jones, eds. African-Americans in the South: Issues of Race, Class, and Gender, Southern Anthropological Society Proceedings, No. 25, Athens and London: The University of Georgia Press, 1992, 111-122; Lawrence Neale Jones, Michael P. Hamilton, ed., "The Black Pentecostal," The Charismatic Movement, Grand Rapids: William B. Eerdmans Publishing Company, 1975, 145-158; Douglas J. Nelson, Paul Eelbert, ed., "The Black Face of Church Renewal: The Meaning of A Charismatic Explosion, 1901-1985, Faces of Renewal: Studies in Honor of Stanley M. Horton,

Peabody, MA.: Hendrickson Publishers, Inc., 1988, 172-191; Hans A. Baer and Merrill Singer, "Toward a Typology of Black Sectarianism As A Response to Racial Stratification," Anthropological Quarterly 54:1, January, 1981, 1-14; David Rees-Thomas, "The Holy Spirit is Color Blind," CAM 27:3 (January 1974), 3-5; Janenne I. Froats and Jennifer E. Kerslake, "Black and White: A Gray Area in the Assemblies of God," Evangel Lance (February 21, 1992), 4-6; Howard Elinson, "The Implications of Pentecostal Religion for Intellectualism, Politics, and Race Relations," The American Journal of Sociology 70:4 (January, 1965), 403-415; Julia Kirk Blackwelder, "Southern White Fundamentalists and the Civil Rights Movement," Phylon 40:4 , Dec. 1979, 335-341; Leonard Lovett, "Racism and Reconciliation," Charisma 18:9 (April, 1993), 14-15; James S. Tinney, "William J. Seymour; Father of Modern-Day Pentecostalism," The Journal of the Interdenominational Theological Center 4:1 (1976) 34-44; Cecil M. Robeck, Jr.; Jan A. B. Jongereel, a.o. (Ed.) "The Social Concern of Early American Pentecostalism," in Pentecost, Mission and Ecumenism: Essays on Intercultural Theology Studies in the Intercultural History of Christianity 75 (Frankfurt am Main: Peter Lang, 1992) 97-106; Cecil M. Robeck, Jr., "Taking Stock of Pentecostalism: The Personal Reflections of a Retiring Editor," Pneuma The Journal of the Society for Pentecostal Studies 15:1 (Spring, 1993), 35-60, esp. 45-51.

1039   THE PAST: Historical Roots of Racial Unity and Division in American Pentecostalism. Cecil M. Robeck, Jr., Ph.D. Introduction.

1040   Cornell Law School. Separate But Equal. Plessy v. Ferguson. Last updated in October of 2018 by Krystyna Blokhina Gilkis.

1041   The New York Times. The 'Some of My Best Friends Are Black' Defense It's a myth that proximity to blackness immunizes white people from doing racist things. John Eligon, February 16, 2019. Mr. Eligon is a national correspondent for The New York Times.

1042   THE PAST: Historical Roots of Racial Unity and Division in American Pentecostalism. Cecil M. Robeck, Jr., Ph.D. Introduction

1043   ORU Archives. Letter from John G. Lake to Charles F. Parham. 1927.

1044   Weekly Evangel. September 2, 1916. No. 155.

1045   https://ag.org/beliefs/statement-of-fundamental-truths

1046   Ibid. Robeck.

1047   https://en.wikipedia.org/wiki/Joe_Friday

1048   "Rolling and Diving Fanatics 'Confess,'" Los Angeles Times, June 23, 1905, I7.

1049   W. J. Seymour. Doctrine and Disciplines of the Apostolic Faith. Pg. 49.

1050   Gary B. McGee, "William J. Seymour and the Azusa Street Revival," Enrichment Journal (Fall 1999), http://ag.org/enrichmentjournal/199904/026_azusa.cfm.

1051   https://christianhistoryinstitute.org/magazine/article/sanctification-scuffles

1052   Craig Borlase, William Seymour: A Biography, (Lake Mary, FL: Charisma House, 2006), 125.

1053   William J. Seymour, The Doctrines and Disciplines of the Azusa Street Apostolic Faith Mission of Los Angeles, California, ed. Larry Martin, (Joplin MO: Christian Life Books, 2000), 29.

1054   James Choung, "Let the Walls Come Down: William Seymour," InterVarsity Ministry Exchange, http://www.intervarsity.org/mx/item/4332 (Accessed April 21, 2007), 4; Borlase, William Seymour, 130.

1055   Florence Crawford, "Beginning of Worldwide Revival," Apostolic Faith. January 1907, 1.

1056   Etta Auringer Huff, "A Scriptural Pentecost," A Herald of Light, July 14, 1906, in Larry Martin, ed., Azusa Street: The True Believers Part 2, (Joplin, MO: Christian Life Books, 1999), 104.

1057   Not only did black and white meet in early Pentecostalism, but the meeting between black and white was at the root of the worldwide revival called Pentecostalism." Walter J. Hollenweger, Foreword to The Black Roots and White Racism of Early Pentecostalism in the USA, by Iain MacRobert (Basingstoke, Macmillan, 1988), xii.

1058   Mattie Cummings; qtd. in Iain MacRobert, The Black Roots and White Racism of Early Pentecostalism in the USA, (London: The Macmillan Press Ltd., 1988), 56.

1059   Mother Crawford. A Profile. The Reverend Florence Louise Crawford. September 1, 1872-June 20, 1936. Amos Morgan. January 2004. See 16 D and C.

1060   Mother Crawford. A Profile. The Reverend Florence Louise Crawford. September 1, 1872-June 20, 1936. Amos Morgan. January 2004.

1061   Articles of Incorporation. Apostolic Faith Mission of Portland, Oregon. October 11, 1909. Also, Ibid. Morgan. Section 16 G.

1062   Ibid. Morgan.

1063   Ibid. Morgan.

1064   Ibid. Morgan. Section 17 A, B, C.

1065   Ibid. Goss.

1066   Ibid. Morgan. Section 17 B.

1067   Ibid. Morgan.

1068   Ibid. Morgan.

1069   Ibid. Morgan Section 18.

1070   Ibid. Goss. Page 90.

1071   https://pentecostalarchives.org/collections/cogicministerialroster/index.cfm

1072   Complete list of white men who were invited to the organizing of the new Pentecostals meeting in 1914. There are a couple of white women on the list. Carothers would deal with that later. Word and Witness. Malvern, Arkansas. December 20, 1913. Volume 9. No. 12. Page 7-8.

1073   Weekly Evangel. Number 103. August 14, 1915. Page 1.

1074   The Apostolic Faith. Charles F. Parham and Francis R. Romack. October 1914. Volume 3. Number 7. Page 8.

1075   Apostolic Faith & Pentecostal Timetable of Key Events 1940 – 1950. 6th Edition. Feb 26, 2020. Bernie L. Wade, PhD. Pages 23-29.

1076   https://www.thearda.com/timeline/events/event_214.asp

1077   https://www.upci.org/about/about-the-upci

1078   Ibid. Morgan. Section 18.

1079   Early Interracial Oneness Pentecostalism: G. T. Haywood and the Pentecostal. Talmadge L. French, Pg. 29.

1080   Ibid. French.

1081   https://www.learnreligions.com/united-pentecostal-church-international-700120

1082   Restoring the Faith: The Assemblies of God, Pentecostalism, Edith L. Blumhofer · 1993. Pg. 172.

1083   General Council Minutes, 1914. 7. A.G.A.

1084   The Weekly Evangel. September 2, 1916. W. F. Carothers. Page 11.

1085   Ibid. Evangel.

1086   https://ag.org/beliefs/statement-of-fundamental-truths

1087   https://en.wikipedia.org/wiki/Black_Pope_(disambiguation)

1088   https://godswordtowomen.org/sloan.htm

1089   Peter C. Nelson, "Are Women Still under Paul's Restrictions!" Unpublished notes. 1931. Peter C. Nelson File. A.G.A.

1090   General Council Minutes. 1935. 21.

1091   Barry Chant, "The Spirit of Pentecost: Origins and Development of the Pentecostal movement in Australia, 1870-1939," PhD dissertation, Sydney: Macquarie University, 1999) 523-542.

1092   She argued that God the Father and the Holy Spirit were one (the Spirit was the influence of the Father), and that Jesus Christ was God's Son (Sarah Jane Lancaster, Good News 1:5, January 1913, 17). In rejecting "trinity" she advocated a "binity.." This is certainly in the spirit of the A.F.M.

1093   Chant, "Spirit of Pentecost," 235.

1094   Sarah Jane Lancaster, "By One Spirit," Good News 18, no. 7 (July 1927): 10.

1095   The Apostolic Faith. Published by the Apostolic Faith Publishing Company. Baxter Springs, Kansas. Charles F. Parham Editor. F. R. Romack, Manager. Page 7.

1096   https://www.merriam-webster.com/dictionary/go%20to%20the%20wall

1097   Ibid. Parham. Pg. 7.

1098   Ibid. Parham.

1099   Colossians 3:17.

1100   Parham. A Voice Crying in the Wilderness. 22-24; Blumhofer, Restoring the Faith. 47 n. 23: Anderson, Disinherited, 176.

1101   The Apostolic Faith. June 1912. Charles F. Parham.

1102   Voice Crying in the Wilderness. Charles F. Parham. Water Baptism. Chapter 2. Page 7.

1103   Parham's position on this, never wavered. He wrote explicitly about this in this 1902 book, A Voice Crying in the Wilderness and made additional references throughout his life in preaching and in a revisit of the topic in print in The Apostolic Faith 1912. He made the point of saying that neither he nor his wife Sarah had ever participated in Triune baptism. Thus, one is left to conclude that the thousand or tens of thousands that Parham baptized were all in the singular name of Jesus Christ.

1104   Goff. Fields White unto Harvest., 153 n. 24.

1105   From Gary W. Garrett, PhD founder of Apostolic Archives. www.apostolicarchives.com "I have been asked many times where the historical proof is that Howard Goss was ever baptized in Jesus' name by Charles Parham. Historical Facts Their Story, 20th Century Pentecostals. Fred Foster. Howard Goss was baptized in Jesus' name in 1903 by Charles F. Parham. (P. 98). Howard Goss was rebaptized in Jesus' name by E.N. Bell on August 15, 1915. (P. 98). E.N. Bell and Rogers were baptized in Jesus' name by L.V. Roberts in the Summer of 1915. (PP. 95-96). Restoring the Apostolic Faith, by J.L. Hall. Charles F. Parham used the Jesus' name formula when he baptized Howard Goss in 1903. (P.29). Dictionary of Pentecostal and Charismatic Movements by Burgess & McGee. E.N. Bell was rebaptized in Jesus' name by L.V. Roberts in the Summer of 1915. (P. 645). E.N. Bell rebaptized Howard Goss in Jesus' name in 1915. (P. 343). Anointed to Serve by William W. Menzies. E.N. Bell and H.G. Rogers were baptized in Jesus' name by L.V. Roberts in July 1915. (P. 114). Early Interracial Oneness Pentecostalism by Talmadge L. French. Howard Goss was baptized twice in Jesus' name! (PP.57-58). 1903 by Charles F. Parham. 1915 by E.N. Bell

1106   Who is Jesus Christ. E. N. Bell 1915.

1107   Britannica, The Editors of Encyclopedia. "Fourteenth Amendment." Encyclopedia Britannica, 22 Oct. 2021, https://www.britannica.com/topic/Fourteenth-Amendment. Accessed 11 Februazry 2022.

1108   Early Pentecostal Visions in the United States. Roebeck. Pg. 15.

1109   The New International Dictionary of Pentecostal and Charismatic Movements. 2002. Zondervan. Pg. 326

1110   https://www.google.com/books/edition/The_New_International_Dictionary_of_Pent/_gJMIFUC?hl=en&gbpv=1&dq=PAJC+CONVENTION+1941&pg=PT2809&printsec=frontcover

1111   Brumback, Suddenly, p. 198.

1112   The New International Dictionary of Pentecostal and Charismatic Movements. 2002. Zondervan. Pg. 326

1113   Ibid. E. N. Bell.

1114   Word and Witness. July 17, 1915.

1115   The Great Controversy and Confusion. Pentecostal Evangel. E. N. Bell. September 6, 1919.

1116   Word and Witness. Malvern Arkansas. Vol. 9. No. 3. March 20, 1913. Page 1.

1117   Word and Witness. Malvern Arkansas. Vol. 9. No. 3. March 20, 1913. Page 1.

1118   Word and Witness. Malvern Arkansas. Vol. 9. No. 3. March 20, 1913. Page 1

1119   http://www.revival-library.org/index.php/pensketches-menu/american-pentecostal-pioneers/charles-parham

1120   https://en.wikipedia.org/wiki/Charles_Fox_Parham

1121   https://biography.yourdictionary.com/charles-fox-parham

1122   https://www.dictionary.com/browse/channeling

1123   https://jonestown.sdsu.edu/?page_id=92702

1124   https://thetencommandmentsministry.us/ministry/blog/articles/30-reasons-for-segregation-of-races/

1125   Christianity Without the Cross. Thomas Fudge. Page 45.

1126   James Craig. Robert Edward McCallister. Canadian Pentecostal Pioneer. Eastern Journal of Practical Theology 3. Spring 1989. 6-24.

1127   Fudge. Pg. 45.

1128   Woodworth-Etter. Life and Testimony of Mrs. M. B. Woodworth-Etter, Evangelist and Woodworth-Etter, Marvels and Miracles God wrought in the Ministry of Forty-Five Years.

1129   Stephen R. Graham. Conservative American Protestantism and the Origins of Pentecostalism A Case Study A Case Study of Andrew D. Urshan. Unpublished M. A. Thesis. 1983. Wheaton College. Pg. 45.

1130   Urshan. The Almighty God in the Lord Jesus Christ (Portland, OR: Apostolic Book Publishers, 1983. Pg. 55. This is a reprint of a book originally printed in 1919.

1131   Personal conversation with Bishop Samuel Smith, Bishop Barney Phillips with the Author, Bernie L. Wade, PhD.

1132   The Surprising Origins of the Trinity Doctrine. Jul 22, 2011

1133   The Apostolic Faith. Baptism. The Apostolic Faith Publishing Company. Baxter Springs, Kansas. March 1912. Page 7.

1134   https://www.apostolicarchives.com/articles/article/8801925/173170.htm

1135   The Apostolic Faith. Baptism. The Apostolic Faith Publishing Company. Baxter Springs, Kansas. March 1912. Page 7.

1136   Ibid. Sarah E. Parham. Pg. 27.

1137   The Azusa Street Revival: No Racism; Only Persecution of Jesus Name...Amen. "Charles Parham, the Father of the Oneness Apostolic Pentecostal Movement. A Brief Life of Charles Fox Parham from Apostolic Archives. Hannah Faith. Pg. 114.

1138   The Azusa Street Revival: No Racism; Only Persecution of Jesus Name...Amen. "Charles Parham, the Father of the Oneness Apostolic Pentecostal Movement. A Brief Life of Charles Fox Parham from Apostolic Archives. Hannah Faith. Pg. 114.

1139   Word and Witness. Malvern Arkansas. June 20, 1913. Vol. 9. No. 6. Page 4

1140   Ibid. Saunders, Gerloff. Pg. 96.

1141   Christianity Today. Facing Our Legacy of Lynching How a memorial could help lead America—and Christians—to repentance from a dark history. D. L. MAYFIELD. AUGUST 18, 2017

1142   Lynching preachers: How black pastors resisted Jim Crow and white pastors incited racial violence. February 10, 2020, 8.57am EST. Malcolm Brian Foley PhD Candidate in Religion - Historical Studies, Baylor University

1143   How a dead U.S. evangelist inspires London's reviled street preachers Pair who shame women are adherents of William Branham, who has links to the KKK and Jim Jones. Andrew

Lupton, Sep 25, 2017

1144 Harvey Paul. God and Negroes and Jesus and Sin and Salvation: Racism, Racial Interchange, and Interracialism in Southern Religious History. In: Schweiger, Matthews, editors. Religion in the American South. Chapel Hill: University of North Carolina Press; 2004. pp. 283-329

1145 Targeting Lynch Victims: Social Marginality or Status Transgressions? Bailey AK, Tolnay SE, Beck EM, Laird JD Am Social Rev. 2011 Jun; 76(3):412-436.

1146 Report on Slavery and Racism in the History of the Southern Baptist Theological Seminary" (PDF). Southern Baptist Theological Seminary. December 2018. Retrieved July 29, 2019.

1147 "The Brethren" as used here is code for white ministers. The A.G. was more than happy for people of color to be divided from their all-white hate group. In fact, they left no other option.

1148 Carothers was busy in the years from 1908 to 1916 with a number of business interests. These had apparently made him of some considerable means so once again he used his affluence and influence to bring the refine the vision of his Texas Syndicate.

1149 https://www.raabcollection.com/jefferson-davis-autograph/oppressed-south-shall-rise-again

1150 Race and the Assemblies of God Church. The Journey from Azusa Street to the "Miracle of Memphis." Joe Newman. Cambria Press. Youngstown, New York. Page 170.

1151 https://ifphc.wordpress.com/tag/g-t-haywood/

1152 Christ Temple Apostolic Faith Assembly founded by Henry Prentiss.

1153 http://www.encyclopedia.com/topic/Assemblies_of_God.aspx

1154 https://www.albany.edu/history/history316/kkk.html

1155 Ibid. Sarah E. Parham. Pg. 75.

1156 Black ministers are not officially licensed by the Assemblies of God until 1969.

1157 Gerloff. Pg.

1158 Parham. Apostolic Faith. June 1912.

1159 Pentecostalism in America. R. G. Robins.

1160 Ibid. Morgan.

1161 Encyclopedia of Evangelism by Randall Herbert Balmer

1162 Encyclopedia of Evangelicalism. Randall Herbert Balmer. Pg. 137.

1163 Encyclopedia of Evangelism by Randall Herbert Balmer

1164 Ibid. Saunders, Gerloff. Pg. 96.

1165 Ibid. Gerloff. Pg. 96.

1166 Lynching: A Weapon of National Oppression (1932). Erin Gray, Harry Haywood and Milton Howard January 9, 2017

1167 Ibid. Gerloff. Pg. 96-97.

1168 https://ifphc.wordpress.com/tag/d-w-kerr/

1169 Timetable of Key Events. Volume 2. Sixth Edition. Bernie L. Wade. Page 54-59.

1170 Ibid. Timetable.

1171 Bishop Monroe R. Saunders, Sr. was the Presiding Bishop of the First United Church of

Jesus Christ Apostolic. Gerloff. Pg. 96.

1172 "Ministerial List," Weekly Evangel, January 8, 1916, 12.

1173 https://originofsongs.blogspot.com/2015/07/i-see-crimson-stream-of-blood.html

1174 A Plea for British Black Theologies, Volume 1: The Black Church Movement in...Roswith I. H. Gerloff. Pg. 88.

1175 https://ifphc.org/index.cfm?fuseaction=history.main

1176 G. Bishop G. T. Haywood. December 1916.

1177 Gerloff. Pg. 94.

1178 The Weekly Evangel. October 21, 1916. Page two.

1179 The Weekly Evangel. October 21, 1916. Page two.

1180 Parham. 262.

1181 http://conjubilant.blogspot.com/2012/03/thoro-harris.html

1182 https://hymnary.org/person/Harris_Thoro

1183 Parham Disfellowshipped in 1916. Midway Tabernacle and the Apostolic Bible Church. Beverly Hicks. Pg. 40

1184 J. Roswell and Alice Flower started the publication in July 1913 as the Christian Evangel, which served primarily a small regional Pentecostal network of churches, known as the Association of Christian Assemblies. In April 1914, J. Roswell Flower helped to lead this network into the newly formed Assemblies of God. He was elected to serve as the first secretary and gave the Christian Evangel to the Assemblies of God

1185 January 1, 1916, Word and Witness merged into the Weekly Evangel. https://pentecostalarchives.org/collections/pentecostalevangel/

1186 Weekly Evangel. September 2, 1916. J. R. Flowers Office Editor. Brother Carothers General Field Work. Pg. 11.

1187 The Weekly Evangel. September 2, 1916. Saint Louis Missouri. Page 8.

1188 'If I did not believe God loved the blackest Negro girl': Responses to American racism among early white Pentecostals, Daniel Silliman. February 26, 2014.

1189 Heaven Below: Early Pentecostals and American Culture. Grant Wacker · 2009. Pg. 232.

1190 The Azusa Street Revival: No Racism; Only Persecution of Jesus Name...Amen. "Charles Parham, the Father of the Oneness Apostolic Pentecostal Movement. A Brief Life of Charles Fox Parham from Apostolic Archives. Hannah Faith. Pg. 123.

1191 The Azusa Street Revival: Hannah Faith. Pg. 196.

1192 Practicing What They Preach? Lynching and Religion in the American South, 1890 - 1929*. Amy Kate Bailey and Karen A. Snedker

1193 Black and White Pentecostals Mend 100-Year Racial Rift During Black History Month Denomination 'birthed in 1919 because of racism in the Assemblies of God' now partner with one of America's largest denominations. KATE TRACY| FEBRUARY 17, 2014

1194 www.awcf.org

1195   www.icof.net

1196   Kimberly Harper, White Man's Heaven:The Lynching and Expulsion of Blacks in the Southern Ozarks, 1894-1909 (Fayetteville, AR: University of Arkansas Press, 2010).

1197   Corum and Bakewell, 125-126. The identity of the street preacher in Joplin is unknown. However, street preaching was a common method of evangelism used by Parham's Apostolic Faith Movement. Parham himself was reported to have preached to hundreds of people on the streets of Joplin. The Apostolic Faith (Houston, TX), December 1905, 13. The preacher was obviously one of Parham's people who were consistent in their stance against racism, segregation and more.

1198   Charles F. Parham, Indefatigable Toil and Launching the World-wide Pentecostal Movement: A New Look at a Forgotten Leader. Jeffery Nelson

1199   Ibid., Loc. 1949.

1200   Apostolic Faith Gospel Mission pastored by William J. Seymour.

1201   International Journal of Pentecostal Missiology 7:1 (2020). Nelson. Pg. 48.

1202   Charles F. Parham, Indefatigable Toil and Launching the World-wide Pentecostal Movement: A New Look at a Forgotten Leader. Jeffery Nelson

1203   See John G. Lake's 1927 letter to Charles Parham.

1204   Proverbs 23:27.

1205   Ibid. Sarah E. Parham. Pg. 85.

1206   Ibid., Loc. 176, 1033, 1304, 1531, 1599, 1736, 3258, and 5024. Loc. 1949. 62 A Standard History of Kansas and Kansans, by William C. Connelly (Chicago: Lewis Publishing Co. 1928); Parham, Loc. 5581. 63 In 1906 before Azusa Street 100,000 people believed, during the first 5 years would be 55 people per day. A year before his death in 1928, 2,000,000 people believed, would be about 202 people per day during the first 27 years. In 2015 with 650 million Pentecostal/Charismatic people would be 15,469 people per day, who have come into the modern Pentecostal Movement since its inception on January 1, 1901

1207   Ibid., Loc. 2036.

1208   Ibid., Loc. 718, 1782, and 1833.

1209   Ibid., Loc. 375, 566, and 701.

1210   Ibid., Loc. 492, 572, and 5380.

1211   Ibid., Loc. 348, 415, 434, 575, 610, 621, 1024, and many others.

1212   Ibid., Loc. 348, 415, 434, 575, 610, 621, 1024, and many others.

1213   2 Timothy 4:10

1214   Acts 7:54-60.

1215   Acts Chapter 7:54-60.

1216   Jeff and Janelle Nelson are missionaries to Africa, currently serving as coordinator of Africa Library Services and Distribution Centers based in Springfield, Missouri. The Nelsons have served as pastors for 16 years and in missions since 2000. Jeff led KA.G. EAST University in Nairobi,